THE BANKER'S LIFE

GEORGE S. MOORE

The Banker's Life

W · W · NORTON & COMPANY · *NEW YORK* · *LONDON*

First Edition

The text of this book is composed in Primer, with display type set in Horizon. Composition and manufacturing by the Maple Vail Book Manufacturing Group. Book design by Marjorie J. Flock

Library of Congress Cataloging in Publication Data

Moore, George S. (George Stevens), 1905–
   The banker's life.

   Includes index.
   1. Moore, George S.   (George Stevens), 1905–
2. Bankers—New York (N.Y.)—Biography.   I. Title.
HG2463.M59A3   1987   332.1′092′4 [B]   86–31123

ISBN 0-393-02458-X

W. W. Norton & Company, Inc., 500 Fifth Avenue, New York, N. Y. 10110
W. W. Norton & Company Ltd., 37 Great Russell Street, London WC1B 3NU

1 2 3 4 5 6 7 8 9 0

For Charon

Contents

Photographs follow pages 41, 61, 221, 269, and 281.

Preface

I record my thanks and praise for Martin Mayer who has helped me perform a miracle, transforming my "memorandum" of my busy life into this book that may be of interest to friends and contemporaries in this changing world of people and action. Martin is the best of our time, and has demonstrated patience and understanding—trying to bring order from the mass of material available. Without his understanding of the fundamentals of banking and our economic system (even when he's dead wrong, which happens), the job would have been impossible.

One of the dividends of this literary venture is getting to know him, albeit rather late in my life. He is a phenomenon, with so many talents—some contradictory: e.g., a scholarly knowledge of the economic pattern of our times, and the struggle of leaders to deal with them, and at the same time, a professional knowledge of music and its performers. Having written the hundred-year history of the Metropolitan Opera, and helped Rudolf Bing with his memoirs, he understood, more than anyone else could have, my own involvement with that great institution. Above all, he can write, he can put complicated situations in simple and understandable harmony. I am deeply grateful for the time he has taken from his busy life, and the pressing demands of others, to try and put Moore on paper.

Above all, I thank my wife, Charon, for her love and understanding and patience. She led and pushed and dragged me into a second career, a second life, after Citibank. Few mortals are given such opportunities. Without Charon and the family and home she has given me, I would have long since passed on to the usual eclipse of retirement. The other reason for my peace and good health is the pride and satisfaction I take in my children and in my relationship with them. I'm grateful to young George, now almost fifty, for my two lovely grandchildren and his wife's welcome into the house I built that is now theirs, and also for telling the admissions committee of the Racquet Club (which I wanted to join after my retirement from Citibank had cost me the use of the dining rooms) that even when I was deep in my overly busy days, I'd always made time to be his best friend. And to Tina and Steve and Pia, all born after I was sixty, for once telling their mother and me that their friends wanted to come see them at their house because we had a real home.

Finally, I record my thanks to my able and loyal secretary, Mary Rieger, who is entirely responsible for what order exists in my busy life—and to Patricia Larsen who did the original research into my files and tapped the memories of my family and friends.

Introduction: George in Retirement

Joe Palmer, who wrote about horse-racing for the *New York Herald Tribune* in the 1940s, once told the story of an eight-year-old horse who ran the first race of his life in a seven-furlong feature event on a western track. Eight-year-old maidens don't attract much betting interest, and the horse went off at better than 65 to 1, with all the tickets on him bought by his owner and trainer. When he came in by ten lengths, the stewards, deeply suspicious that they were dealing with a ringer, called in the owner and asked what the hell was going on. How come this horse had never raced before? This was a damned fast horse. "Yessir," said the owner, a little shamefacedly. "He's a fast horse all right. We couldn't even ketch him until he was seven."

Men have many reasons for employing a writer to help them with their memoirs. George Moore's reason is that at the age of eighty-one he's still moving too fast. When I told people in the banking business (who knew me because I once wrote a book called *The Bankers*) or people in the opera business (who knew me as the author of the centennial history of the Metropolitan Opera) that I was helping write the memoirs of George Moore (retired president and chairman of Citibank and Citicorp and former president of the Met), I would sometimes receive the response, "Is Moore still around?" For someone like myself, who was more or less frantically trying to ketch him, it was a flabbergasting question.

Moore now keeps his residences in Spain (five of them) rather than New York or New Canaan, Connecticut (though in 1986 he had a new house built in New Canaan for the use of himself and his teen-age children). He is no longer president or chairman of Citibank or Citicorp, of course: the bylaws of those organizations compel resignation at age sixty-five. And he is no longer president of the Metropolitan Opera (though he is still a director and makes his presence felt at meetings when he's in New York). But he's still sole trustee for the Onassis interests in the United States, and a director of several major American corporations, and active if "honorary" chairman of Commerce Union Bank in Nashville, and founder and chairman of a bank he just opened in Gibraltar in partnership with Credit Suisse, and founder and now also "honorary," chairman of Banco Hispano Americano in London. In Spain, he plays a role in supervising the second-largest department store chain in the country (which he helped friends in Venezuela acquire in 1984), he's working with Bechtel and Six Flags to create a theme park, Disney style, on the Costa del Sol, and he is trying to organize, as an adviser to the Andalucian government, a Bay of Algeciras Authority like The Port Authority of New York and New Jersey, to bring prosperity to what is still a relatively underdeveloped part of Spain.

Working with George means subjecting yourself to boundless enthusiasms and careful flattery ("I tried to think of what I would want to hear if I sat in that man's chair," he said, explaining his success as a calling officer who made loans for National City Bank in the 1940s). It also means learning a number of angles you might not have thought about before from a masterful, always shrewd analyst of business conditions and business deals. But the overwhelming recollection is the pace of activity. George gets things done, and then gets the next things done, and the next, and the next, and he doesn't pause to relish his handiwork.

Let us regard, for example, Moore's schedule for two weeks in April, 1986.

He arrived from Spain late Wednesday afternoon, April 2d, dropped his luggage at the River Club, and went off for dinner with Edmund Eisner of Foster-Wheeler, which was considering sponsorship of a natural-gas pipeline to feed a liquefication plant to be built in Argentina for transport to the United States. This was a major project, which would cost several billion dollars. Moore thought banks might help

Argentina finance it by swapping the Argentine loans and bonds for equity in the LNG (liquefied natural gas) lines and plant.

Thursday morning a little after 5:00, Moore went over to his office in the retired-top-executives' suite in the Citibank building at 399 Park Avenue to make calls to Europe. Then he had a 7:45 breakfast and Finance Committee meeting of Mercantile Stores and a board meeting until 10:30, when he huddled with his tax counsel. At 11:00, he had a talk with someone from Citibank España in Madrid, who was in New York and wanted advice. Lunch was with Tom Lincoln, the president of Victory Carriers, the holding company for the Onassis enterprises in America.

At 2:00 we met for a three-hour session on the memoirs, at which he told me that he had a 5:30 cocktails date with Stanley Osborne, who had been with Eastern Air Lines before becoming chairman of Olin Mathieson and then general partner of Lazard Frères. Moore sits with Osborne on the board of New York Hospital, and likes to twit him about being five days older than Moore is. After drinks, he was dining with a young man named Tone Grant, who had taken a job at Commerce Union in the 1970s to sit at George's feet and learn, and is now president of Refco, the largest broker on the Chicago Board of Trade and the Chicago Mercantile Exchange, specializing in the financial futures that more or less drive the world. After dinner, his evening was free. He asked me what my wife and I were doing that night, and I said we were going to the Met to hear Pavarotti sing Radames in *Aida*. He nodded. "I'm still a member of the board," he said, "and I have the use of the director's box. I'll meet you at the bar upstairs for a drink between the third and fourth acts." And he did. This was maybe thirty hours since his plane had arrived in New York. I was a little tired. Not George.

On Friday, April 4th, George had a 7:30 meeting with a personal attorney, then a 9:15 brief appointment on Onassis business, and at 9:45 we got to work. At 11:30 he met with Jim Grant of *Grant's Interest Rate Observer* to discuss a speech he was going to give the next week at a luncheon in the Plaza sponsored by the Grant publication; at 1:00 he had lunch with Manuel Sassot, the Spanish consul general in New York. Thence to the River Club, to pack, and to Kennedy for a plane to Spain. Saturday evening and Sunday he saw his wife and children on what was, in fact, his birthday weekend. Monday and Tuesday he was in Gibraltar renting premises, negotiating charters, and interviewing possible managers for the Gibraltar Trust Bank he was in process of creating. Wednesday the 9th he came back to New York. Fortunately, the plane was on time, for he had two dinners that night at the River Club, one the New York Hospital Medical Board and one with Captain Paul Ioannidis of the Onassis group in Europe.

Thursday the 10th George had a dentist appointment at 8:30, and from 10:00 through lunch a meeting of the Victory Carriers board (for which he had prepared the night before with Ioannidis). Then at 2:00 we met for work on the memoirs, until after 5:00, when he went off for a half-business cocktail party and dinner. Friday morning at 8:00 he saw John Reed, the current chairman of Citicorp, and then he worked with me until he left to give his speech on banking and its regulation to Grant's conference at the Plaza. At 2:15 he had an appointment with a youngish friend at Merrill Lynch, who had been one of George's white-haired boys when George was judging candidates for high office at Citicorp. That night he returned to Spain because there was a dinner party Saturday to which his wife wished to go, and could not go without him. They were both committed to a dinner party at my apartment on Sunday, however, so George turned around the next day and came back to New York.

Early Monday morning the 14th George flew off to Nashville for a Commerce Union Bank board meeting, returning in time for dinner on the 15th with a European client whose dollar holdings George invests. The next day's appointments included meetings with the lawyer, with Greek shipowner George Livanos, with someone who had a venture-capital idea, and with the architect who was designing the new house George planned to build in New Canaan. At the end of this day, George flew off to London, where he had appointments with the manager of the syndicate at Lloyd's to which he belongs, and a dinner with the directors of Banco Hispano Americano, and then, the next morning, a meeting of that board . . .

"Is George Moore still around?"

Yes. It's just that he moves so fast it's hard to see him.

MARTIN MAYER

New York, New York
October 6, 1986

THE BANKER'S LIFE

1
Surveying the Bank

In the history books, 1948 goes down as the year when my fellow Missourian Harry Truman unexpectedly beat my candidate for president, Tom Dewey. In the economy, 1948 was the year when the postwar boom began to slow. It wasn't a great year for the National City Bank of New York, where I was a forty-three-year-old vice-president, because business at the banks usually slows down just ahead of the economy. Our total assets didn't go up much in 1948, and our total profits, so far as we could measure them in those days, didn't go up at all. But in one way it was our most successful year in a long time, for it was the year when the senior officers of National City finally shook off the guilt complex of the 1930s. Washington was still blaming the banks, and especially us, for 1929, but we had begun our moral reconstruction. The change in the psychological climate of the bank made 1948 a great year for Moore, because when the bank began to look forward rather than backward its leaders realized they didn't know enough about what was going on in their own organization. They decided they needed a "new look" at their own bank, and they asked me to choose and chair a "new look committee" (later we called it a "survey committee") that would tell them where we were strong and where we were weak, and where they would have to shake things up.

National City in those days was a personal bank. The chairman or president was boss and called the tune, and the bank followed. Founded in 1812 by a former Secretary of the Treasury, Samuel Osgood, it had been a personal bank for more than a hundred years, from 1837, when John Jacob Astor's friend Moses Taylor took over what was then called the City Bank of New York and ran it as an auxiliary to his commercial empire. Taylor's son-in-law became president when he departed, and a few years later turned over the bank to James Stillman, who had been a protégé of Taylor's when young. Stillman in turn, relying considerably on his friendship with William Rockefeller. John D.'s brother and partner in the Standard Oil empire, built National City from a bank for New York merchants to a bank for nationwide industries, and made it the country's first billion-dollar bank and the most important in the United States. In 1948, City Bank was no longer the nation's largest. Chase, through various mergers, had outgrown us in New York, and Bank of America, with its branches all over California, had easily skipped past banks like ours that were restricted in our deposit-taking to the five boroughs of New York. But we still considered ourselves to be what Stillman had made us: the most important bank in the country.

Stillman's had been an exceptionally strong bank, conservatively financed and run, perhaps the only bank in New York to grow in size and profitability in the terrible panic of 1907. It was also the nation's most international bank. As early as 1902, its advertising had bragged that through a network of correspondents National City could pay out "any sum of money in any city in the world within 24 hours." When the Federal Reserve Act permitted nationally chartered banks to open foreign branches, National City was the first to do so, and in 1915, in a coup that still echoed in our structure in 1948, Stillman had acquired the International Banking Corporation, a Boston group run by Britishers with offices all over Europe and Asia, and special strengths in China. Until World War I chased him back to New York, Stillman lived in France and ran the show by remote control.

People not in descent from a Taylor connection were chief executive officers at National City at various times in this century, and there was even a brief period during and just after World War I when operating authority was split among a group of four "executive managers," but it could be argued that the personal tradition at Citibank didn't end until I became chairman in 1967. My immediate predecessor was Stillman's and Rockefeller's grandson, James Stillman Rockefeller, who had been leapfrogged over a number of somewhat more productive executives (including me) because the executives of the Stillman Trust and the senior partners of Shearman and Sterling, the law firm that represented both the trust and City Bank, decided he had the necessary ability as well as the desired bloodlines.

Though Rockefeller chose me to be his number two and the president of the bank, we were in all honesty very different personalities; when he was chairman and I was president, Fred Donner, chairman of General Motors, said that the bank had a chairman who never talked and a president who never listened. We respected each other, Rockefeller and I, but I can't say there was great affection between us. He was totally lacking in youthful drive (I used to say he was fifty the day he was born), and he thought I had too much of it. When the rules of the bank forced him to retire at age sixty-five, and I became chairman, he staged a strange little personal drama to keep me from having the title "chief executive officer." He stayed on the board, which no retiring chairman had ever done before, and *nobody* got the title of CEO. It was, I suppose, a kind of way for Rockefeller to get even, because— with a lot of help from my assistant and then successor Walter Wriston—I'd been in effect running the bank for some time while Rockefeller had the title of CEO.

People weren't so conscious that Walt and I had been making the moves while Rockefeller was CEO, transforming the bank into a global financial services institution, because I didn't give orders—James Perkins, my first boss and sponsor at the bank, had taught me that the way to manage was never to give an order but to lead people, get them to think that what you wanted them to do was their own idea. Rockefeller was authoritarian and secretive, and if that's the way you relate to the world around you, you give orders. Sometimes you then have a problem finding out whether they were obeyed. I can't say Wriston and I didn't need Rockefeller, or that he didn't make an immense contribution, mostly by his willingness, in the end, to be persuaded that Citibank could not keep its old ways but really needed new plans, new life, new blood. Rockefeller had his brave moments, too: overcoming the doubts of Moore, among others, he pushed the bank into its pioneering move from Wall Street to midtown. But compared to Wriston and me, he was a conservative, which was an advantage. In the minds of some members of our board, even as late as the 1960s, Citibank was still living down the aggressiveness of the 1920s, and without Rockefeller, who was so obviously solid and sound, Wriston and I might not have won approval of our strategy to create a universal bank.

The Rockefeller years, of course, were still in the future when I was made chairman of the survey committee in 1948. Wriston was still in the comptroller's office, where I found him a couple of years later when I was head of the domestic division and looking for good men for the banking department. Rockefeller was running the New York City branches. I was a vice-president in the domestic division, in charge of our banking relationships in the middle west. But I was successful and I was ambitious. If you'd asked me then who was going to be chairman of the bank when the time came for my age cohort, I'd have said, "Moore, I hope!"

In the mid-1930s, I was often in and out of St. Louis, where I'd grown up, working through the problems of the bankrupt public transit system, of which City Bank was the lead creditor. In 1936, when I was all of thirty-one, and then again in 1938, I was offered the chance to go back to the town where I'd gone to school and be president of the First National Bank of St. Louis, the biggest in the city. Walter Smith, the chairman of the bank, made the offer. I told him, "No. I've tasted New York. I don't want to go back. Doesn't matter how much money you want to pay—I'm spending only a third of my salary now. I'm in a big bank, I'm not going to leave." Smith went and told Gordon Rentschler, then president of City Bank. Sometime later, he relayed to me the comment from Rentschler (to whom I had said nothing): "Of course he turned you down. He's too smart to leave City Bank—he knows he's going to be president here some day."

What you can only glimpse from a distance until you've done it, of course, is the fun you can have when you're part of the most important bank in the country, eventually the most important bank in the world. It's exciting to be Onassis's banker; to open bank branches in Europe and Asia and Africa and Latin America; to have George Woods of First Boston come in with Henry Kaiser, who'd been turned down at Chase, and tell them what he'd have to do (which he did) to get his money at City; to encourage United Airlines to keep paying a preferred dividend they had planned to pass, which would have endangered their eligibility as an investment for insurance companies. It was exciting to be a director of Union Pacific as it first began to exploit its fabulous wealth of land and minerals, and of United Aircraft when that company and Boeing were creating the jumbo jet, the 747, and of U.S. Steel as it laid its plans to diversify, to acquire Marathon Oil, and reduce its dependence on steelmaking. It's exciting to be received on one's travels by the heads of state—by Winston Churchill, by Nehru and later his daughter Indira Gandhi, by Khrushchev, Perón, Chiang Kai Shek, Suharto, Nasser, the Shah. (I didn't really collect heads of state, the way David Rockefeller did—I found it more useful usually to meet with the central bankers—but I didn't avoid them, either, and the experience was fun.) It's exciting to be president of the Metropolitan Opera, and in "retirement" in Spain to play golf with the King of Morocco as representative of the King Ranch group that was starting a cattle-raising venture in his country, and to stimulate an effort to create a sort of New York Port Authority in the Bay of Algeciras, to become someday one of Europe's premier ports. It's exciting to advise the Cisneros family of Venezuela in their acquisitions of banks in Florida and Tennessee, of Spalding, the sporting goods house, and of Galerías Preciados, the second-largest department store in Spain; to chair a merchant bank in London and serve on the board of the new Merrill Lynch leveraged buy-out fund; to have Credit Suisse give you an eightieth-birthday party in London to which the heads of Deutsche Bank and Fiat and central bankers and corporate leaders from all over Europe come, just to be nice. All that didn't start in 1948—a little of it had already happened and some was far in the future—but the eighteen months of the survey committee gave it all a big push.

2

In 1948, I had already been with the bank—or, to be precise, with an institution that became part of the bank—for more than twenty-one years. For half that time I'd been personal assistant to James Perkins, chairman and CEO from 1933 to 1940, a very formidable figure, well over six feet tall and heavy, with a thick brush moustache and bald head, a man whose strengths of character, real and reputed (widely reputed, for he had been head of the American Red Cross in France during the war), had made him the savior of the bank in the 1930s. City Bank was on the way to going over the hill in the 1930s, before they made Perkins chairman.

As the boss's assistant, I'd been all over the bank. He'd made me assistant secretary of the board of the trust company, preparing the black looseleaf book for the meetings of the directors. He put me in the investment management department of the trust company to learn how the bank handled investment portfolios, and then he gave me the job of managing the loan fund from which officers of the bank could borrow to carry their margin payments on stock (including National City Bank stock) they had bou ght on credit before the bottom dropped out of the market. He made me one of the liquidating trustees of the National City Company, our securities affiliate, which we could no longer operate because of the Glass-Steagall Act, and couldn't sell. He sent me down to Florida to help bail us out of the banks we had acquired there during the land boom, before the McFadden Act prohibited interstate banking. He assigned me to work with our lawyers defending the directors in a stockholder suit, and to help persuade Congress to write the reform legislation so we could live with it.

Then Perkins also put me to work part time with what we called the "suspense department"—now it's called the department of non-performing assets, but it's still the place where people work out the loans that have gone bad—which was an education in how Charles Mitchell, Perkins's predecessor, had run the bank in the 1920s. It was an eye-opening experience, going through the documentation on the loans Mitchell had made: the only thing in a file on a $30 million loan to the Van Sweringen interests in Cleveland, for example, was a memo from Mitchell saying he had talked on the phone that day with J. P. Morgan & Company and agreed to participate in a loan they were arranging. By the time I was done, I was (and I still am) a convert to the rule that it isn't the business of the chief executive officer of a bank to make loans—that's for lending officers to do, after analysis and consideration.

Throughout this time, I was spending about half my time working directly for Perkins and the other half on assignments he gave me elsewhere in the bank. He taught me, among other things, never to give myself the luxury of disliking anybody with whom I had to work. I learned how to be careful in dealing with people, learned how to build my credibility. He told me, "Everywhere you go in this bank, they'll think you speak for me," and it was true. If I went down and asked someone the time of day, he would say, "Mr. Perkins wants to know the time." Perkins said, "You have the power to do anything, provided you don't abuse it." I had a temper in those days—those who think I have a temper now should have known me then—and I used to blow a fuse at people who were stupid. I learned not to do that.

Perkins was a great man, next to my father the most important influence on my life. He had only one weakness: sometimes he thought he could carry second-grade guys in top jobs. There wasn't any side or show-off or self-indulgence to Perkins. Charlie Mitchell when he traveled around the country had to have a private railroad car, because he was the chairman of National City Bank and that was how so important a man traveled. Once he made the Chicago and Northwestern rebuild the car he had borrowed because he didn't like where the partitions were. Perkins when he traveled took a room on the Twentieth Century like anybody else, and sometimes we shared it.

His reputation was one of great dignity, but in fact he could relax and he always had time to tell a story. One of his favorites was about Charles Hayden of the Wall Street house of Hayden, Stone, whom I came to know because the American Museum of Natural History was one of Perkins's favorite charities and I represented him in the meetings that led to Hayden's giving the museum what is still called the Hayden Planetarium. (All he had to put up in those days to get his name on that institution was three hundred thousand dollars.) Hayden was as tiny as Perkins was big, and he was hugely self-important; he must have been a director on a hundred corporate boards. Perkins was going up to the old Bankers Club in the Equitable Building in the same elevator with Hayden, who was being importuned by some fellow who wanted to make an appointment with him. Hayden kept saying he was busy this day and that afternoon and the other morning, until finally he said something like, "Come in Monday morning at ten, and don't be late because I've got an appointment at eleven with God." As they left the elevator on the top floor, the elevator operator muttered to Perkins, "Busy little s.o.b., isn't he?" Perkins liked the story as evidence of how the most important people look in the real world. And he honestly cared about people like elevator operators. He would say, "You may be the president of the bank and he's just an elevator man, but when his wife is sick it's as important as when your wife is sick."

Perkins and I were very close—I remember he used to squeeze his big frame into my little Ford convertible coupe, waving off the bank's big black car, so I could drive him home and we could talk on the ride uptown at the end of day. I remember moments of special kindness. One day I handed in a report I had prepared at his request. I had worked hard, and I was proud of it. Before looking at it, he said to me, "George, there's one aspect of this subject that especially interests me"— and then he mentioned something I had not included. I was crestfallen. He laughed and told me a story about "my old pal George Murnane, who represented Morgan in Paris during the war, on the French debt arrangements. One day he received a wire from H. P. Davidson, the senior partner of the firm, asking him to buy the best chow dog in Europe and ship it immediately to New York. Murnane decided this had to be important to Davidson, and he worked on it as though it was the French debt itself. Finally, he located what everyone agreed was the best chow, in Vienna, and he gathered a portfolio on the dog's pedigree, all the prizes it had won at the best dog shows, what its dietary preferences were, and so forth. He sent his man to Cherbourg to put the dog on the fastest boat, and he said to himself, I have done this well, Mr. Davidson will be pleased. Then a couple of days after the dog had arrived in New York he got an irritated telephone call from headquarters: 'Murnane, what the hell is that dog's name?'—because the dog wouldn't respond unless called by name. The boss," Perkins said to me, smiling, "always asks the question you don't expect." Once I asked him why he never got mad at me, and he said that if he got mad at me I'd get upset and I wouldn't get my work done.

In 1937, as a final mark of his helpfulness, he moved me out of his office and placed me in the domestic lending division. "An old man with a bum heart is a bad risk," he said; "you ought to get out of the front office and learn to be a line banker, deal with customers and negotiate loans."

He assigned me to DeWitt Arthur Forward, a sound and careful banker who had won his stripes running the Brooklyn branches, who had nursed along such difficult credits as the Brooklyn *Eagle* and the Schaefer breweries—thanks to Forward, without a loss to City Bank. He was a fine instructor and a kind boss, though I always felt he had a weakness of paying too much attention to what his bosses thought: he would jump across the room if one of them spoke to him. I became a vice-president under Forward shortly before Perkins died. That was in 1939, when I was thirty-four, which was very young to be a vice-president of City Bank* in those days—there were only about twenty-

---

*What was originally City Bank of New York, chartered under state law, became the National City Bank in 1865, when a federal charter was awarded under the terms of the then recent National Bank Act. That was the name until 1955, when we merged with First National Bank. On my watch, in 1968, we formed First National City Corporation to own the bank and other companies; in 1974 my successors changed the name of the holding company to Citicorp; in 1976 they changed the name of the bank to Citibank, N.A.

five vice-presidents; we all met together in the boardroom once a week. By the time I left Citibank, we had five hundred vice-presidents, and the only place we could hold a meeting of vice-presidents was the auditorium.

Before going to Forward, I'd done one self-indulgent thing that later turned out to be valuable: in 1936, I'd gone around the world. I'd been involved in an acquisition by one of our trust customers of the infant Western Airlines, which then ran from San Diego to Los Angeles to Salt Lake City, and the business excuse for my trip was that I wanted to see how airlines elsewhere in the world were run. Some of that was interesting. In my mind's eye I can still see the Lufthansa pilots lounging around Athens airport—military fliers every one of them, preparing to take over the world.

I also learned some aspects of banking that you wouldn't find out about in America. I visited our branches in India, and found that much of their business was importing and exporting silver. "These people," one of the managers told me, "have a fantastic sense of value, know whether a silver bracelet is worth two goats or three goats. When the price is two goats, they buy silver; when it's three goats, they sell." We had a manager in the Persian Gulf. I asked him what his customers did. "White slavery and piracy," he said casually. "And smuggling narcotics, gold, and silver into and out of India." I remember we were handling payments for the oil companies to the Saudi government, which demanded gold sovereigns. Britain wouldn't mint them for us, and we had to scramble to buy them, in Argentina and elsewhere. The Saudis didn't want sovereigns with portraits of Queen Victoria on them, and it was explained to me that Arabs are prejudiced against women. Then a Lebanese banker gave me a better explanation: the Victorian coins are older, he said, and they've been handled more, and some of the gold has worn off. The Arabs value gold coins by weight, not by face value, and the Victoria sovereigns weigh less! Lesson: you mustn't accept the first explanations you hear.

3

The chairman of the bank in 1948 who had the idea for the "new look committee" was William Gage Brady, who had come into office only six months earlier. In the politics of the bank, the committee was early witness that he planned to make big changes. Brady had started in the bank's Cuban branches in 1914, and he was a precise, thorough, hard-working credit man. And tough. He understood numbers and he understood banking and cash flow. Nobody ever accused him of doing dumb things. He was a better banker and a better administrator and in general a bigger-league fellow than anybody else in the bank, and that was why he'd become chairman.

In 1948, I was known to Brady mostly as the officer in domestic division who had brought in all those new customers out in the Midwest. He had traveled my territory with me occasionally to visit the bank's major customers. Brady was also pleased, I suppose, by my conformance to his wishes. When I'd worked for Perkins, I'd always worn a comfortable collar, but Brady thought all officers of City Bank should wear a snap-on stiff collar, so I changed to a stiff collar. I kept my shoes shined, too, and wore dark suits and white shirts, because Brady thought a banker ought to look like a banker. And I was thin, and stayed thin, which Brady liked; he used to say, "George, if you get fat, I'll know you've got a fat head."

Howard Sheperd, whom Brady had selected as his president, was a different sort, more easy-going and gregarious. His personal popularity had been a big asset to the bank in the metropolitan division and the overseas division, which had been his responsibilities before he moved up. He and Forward had been direct rivals for the presidency—and earlier: they had both come to the bank in 1916, and shared the same training classes, and lived in the same Brooklyn dormitory. He was also a man of determination and principle. Of those I knew about from my custody of the loan fund, he alone among the vice-presidents of the early 1930s had paid off every penny of the loans that had been made to him to buy National City and other stock, though it meant he was still living modestly when he was a senior vice-president. That's guts. So far as I know, Brady had never borrowed money to buy his bank's stock: he was too smart.

In choosing me for the committee job, which clearly put me on a fast track for future advancement, Brady and Sheperd had had to overlook one disadvantage: the fact that I had arrived at the bank (with Perkins) from Farmers Loan and Trust, also one of Moses Taylor's companies, the oldest such institution in the country, which had been controlled for years by some of the stockholders who also controlled National City, but had not been taken over by the bank until July, 1929. Even after that, the bank and the trust company remained separate corporate entities until 1960. After the Depression hit, when the bank had problems and its directors were sued, when the trust company suffered defaults on 80 percent of the mortgages in which it had invested clients' money, the two organizations were strictly divided in attitude: trust company people looked on bank people as overly aggressive adventurers, whose reputation was scaring the old-line clients of Farmers Trust, while bank people looked on trust company people as dead from the neck up.

Morale at the trust company was even lower than it was at the bank, and trust company people were poorly paid. The man proposed to succeed me as Perkins's assistant at National City in 1937 was Alfred Hayes, later the distinguished president of the Federal Reserve Bank of New York, already considered one of the most able young officers at Farmers Trust. To mark the promotion, Lindsay Bradford, president of the trust company, offered Hayes a small raise. At about that time, New York Trust came to Hayes and offered him a vice-presidency at double his salary. We were good friends; my roommate and I had introduced him to the girl who became his wife. He came to me for advice, and I told him to take the offer: the Hayeses already had two children, and they needed more income. Bradford heard about this, called me down, and accused me of disloyalty to the bank. As a result of such penny-pinching, the reputation of the trust company stayed low. Even as late as 1948 there were still some people in the bank with whom I had to live down the fact that I was an immigrant to the bank from Farmers Trust.

4

The problem Brady and Sheperd wanted me to solve can be simply stated: National City didn't have a game plan, didn't have yardsticks, didn't have a P&L (profit-and-loss statement), really. It was being run on the assumption that anything that made the bank bigger would also make it more profitable. Our committee's mandate was to look at the bank from scratch. I started by listing the businesses the bank was already in:

1. The New York City branch system.
2. The Domestic Division, comprising banking business outside of the city of New York. [This was necessarily done by traveling men and remote control: the McFadden Act prohibited banks from branching interstate.]
3. Head Office Metropolitan Division, comprising the original basic business of the bank, i.e., New York City business not handled by the branches.
4. The foreign banking business handled directly in New York City. This comprises the foreign deposit accounts and loans at Head Office and the departments handling our foreign trade.
5. The foreign branch system.

6. The Compound Interest Department [i.e., consumer savings accounts: we weren't in those days allowed to use "savings" in describing our time deposits, because that word was restricted for the use of savings banks and associations. Strangely, in the City Bank system, the "C.I.D." money, the longest-term funds in the bank, was allocated to the Wall Street office for use in overnight brokerage lending].

7. The Personal Loan Department.

8. The Special Checking Department.

9. The Travelers Check Department.

10. The capital account (if we were not engaged in any of the foregoing businesses, the stockholders would nevertheless make a return on the investment of their capital). Earnings on this capital do not properly belong to any of the foregoing functions.

It will be the purpose of this committee to analyze these separate businesses on their individual merit . . ."

I had known for years that there was a lot wrong with the organization of National City Bank. When I first came over from the trust company, I found that the basic profit-and-loss statement did not express what had happened in the bank over the period it was supposed to reflect. Each division kept its own numbers according to its own traditions, on a memorandum basis, and the profit they reported to the chairman usually added up to about twice what the bank had really made.

Nobody allocated overhead. Nobody assumed any part of the cost of the headquarters office. When our committee studied the profitability of the New York branches, for example, we found that their reported earnings of $8,556,000 in 1948 had to be reduced to $4,843,000 by charging a pro rata share of bookkeeping, comptroller's expense, legal costs, publicity, night operations, and so on. The branch managers would say, "Why should we be charged with the costs of the annual report? We don't need an annual report." Each branch kept its own books, often enough in its own individual way, and the people who ran the branches were little kings. Some years later, when I became president, we commissioned a study of what people thought of the personnel in the branches. They thought the guards were the most helpful, the tellers next, the lending officers after them, and the manager always unavailable.

Other divisions could be fiefs to a breathtaking degree. Soon after Perkins became chairman of the bank, I made out a form that could be used for daily reports to him. I went to Bernie Duis, the bank's chief foreign-exchange trader, with a request that his people price out our foreign-currency holdings at market every day and send the information upstairs. He flatly refused; he told me to tell Perkins that the bank's foreign-exchange position was "none of his business." He had never, he added, told his position to any of Perkins's predecessors, he had always made money, and he had always kept a hidden reserve. A popular story in the bank told of a crisis in 1921 or thereabouts, when a $5 million fraud was discovered in the foreign exchange department in Brazil—and Duis simply reached into his reserve, which he had gathered by selling sterling short during World War I, and absorbed it. He still had a hidden reserve in 1933, and he had no interest in helping other parts of the bank help themselves to what he considered his money. Perkins just smiled at Duis's response. (The only restriction anyone had ever imposed on Duis was that he was kept off the phone. He had six assistants who actually did the minute-by-minute trading, while he supervised at the head of the table. A call would come in: "Guaranty wants to buy two million pounds at five-oh-one." Duis would say, "Tell him to go _____." The trader would say smoothly into the phone, "Mr. Duis thanks you for your inquiry, but he is not interested in making that purchase today.") It was not until after Duis retired that Perkins could really get complete figures on the positions held by the foreign-exchange department.

Some routine matters were problems. We did not have a central file you could call and find out whether Moore was a customer of the bank. At Farmers Trust, we'd established a central information file in 1932, consolidating material that had been in filing cabinets on four different floors into one room, and in the process got the people who worked on the files down from fifty to ten. But it was a new idea at the bank, and to a man, the divisions resisted it. Everybody wanted his very own files. To prove my point, I gathered together in one room the documents relating to one customer, Westinghouse, that were being kept in all the branches and divisions. They covered the big table, and many of the files were duplicates. And this was in the days before Xerox, when making these copies was expensive. The same problems afflicted the securities departments. We had four different places where we kept customers' securities, depending on whether we had them as collateral for a loan and clipped the coupons for the owner, or in a custodial account, or in a trust account, or as the trading inventory of people and correspondent banks to and from which National City sold and bought securities.

There was something to be said for the informality of our opera-

tions: business was done differently in those days. In 1948, after I had
been a vice-president for nine years and had large responsibilities, I
was still formally a "platform officer" and my office was in open space
on the huge, block-square, high-ceilinged banking floor at 55 Wall.
Once because I was on the platform on a Saturday morning when
William Keck of Superior Oil walked into the bank, we made a $5
million loan that otherwise would have gone elsewhere, and picked up
an important customer for the long term. Keck came to us because
another bank had treated him badly, and Jessie Jones, then head of
the Reconstruction Finance Corporation in Washington, suggested that
he try City Bank. Keck said he would do it, but he didn't want anyone
to give us any warning, so he could make a true test of our service.
After he left, I called Rudolfo Ogarrio, a friend who was vice-president
in charge of production at Texaco—Keck had said he had a kind of
partnership with Texaco, because they relied on what were then his
unique skills at deep drilling to reach some pools of oil under land they
owned along the Gulf Coast. I asked Ogarrio whether it was safe to
lend Keck $5 million, and he said, "We'd take his position today for a
hundred million." So I didn't have to do any credit analysis, and I could
call Keck on Monday and confirm to him that he had the loan.

Still, the fact was that we were already a $4 billion bank, with 4
percent of all the bank deposits in the United States. That was too big
an organization to run without a plan. "Take what time you need,"
Brady said when he asked me to be chairman of the new look committee, "but this ought to be done yesterday."

Regular meetings of the full committee were first held every
Tuesday afternoon from 2:00 to 3:30, and then that same afternoon
after the close of day. "Special meetings" were more frequent, and
longer. The minutes repeatedly begin with the statement that ". . . all
were present. Meeting started at 5:30 and adjourned at 11:40 with a
recess for dinner." I asked committee members to set aside three afternoons a week for the work of the committee, and it is a measure of the
commitment of top management to the survey that most of them did.
Brady had not, of course, relieved me of any of my other obligations. I
was still on the road one week a month, traveling the midwest and
making my calls and supervising the lending officers of the district.
Brady and Sheperd knew that the busy guy is the guy you give the job
to, because he's organized. You couldn't overburden Moore; he got it
done. While I was chairing the survey committee, I was also handling
accounts like International Harvester and Standard Oil of Indiana and

United Airlines and Greyhound Corporation—a favorite of mine: all the executives were former bus drivers, turned into hard-bitten businessmen; good fellows; they once asked me to be president of the company.

There was one particular hobbyhorse, growing out of my experience in the domestic division, that I rode throughout the eighteen months of the committee's work. It was the importance of recognizing the soundness—indeed, the necessity—of bank term loans to American industry. We were helping the country build the airlines and gas pipelines and power plants it would need in the future, and it seemed unwise to pretend that such expenditures could be financed by short-term loans under conventional credit lines. These loans required an analysis quite different from what a traditional banker did when he helped a department store stock the shelves for the Christmas season or a shoe manufacturer buy the leather and pay the workers to make shoes. Moreover, term loans paid higher interest rates.

Both Brady and Sheperd were traditional bankers, who distrusted term loans, and they had made a relatively formal commitment to decrease the proportion of the portfolio that was in term lending. A touch slyly, I set up as one of our "projects" a study of "Term Loan Liquidity and Earnings Projection." The memo to Brady from the committee noted that "the liquidation of our term loan portfolio, which is now taking place and is in further prospect, may have a substantial adverse effect on interest income." The project had the desired effect. As the minutes of a meeting have it, "Mr. Moore reported that the term loan study had been referred to Mr. Brady who had commented that term loans with a maturity no longer than five years were desirable if the interest rate was sufficient." With the passage of time, we would get that limit up to seven years, and then, in exceptional circumstances, ten. When somebody wanted to borrow money for an investment that wouldn't pay off for more than ten years, I agreed with the old-timers that there's a limit to how long bank loans should run, and at some point we had better leave the longer maturities to traditional long-term lenders like insurance companies.

I also argued strongly for the full merger of the bank and the trust company. The distrust between the separate institutions was doing real harm to important banking relationships and holding back development of profitable trust business. As structured since 1929, National City contracted out to Farmers Trust for trust services. If you were a trust officer, you were an officer of both entities, but for most men their first loyalty was to Farmers. And the orientation at Farmers was still toward the old families in Oyster Bay and Tuxedo Park who didn't trust City Bank. But the most important business wasn't going to come from the old families any more, it was going to come from the corporate pension funds, and they thought Farmers Trust was full of old fogies who didn't know how to make money with money. Our investment officers had declined to buy common stocks for the Ford funds, and Henry Ford II was once quoted as saying it was a pity that the best bank in the world had the worst trust department. William Lambie, head of the domestic division in the eastern part of the country, refused to permit the trust company to solicit pension management business from the large corporations in his area, for fear that incompetent management of the pension account would jeopardize relationships. Meanwhile, competitors like Bankers Trust, which managed the AT&T pension funds, were leaving the Farmers in the dust.

The solution, obviously, was to improve the trust company, not to bury it. National City had to take it over formally and make it part of the bank. When I became president in 1959, one of my first acts was to push forward the process of shareholder approvals needed to make the trust company a component of City Bank. When the consolidation was announced, I received a note from Halsey Cook, who ran the bank's relations with the Wall Street investment houses and had been a member of our committee eleven years before. "Now," he wrote, "the bank has followed through on all our recommendations. . . ."

5

I have enjoyed saying that everything I did as president and chairman of Citibank was simply a follow-through on the work of the survey committee, and in 1985 one of the senior executives of Citicorp said to me that they really had to have another "Moore committee," because the impetus that such a study gives doesn't last more than a generation. But it's also true that we missed a lot. We did a lengthy study of the bank's municipal bond underwriting and trading department, for example, but never thought to suggest that City Bank should become a dealer in Treasury securities. We were constant buyers and sellers of such securities for our own account, and we were 20 percent owners of Discount Corporation of America, which we had helped to start some years before, and we didn't look beyond that.

The committee failed also to recommend that we reorganize the domestic division into industry rather than geographic groups. I already knew we should do that, because I'd been the chief officer for the Midwest, and I had found that my team of geographical lenders couldn't be expert in twenty-one industries. The First National Bank of Chicago had already divided its officers into industry cadres, and Chase had established "special industries groups," for oil and public utilities. But Forward felt that such arrangements made loan officers the prisoners of their contacts, and meant also that you lost flexibility in deploying your officers—you couldn't move them around. It wasn't until Rockefeller took over from Forward (because the board had to give him some feathers before they made him president), and I had a pretty free hand to run the division, that we acquired our first special industries groups. Even then, I couldn't persuade Rockefeller to let the oil division handle the Mobil account; that, he said, would be "unfair" to the 42d Street branch. Whether we could have moved faster with a boost from the survey committee, I don't know. Doesn't matter: I didn't try.

We were handicapped by City Bank's weakness as a "banker's bank," a correspondent for out-of-town banks that needed reserve city and foreign banking services. I knew why we were weak, because I had heard the story when I started traveling for the bank in 1937. Back in 1922, someone had sent a letter to all City Bank's correspondents, which said, in effect, that if you're not prepared to leave a hundred thousand dollars minimum in the correspondent account, we don't want your account. One of the best ways to get business as a lending officer is to have local banks introduce you to the customers whose needs are too big for them to handle, but when I traveled and called on local bankers, the president of the bank would sometimes pull out of his desk this twenty-year-old letter about why City Bank wasn't interested in doing business with them. There were some towns where *all* the banks were Chase correspondents, because Chase had been formed by an amalgamation of New York banks that had strong correspondent networks, and it was a handicap for the City Bank representative to carry. (These "correspondent accounts" added up to something more than 15 percent of Chase's total deposits.) In retrospect, the survey committee should have urged a campaign to convince the country banks that it would be worth their while to leave a hundred thousand dollars or more at City Bank.

We did strike a blow for the expansion of the retail branches. In 1948, we had only three branches in the whole of midtown Manhattan—42d and Madison, 57th and Park, and 39th and Broadway. We recommended that City Bank concentrate its new branches "in the profit yielding middle and lower Manhattan areas" and take advantage of what we had learned since the Mitchell days (when we had built freestanding buildings of our own rather than rent ground floors in office buildings), that tenants in a large office building are a captive market for banking services and often provide so much business that the branch can be profitable just with the customers who come in through the door from the building lobby, even if nobody ever walks in from the street.

One subject we dealt with exhaustively and unhappily was still around to haunt me when I became president a dozen years later. That was City Bank traveler's checks. We'd had a project on that subject, which had, very surprisingly, turned up an accounting study that proved we were losing money on our traveler's-check business. This was hard to believe, because traveler's checks looked like a natural profit center. You got the use of the purchaser's money without paying him interest, and the costs of having someone else supply him with the cash far away were paid by the fees collected when the checks were sold. The importance of the business as a cement in our foreign network made us reluctant to recommend that we drop it, but the committee some-what sourly suggested that marketing expenses be held to 0.05 per-cent of the previous year's total sales, which would at the least have guaranteed against expansion.

Years later, when I became a member of the Citibank board, I often sat in alphabetical order at banquets next to Neil McElroy, the CEO of Procter & Gamble and a great marketing expert. One evening we had a dialogue:

"How's your traveler's-check business going?"

"Not well."

"What share of market do you have?"

"About 15 percent."

"At P&G we won't be in any product line where we don't have 35 percent. We didn't start Crest and Gleem, our toothpaste brands, until we had confidence we would get a 35 percent market share. What share does American Express have?"

"About 65 percent."

"How many sales agents do you have?"

"About three thousand."

"How many does American Express have?"

"Ten thousand."

"Why?"

"Because we don't think the travel agents and other retailers who sell Amex checks are a good credit risk."

"They pay American Express, don't they?"

"Yes."

"What do you spend in advertising?"

"About three hundred thousand dollars a year."

"Amex?"

"About three million."

"We use your checks," McElroy said, "but I think you're lucky you have 15 percent. Our experience is that to be in business you need product, shelf space, and advertising. You don't have any of them. You'd better give your traveler's checks some special gimmick, get more agents and spend more money on advertising. You have more capital than American Express. Use your muscle—we do!"

Goaded by McElroy, we came up with the idea of instant refund if you lost your checks—such a good idea that in recent years American Express has walked away with it. We went to the National Education Association, the organization of teachers, and asked them to choose a teacher and spouse for a free trip around the world. The one thing the couple would have to do is go into the correspondent banks that cashed our traveler's checks abroad, say they'd lost theirs, and see if they got the service we advertised. I saw the couple just before they left, and told them that even though we were sending photographers to take pictures of them on their travels, I wanted them to be honest— if they couldn't get their money easily, I didn't want them to perjure themselves for the sake of our advertising. Some people at the bank thought we'd be stolen blind, but we never were. Even in the days when you had to post traveler's checks by hand and it was weeks before you knew whether a check had been cashed, very few people tried to beat the bank by cashing checks and then reporting them as lost or stolen. Now, of course, the computer enables you to verify instantaneously whether that check is still outstanding,, and you don't have these risks. But we're still a distant second in the traveler's-check business, though our market share has increased.

6

One of the things I learned while exploring the bank for Brady and Sheperd was that many of the legal restrictions under which we had to operate were our own fault. The businesses we would have liked to be in were businesses the bank had done at one time or another and had abandoned or cut back. City Bank had pioneered personal loans in New York. (I remembered Roger Steffan, who had started that business a year or two before I arrived at the bank, saying that "our credit losses are about three-tenths of 1 percent, and our costs of analyzing borrowers run about 3 per-cent, and that means we must be wasting a lot of our money asking stupid questions.") But we didn't make mortgage loans, and our presence in the consumer business generally had been much reduced by our refusal to help automobile dealers "floor plan" their own inventory. Obviously, dealers would send customers who had to finance their purchases not to us but to the finance companies and other lenders that lent them the money to carry their stock. We didn't understand factoring. Though we advertised "compound interest accounts," we had permitted the mutual savings banks to get exclusive use of the vital word "savings." Increasingly, others, including some who weren't bankers, had built up these businesses as separate institutions, and they had been successful over the years in persuading the government to erect legal barriers to keep banks out.

The bank was willing to spend money for marketing new branches, but few wanted to spend money to develop or market new products. There was always somebody around who remembered that we had tried it in the old days. I share the management theory that nobody should stay in the same job for more than ten years. After ten years you know all the answers, and you start making mistakes. Somebody comes in with an idea and you say, "Won't work. We tried it." But your wisdom is ten years old, and times have changed.

In our final report to Sheperd in July, 1950, I wrote that "our projects and recommendations must be regarded more in the nature of a catalyst, or a series of ideas and possibilities, rather than a finished product on which a final decision could or should be made . . . It was clear to us that our existence, and our work, was stimulating many to reexamine their own work in a similar inquisitive light." Such inquisitiveness came naturally to me, and the opportunity to exploit that trait had been a godsend. By 1950, I really knew the bank, from the cages to the chairman's suite. When I became president, people would speak of "Moore's needle," warn each other to beware. I knew where to put the needle in part because of the survey committee. It was, if you like, the postdoctoral part of the training that had been generously arranged for the man who would become the first chairman of Citicorp.

2
Hannibal to New York, via Yale

I was born in 1905, and spent my first seven-plus years in Hannibal, Missouri. The three children of my second marriage, Cristina and Steve and Pia, were born respectively in 1968, 1970, and 1972, and they spent their childhood mostly in Spain, which is where I retired—presumably retired—when I left Citibank. Because I was in and out of the United States all the time on business, we took our vacations in Europe. When my wife Charon and I began talking in 1981 about what we would do that summer when the children were out of school, they complained that they didn't know anything about where they came from. They'd seen Russia, China, Japan, South America, and India, they'd been all over Europe, but even though both their parents were American they'd scarcely seen anything of the United States. And they were right.

But if the purpose was to have them meet their homeland, I didn't want to take them on the kind of trip where the airplane touches down here or there and you walk through an airport just like the last airport and get into a cab to see what are supposed to be the sights. I wanted some sort of land yacht that we could all live on, so we could see the country as it was made to be seen, by road. We were still thinking about this when I made one of my regular trips to Nashville, where I'm honorary chairman of the board and share strategic planning duties for Commerce Union Bank, which is not the biggest bank holding

company in the state, but it is the most profitable. Somebody in Nashville told me about a Greyhound bus the country-and-western singer
Kenny Rogers had converted to a traveling home when he had to go
on the road as an entertainer. It had a big queen-size bed in the back
compartment, then front sections with six bunk beds, a fully equipped
kitchen, bathroom, dining facility, lounge, and so forth. This was in no
way economy-class travel. Rogers didn't need the bus that summer,
and we rented it.

The plan was that we would live in the bus on weeknights but
stay in a hotel on the weekends. Our driver, Jim Boatman, had sung
with Rogers before becoming his driver, and he was used to theatrical
hours. This was summer—it was light until after 10:00; the others
would go to bed early and I'd sit up in a kind of comfortable armchair
Rogers had installed beside the driver's seat, as Boatman drove through
the night. He rolled that bus at 110 miles an hour, and the only time
we were ever stopped was once in Nebraska, when a police traffic
airplane got us. The first weekend we stayed at the Broadmoor in Colorado Springs, then we went north and stopped during the week at
Aspen and at Laurance Rockefeller's place in Wyoming. On the way
across Montana we lunched with a friend who used to run Montana
Power & Light. Next weekend we were in Lake Louise, and then we
came down through Vancouver and Seattle, where we visited the Boeing
plant, and across Oregon where we visited a Georgia Pacific paper mill
I had first seen with Owen Cheatham, whose financial backing when
he built that company's timber resources included loans from my bank.
(In fact, he and I had worked out the first "timber production loan,"
like an oil production loan, with royalty calculated per thousand feet of
timber rather than per barrel of oil. Those loans were one of the vehi-
cles Georgia Pacific used to become the largest owner of timber land
in the United States.) Then we had a run through the California wine
country, where we visited the Chandon winery because my friends at
Moët-Hennessy own it. They don't call the product champagne, but
they told me it is as good as their Moët-Chandon. We lunched at their
restaurant, which is one of the best in California.

We broke the wine tour with a weekend at the Lodge in Pebble
Beach, then went on to Modesto where we dined with my friend Ernest
Gallo and his family, and visited his incredible winery. Then we saw
Yosemite and the sequoias, and went on to Los Angeles, where we saw
the Paramount studios, where they were shooting *The Winds of War,*
with toy battleships firing real ammunition. We stayed overnight in

the bus in the parking lot at Disneyland, right at the entrance. We saw Grand Canyon, Boulder Dam, and Las Vegas, and drove to Salt Lake City, where we looked in on the Mormon Temple with George Eccles, a longtime friend from work together at the Association of Bank Holding Companies, and visited the big U.S. Steel (now USX) mill—as a former director, I regularly attend their semi-annual management meetings. A fast run to Chicago, then back east to Connecticut. The kids really saw the West.

I saw it too, as I hadn't for a long time. In 1924 and 1927 I'd made trips on gravel roads with my schoolmates at Yale, and back in the 1930s I'd gone fishing in the Wind River Mountains, where John Hay, who owned the bank in Cheyenne, had most of the sheep in Wyoming. During the years I traveled for City Bank I'd been west every ninety days, but when you're traveling for a bank you don't see much. The changes in the country over the half-century were beyond imagining. I'd first seen Rock Springs, Wyoming, in 1933, when it had been a railroad stop, no paved streets, a frontier town like those in the Western movies. Now it was full of shopping centers and offices and apartment buildings. Most of this had happened since 1953, when I'd taken my eldest son George, the son of my first marriage, for his swing through the West, also by car.

But the great moment of this trip with the kids in 1981 was not the mountains or the canyons, the movie lots or the factories, or even the sight of the country rolling past the windows of the bus. It was our visit to Hannibal, where we went first from Nashville. I went to the cemetery where my mother and father and sister lie buried (and I noticed again what I had always thought to be a peculiarity of Hannibal, that the tombstones told you either of youngsters who had died early, of diphtheria or scarlet fever, or of very old people who had lived into their nineties: few people in Hannibal—few people in my family, wherever they live—seemed to die in middle age). My children, one of them not yet ten, met their father's relatives, my mother's sister's daughters, other than myself the last of my generation, who were already in their nineties, and who died not long after.

2

In physical appearance, Hannibal has changed less than most of the country. The population today is almost exactly what it was eighty years ago, about eighteen thousand. It still has the Mississippi, and the hills to north and south, the houses with the deep porches, broad streets, and lawns with sheltering trees. Of course, in nearly all the ways that count it's very different from the Hannibal where I was brought up, which you probably know a lot about already, if you've read *Tom Sawyer* and *Huckleberry Finn*. My Hannibal had a number of people living in it who knew Mark Twain, and even more who were characters out of his books, like Molly Thatcher and "Injun Joe."

The Hannibal where I was born was a railroad town. The real money in Hannibal was lumber money, which is perhaps the reason I've always been interested in timber properties, and there were factories that made everything from iron stoves to candy, including a U.S. Steel plant that produced the cement for the Panama Canal locks, and a Du Pont powder plant. But the major employment in the city was in the railroad, in the works that manufactured and repaired locomotives, in the divisional offices of the railroads, in the train crews and work crews that were based at this crucial junction point, where the line between Chicago and Minneapolis and St. Louis met the main line going west. The year of my birth there were fifty-four passenger trains a day that stopped at the Union Station in Hannibal. (In 1986, there wasn't one.) Running the railroad in Hannibal was a step on the executive career ladder of the Hill railroads: four men who had been district superintendent in Hannibal later rose to be president of the Burlington Railroad or its affiliates Northern Pacific or Great Northern. Long years later, I would serve on the board of Northern Pacific.

My father, who had been born in Hannibal, worked for the Burlington, the "K-line," so-called from the shape of its route map, and had since he was in his teens. Eventually he rose to be chief of the claims department, a position of some substance; he couldn't go any higher—this was talked about at home—because he'd never been to college. While we were in Hannibal, he was still just a claims examiner: if a farmer said his carload of wheat had got wet and ruined in Burlington's boxcars, my father went off to investigate and settle. That meant he was away from home quite often, perhaps two, three days in the normal week. As a significant employee of the railroad, by the way, he had to wear a watch that was accurate within thirty seconds a week, and the Burlington specified its construction: no less than seventeen jewels, a steel balance, nickel movement. There were only two acceptable brands, one of them Hamilton, which he wore. He gave me that watch when he retired, and the railroad gave him another.

We lived in half of a nice double-house in a good neighborhood, on Center Street. The house is still there. One of our near neighbors across the street was George Dulany, whose family were lumber barons and also controlled the Hannibal National Bank. George Dulany inducted me into what he called the Society for the Prevention of Calling Sleeping Car Porters George. George Washington was its patron saint, Senator George of Georgia was its president, and all members had to be named George. To become a member one had only to pledge that if he heard any traveler call, "Hey, George, take my grip" when addressing a sleeping car porter, he would intervene and ask the porter his name. If it wasn't George, the member was then obliged to turn to the offender and say, "Pardon me, sir. This man says his name is Charlie. Please call him Charlie." I am among the last survivors of the club, which has of course lost its function.

We didn't have much money. I remember my mother made most of her clothes, and my sister's and some of mine, too. I think all my uncles were richer than we were, including my mother's brother, who had married a rich girl from Chicago. Aunt Sada married H. A. Allshouse, the Kansas City manager for Parke-Davis, and they had prospered on its stock. Their son Harry, Jr., became a pioneering orthodontist and straightened my teeth with braces. We didn't have our own carriage, and few had a car in Hannibal in my childhood, though my Aunt Luna and her husband John T. Holme did; they had a Cadillac. He was the largest stockholder in the Farmers and Merchants Bank and ran it. (The cashier of the bank and his family occupied the other half of our house.) We called him "Uncle Dode," and like most people in Hannibal we relied on him for financial services. He and his son-in-law owned an insurance agency, Holme & Hickman, and what amounted to a savings-and-loan association where people left their money and Holme lent it out for mortgages, and made other investments for them. Uncle Dode always came home for lunch, then took a brief nap (siesta, we'd say in Spain), and walked down our street back to his office. His only son had died in childhood of scarlet fever, and he was especially nice to me.

Among our other rich neighbors were the Rendlens, who owned the local stable (later, showing you how things change but still they stay the same, the Rendlens became the Chevrolet dealers). But we weren't by any means poor. We could rent a carriage if we couldn't borrow Aunt Luna's, and we had something other people didn't have, not even Aunt Luna, which was a pass on the railroad. One summer before I left Hannibal, in fact, the district superintendent lent us his own private railroad car so my mother and my older sister and I could

The six Stevens sisters, ca. 1900; my mother Etha to the far right.

My sister, my mother, and me, 1910.

In front of our house on Forest Park Boulevard in St. Louis, about 1915.

Yale freshman before his dormitory, fall 1923.

travel to Colorado on vacation in style. My father, as I remember it, didn't take vacations in those days.

He was George Moore, too; in fact, my son is the eighth George Moore in direct descent, according to records in Lancaster, Pennsylvania, which is where the family lived before my grandfather Moore went west. My mother always called my father "Mr. George," probably to distinguish between the two of us, but he was George Victor Moore, so I wasn't a junior. I was George Stevens Moore, and for a while in my first years at college I even signed myself G. Stevens, because my mother liked that. Stevens was her maiden name; the pretty Stevens girls were among the leaders of Hannibal. Their grandfather was a legend; he had gone off to California to make his fortune in the Gold Rush of 1849, and had come back without the gold—it had been stolen from him, he said, on his return trip—but with a diary full of stories about Indians and cowhands and miners and mining towns.

The Stevens clan gave their daughters strange names: my mother was Etha, and her sisters were Luna, Valley, Sada, and (the one common name) Jessie, who died young. They had been Virginians originally. When I was ten, my mother took my sister and me on a vacation to Winchester, Virginia, where the family mansion was still in the hands of *her* mother's people, the McLeods. Half a century later, when I was president of Citibank, I went to Martinsburg, Virginia, about two dozen miles away from Winchester, to help the Old National Bank of Martinsburg celebrate the hundredth anniversary of its founding. Old National had been a correspondent of City Bank from the day it opened its doors. I told the story of my childhood visit to Winchester, and one of the men on the dais for the banquet rose at the end of my speech and said, "I am your cousin . . ."

Like other Missourians who had arrived from the South, the Stevens family were Southern sympathizers, and I remember them telling me about the Yankees' coming through Winchester, and the young men, hiding in the attic till they were gone. The Civil War was still in people's memories when I was a boy in Hannibal, which had been a border town, fought over, with members of the same family on different sides. There were in effect two county seats for Marion County: Hannibal (which had lost its primacy as punishment for mostly taking the side of the South) and Palmyra, which had been Union country through and through, where, according to firm belief in Hannibal, Union soldiers had staged a gruesome massacre of Confederate prisoners.

I remember the winters best. There was always a big Christmas party at Aunt Luna's, with fifty or seventy-five people from the Stevens clan. Our neighbor across the street, Bob Hogg, had a homemade bob-sled, a plank ten or twelve feet long with steel runners attached to it front and back, and ropes that could steer the runners. All the boys would pull it up the hill from Center Street to the Cruickshank mansion atop Tenth Street (this was another lumber baron), and lookouts would be stationed at the cross streets to make sure there was no traffic coming in the snow. The bobsled would come careening down the hill, almost out of control, and sometimes would make it almost to the rail-road tracks, more than half a mile away. When the snow was light and the metal runners hit rocks in the roadway, you could see the sparks. I would watch the bobsleds from my window. The boys would give my sister Louise a ride once in a while. I was only six years old the winter before we left Hannibal, and I didn't qualify for the bobsled gang, but I remember, or I think I remember, that at least once the big boys gave me a ride, too.

In the summers there were boat rides on the Mississippi in the great sidewheelers, and my sister, who was six years older than I, would talk about the dances on the boats and at the Labinnah Club (Hanni-bal spelled backwards). Mostly, for me, there were the circuses, three to six of which came to Hannibal every year—the Lemon Brothers, the Sells-Down, the John Robinson, the Barnum & Bailey, Wallace and Hagenbeck, and Ringling's Circus, of course, which came every year. Ringling also owned the Hannibal & St. Louis Railroad, because the tradition of the industry was that people who owned (or worked for) one railroad got special privileges on other railroads, and the Hannibal & St. Louis was good for concessional fares for the circus all over the country. In itself, it wasn't a very successful railroad. Wags used to say that trains left Hannibal for St. Louis "tri-weekly—they left on Monday and tried all week to get into St. Louis." In fact, Ringling's tracks never did make it to St. Louis; they ended in Alton, Illinois.

The summer when I was four, the Wallace and Hagenbeck Circus came one night while we were asleep and had its tents pitched before we woke. They paraded down Broadway to open the run, delivery wagons fighting their way for position against the elephants, the horse-drawn lion cages, the clowns and trapeze performers, the calliopes and the band. The street was all churned up. We went, of course. I saw the show in the big tent, the bands, the fat lady, the tallest man, the dwarfs, the Siamese twins, and I ate popcorn and candy canes and cotton candy. Every summer, some Hannibal boys "joined the circus" and left town.

I don't suppose I ever would have done that. We were too close a family for me to run away, and my mother was too ambitious for me. And I always was fond of Hannibal. I loved the Mark Twain Cave where we could pretend to be Tom and Huck, which wasn't hard for us because that's what we were like ourselves. I enjoyed the carriage rides to the railroad station, with a stop at the ice cream parlor for a chocolate soda. I can still remember my Aunt Lou making apple butter in a big copper kettle, with a big ladle stirring it, and how good it tasted. I can still hear in my mind's ear the midnight sound of No. 4, the fast train to Colorado, whistling as it came to the grade crossings, the whistles coming closer and closer together as the train picked up speed going through the town. But something extra would have had to be done, I suspect, to let me broaden my horizons, if the Burlington hadn't transferred its claims department to St. Louis. To St. Louis, then, we moved, in fall, 1912.

For some years we lived in an apartment on Forest Park Boulevard, a gravel street with a strip of parkland down the middle. It was a good neighborhood, and when my father became chief of the claims division and we could afford something more, we stayed, renting a house very near the old apartment. Even so, it was a tight squeeze, and my mother helped ends meet by renting out a room in the attic, at twenty dollars a month, to a young salesman from the Ralston Purina Company, a great St. Louis company, which made corporate loyalty a religion before anybody ever heard of the Japanese—everybody who worked for Ralston Purina wore the company's red-and-white checked jacket, and not just on the job, either. He gave me my first lesson in salesmanship, showing me how he put together a marketing plan. This is still a great company, founded by a man named Danforth, a Tom Watson, IBM-style promoter. One of his grandsons is now a United States senator and another runs Washington University, which inherited part of the Purina money. The other fountains of fortune in St. Louis were the shoe business (led by Hamilton Brown, predecessor of International Shoe, which became the GM of shoe manufacturers), the Anheuser-Busch brewery (though it wasn't yet the biggest beer company in the country), and Lambert, which made Listerine.

My mother's reward for moving to the big city, away from her family, was a little Dodge sedan she loved, and I did, too; it was my job to wash and polish it. Another luxury was the Steinway piano, the status symbol of the middle class. When my sister married, she and her husband bought one, too. Then when my mother's house was broken up after her death and my sister found herself with two Steinways, she sold them both—nobody played them, anyway.

I went to the Duncan Avenue School, a block away, and my best friend there was Finley McElroy, whom I met playing marbles in the neighborhood. We both remember that I won all his marbles and followed him home in hopes of getting more. The next time I showed up at his house, he remembers, and it may be so, it was to sell his father a subscription to the *Saturday Evening Post,* and I did, though I was only about eight years old. Finley lived in a three-story mansion of twenty-five rooms and a ballroom, with a side yard big enough to play football in, which we did—and a basement, where we could make gunpowder, which fortunately nobody ever found out about. When the world war came, we were intensely patriotic, dug trenches in the yard, played games in which many Huns were killed, and knitted scarves and even warm socks (our teachers "turned" the heels) for the boys at the front. That's been a long friendship, Finley and I: we didn't go to school together after the age of ten, because Finley's parents had the money to send him to St. Louis Country Day, and mine didn't, and he was at Princeton while I was at Yale, but his younger brother David and I roomed together in New York before I was married, and over almost three-quarters of a century we've never lost touch. When I took my children on the bus trip, our first stop was at Finley McElroy's house in rural St. Louis.

Warren F. McElroy, Finley's father, was a classic Horatio Alger story. A farm boy, he had walked 120 miles to St. Louis from Rensselaer, Missouri, not far from Hannibal, looking for work. He applied for a job in the shipping room of the Hamilton Brown Shoe Company, and when told that there were no jobs, he offered to clean up the shipping room without a job, because it needed cleaning up. The boss, A. D. Brown, happened to hear this, and told McElroy that when he was done tidying up he should come to the office. Hired, he worked hard, became plant manager at the age of twenty-eight, and (this was, as people forget, a key part of the Alger legend) married the boss's daughter. That boss's daughter, by the way, lived to be 103 years old. Widowed at age seventy-one, she took up ballroom dancing, which she had never done before, and in the words of a tribute to her in the Mary Institute alumnae magazine, she "quickly learned all of the steps, new and old . . . won every medal offered by Arthur Murray and gave an occasional ballroom exhibition." The boss's son, unfortunately, was less talented. When he succeeded his father as president, McElroy moved out to start the McElroy-Sloan Shoe Company (and some of the other executives left to start International Shoe, which became the biggest shoe company in the world). Brown's will had instructed the bank as executor and trustee to sell Hamilton Brown, which they failed to do, and after the shoe company went bankrupt in 1927 for lack of management, the heirs successfully sued the bank for negligence, an interesting case that stayed in the back of my mind when I was doing trust company work.

Mr. McElroy liked me; I guess he saw in me some of himself when young. I remember he liked to say that while the world had changed a lot, "the same rule still prevails, that energy and industry are rewarded, and laziness suffers." From the age of twelve, I always worked, weekends and summers, selling magazines and delivering orders for Freedman's Delicatessen. I also sold honey, which I bought for ten cents a pound in five-gallon jugs and peddled at thirty-three cents a pound in quart glass canning jars I'm afraid I filched from our pantry. On hot weekends, I'd make lemonade and set up a street stand on the corner of Forest Park and Euclid. I had my own bank account from the age of twelve, and thought of myself as financially self-reliant.

One of my teen-age summers, Mr. McElroy gave me my first real job, as a "sole stamper" in what had become the McElroy-Sloan Shoe Company. I ran a stamping machine that cut out sole leather with a steel cutting die, for fifteen dollars a week. The work was dull, but the experience was intensely interesting. I met other workers and learned how shoes are put together, and how hard ordinary people had to struggle for a bare living. Another summer a road crew was working on Forest Park Boulevard and I went out and asked if they needed another hand, and I wound up driving the big grader—it wasn't very hard, I had learned to drive my mother's Dodge, but it was exciting.

One summer I had a political job: a friend of the family knew Louis Nolte, the comptroller of St. Louis, and I worked in City Hall writing out water bills at a penny a bill from huge piles of looseleaf ledgers. Another year I was a meter reader for the Laclede Gas Light Company. After a month I was promoted from being a meter reader with a block to cover to being a "special" who went out on problem cases, riding my yellow bicycle around a whole neighborhood. Some of these were houses where people threw their garbage in the cellar and it smelled so bad I wouldn't go in; I'd send a notice that if they didn't clean out their cellar we'd cut off the gas. Another of the problems was at a mortuary where they'd built the freezer against the wall that held the gas meter. They told me to go right in and read the meter, and there were corpses in the icebox. . . .

The story the McElroys liked to tell, however, the one that tipped them off to the fact that I might have some unusual business talent, happened at their country place, Blackburn Villa, on their large farm about fourteen miles from Hannibal. I spent many weekends and several weeks every summer with the McElroys on this farm, which boasted a tennis court and one of the earliest swimming pools in the state of Missouri, sixty feet by twenty-five feet, with fish in the water to eat the tadpoles. The high point of the summer was always Fourth of July, when the McElroys had a giant fireworks display and people by the score came out from Hannibal for the party. To guide them and add to the festivities, the McElroys always hung Japanese lanterns on the elm trees beside the road to their house. This year they forgot to buy the candles for the lanterns, and Mr. McElroy gave me a twenty-dollar bill and sent me out with the chauffeur to go into Hannibal and buy candles. I went to hardware stores and grocery stores, but everyone was out of candles. Somebody mentioned that candles could be bought at the Hannibal office of the Standard Oil of Indiana, so I went there, and found that they sold only by the gross. So I bought a gross, went back to the hardware stores and grocery stores and sold half a gross of candles to them, and returned to Blackburn Villa with both the twenty dollars and the candles.

Most years, we took a real vacation for part of the summer. Often my Aunt Sada would come with us and help pay the bills. She was a widow then, and her friend Mr. Harry Walpole, a rich landowner from Kansas City, would sometimes join us, and maybe he picked up some of the check, too—I never knew. We went to Colorado many summers, and then we got passes on the Santa Fe all the way out to California. We visited Los Angeles half a dozen years in a row. I remember the big hotel, the Ambassador, which is still there. Now it's virtually in downtown Los Angeles; then it was out at the end of Wilshire Boulevard, with nothing but open countryside between it and the Pacific Ocean at Santa Monica. The movie industry had already settled in, and we went to see Tom Mix make movies. We stayed at Santa Monica and at Ocean Park, where we could swim and visit the "piers," which were the forerunners of today's amusement parks.

Before I entered high school, then, I had been to Colorado and to California, and to Virginia to visit with my mother's family. And I had been on the trains back and forth to Kansas City many times, riding on the family pass, going to the dentist. Unlike most youngsters of that time, I already knew something of a larger world. Even in high school, which was still in those days a rather selected group of adolescents—the proportion of teen-agers who went to high school in the 1910s was much smaller than the proportion of young adults who go to college now—you were pretty well-traveled if you had seen California and Virginia. Thanks to my mother's ambitions for me and the position of the Stevens family in Hannibal, I was also moving in somewhat more exalted social circles than my companions at Soldan High School, which was considered the best public high school in St. Louis, but which was still just a public high school in a city where the top families sent their children to Mary Institute and St. Louis Country Day.

I met those children of the St. Louis social set at the McElroy's, and also at Jacob Mahler's dancing school, where my mother arranged for me to be accepted. There were classes on Friday afternoons, and for the older students there was the "Fortnightly," a formal dance usually preceded by dinner parties at the leading homes. At the dance, you tried to get "seasons"—reserved dances—with the pretty girls, and to fill your program as soon as possible, or else Mr. Mahler or one of the mother chaperones would collar you and make you dance with the wallflowers. Even then, I was conscious of how those homely girls suffered waiting against the walls for someone to arrange a dance. My girlfriend my last year in St. Louis was a girl whose grandfather, Rolla A. Wells, had been mayor of St. Louis, and whose mother was upset that we were holding hands at Jacob Mahler's. Maude Street: she was a very beautiful girl, exactly my age, and the year of her debut she was Queen of the Veiled Prophet Ball, the big coming-out party in the city of St. Louis. She was married the year I went away to college, though the two events weren't related. Last I heard, she was still around, though we didn't look her up on our bus trip. I hope she has as happy memories of those days as I do. Jacob Mahler's, of course, is long gone, with so far as I know nothing to replace it, which is very sad. The building survives; it's used by an undertaker.

The academics of Soldan High School never gave me any trouble. I was one of the best students, especially in math, and in English and history, though I was also a member of the school's chemistry club and I liked science. My mother kept some of my report cards, and looking at the ones for the spring of my junior year—with my father's signature on them to prove that he had seen them: "Mr. George V. Moore"—I find that I was also very healthy, no "times absent" at all.

The big thing at Soldan High, however, was sports, and I wasn't much good at any of the sports. I was small. So I did the next best thing: I wrote about them. The school had a weekly paper supervised by a bachelor English teacher, Bruce Smith, who had to read every word before we could go to press. It was Smith who had given the paper its rather obscure name *Scrippage*. This came from Shakespeare's *As You Like It* (recent research has been done on the matter), where the court fool Touchstone contrasts a military retreat with "bag and baggage" to his own exit with "scrip and scrippage." The Yale edition of Shakespeare, which was published as early as 1919, says that "scrip" is a wallet and "scrippage" its contents. It's a suitable name for a paper of which a future banker was manager, but I doubt that was on Smith's mind.

I was never the editor—I was the "manager," responsible for getting the ads sold and the paper printed. But I wrote the sports stories that took most of the front page, and I wrote a humor column, under the title "The Nutmeg Grater." (The masthead of the paper carried a motto reading, "The greatest nutmeg ever grown will some day meet a grater.") I cared about the newspaper more than about anything else in my high school years. Late every Sunday afternoon, I would take all the copy and the layout of the new issue to Smith's rented room in a house near the school. He would approve it (we never had a censorship problem), and I would see it through the press. My successors on the paper the next year wrote of me "as the indomitable spirit who made SCRIPPAGE a real paper, who gave it an artistic as well as a peppy appearance." Even in those days, I had a reputation as someone who got things done: in my high school yearbook under my picture, the legend is "Efficiency—George all over."

At my high school commencement, six graduating seniors spoke. The others chose as their subjects Loyalty, Ideas and Ambitions, Essential Qualities of Leadership, Mothers of Humanity, and The Far Goal. My subject was The Newspaper and the American Ideal. I have no memory of what I said, but I must have been impressive, because at the end of the ceremony the principal, John Rush Powell, asked me to come to his office, told me that he was chairman of the scholarship committee of the St. Louis Yale Club, and that he was authorized to offer me a five-hundred-dollar-a-year scholarship to Yale.

Finley McElroy was going to Princeton and several of my friends from Mahler's classes were going to Yale, but it had not occurred to me that I might go east to college. My parents could never have afforded that. (I would necessarily have gone to one of the universities in St. Louis, probably Washington University.) When I told them about the scholarship, they were almost as much concerned as they were pleased. My mother thought that at seventeen I was too young to go east by myself, and my father thought five hundred dollars might not be enough money. Both were worried that my academic preparation at Soldan might not be good enough to make me ready for the work at Yale, for in those days two-thirds of the students at Yale came there from the ambitious prep schools. Mr. Powell decided that they might have a point, and agreed that I should take a year first at Washington University in St. Louis, near my home. I could live home, work and save some money for Yale, and make sure I was ready to handle a Yale program. He not only arranged my admission at Washington on those terms, but found scholarship money to pay the Washington tuition so that my funds for Yale would not be diminished. After a year at Washington University, where I also put much of my time into the newspaper, *Student Life,* I had the great good fortune of a five weeks' summer job on the *St. Louis Globe-Democrat,* filling in for the beat men at City Hall and the city hospitals and the county court house. Then I went off to Yale in fall 1923 with a new blue suit my parents had bought me, riding as usual on my father's railroad pass.

3

The first thing I learned at Yale was that my blue serge suit wouldn't do, and that five hundred dollars a year wouldn't do, either. There were twelve of us from St. Louis in the class of '27. The other eleven had gone to St. Louis Country Day or to one of the eastern prep schools. I was assigned to a suite in Farnham Hall on the Old Campus, sharing it with a boy from one of the nearby Connecticut mill towns. He was an outsider, too, a "townie." I took care of the suit problem first, my second day in New Haven: I went to J. Press and spent forty-six of my last fifty dollars to buy a suit that looked like what the prep school boys wore. Then I went to the bureau of appointments for a student job, and found that all the good jobs, those running the laundry, for example, had already gone to people who knew somebody. What was left for me was a job as waiter / dishwasher in the Commons, the student dining room. The hours were 5:30 to 9, which meant I couldn't enter the competition for the *Yale Daily News.* The job was tough, time-consuming, and socially downscale, too. This was the first time I had been away from my mother and my family. I was confident I could make friends, and I did; but I never succeeded—no one ever really did—in breaking into the prep school crowds. Those first weeks were pretty painful.

Fortunately, I found out about Mrs. Porter's on High Street, where the boys who could afford something better than the Commons ate their meals, at eight dollars a week for three meals a day, and excellent meals, too. The Porters had an arrangement whereby they gave any student who signed up ten others to eat at the restaurant free meals for as long as the ten remained patrons. I went out and found ten of my classmates who could afford to eat at Mrs. Porter's, quit my job at the Commons, and was free to compete for the *Yale Daily News,* billed as "the oldest college daily," which I believe it is. Two older alumni, one the uncle of one of my "favorite's" at Mahler's, the other one of the St. Louis Yale Club sponsors, had advised that I get into the first of the year's three competitions, the one that ran from September to Christmas.

Candidates for the board of the *News* were called "heelers." They were messenger boys for the editors, they reported the news, they wrote the stories and they sold the ads. You got "points" for every hour running errands, every dollar of advertising sold, and every story the paper carried. There were forty-three candidates in my competition, and by the rules only three were to be elected. I was told that the winners would likely be reporters who had placed sixty to seventy thousand words of copy in the paper during the three months, performed three hundred hours of errand work, and brought in about eight hundred dollars of advertising (this was easier for candidates whose parents or parents' friends had businesses that advertised). To keep up with that schedule, I had to work at the newspaper until two or three every morning, and begin preparing my classroom work after that. But I never regretted it. Heeling the *News* was a great way to learn the ropes at Yale, because the members of the board of editors were influential men on campus and the process of reporting opened doors where I could never have entered otherwise. In a matter of days I met most all the key people on the campus, the men who were active in sports and student activities, and I could begin to think about what I should do to build my own place in that power structure.

And it was a great experience in itself. I knew the thrill of a scoop and the disappointment of a failure to sell advertising space (I didn't have my rivals' captive customers). I felt the joys of receiving a bonus on my record for a well-written article, and the horror of being docked for an error. This was a sterner competition than anything in athletics, let alone academics. And reporting built character: a reporter who is unceremoniously expelled from a dozen places in a single afternoon, which can happen to someone from a college paper in a place like New Haven, receives an unforgettable lesson in managing adversity. It was also, though this would never have occurred to me at the time, excellent training for the life of a calling officer at a bank. Finally, heeling for the *News* taught a convincing lesson that it was not only possible to work twelve hours a day at a job—it was, sometimes, enjoyable.

My sponsor at the Yale Club had warned me that successful heelers were almost always boys who had been on the boards of their prep school papers or had worked for real newspapers in their home towns. My time on the *Globe-Democrat* proved invaluable, and I held on against the prep school crowd. Of the forty-three original candidates, only twelve stayed till the end. Two of these were disqualified for some reason, and of the other ten the editors elected four instead of three. I came in third; I hadn't sold much advertising and I hadn't run many errands, but during the three months I had written ninety thousand words and the *News* had printed seventy-five thousand of them. They elected a fourth because on the editors' record books I had finished with five thousand points more than the younger brother of one of the senior editors, who was going to be elected pretty much whatever happened (he was also, in fact, well qualified, and had been editor of the paper at the Taft school).

I was still not quite home free, because a faculty rule required that a new member of the *News* board had to pass all his courses in the term of his competition, and I was in bad shape in English and French. I signed on at Rosenbaum's Tutoring School and just scraped by in the term exams February 1st, with a sixty in both. Sixty was passing. I was so exhausted after the exam that I went to the Yale clinic, and a doctor told me to take a week's rest. Finley McElroy was also at end of term in Princeton, and his father was taking him to Atlantic City for a celebratory weekend; and he took me, too.

When I returned, life was pretty soft. Editors had to do much less work than heelers—and, in those days, editors earned money for the work they did, because the *News* in those days was a profit-making enterprise. Subscriptions paid the cost of publishing, and all the ad sales were profit. The organization was a partnership, which was dissolved by the outgoing editors every January and immediately reconstituted by the incoming board. The departing board would make some of the profits of its year available as a loan to the new board to provide working capital until graduation, when the loan was repaid to the graduating board members. Meanwhile, editors were paid three-fifty or five dollars a night for their labors. Each editor worked one night a week, three of them at a time, reading what the heelers turned in, deciding what to use, laying out the paper, and recording the heelers' credits for the night. I worked on Thursdays, which meant I had the rest of the week free. I even had time to attempt something athletic, and I rowed in the class crew.

Now that I had time to burn, I was determined not to burn it. I drove at my studies, and I went out for debating, which I felt would do me more good than any other available activity. I was one of the three Yale debaters in the Freshman Triangular Debate in Sanders Theatre at Harvard, where we defended the affirmative to the resolution "That the Platt Amendment concerning Cuba should be applied to the Philippine Islands." Remembering the fury that later descended on the United States from the Latins, who resented this provision empowering the United States to prevent any change in the Cuban constitution, it's interesting to note that ours was the "progressive" side, because we were in effect arguing the case for Philippine independence. It was quite beyond anyone's imagination in those days that we would turn our colony loose without some requirement similar to the Platt Amendment, retaining our right to intervene. We won the debate, but the Philippines would not receive their independence for another twenty-odd years. (Forty years later, incidentally, I would be the American president—Carlos Romulo was the Philippine president—of a splendid organization called the Philippine–American Friendship Society, which met only when there was something to do. We built a memorial to MacArthur, helped build a hospital, and financed a meeting arranged by Columbia University's American Assembly that helped the State Department convince Congress that we should permit to expire a treaty that guaranteed American business in the Philippines the same treatment native businesses received.) I didn't debate again. Yale in those days leaned toward the English style of debating, which meant making wise puns and jollying the judges, but I didn't do enough background reading to debate that way.

At the end of my freshman year I was faced with the major Yale decision: was I going to take what we would now call a liberal arts program (then it was called the "academic" program), which meant living and taking classes on the main campus—or was I going to take the scientific program, which meant living and taking classes up the hill at the Sheffield School? That first year, I had been stronger in science courses, and I liked the idea of more practical studies, but the truth of the matter is that I made the decision on social grounds. At Washington University I had joined Alpha Tau Omega, a national fraternity, which disqualified me from joining any of the fraternities at Yale College, all of which had other national affiliations. But five of the eight Sheffield fraternities were local to Yale, and couldn't care less about ATO. One of the St. Louis alumni, a Sheff product himself, warned me about this problem in January of my freshman year, suggested that I would be happier with a social home at the Sheff than as a non-fraternity student in the academic program, and offered to introduce me to his own Berzelius Society. This was a "secret society" in the Yale tradition, but it operated an open and aboveboard residential house called the Colony Club, on Hillhouse Avenue, in a stretch of great mansions that still looked much as it had when Charles Dickens described it as "the most beautiful street in America." The Berzelius meetinghouse, an impressive brownstone building on Congress Avenue, still standing, was called "the tomb." My sponsor in St. Louis not only arranged for me to be tapped by Berzelius (which I was told about long before Tap Day), he also arranged that I would have the right to recruit my friends to the society. That was really the way it worked, and still does despite all the mystique.

Before that I had to get through sophomore year in the Sheff dorm, which meant new eating arrangements—Mrs. Porter's was a little far away for Sheff students. I went to Mrs. Porter, and promised that if she would start a restaurant in Sheff I would deliver enough customers to make it profitable. Some friends of mine and I started a "Sheff Club" to which we "elected" the customers, and it worked! Mrs. Porter then had two establishments. As the organizer, I received my meals free, plus a commission on each week's take.

During that year I found the job that would take care of my money requirements for the rest of my time at school, and give me a lot of fun and recognition, too. Lyman Tucker, Sheff '25, was an editor of the *News* and also sports correspondent at Yale for all the newspapers other than the *New York Times*—for the *New York Herald Tribune* and the *New York Sun,* the *Boston Herald,* the *New Haven Journal-Courier* and *Register,* and the Associated Press. The local papers paid a quarter of a cent a word, the other papers paid a half a cent, and the AP paid by the item on some formula I never did understand. Once the football season was over, Tucker was tired of the job. He made me an offer: if I would do his writing and file it under his name, he would pay me fifty cents an hour and turn all the jobs over to me when he graduated that June. I accepted. By April I was the Yale correspondent for all those papers. I also attempted to create a magazine, which I called *Intercollegiate Sports;* we published only one issue, because we couldn't sell any ads.

These activities won me various perquisites. I was, for example, allowed to have my private phone at the Colony Club, which was otherwise forbidden (I had to lock it up to keep my brothers from using it). I had a desk and a typewriter at both the Western Union and Postal Telegraph offices, so I could get my "takes" on the wire as I wrote them. The *New York Times* correspondent, an older man named Sedgewick, also had a desk at the wire offices, but the boys, especially those at Postal Telegraph, liked me and they didn't like him. So if he "filed" a story I didn't have, or if I was away for some reason, they would rewrite his story and put it on the wire to my papers—Sedgewick never had a beat on me. I had some on him, though, for which the *Times* chewed him out.

Sedgewick had a hard time in general, because I had so many papers. Once at a hockey game I was so busy writing my story that I didn't notice the last goal. I reported that Yale had won 7 to 6 when it was really 8 to 6. He got it right, but the *Times* was angry because his editor was sure he had it wrong—the AP, for which I was the stringer, had the score 7 to 6. In my senior year, I also wrote two columns for the *Yale Alumni Weekly,* one called Campus News and Views, the other Sports of the Week. Deadline was 7:00 Monday morning. Many was the Sunday night I got back from visiting some girl at Smith College, or a weekend in New York, wrote my columns in the early morning, and slipped them under the door at the *Weekly* at 4:00 A.M. before snatching some sleep and getting up at 7:30 to make breakfast and class. I also did some publishing work for which I didn't get paid, writing the newsletter of the Berzelius Society, and editing the journal of the Yale Engineering Association, and serving as one of the editors of the 1927 class yearbook.

Of course I also had an annual pass from the athletic department for all sports events, and I sat at the press box in the Yale Bowl. Reporting on a football game is harder work than people think. You have to keep a chart of what happens on every play to make sure you get the summary right, with the names of the ball carrier and tackler—there wasn't so much passing in those days—and the kind of play. Afternoon papers and the AP expected a running story, too, so while keeping the chart I was usually dictating a play-by-play to two different wire operators. And then at the end of the game I would dictate a summary. That was the time when Ivy League football was the national story, and the big names of sportswriting sometimes sat beside me. Grantland Rice was the senior football writer for the *Herald Tribune* in those days. Usually, he would write some color for the opening paragraph— "As the red, red sun went down behind the purple hills, the big blue team did it again"—and then he'd say, "George, you finish the story," and he'd go have a drink with the Yale coach, Tad Jones. But he saw to it that the *Herald Tribune* paid me my space rates (a half a cent a word) for the whole story, including what he'd written.

Another good earner for me at Yale was the "Yale Press Club," a trade name I used to sell articles to newspapers across the country. For example, the Yale Prom comes around February 1st each year. I would write a full article about this undergraduate glamor event, and then get a list of the girls who had been invited, their home towns, and who had asked them. The article I sent to the *New Orleans Times-Picayune*, for example, might start, "Betty Boop, daughter of Horatio and Evangeline Boop of New Orleans, will attend the Yale prom as the guest of Charlie Whoosit, captain of the Yale football team and a member of the promenade committee." There followed a thousand-word article about the committee and the prom, and so on. I would send this with a letter on "Yale Press Club" stationery, asking them to send me twenty-five dollars if they used the article. They usually did, and they always paid. I did the same sort of thing to the home-town papers when a local boy received a campus honor. This was a good income-producer.

I found a number of other ways to make money at Yale. My senior year, for example, Brad Smith, another *News* editor, and I formed a partnership to promote events. We organized dances at the New Haven Lawn Club, hired Rudy Vallee or Ben Cutler (who were Yale men) to play at the dances, formed "committees" of the prettiest girls from Smith, Wellesley, Bryn Mawr, and Vassar who were sure to be asked to Yale dances to promote the event, and sold tickets, scheduling the event for the nights after big football games or spring crew races. To make sure too many fellows didn't come with the thought of taking home somebody else's girl, we priced the tickets at two dollars for a couple and five dollars for a single. Some of these dances netted us as much as a thousand dollars.

In November, 1926, we bought out the Ambassador Theatre in New York for the hit musical *Queen High* the night after the Yale-Princeton game, held that year in Princeton. We advertised "Yale night on Broadway"—catch this year's hit musical on your way back from the game—in the *News* and the *Alumni Weekly* and at the Yale Club in New York, and we sold all the tickets at a one-dollar premium, with a profit of about twelve hundred dollars. I saved the stage box for myself and my friends. We had to give back two hundred dollars of our profits in overtime payments to the stagehands, however, because we had to ask the theater to hold the curtain until the team finished its dinner at the Vanderbilt Hotel and all the special trains got in from Princeton Junction. But that was a great night.

The most memorable of my money-makers was a Grand Tour of Europe. Mac Lewis, a St. Louis boy my age, friend of McElroy's at Princeton, had a friend named Jack Wyngaard who'd been a soldier in the war and stayed in Europe, married a French girl. He had a Cadillac limousine that would seat six in addition to the driver, and he was looking to rent it for the summer at twenty-five dollars a day, including the gas and his services as driver. Lewis and I gathered four fellow students, rich pigeons, to take an all-inclusive two-and-a-half-month guided tour of Europe, which we described in the most glamorous terms, at around twenty-five hundred dollars each. We didn't tell them we'd never been to Europe, either. Lewis and I earned free passage for ourselves from the Holland-America Line by serving as "recreation directors" on a student third-class passage, over on the *Rotterdam* and back on the *Nieuw Amsterdam*. We met our tour buyers in London, took them to Oxford and Stratford, left them in London for a few days while the two of us stole a side trip to Ireland to kiss the Blarney Stone and visit Killarney, then went to the continent to tour in the Cadillac through France, Switzerland, and Italy. That was the year the French franc collapsed; it went to fifty to the dollar. You didn't need reservations at the hotels and the rooms were cheap, champagne was ten cents a bottle, and Europe was full of American college boys and girls living like kings and queens.

The typical routine would be as follows. We would arrive at, say, the Palace Hotel in Lausanne. Wyngaard would go in and say we wanted dinner, bed, and breakfast for four passengers, two double rooms, and get a price. Then he would insist that the "courier" (Mac) should stay free, ditto for the driver, and for me as "second courier." Sometimes they balked at three freeloaders for four paying guests, but usually we could make a good deal. Then Wyngaard would go to a nearby jeweler to arrange a commission for us, and we would suggest to the boys that they buy Swiss watches for their families and friends: which they would do, and Jack would come back later to collect our percentage. Then we'd go out in the evening, sometimes with the boys and sometimes just the three of us, to find the college-girl crowd. The boys were poor little rich boys, very dull, and their families were glad to get rid of them for the summer. And they were glad, and lucky, to have Mac and me take them for a fabulous tour. That's the way they felt, too—years afterward, when I would run into one of them, he'd thank me.

This was Yale in the twenties: speakeasies, mocking Prohibition; flappers; flaming-youth time and no denying it. I can't quarrel with the statement that it wasn't good for everybody. My senior year one of my roommates at the Colony Club was T. D. Buhl, whose father had been founder of Parke-Davis and whose mother was a sister of Florenz Ziegfeld. He was in love with one of the Ziegfield girls, Anastasia Riley. We'd go down and see the Follies and go out afterwards, T. D. and his Stasia and a girl for me. Buhl was very bright but also very lazy; he never worked, and he became the dullest guy in town. He married Stasia, and they lived in Palm Beach and raised cats until they both drank themselves to death. But I could have a ball in the evening, late into the night, and get right back to work the next morning. I did, all through my years at Yale.

4

When I think back on Yale I don't think about any courses I took, and the only professors I remember were English teachers—William Lyon Phelps and Chauncey B. Tinker, both great characters and great lecturers, whose classes usually drew alumni visiting New Haven and seeking to recapture what they best remembered about their college experience. I went to my classes and took my exams. They were the price I paid for what I wanted to do. They didn't have much relevance to what I planned to do in the future, because the fact was that like nearly everybody else I knew at Yale, I didn't have much idea of what I wanted to do in the future. In the end, though, it turned out that my training at the Sheffield School was continuously useful to me as a banker. I'd studied industrial engineering and industrial chemistry.

When customers came to me with projects to finance in energy, chemicals, machinery, they didn't have to draw too many diagrams for me to make me understand what they were talking about. Reading their annual reports, I knew the difference between shoe polish and mouthwash. When I ran into the Solvay process for making ammonia, I remembered it as something I'd studied in school. I learned enough French so that when Citibank opened its Geneva branch I thought I could give a brief talk in French, and I thought I did, though I gathered that the French-speakers in the room were not so sure; I didn't try that again.

The Yale that developed after the Depression and the war is a very different place from the college I attended, and I'll admit I like it less—it's too intellectual for me. My friends and I got deeply involved in academic questions at Yale only once, when the *News* picked a fight with the president of the university, James Rowland Angell. He was the first non-Yale man who had ever held the job. The trustees had recruited him from the University of Chicago, which was importing a more European, research-based model of education into the United States. Angell recruited some Nobel Prize-winners and other famous academics, but the weakness in that, as we saw it, was that these great men did not teach undergraduates. Angell seemed to be building up the graduate schools at the expense of the college, and we were a college paper.

During the year when my class ran the board of the *News*, the administration began a major fund-raising drive. We went to Dr. Angell and said that we thought he should tell the alumni before raising the money where he planned to spend it. After all, the alumni of the undergraduate college were likely to be the major contributors. They weren't interested in giving to Yale so that professors could be recruited to teach graduate students who had done their undergraduate education elsewhere. He said, No, no, they couldn't do that, he wasn't ready to announce a plan yet. So the *News* editorial criticized the pending endowment campaign, which as I look back was rather impudent of us. Eventually, Angell did make a commitment to spend most of the money to be raised on the undergraduate colleges.

When I was chairman of Citicorp, my colleague Walt Wriston and I went up to New Haven and asked the then president of Yale, Kingman Brewster, to join our board of directors. He gave it some consideration, but decided he didn't want to soil his hands with thoughts of commerce. I left with Walt, whose father had been president of Brown

University, and we both wondered if we should feel ashamed of ourselves, though not for long. (We offered the post we had set aside for
an academic to Lawrence Fouraker, dean of the Harvard Business
School, and he accepted with pleasure; he used to tell me those Citibank board meetings were "my only contact with the real world; otherwise I live in a world of theories.") When I visited Yale in 1983 with
my children, I asked Brewster's successor, Bartlett Giamatti, whether
Yale still turned out *leaders,* and he said that he thought it did. Moreover, he said, when he hired Nobel Prize-winners it was with the
understanding that they would not only teach undergraduates but would
take some of their meals in the Commons and hold court in the lounges
before dinner so the students could meet and talk with them. Some of
them live in the colleges with their families. I think that's excellent,
and maybe it would have made a difference in my education if something of the sort had been true in my time. Probably not. Anyway, as a
past president of the Metropolitan Opera and the Hispanic Society in
New York and a founder of the Monjo Museum in Barcelona, I guess
I can say that my education managed to equip me to appreciate what
we used to call the finer things in life.

What Yale really taught me was how to communicate, and you
can't learn anything more important. You can be the smartest guy in
the world, and it doesn't do you any good if nobody listens to you.
That—and reliability. You've got to file to the newspapers on the football game at 4:45 P.M., and you can't be late.

I did well enough in my courses to be chosen in my junior year
for Torch, an honor society at the Sheff, which had an interesting custom. At some time during his senior year, every member was the subject of a meeting of the society. He would speak for ten or fifteen minutes
or so about himself, and then other members would comment, making
suggestions about how he could improve his efficiency or his sociabil-
ity or his plans for the future. It was an instructive experience. These
fifteen guys who were telling you about yourself had known you for
four years, they're pretty smart fellows, and you know they mean well;
the system gets you in the mood to accept criticism without jumping
out the window or getting your fur up. What they said about Moore
was that his arguments were too set and he was too inflexible, that he
was too hard-headed, that he joked too much, that he's too much for
himself rather than for the group, that he's not around his fraternity
house enough, that he tries too much, and that he cares too much for
money. I guess the session didn't do much good, because these same

criticisms have been made of me for all the almost sixty years since; but at least I knew they were coming.

Membership in Torch led, oddly, to my last commercial venture at Yale and my monument at the school, for succeeding generations of students kept publishing the magazine I revived (a similar magazine had been published early in the century) at the behest of the Torch alumni. This was the *Yale Scientific Magazine,* which was an effort to communicate to the world, and especially to Sheff alumni, what was going on in the sciences and especially Yale's contribution to scientific advance. There was no *Scientific American* or *Science Digest* in those days, but a number of other universities did have scientific magazines. Yale had tried a few years before, and failed. I guess I was tapped for Torch, despite the fact that my grades weren't that great, because some of the recent graduates wanted to try the magazine again, and thought I was the most likely man to do it. They raised a purse of two thousand dollars to pay for a secretary and for my trips to New York to sell advertising and work with the Yale Engineering Association, a Sheff alumni group that had about five thousand members and offices in New York. I didn't spend much of it.

Starting a magazine puts you in a vicious circle. You can't sell a magazine until you've got one, and you can't afford to put out a magazine if you haven't got advertisers, and you can't sell advertising until you have a magazine. All three legs of the tripod have to sort of appear simultaneously, or somebody has to hold the bag for the costs until they do. But I had an idea. The Yale Engineering Association was collecting dues, but it hadn't been doing much. I went down to New York and outlined the magazine I proposed to put out, and suggested that they buy subscriptions for all their five thousand members—and they agreed. Then I went to the advertising representatives who sold space in all the other university science magazines, treating them as a unit, which made it worthwhile for, say, General Electric to take an ad that would run in thirty places. I told them what I was going to do, and they liked the idea of adding Yale to their list; and they promised me twenty pages of advertising for the first issue.

Then I went to the faculty and told them this was going to be good for the Yale Engineering Association and the Sheffield Scientific School, and I formed an advisory board of professors who agreed to write some articles and screen the others. The advisory board gave the magazine some professional pizzazz. Finally, I had to assemble some fellows to do the work. I started the project in my junior year, but it wasn't until

Greece in 1936, on my airline inspection trip; me at far right, William Coulter, owner of Western Airlines, second from left.

David McElroy, me, redwood tree, and touring car, summer 1927.

the May just before I graduated that the first issue came out. It was a magazine for the layman—the first issue, for example, featured an article on how Movietone was making the new talking pictures—but the faculty advisors assured its probity. Thanks to the twenty pages of advertising, it was profitable. I took about eight hundred dollars out of it as my share and left the rest to the fellows I had chosen as my successors, to keep the magazine going.

That year, counting the receipts of the special fiftieth-anniversary issue that commemorated the founding of the nation's oldest college daily, the *News* made about thirty thousand dollars. Through calendar 1926 I had been assignments editor in title and for most of the year I had been managing editor in fact, because the managing editor was sick. My share of the profits was four thousand dollars. I had eight hundred dollars from the scientific magazine, plus my share of the proceeds of the dances and *Queen High* and the previous summer's Grand Tour, plus the money I'd saved from the sports reporting and my columns in the *Alumni Weekly*. Having arrived at Yale with no money at all, a blue serge suit, and a five-hundred-dollar-a-year scholarship that would pay tuition and dormitory room and absolutely nothing more, I would depart Yale with a Yale man's wardrobe, grand memories, and about ten thousand dollars in the bank. One way to illustrate how much money that was is the fact that a new car cost about four hundred fifty dollars in 1927. Another is the fact that the job I took in New York carried a salary of eighteen hundred dollars a year. All my life since then I have had a luxury my father never knew— enough in the bank so I don't have to worry about what happens next.

My success as a businessman at Yale turned out to be the determinant of my future. That spring, Sloan Colt, Yale '18, a vice-president at the Farmers Loan and Trust Company of New York, came to New Haven on a recruiting mission. He asked Albert "Baldy" Crawford, who ran the bureau of appointments, to recommend the student in the class of 1927 who had been "most successful at self-support." I didn't know Crawford particularly, but he knew about me. He called and said he had suggested that Colt lunch with me. I told Crawford I didn't want to be a banker—banking was dull. He told me I didn't know anything about banking, which was true, and he scheduled the lunch.

Colt took me to the Alumni Club and charmed me. He told me that being a banker was much better than being a businessman, because a businessman made decisions only about his own business while a banker made decisions about everybody's business. He promised me that he would personally follow my career and teach me banking. The next morning I wrote him a letter accepting his offer, noting that we could arrange the details later. I didn't ask him what he was going to pay me—that's one of the advantages of having ten thousand dollars in the bank.

When I went home to St. Louis and told my mother, she said she could understand why I wanted to work in New York, but she wished I had taken something in St. Louis, instead. The fact is that nobody offered me anything in St. Louis, though I'd met with people from the Yale Club to report on how I'd used my scholarship and they'd had chances to talk with me about my plans. The president of the First National Bank of St. Louis, in fact, had sort of run down the job I was taking in New York, but he didn't offer me one himself.

The summer after my first year at Yale, I'd taken a circle tour around the country with a classmate from Cleveland, Lyman Treadway. We drove through Wyoming and Montana, saw Lake Louise and Vancouver, then traveled down the West Coast to Los Angeles and back via the Grand Canyon and Colorado. That had been a grand time, and following my graduation I more or less repeated it, with Finley and David McElroy, carrying tents and sleeping bags in a touring car, for six weeks in Colorado and Montana and the Pacific Coast. We came back to St. Louis and dropped the car, and I had a last night at home.

I saw my mother twice more—when she visited me that Christmas in New York, and when I went to St. Louis on my vacation the summer of 1928. She took sick without warning while my train was taking me back to New York, and before I could return, she was gone. My father moved in with my sister. Suddenly the only home I had was in New York.

3

Becoming a Banker in Boom and Bust

Sloan Colt had promised that if I signed on with Farmers Loan and Trust he would make me a banker. The first thing required of a banker is judgment about whether someone who is borrowing money, or wants to borrow money, can and will pay it back. When I reported for work in August 1927, therefore, Colt had me assigned to the credit department, which was *the* apprenticeship for becoming a banker. It's like being a young doctor—you want to be in the hospital; that's where the patients are. Colt liked to say that a banker was a business doctor.

Unlike the doctor, of course, the banker risks his own health on his diagnosis, and the first lesson of banking is that you mustn't, ever, place a bet you can't afford to lose. The banker is a person who diversifies his risks, and never steps on a soft plank. That's something you have to know instinctively when you come to work in a bank. Then you can learn in a credit department that there's more to banking than balance sheets. A balance sheet is nothing but a photograph taken on December 31st. It shows you how that racing car looks as it zooms past the stands in front of the crowd. But if you're going to put money in it, you'd better go round the whole track with this fellow a couple of times, take a look at those places where he skids and the turns he takes on two wheels.

Colt was a good sponsor to have. He came from old families on both sides, he was wealthy, he was intelligent, he was handsome, he was a good fellow, with friends all over. And when he said he would take care of me, he meant it, within reason. One of my first weekends after I started with the bank, he invited me to his lovely home in Tuxedo Park, a guarded-community hideaway for New York's rich and powerful (the place gave its name to a way of dressing for dinner). That set me up with the other juniors, and with the seniors, in the credit department: they'd never been invited to Sloan Colt's weekend place. There was one junior, though, who wasn't impressed at all: William Waldorf Astor, later Lord Astor. Farmers Trust had managed the Astor money for more than a century, and the family had sent Bill our way with the thought that he might find it useful some day to know about banking. It wasn't a thought he particularly shared. Bill worked at the next desk, so I knew what he was doing. He was on the phone, ordering champagne from his bootlegger and making dates with girls.

The rest of us worked pretty hard. My second day on the job, I went to the number-two man in the department, Edward Crabbe, and asked him what he thought somebody starting out should do in his off-time, to give him a head start in a bank. He said, Well, you'd better learn accounting, and you can't teach yourself accounting. So I quickly signed up at New York University to take an accounting course two night a week.

Farmers Loan and Trust was an important institution on Wall Street because it managed the money of the Astors and the Whitneys and the Dukes and many of New York's oldest families, not because it was a power in the great world of commercial banking. It was the oldest and at that point the largest trust company in the world. Founded in 1822 as the Farmers' Fire Insurance and Loan Company, Farmers Trust had long been a sort of partner to City Bank, which as a nationally chartered bank hadn't been given trust powers until 1919. The Moses Taylor family had controlled both institutions, and into the 1910s James Stillman had run them in tandem. Then they split up and even began to compete: the bank had acquired a trust department and the trust company had built a banking division. Even in 1927, the two institutions still had many of the same stockholders and directors, but we did compete. Though Farmers Trust was quite a small bank by comparison with City Bank, we had some big borrowers and some even more sizable lines of credit—agreements with companies that when and if they needed money "during the current season," up to the limit of this line, they could simply come in, sign the note, and take it at the interest rate prevailing on that day. The line-of-credit letter usually gave the bank an out if there were any "material adverse change" in the company's affairs, though I cannot recall a single instance where we actually invoked this clause to refuse the use of a line.

What the credit department did was described as "revising the file." Whenever a lending officer saw a customer, he wrote a memo on the meeting, summarizing the information received and what the company wanted (and what he had promised) with respect to its borrowing needs. That memo came up to us, and we analyzed the statements submitted and compared any new data with what we had before (remember that these were days before the Securities and Exchange Commission, when you didn't get anything like the information you get today). We called around to the other banks, City Bank, Guaranty, Chase, whatever, to ask whether they had loans outstanding to this borrower and what their experience was with them. We wrote to out-of-town banks, asked what sort of balances these borrowers kept, did they expect to renew their lines of credit, and so on. We asked trade creditors whether the customer paid his bills promptly, and what limits they put on his line. Usually we also went to one of his competitors to get another view of conditions in the trade and, discreetly, what our borrower's reputation was. The credit department didn't *decide* whether the bank would make the loan, or even make recommendations. It sent the file back to the lending officer with the "revised" information he needed to make the decision himself. Everyone in the credit department hoped and expected to be a lending officer himself, some day.

Not long before I arrived, Farmers had learned the hard way, humiliatingly, about the importance of credit analysis. One of the bank's biggest borrowers, Bacon & Company, a factor in the textile industry, had gone bankrupt, and ultimately paid off less than five cents on the dollar. Its president, Francis M. Bacon, was one of the largest stockholders in Farmers Trust, not only a director, but chairman of the directors' examining committee. We not only gave him a large line of credit ourselves, we vouched for him with other banks. He went under mostly because he concealed losses Farmers could have helped him recover or stop if he had been candid with us. New York law in those days gave state-chartered banks the power to seize the stock a borrower might own in the bank and apply its book value to any losses on his defaulted loans. We did seize Bacon's stock, but our president, James H. Perkins, was so embarrassed by what had happened that the Farmers donated the stock to the other banks that had lent Bacon money, accepting a total loss on our loan.

Still, the fact is that when the borrower is big enough and well-enough connected, lending officers often don't want to listen to bad news from the credit department, even when the taste of a Bacon & Co. disaster is fresh in their mouths. I learned that only a few months after I started work, when I was handed the file on the L. C. Gillespie, Rogers Pyatt Shellac Company, which borrowed from Farmers as much as the banking law allowed us to lend. Hugh Brooks, a Farmers vice-president, was the officer on the account. His memo on his meeting with Gillespie included a statement from the company that its accounts receivable were all "good and collectible," due from customers in the "ordinary course of business." The fact was, however, that those accounts receivable included millions from an Indian subsidiary of the company that was a shell and a fraud, with no resources from which to pay its liabilities.

The Gillespies were supposedly very wealthy people. John T. Gillespie was, among other things, president of the Yale Club in Morristown, New Jersey; his son Lou had been in my class, and I knew him. Nevertheless, I went off and did my job, which included what we called "competitive checking," making discreet inquiries at the borrower's rivals. My experience as a reporter on the *Yale Daily News* came in handy for this purpose. I talked my way into the offices of Gillespie's leading rival, Ralli Brothers, and questioned one of the principals. Mr. Ralli said he thought Gillespie had lost more money than its net worth in shellac dealings with Ralli alone in the previous twelve months. He showed me the numbers and the documents, and I wrote a memorandum for the lending officers. But Colt had been Gillespie's friend at Yale, and he couldn't believe a member of the old blue team would cheat his bankers. Brooks and Colt initialed my memo, filed it, and ignored it. Six months later, the company went broke. My memo had disappeared from the files, but fortunately I had kept a carbon, and had shown it to some people.

It would be nice to think that because I got this one right they gave me more significant things to do, but the truth is that the assignment that gave me my big break was an accident. Mr. Perkins—it's a prerogative of being president—wanted someone from the credit department to take a look at a business proposition he had been offered as a personal investment. He called the department at lunchtime and spoke with Paul Jacoby, who was the head of the department (and a survivor: he was a senior officer of what was functionally the same department at Citibank a quarter of a century later, when I was a senior officer). Perkins was in a hurry. Everybody in the department was out to lunch except Jacoby and me. Jacoby described the job to me and said, "This is for the boss. Make it good." I think Perkins had a hunch that the fellow he was asking me to look up was a bum risk. What you find once you're suspicious is that bad guys leave a trail. You can save yourself a lot of pain by following it. I went to fellows this man had cheated, banks that had lost money on him. *Everybody* said, "Don't trust him." I brought Perkins my report, and he got word to me through Jacoby that he thought it was a good job—and a few weeks later, he called to ask me to do another one for him.

Though I didn't feel it in my lowly position, through 1928 Farmers Loan and Trust was under continuing and growing pressure to sell out to National City Bank. Charles Mitchell, who ran City Bank and had built its associated National City Company into one of the largest securities houses on Wall Street, was embarrassed by the weakness of his trust department. Mitchell argued that by combining City Bank and Farmers Trust you could get major improvements and better earnings in both the bank's trust operations and the trust company's commercial lending business. The collapse of Bacon & Co. and the Gillespie bankruptcy, and some other credit mistakes at the Farmers, lent a good deal of force to Mitchell's position. The market price of the City Bank stock he offered in the exchange was more than double the market price of the Farmers Trust stock that would be surrendered.

Perkins had no great desire to work for Mitchell—he had hired Mitchell into City Bank originally, in 1916, during the period when he had been one of the four "executive managers" of the bank, before he went off to head the Red Cross in France in World War I. He knew Mitchell was primarily a salesman, and might make really serious mistakes if not controlled. I found in Perkins's files a memo he had written in 1916, recommending Mitchell's employment as "just what the organization needs to put its new securities affiliate on the road . . . a good salesman, developer, but possibly prone to take excessive risks, which would necessitate supervision, lest he get the company into trouble." The arrangement that was worked out in 1929 when City Bank took control of the Farmers provided that Perkins would retain a fair amount of independence as the president of a separate trust company, to be operated entirely for the benefit of the stockholders in City Bank, but in no way consolidated.

The creation of the new City Bank Farmers Trust Company was to occur on June 30th, 1929. When this development was announced in March, Perkins found himself overwhelmed with correspondence from customers and shareholders of the trust company. He asked me to come down from the credit department and become his assistant in handling the correspondence. He gave me a box of correspondence signed in blank, and told me to use it with discretion, checking in with him if there was any doubt about what he should be saying. Sloan Colt was very pleased with my new position, which seemed to testify to his good judgment, as I was identified as someone he had brought in. Perkins used to tease both of us—he was from Boston and a Harvard man, and he liked to say that he'd never met anyone from Yale who could read or write the English language, but sometimes they were good at business so he liked to keep a few of them around.

The day before the reorganization was to take effect, Perkins's secretary Anna Shepard saw me outside his office and said, "Where is our nice Mr. Moore going tonight?" Perkins called me in. He'd been busy, and he hadn't thought about me. I told him I expected I would follow Colt to the bank, and resume my work in the credit department. Perkins said he felt abandoned, and he wanted me to stay in the trust company as his assistant. He called in Colt to suggest that I stay with him, but Colt disagreed: he thought I'd learn banking better with him at National City. But Perkins was a very important person, and the chance to work as his special assistant was an unusual opportunity, and I happily accepted his offer. What I had seen of National City up to then I hadn't liked very much—it had seemed to me a big, impersonal organization. I thought Colt himself might get lost there. I already knew a little about Charlic Mitchell, who ran National City in a very personal way, and it seemed to me he wouldn't tell Sloan Colt the time of day. What happened, in fact, was that after only a few months at City Bank, Colt was recruited to be the new president of Bankers Trust, the youngest president of a big bank in New York. Maybe he would have taken me with him if I'd gone to the National City when he went, but I don't think so.

Anna Shepard, incidentally, stayed with Perkins to his death in 1940, and then retired. At this writing she is still very much alive, 103 or so. When I was president of the Metropolitan Opera and she was more up and around, I used to give her opera tickets, and I still send her flowers every year for Christmas, and every year I get a nice note of thanks.

I was happy doing chores for Perkins, who kept giving me new assignments with growing responsibility. In January 1930, before my twenty-fifth birthday, Perkins made me an officer of the trust company. The title was only assistant secretary, but there weren't many twenty-four-year-olds who were officers, and it meant that my pay rose to more than I could spend, which has been true all the rest of my life and probably accounts for my good health and cheerful temperament.

2

People who did not live through it can scarcely imagine the Wall Street of the late 1920s. It seemed that money was something you played with: everybody had it. If you were a senior officer of a bank, with lending powers, you benefited by what could almost be called a conspiracy to make money for you. One incident I happened to know about was the first offering of a stock trading company, the Goldman Sachs Trading Company, to be operated by Goldman Sachs & Co. It came out at something like twenty dollars a share, and immediately went up in price, because, then as now, people thought Goldman Sachs had a golden touch. That afternoon, a senior officer I knew at the bank received a call from a partner at Goldman Sachs, who said, "We allocated so-and-so many shares to you at the offering price. Would you like to take them? If not, we'll sell them for your account and send you a check for the profits."

The president and two senior vice-presidents of Farmers Trust rode downtown together in a taxi every day. One of them would poke a pin through the *New York Times,* then open the paper to the financial section. When they got to the office they would buy a hundred shares of the stock that the pin had punctured. Before the close of the market that afternoon, they would sell the stock, and the profits from the day's trading would be added to (or, less frequently, the losses would be subtracted from) what they called "the taxi fund." Over the course of the year, the taxi fund more than paid the cost of their transportation to and from work. It was that easy!

Everybody seemed to have money. The messenger boys from the floor of the stock exchange would pop out for an ice cream soda, and tip the counterman a quarter, which was more than the soda cost. In his first appearance as chairman of the City Bank Farmers Trust board, after the reorganization had gone through, Mitchell boasted that every vice-president of National City was worth at least five hundred thousand dollars, thanks to the National City stock the bank's officers had been encouraged and helped to buy. He said he would "take care of the trust company people" when he had some time.

Fortunately, I didn't need much money, and I wasn't tempted to gamble. One of the advantages I gained by working in the credit department was a thorough understanding of the fact that companies, lots of companies, can get in trouble even in prosperous times, and you can't predict which they are until after you've done some probing. I bought ten shares of United Corporation, a public utility conglomerate, for about a thousand dollars, because somebody told me something I shouldn't have believed, but I kept the rest of my ten thousand dollars in the bank. What it adds up to, I guess, is that if you work in the undertaker's parlor you're a little more careful about how you cross the street. I never put any real money into securities until it was very unfashionable, in the mid-1930s, when I picked up a bunch of bonds of bankrupt railroads at about five cents on the dollar, because I thought that the underlying assets would be more than enough to make the bonds worth far more than what I was paying. The profits on that play built my house in New Canaan, but that was a few years off.

In the eleven years between my arrival in New York and my marriage, I lived on the east side of Manhattan with a succession of roommates, most of them from Yale or on Wall Street or both. From 1930 to 1938, my partners were Ken Ryan, who had been my senior-year roommate at Yale but had gone to law school rather than banking, and David McElroy, younger brother of my old friend Finley from St. Louis. We had a succession of two-bedroom apartments. I always had a bedroom to myself, and I always paid half the costs, because I was doing better than they were, having started my business career three years earlier than they had. The costs weren't much. For rent, food, liquor, and telephone, and the services of a Chinese butler, the three of us together paid a total of three to four hundred dollars a month: I could easily afford half of that. Our last apartment, which we took in 1936, was a duplex in one of the Phipps houses on Sutton Place, on the East River above what is now East River Drive, and it was grand enough so we thought we should spend some money furnishing it. We got W. & J. Sloane's decorating department to do it for us, and I remember that the whole bill—beds, dining room furniture, living room furniture, rugs, and drapes—ran about a thousand dollars. We lived like kings. Ken and David and I still have reunion dinners once in a while, most recently, at this writing, in September 1986.

We were all veterans of Prohibition, of course. We knew the speakeasies. I remember the bellcord that hung beside the back of the bar at the old "21." They told us that was there so if the Prohibition agents raided, they could knock the pins out from the shelves and the bar itself with a single pull, and all the bottles would fall down into the cellar and break on the cement floor, allowing the guilty contents to wash away into the sewer. I never had occasion to find out if that was true, because they took care of things so they were never raided.

After 1930, when my eminence as assistant secretary of Farmers Loan brought me a salary of five thousand dollars a year, I kept a car, a little Ford coupe I'd won in the raffle at the annual bond club outing. I wasn't a bond trader, but Perkins had put me in the investment advisory department for bookkeeping purposes, and I worked with that group when he didn't need me, so I thought it best to get into an organization where I could meet all the boys who were in the investment business. This was a special kind of raffle, where a certain number of tickets were eliminated at each drawing, and the holders of the tickets still in the hat could then auction them off to the audience. The last ticket in the hat won the car. We got down near the end, with only two tickets in the hat, and one of them was mine. I looked up the fellow who had the other ticket, and bought it from him for two hundred dollars to be sure I got the car, which was worth about four hundred and fifty dollars. My ticket was in fact the winner, but I had played it safe, as usual.

For people situated as we were, New York was a comfortable place in those days. There were piers side by side in the East River; one of them was where they set the play about Dead End kids, and the other was the pier where the Wall Street brokers docked their yachts, in front of the River Club, to get in their cars and be driven to Wall Street. When they built the East River Drive, they had to include a passenger walk over the highway for the big shots who left their yachts at the River Club. (The bridge was later removed: even the River Club members who have them don't use their yachts to commute to work anymore.) People didn't have the sort of worries about crime then that they have today. My friends and I would go up to the Cotton Club at 125th Street and Eighth Avenue and hear Duke Ellington, and then walk home through Harlem and never think twice about it.

I had a number of girlfriends; life was good.

I also worked hard. I got into the bank as soon as they opened the doors, and I didn't look at the clock. You went to the office six days a week in those days, and my first four years at the bank I didn't take a day's vacation. I studied accounting at night, and when I was finished with that, three other young men and I formed a self-study group that met two, sometimes three times a week, while we educated each other on public utilities and railroads, municipal borrowings, loans to major corporations. I drew charts of the public utility holding companies and the individual companies they controlled, and having that information in my head proved quite valuable to me as a banker in the 1940s and 1950s, when the groups were being broken up according to the provisions of the Public Utility Holding Company Act of 1940.

I spent a year's midnight oil working on the debt structure of railroads. That was why I was able to buy the bonds of busted railroads so confidently in the later 1930s. And parts of that work were still worthwhile forty years later. I had made a map of the Pennsylvania Railroad, and I drew on it, in crayon, the mortgages and subsidiaries the company had acquired in the course of putting together its system. There were some 220 of them, and they were the financial foundation of the system during the Depression, for mortgage bonds on good property were salable assets when almost nothing else was. For forty years, that knowledge was worth little to me. Then, a few months after I had retired from Citicorp and could make whatever investments I wished, Penn Central went bankrupt, partly because the Pennsylvania's merger partner, the New York Central, had been much less skillfully financed and nurtured. Because I had confidence in the basic values of the underlying assets, largely real estate, I was able to buy half a million dollars' worth of Penn Central bonds at five cents on the dollar, and wait for them to pay off after the reorganization, as they did, at par.

Being in Perkins's office, first when he was president of Farmers Trust and later when he became chairman of National City Bank, I felt I needed a grasp of business conditions in general, not just the prospects of specific borrowers or even specific industries. I kept my own black book, in which every month I filed charts from the *New York Times Financial Analyst,* the leading financial journal of the time, with a page for each component of their "Analyst Index"—steel and coal and autos, retail sales, railroad carloadings, electric power production, paperboard production, and so forth. Then I filed key financial data from the Federal Reserve, a section on significant international trade and financial data, and finally a section on commodities, production, and prices.

Perkins used to tell me, "Follow the numbers—don't read the commentaries." I formed my own conclusions, didn't have to rely on some clown to tell me what was going on, and compared those conclusions with the contemporary judgments of the few analysts whose opinion I respected. Later, I'd tell my young people, "Don't waste time reading the opinions of people whose opinions you don't respect." The important thing, Perkins liked to say, was not what you read but what you decided not to read from the mountain of economic data—a mountain that has grown far higher. I posted information in that black book of mine for more than twenty years. Then I had all those trend lines in my internal computer, and I didn't need the book anymore.

I had certain advantages. Because I was at City Bank, working in the boss's office or a senior executive myself, I had access to a broader spectrum of information on what was happening in the economy. One instructive record the bank then kept was a monthly tabulation of depositors who kept more than half a million dollars at the bank (later, of course, with inflation, the average deposit required to qualify for the list went up sharply). This list told you the dramatic changes taking place in the business world. Every year, about 10 percent of the names dropped off and a new 10 percent came on. You could see the wholesale distributors of hardware, grocery, dry goods dropping off the list along with the railroads, while the chain stores and the airlines and natural-gas companies and eventually high-tech companies came on. And you learned from the bank's customers. I remember how impressed I was when I learned that Sears had a demographics research division, and planned the size of the infants' departments in the stores according to its predictions of the birth rate. Many years later, Gordon Metcalf, the head of Sears and a Citibank director, visited me in Spain and said, "We're in trouble, George. The market expects us to grow 10 percent a year, but we've already saturated the suburban markets where the growth is, and the country's growing only 5 percent a year." I said, "Well, you're also in financial services, which are growing at a rate of 15 percent a year. If you increase your emphasis there, you can reach an average of 10 percent." They followed this advice—but ten years late; and then they paid too much for what they bought, and they didn't develop the management they needed. Researchers can help you decide what to do, but they can't tell you how to do it.

3

My first major assignment for Perkins brought me face to face with real financial disaster. That was the collapse of the Florida land boom that almost buried, among other things, some banks owned by Farmers Trust. This venture had started in 1926, the year before I arrived, when Farmers and Central Union Trust (one of the ancestors of what is now Manufacturers Hanover) had joined together to form the Central Farmers Trust Company in West Palm Beach. It was a largely defensive action, designed to keep the money the trust companies feared they would lose as customers moved their residences to Florida to retire and to escape New York inheritance tax, which was punitive in those days because it was not deductible from federal estate tax. The New York carpetbaggers in West Palm Beach made their move at the peak of the boom. They bought an expensive downtown corner, built an expensive building, bringing workers down and housing them in tourist hotels because there wasn't enough construction labor locally . . . and found themselves without the business they had come to get.

First the tax laws were changed to make the state inheritance taxes deductible, and then the Florida real estate market sank like a stone. In all of Florida, there was only one important banker who had seen what was coming—Ed Rompf at the First National of Miami, who correctly diagnosed the unsoundness of the real estate loans and did not participate; this was before the days of deposit insurance, and his reputation for soundness was such that he was able to charge customers a fee to keep their deposits at his bank, which impressed me then and still does. At the end of 1926, there were sixty banks in Palm Beach County. By the middle of 1927, only two were left—ours on the mainland side and the First Bank and Trust Company in Palm Beach itself. Then the Palm Beach bank got in trouble, and in an overnight rescue, from 5:00 one afternoon to 9:00 in the morning the next day, we and Central Union took it over, acquiring all the assets and assuming all the liabilities, forming a new First National Bank of Palm Beach.

The Florida banks were part of Sloan Colt's empire at Farmers Trust, run for him from New York by Charles Wight, a vice-president in his division and another Yalie. Colt and Bill Gray, president of Central Union, had chosen the banks' very distinguished boards, which included such big New York names as E. F. Hutton and John Phipps, John W. Harris of Harris, Upham, and Wiley Reynolds, plus Leonard Replogle, one of the most knowledgeable businessmen in Florida. Colt had also chosen the operating staff of the banks, mainly from old friends who had been through Yale with him. Perkins hadn't paid much attention: he knew the situation in Florida was risky but he assumed Colt and Wight were taking care of it. When Colt went off to Bankers Trust and took Wight with him, there was nobody left at Farmers Trust to handle the problem. It appeared we were losing a lot of money; nobody knew. It was on Perkins's back. He asked me to go down there and see if I could pull things back in shape: Central Union had agreed to give me carte blanche.

Our people in Florida were not happy to see me. They were mostly forty years old or so, Yale men, and they were upset that this twenty-five-year-old whippersnapper was being given such power over them. I was even more unhappy with them, once I looked at the situation and discovered that realistically these banks were bankrupt. The people Sloan Colt had sent down to run the bank, while many of them were very charming and well connected, hadn't the vaguest notion of what they were doing. Still, most of what was wrong was that all Palm Beach was bankrupt—Florida land had gone from the heavens to zero and taken everyone with it. The Everglades Club and the Bath and Tennis Club were virtually bankrupt, and we handled them both in our trust department. The former had a net worth of about eighty thousand dollars; the latter, about fifty thousand dollars. Both had to be reorganized.

The failure of the Florida banks, if anyone had wanted to put them under, was an especially serious matter for us in New York because under the law as it then was, the eminent directors of the bank might well have been declared liable for its deficiencies, ruining some of our proudest and most profitable relationships. Farmers Trust's and Central Union's names were on these banks, but the law forbade us to put more money into them to keep them afloat. On my first day visiting the West Palm Beach operation I could see that our president there, a former Baptist minister, was both incompetent and, to put the matter charitably, insensitive to problems of conflicts of interest. I called Perkins and said, "The bank's in bad shape—the president has been taking commission on loans." He said, "Fire the man," then thought better of it (because I was so young), and told me to send the president to New York so he could fire him. Under the circumstances, it wasn't surprising that his platform officers, the men who actually made the loans, were both incompetent and overpaid, including those who were friends of Colt's.

The only man in the bank who seemed to know what was going on was the cashier, a fellow named Robert McNeill, who was being paid $1,200 of the $129,000 a year the bank spent for officer salaries. We hired John Borden, a national bank examiner and the brother of the National City Bank comptroller, to take the president's job, and we made McNeill his number two. We paid Borden ten thousand dollars a year and McNeill five thousand a year, and we had no other officers at all. By saving 90 percent of the officers' salary overhead, we immediately brought the bank back to profitability. It turned out we were right about McNeill, by the way: he went on to become chairman of the board of Manufacturers Hanover, one of the best bankers of my day, and a strong competitor in New York.

Once you understood that there was no easy way out, there were many things to be done. We'd foreclosed on houses on the beach, some of the fine homes of Florida; we sold them for what we could get. I remember a beautiful house near the beach on Seaspray Avenue that we sold for eight thousand dollars to John Rovensky, a National City vice-president, lending him 100 percent of the purchase price to get it off our books. We traded one house for a yacht, on the theory, which was true, that it would be easier to sell a yacht than a house, because we had too many houses; McNeill and I and some friends took it on a weekend trip to the Bahamas for R&R, and then sold it. In another instance, a builder named Hap Hall had built about thirty houses in West Palm Beach on the wrong side of the tracks. We got a contractor to saw them apart and reassemble them on some vacant lots we held along the shore of Lake Worth, and then we found buyers more easily. I never understood how they glued those houses together, and why they didn't just blow away in the hurricanes, but they didn't.

Our other bank, the First National Bank of Palm Beach, was a more interesting story. There the president was a canny banker named Frank Shaughnessy, who had been cashier of the Central Union and had taken the Florida job more or less as a form of early retirement. He was a sound banker and a dapper and charming fellow, who wore the smartest clothes and went in the best circles. In fact, he had married the great catch of Palm Beach, the widow of Harry Bassett, the inventor of the valve-in-head automobile engine, who had been president of Buick and then General Motors. She was reputed to be the largest single stockholder in General Motors, and it was said that she could go to Detroit and walk into Alfred Sloan's office without knocking. First National was much better run than the West Palm Beach bank, but there remained an overhang of five hundred thousand dollars of bad loans from its defunct predecessor. In theory, this had been guaranteed by the directors of the old bank before we took it over, but in fact they had all disappeared somewhere up north. What we did have, and what ultimately bailed us partway out, was a piece of beachfront property one of the directors had left in pledge. It was at the southern tip of Palm Beach, about four hundred feet wide, running two thousand feet out to the yacht channel. The New York banks took this land off First National's books, to clean them up. By adding some sixty acres of underwater land the state of Florida was willing to sell to us, we made a package valuable enough to recover about half what it had cost us. With this doubtful asset off First National's books, we had a clean bank we could sell, finally, at an apparent profit.

That was still some years in the future. For most of the early 1930s, I was on the telephone every day to McNeill and Shaughnessy in Florida, and I took the train down to West Palm Beach just about every month. On one of my early trips, I remember, someone took me to Colonel E. R. Bradley's casino for dinner. It was just over the bridge from the mainland in Palm Beach, and probably the ritziest roulette parlor in America. Colonel Bradley raced horses at all the great tracks under his own silks and owned the Idle Hour Farm in Kentucky, one of the nation's great horse breeding establishments. He won the Kentucky Derby four times. There was nothing Mafia about E. R. Bradley: he was a leading citizen of Palm Beach. Gambling was illegal in Florida, but it was understood that Bradley's place refused admission to Florida residents. He contributed generously from his takings to the local churches and hospitals, so the state left him alone. He was a pillar of the community.

As I was finishing my dinner, the colonel asked me to his elegantly decorated office and politely suggested that I leave. "Your customers," he said, "are in this building at the gaming tables. They won't want you to know they are here, and, frankly, they will wonder why a banker is in a gaming establishment." I crawled out the door—but the colonel was right. Years later, I was embarrassed on a trip to Mexico when a newspaper printed a picture of me at a racetrack soon after we had fired an officer in one of our branches for frequenting the track, which was off limits. Even after I'd retired from the bank and my host was Bob Kleberg's King Ranch—and the occasion was a glamorous match race at Belmont Park, the most social of racetracks, between Kleberg's Canonero II and that year's Kentucky Derby and Preakness winner Riva Ridge—I was a little reluctant about being seen at the track, remembering Bradley; but I went.

Early in my connection with the Florida banks, I learned an important lesson in the management of bank funds. In 1931, there was a large issue of U.S. Treasury bonds, Andrew Mellon's famous 3 percent bonds. We had a hundred thousand dollars to invest, and decided to buy the bonds. National City's bond department was advising us on the bond account of Central Farmers, and they strongly urged us to bid for three hundred thousand dollars, because the issue would be oversubscribed and allocated, with each bidder receiving only about 30 percent of what he asked for. We did as advised, and it turned out that the issue was not oversubscribed, and we had three hundred thousand dollars worth of 3 percent government paper instead of the ninety thousand dollars we wanted. For the same reason that the subscriptions were light, the price went down soon after the issuance. We held the bonds for a while, hoping that they would come back up, but eventually we had to sell them at eighty, with a sixty-thousand-dollar loss to the bank. Perkins accepted my explanations, and said he thought this experience would probably save the bank money later on, because I'd learned two important lessons: don't subscribe for more than you can afford to take, whether or not you expect your allocation to be well below your subscription—and when you've got a loss, take it fast. The bonds had hung around ninety-eight for three months, and if I'd accepted the fact that we'd made a mistake I would have lost only two points instead of twenty.

After the Banking Act of 1933, our continued ownership of the Florida banks was illegal, and the comptroller of the currency kept pressing us to find a buyer. We couldn't just close them down: they were the only banks in Palm Beach. But as the Florida economy came off the floor, so did the Florida banks, and by 1936 we were able to sell the Central Farmers Trust Company in West Palm Beach to Atlantic National, which still owns and runs it. The next year, we sold the First National Bank of Palm Beach to one of its directors, Wiley Reynolds, who had owned the Reynolds Spring Company in Michigan. By then, Perkins and thus I were working for National City Bank rather than for Farmers Trust, where Lindsay Bradford was president. Bradford had never been to Florida, and thought that the party celebrating our disposal of our last Florida affiliate would be a good occasion for a visit. Reynolds hosted the affair, at the Everglades Club, prosperous once again, and most of the old-timers came. Bradford at the dinner table mentioned that he'd often heard about the land boom, but he didn't have any feel of how it had actually happened. Could someone give him a typical transaction to help him understand those days?

Our director, Replogle, was glad to oblige. "I was in my office one morning in 1926," he said, "when Ed Hutton called me and said, 'There's a piece of land in West Palm Beach that's for sale for fifteen thousand dollars. It's a corner and it looks interesting, and I've decided to take it. I've already got a partner for a third of it; would you like the other third?' And I said, 'Fine.'

"Several hours later, Hutton called me back and said he'd been offered twenty thousand dollars for the property; did I want to sell? I said No. He called back again after lunch and said he had a new offer of twenty-five thousand dollars; what did I think? I said, 'Well, I just bought my wife a new car, that cost about four thousand dollars; I think I'll take my profit.' Hutton said, 'Okay. I'll take over your interest and send you a check for your profit.' He sent me the check, and I went down and paid for my wife's car. The next morning I took a look at the lot, and I liked it, so I called Ed Hutton, who said, 'We've just been offered thirty-five thousand dollars, but we still don't want to sell.' I told him I would like to get back in if I could, and he said that was all right, so I sent him a check for a third of thirty-five thousand dollars. We kept getting new bids for that whole month, and finally we sold it, about thirty days after we bought, for $150,000."

Bradford said, "Was this some sort of swap? Did people actually pay you one hundred fifty thousand dollars for a piece of land you had bought for fifteen thousand dollars only a month before?"

"Oh, yes," Replogle said. "It was a cash transaction."

"Who bought it?" Bradford asked.

"Your bank in New York bought it," Replogle said. "That's the land on which your West Palm Beach bank was built."

That about tells the whole story, but there are two items to add. One is that this building was not the place the bank had occupied when we sold it in 1936. We had traded the old site to the state banking department for a larger, then-vacant bank building in the absolute center of town, which the department had taken over as part of one of the 1927 bankruptcies. The bank that had occupied that site had been started and run by a croupier from Bradley's. The banking department had then sold our old building to the Second Baptist Church of West Palm Beach—for fifteen thousand dollars, exactly what the original empty lot had cost us in 1926, with the building thrown in as an extra.

The minister wrote me a few years later and asked if I had plans for the building, because they were turning the vault into a closet for their vestments.

The second item is that a few weeks after my first trip to Palm Beach I sat down with our people to see if there was anything I didn't know about that could explain all the real estate investments we had financed, with nowhere near enough people in Florida to use the buildings. One of the officers explained: the theory was that the population was getting older, and older people were getting richer, and a lot of them would come down to Florida to retire because of the sunshine and the climate, and a lot of business would come down with them. The theory was absolutely right; it was just a generation too soon. There is a lesson in that, too.

4

The history books teach that the good times came to an end in October 1929, but as we saw it at the time the economy seemed to right itself in early 1930. When I received my appointment as assistant secretary that January, I had no thought that I was being given a berth on a sinking ship. Perkins, however, was not sanguine. In 1929, he had been asked to manage some two million dollars in a stock fund for the Solvay group in Belgium, proprietors of one of the world's most important chemical companies (it still is). Despite the losses the fund had taken in the crash, the rebound in the spring of 1930 had generated a net profit of about a hundred thousand dollars on the account. Perkins cashed in that profit and sent the money back to them, saying that he did not feel this was a good time to be investing in the American stock market. He had made me treasurer of the special Solvay fund, and when they received their profits the Solvays insisted on giving me a thousand dollars as a special payment for my work. I refused, saying I had done this job like my others as an employee of Farmers Trust, but they went to Perkins, who approved, and then I gladly took the bonus. If Perkins was pessimistic, I at age twenty-five was prosperous and pretty cheerful. I knew about what had happened in Florida, but that seemed a special situation, not a precursor of trouble everywhere.

By the end of 1930, however, it was clear that the country had entered a long, dark tunnel, and the banks, even the biggest of them, were going to be in trouble. In December, Bank of the United States, the twenty-eighth largest in the country and in terms of the number of its depositors the fourth-largest in New York City, closed its doors, leaving a tenth of all the New York families that had bank accounts without access to their funds. (Led by National City, which finally liquidated the bankrupt bank, the New York Clearing House members advanced depositors immediately up to 50 percent of the value of their accounts, which helped but not enough.) Deflation shrank the value of the assets pledged against bank loans: more than three-quarters of the mortgages Farmers Trust had written or invested in for its customers went into default. At National City, the problems were compounded by the unpopularity of chairman Charles Mitchell, whose arrogance was legendary inside and outside the bank; by the existence of a securities affiliate that had sold the public a lot of what turned out to be worthless paper; and by the way that Mitchell had used the securities affiliate, and the bank's immense customer base, to push the stock of National City itself, which dropped from more than five hundred dollars a share in 1929 to less than twenty dollars a share in 1933.

Mitchell's aggressive use of National City stock put the bank in embarrassments while the first crash was still resounding, and later became the instrument of his disgrace. In summer of 1929, Mitchell had bullied an agreement to merge out of the board of the Corn Exchange, a bank with a large New York City branch network. The merger was hailed in the press: the *New York Times* noted editorially that it "undoubtedly interests most people chiefly as giving America, for the first time, the largest bank in the world. In a way, it has been a matter of mortification that, with the post-war United States outstripping Great Britain in the field not only of industry but of home and international finance, London should still possess the premier institution, measured by total banking resources. With this new merger at New York, $2,386,000,000 resources pass under a single management, as compared with $2,303,000,000 shown in its last report by the Midland Bank of London." The strength of Mitchell's sales pitch in the negotiations had been the market value of the National City stock to be exchanged for Corn Exchange stock. On the day the deal was agreed, National City stock was trading at $492, a remarkable price even in 1929 for a company with a book value of fifty dollars a share and a dividend of four dollars a share. Walter Frew, the chairman of Corn Exchange, didn't like the deal, and insisted that the National City Company, which was arranging it, pledge to purchase at $450 the National City Bank shares that would be issued to effect the takeover, so that Corn Exchange stockholders who preferred cash had a guaranteed value. The stockholders' meetings were to be in November. In October, National City stock plunged through Frew's minimum price.

At Mitchell's instructions, to support the stock price and keep the deal alive, Hugh Baker, president of National City Company, ordered his traders to buy all National City stock offered at $450. One day not long before the stockholders' meetings, Mitchell called Baker to find out how the stock was behaving. Baker said he'd had a rough day, and had been forced to buy some fifty thousand shares. Mitchell knew that National City Company had used up its line of credit at National City Bank, and had few other resources available for that size purchase. "How," he asked Baker, "are you going to pay for it?" Baker said he hadn't thought of that.

Some years later, when I was one of the liquidating trustees of the National City Company, I learned that Mitchell had left his office immediately after his talk with Baker and walked alone from Wall Street to his uptown home, reflecting on his problems. The next day on his way to work, he stopped in at J. P. Morgan and borrowed $12 million on his personal line of credit (secured to a large extent with his own holdings of National City stock) to take over Baker's position. These transactions wiped out Mitchell's personal fortune, and for some years after leaving City Bank, he devoted his earnings from his new post at Blyth & Company to repaying his loan from Morgan, which he did.

But nothing could help the stock of National City. By the time the stockholders of Corn Exchange and National City were to vote on the merger, the cost of redeeming the new shares at $450 would have embarrassed City Bank, to say the least. Mitchell took the proxies he controlled and voted them against the merger, killing it. The Corn Exchange people, who had been licking their chops at the profits they were going to make in this down market, complained that Mitchell had welshed, which was true, but he didn't have any choice.

One of Mitchell's transactions in the down market for our stock did serve the bank very well. In autumn 1931, National City, simply by issuing stock, acquired the old New York-based Bank of America from Transamerica Corporation, the holding company built on the San Francisco-based Bank of America. (The New York bank was the original: A. P. Giannini, who had created the California bank, had called it "Bank of Italy," and had changed the name to Bank of America only after Transamerica bought the old institution in New York.) The acquisition of Bank of America gave Citibank thirty-two additional New York branches, making National City for the first time the most convenient retail bank for New Yorkers. More than that, it came with $81 million in sound capital, which National City used immediately to write off bad loans on its books. The danger was that the transaction made Transamerica, with 8.7 percent of the shares, the largest stockholder in National City. Fortunately, the economy turned up before bank stocks did, and Giannini found it in his interest to sell off his National City shares at a loss to reduce taxes on the profits from Transamerica's other interests. I have no doubt that Giannini had in mind to take over National City, but changes in the times and the law made that impossible.

In the end, the manipulation of National City stock brought Mitchell down, and could have brought down the bank. At the time of the crash, National City Company, the bank's brokerage and underwriting affiliate, had capital of $100 million and unrealized profits of probably another $100 million—and it had large holdings of National City Bank stock, some of it carried by loans from the bank, some of it stock the customers' men had ordered for their customers because they had discretionary authority over the account or because they were in the habit of making friends (or making money for themselves) by buying and selling for one-day profits in a rising market. A good deal of that had simply settled into the company when the customers refused delivery in a falling market. Other loans from the bank had supported holdings of National City stock by officers of both the bank and the company.

In 1931, the bank set up a $2 million fund, with three outside directors as trustees, to help officers meet their brokers' margin calls and carry securities holdings in situations where otherwise their losses (this was the excuse) would impair their performance in their job. I was made administrator of this fund. In effect, I ran a small private bank. The officers who wanted loans from the fund would give me their financial statements and whatever collateral they had available, which I sent down to the vault every night in my tin box, insisting that a deputy comptroller of the bank count the securities and see that everything was in order. I told Perkins when he gave me the assignment that I wanted one of the bank's auditors in to examine my books once a week, so that everything I did would be fully documented and verified. Some day, I said, we might have to defend these actions in court; and we did. What I didn't know until several years later, when I became a liquidating trustee of the National City Company, was that the company had a parallel fund. Both funds were a mistake. The officers who borrowed from them would have been better off if they'd let their brokers sell them out of all the stocks they owned, for few of them ever came back to where they had been. And the bank would have saved some money, because both these funds showed losses of much more than half of what they lent: Howard Sheperd, the future president and chairman of the bank, was one of the very few who repaid all they had borrowed.

What made the trouble in the press, however, was something entirely innocent. In the course of its operations in the market for National City stock, the company naturally sold as well as bought: any trader whose activity remains entirely on one side of the market will get killed by those who deal with him. To make deliveries on some of the sales, it was necessary to borrow stock that would be returned when certificates representing purchases from holders in Texas or overseas were delivered. This meant that there were days when the company apparently made short sales of National City stock, profiting by its decline. The day in 1933 when this fact came out at the congressional hearings on the role of the banks in the Depression was the blackest day of all for National City. If the congressmen and newspaper editors who made so much of these alleged short sales had added up the company's transactions for the entire week involved, they would have found that National City was a big net purchaser of its own stock, but that was not the way the political and publishing game was played.

Meanwhile, it was discovered that Mitchell himself had sold some stock in late 1929, enough to erase his taxable income for a year in which he had truly suffered devastating losses. It was clumsily done: Mitchell didn't want to sell his stock on the open market because he was afraid people would hear about it and believe he'd lost faith in his own bank, so his lawyers arranged that he would sell the stock to his wife. They then failed to affix a tax stamp, destroying what claims to validity the transaction might have had. Another banking Charles— Wiggins of Chase—had in fact sold his bank's stock short as the market collapsed and made money on the disaster, so it was easy to hang an albatross on Mitchell. A month later Mitchell was charged with tax fraud (he was acquitted, and properly so, though Franklin Roosevelt was reported to have disliked the verdict). By then, Mitchell was out of the bank: the day after the news of the City Company's alleged short-selling of its stock hit the papers, the board of directors decided that he had to go.

In theory and for the most part in fact, Perkins had been removed from all this, though he sat on the National City board. Directors were not given much information in those days: it was not until he became chairman that Perkins saw a bank examiner's report or was given a statement of the market value of the bank's bond account. Farmers Trust had been an independent institution until mid-1929, and even after that it was a separate organization. Perkins had been immensely careful not to let his investment department do business with the underwriters at National City Company: through the years, despite occasional pressure from colleagues when the offerings market dried up in 1930–31, Farmers Trust had only once purchased a bond NCC was marketing—and that purchase, a New York City issue, had been reversed as soon as Perkins heard about it. I was at Perkins's side in the congressional hearing room, where he had gone with the officers of the bank and the company, expecting to be called, when Ferdinand Pecora, the counsel to the committee, came up to his seat and told him that his investigators had been combing through the accounts of City Bank Farmers Trust, and had found nothing wrong, and Perkins could consider himself excused.

When the board decided that Mitchell had to go, then, the natural candidate for his replacement was Perkins. In the last week in February 1933, Guy Cary, senior partner of Shearman & Sterling and a director of the bank, called Perkins in Washington to tell him, and to summon him to a meeting that night at Cary's house. I rode back to New York with Perkins on the train, and he told me he had decided to accept, on two conditions—first, that Mitchell's president, Gordon Rentschler, should stay, because he was a good businessman, knowledgeable about the sugar industry which was our worst lending headache, and not implicated in Mitchell's excesses; and second, that the incoming president, Franklin Roosevelt, with whom Perkins had long been personally friendly, would give his approval. Both conditions were met.

Four days after Perkins took over as chairman of National City, on a Friday night before a Saturday when the New York banks would face an unprecedented demand for cash from frightened depositors, he and the then chief executive of the Federal Reserve Bank of New York led a delegation to Governor Herbert Lehman to request that New York State join lesser states around the country in declaring a bank holiday. At 3:30 Saturday morning, an agreement was reached on the terms of a temporary suspension of banking business in New York, and at 8:00 Lehman issued the order closing the banks. Perkins had gone home to sleep, and I was covering for him that morning at the bank, when a telephone call came from the chairman of Midland Bank in London.

He had seen the story about the moratorium on the news wires. He reminded me that we had branches in London and Panama and elsewhere that had remained open—and that had no way to draw funds from the home office. "Tell Mr. Perkins," he said, "that I have instructed our branches to keep in touch with yours, and to extend them any assistance they may need." I thanked him, and in later years remembered that our relationship with Midland Bank should be something more than purely commercial.

On Sunday, March 4th, 1933, Franklin Roosevelt was sworn in as president and vowed to drive the money-chasers from the temple; on Tuesday, he declared a nationwide bank holiday. Perkins went down to Washington that day, taking me with him, and I sat on a bench in the park across the street from the White House while he took tea with the president and Mrs. Roosevelt. He wanted assurances that the wave of attacks on National City would stop, and that the authorities would cooperate with him in his efforts to get the bank back in order. He emerged to tell me that the president had been entirely supportive, and in his presence had called Senator Glass and Congressman Steagall, Chairman of the Federal Reserve Board Isaac B. Newton, the comptroller of the currency . . . and Pecora, to make sure the committee would call off its dogs. All of them, Roosevelt had told him, had spoken well of Perkins as a leader for City Bank, and agreed.

Returning to New York, Perkins called all the officers of the bank together, told them that he had been to see Roosevelt, and said, more or less, "Our bank is in the doghouse, and considering some of what's come to light, it should be. But this will all be over someday, and the bank will be stronger than ever." Everyone believed him: he had universal acceptance for integrity and soundness.

About a month later, after the Congress had rushed through the Emergency Banking Act of 1933, which validated what the president had done, and Roosevelt had permitted the reopening of those banks the Federal Reserve could certify as solvent, Perkins took me with him to his home at Mishaum Point in South Dartmouth, Massachusetts, and I helped him go over the most recent report on our bank by the national bank examiner. It was a shocker. In their official history of Citibank, Harold van B. Cleveland and Thomas E. Huertas report that "total losses incurred by the Bank" from autumn 1929 to January 1934 were "$167 million net of recoveries, or 68% of its stockholders' equity at the end of 1929." My calculations, which included the entire enterprise for the whole period, were worse. I calculated losses of $433.5

million, including the loss of capital and unrealized profits at National City Company and the $81 million of Bank of America capital written off against loan losses in 1931. What was left was capital and surplus (in the bank and the trust company) of $137.5 million.

In January 1934, the Reconstruction Finance Corporation (RFC) bought $50 million of National City preferred stock as part of the New Deal campaign to shore up the entire banking industry. The line was that National City sold the RFC that stock *noblesse oblige,* that we didn't really need the money but believed it would be helpful to banks that did if the world saw us in effect borrowing from the RFC. The fact was that we still had problems—the German loans I will discuss later, the sugar loans, and the holes in the bond portfolio, and we really needed some of that money if we were going to meet the require-ment of the new Federal Deposit Insurance Corporation that a bank have capital to the extent of 10 percent of its assets. Once that $50 million was in hand, Perkins wrote off another $24 million, telling the board of directors, "Let's clean up this bank once and for all." These last write-offs were, quite deliberately, overdone, because Perkins wanted to make sure that there would never again be an announcement of losses that would be bad publicity for the bank. And there was not another year in Perkins's time when our charge-offs exceeded our recoveries on loans previously written off. From January 1934 to the end of the decade our capital grew by a net $50 million from recoveries on loans we had declared a loss.

5

Supervising this portfolio of problem loans was also part of my job at National City Bank in the next five years. Perkins had not made any formal arrangements to take me with him when he became chairman, but his first afternoon on the job, looking around, he inquired where the hell Moore was, which amounted to the same thing: except that I worked the next two months at City Bank without being paid, because nobody had done the paperwork to accomplish my transfer from the trust company to the bank. Finally Perkins found out about it, not because I had told him, and with impatience and some amusement asked Rentschler to set my salary. This got me an increase to eleven thousand dollars a year, which was princely money in 1933. I had a large office adjoining Perkins's office on the seventh floor at 55 Wall Street, and many responsibilities—for the loan fund, the liquidating of the City Company, the Florida banks, our activities in Washington with relation to the shape of new legislation, much else. I was just twenty-eight years old.

Among those who thought they could do some of these things better was Dan Borden, the comptroller of the bank, who was responsible for collecting what are now called "non-performing assets" in what was then called the "suspense department." He persuaded Perkins that the chairman of National City needed two assistants, one of them expert in the management of problem loans. As the senior man, he got the big office, and I moved to a smaller office next door. But my real source of influence, of course, was my personal relationship with Perkins, and that Borden never had. He was an able, tough comptroller, but sometimes when he turned around he broke the windows.

That characteristic of Borden's wrecked the deal to merge National City and Marine Midland, back in 1938. The state in those days permitted a bank to have offices only in one county (or, if it was a New York bank, one city: New York had five counties in its city limits). But Marine Midland, which was based in Buffalo, was an established state wide holding company, and its power to open subsidiaries anywhere in the state was grandfathered into the law. Perkins came up with the ingenious notion of making Marine Midland the parent company (though the name would be changed to National City), allowing us to have the only statewide bank holding company. Perkins and Frank Rand, then chairman of Marine Midland, worked out a deal with shares to be valued on the basis of book value, and then turned the details over to subordinates, Borden for us and Walter Scheckenberger for Marine Midland.

Borden insisted that Marine Midland give us credit in the share calculations for some loans we had written off that he said we were going to collect. Scheckenberger said that if we were willing to restate our books so that the loans were carried as good assets—which meant we were confident the examiners would approve—he would be willing to include them in our book value for purposes of share valuation. If we thought they were too iffy to carry on our books, we shouldn't ask Marine Midland to give us credit for them. By the time Perkins and Rand returned to the scene, the atmosphere was so bad that the deal fell through. "George," Perkins said, "never let anybody promote you out of a job you're good at." The failure of the merger cost us what would have been a forty-year jump on statewide banking, and a useful increase in our capital. (A year later we just missed acquiring Irving Trust, which would have improved our capital even more; before the deal could be announced—or even put in the rumor mill—the Irving executives rebelled against it, and Perkins backed away.) Not until 1975 did First National City receive statewide branching powers, and in fact we were never able to break into the cream-of-the-crop upstate business Marine Midland (now owned by Hong Kong & Shanghai Bank) still commands. Borden eventually moved back to his comptroller job. Perkins said he was the best comptroller the bank ever had, though that didn't make him a good assistant to the chairman.

Borden was a great pro at managing defaulted loans. National City had long had a rule that the lending officer who made a loan should not be the man responsible for collecting it if it got in trouble. What was needed then was somebody who had no stake in defending the loan, and would be more willing to take a small loss on it if necessary. Perkins insisted that Borden continue to supervise this work after he came to the seventh floor. That was my opportunity. I asked for the chance to help him. It was agreed that subject to Borden's direction I would supervise all loans in default for more than a hundred thousand dollars. It was great training. I learned how banks come to make bad loans. I learned about human behavior, about the bankruptcy laws and reorganizations, about how to work with lawyers, and especially about how to turn a problem into a success. Unlike colleagues in Chase and Guaranty Trust, whose tough actions often antagonized borrowers, Borden and I were always conscious that if the company survived its reorganization we wanted to be its banker. And we almost always were. The fact is that there are very few big customers of Citibank today with whom at one time and another we didn't have to go around some sharp corners—that's what a banker-customer relationship is all about.

For so opinionated a man, Borden was capable of great patience in a negotiating situation. Early in our time together, we went to the creditors' meeting that was going to divide up the surviving assets and reorganize the Long Bell Lumber Company. There was no way this one could survive: it was a timber company with forests, lumber mills, and a nationwide chain of lumber yards with heavy inventories carried on borrowed money—and there was virtually no construction industry to supply. Chase Bank was the principal creditor, but there were many banks and suppliers and landowners who had leased timber land to Long Bell and had not been paid. Some seventy-five people were at the table in Chase's directors' room, representing bondholders, creditors, and shareholders. The lawyers for the company explained who would get what under their reorganization proposal, and the meeting was thrown open for discussion, which went on and on. Obviously, compromises would be necessary. I grew restless and nudged Borden, saying that I thought I had a compromise I could sell.

Borden took me outside the room and said, "Let me explain about these meetings. Everybody came here with a speech to make. Before they left home, they told their bosses, 'I'm going to tell them this, and I'm going to tell them that, and I'm going to insist on this, and I'm going to insist on that.' A lot of them haven't spoken yet, so you don't know what problems your compromise may have to face. And whatever you say now, they will insist on speaking. Furthermore, these men came here for the day. Some arrived from Chicago this morning, and they expect to be here at least until tonight. What you want to do is sit patiently until the most difficult man in the room looks at his watch. That means he's got another appointment, or he has to catch a train, and he's going to be more susceptible to compromise. The Twentieth Century Limited leaves for Chicago at 6:00. We should be ready to propose our plan at about 3:30." Sure enough, at 3:30 a man from one of the Chicago banks, who had been talking very tough, looked at his watch. We proposed our compromise, and he objected, but at 4:15 he looked at his watch again, and he accepted, so he could catch his train.

The reorganization of Long Bell Lumber was rather successful, under the circumstances, and most of the assets were sold. Weyerhauser, I remember, took in settlement of its claims a million acres of cutover timberland that was considered to have a very low value. Later, Frederick Weyerhauser said to me, "I made a very big bet on capitalism." Today all that timber has grown back, and that land is now worth a fortune. Working on the Long Bell situation gave me an interest in timber that I never lost, and led me almost half a century later to an investment in Arcata, a West Coast company with major redwood interests that was one of the first leveraged buy-outs and should be one of the most profitable. I remember a visit to California redwood country some years ago, and a tree on the ground, in the fork of a trunk that had grown around it, felled by a storm two thousand years before, still as good as new because of the impermeable vinyl resin in the grain. I was out at my son's house in New Canaan not long ago, and I noticed some redwood chairs around the pool, and suddenly I realized that I'd bought those chairs when I built the house, almost fifty years ago.

Going through the files of the "suspense department," I soon became conscious that only a small fraction of our final losses, perhaps $25 million all told, had been the result of the normal ongoing lending activities of the metropolitan division or the domestic division that lent to businesses outside New York. The reason our basic bank had lost so little when the auxiliary activities (and the city's other banks) had lost so much was senior vice-president William A. Simonson, the best commercial banker I ever knew. They said that Mitchell always called him "Mr. Simonson," and it may be true. He was the senior lending officer of National City from 1910 to 1936, and he had both the strength of character and the political clout at the bank to turn down even some of Mitchell's most cherished projects. I had an opportunity to see Mr. Simonson in action when one of our Cleveland correspondent banks wanted a line of credit from National City, to be secured by their mortgage portfolio. "We don't do that," Mr. Simonson said, stiff-backed. "The day they want to use that line will be the very day you don't want to make the loan—and on that day, those mortgages will be no good." He was right, of course; we didn't give the line of credit.

I will deal in other chapters with some of the loans I worked on in 1933–38. Those that related to the activities of the National City Company, for example, belong in the next chapter, on why the banking laws were changed and what should be done about them now. And the chapter on international lending is the place to deal with my experiences involving National City's Cuban loans, our tangle of deposits and loans relating to Czarist Russia, and the German "standstill agreement." Other aspects of my work for Perkins—my introduction to the world of commercial aviation, for example—are best considered in the chapters on domestic lending. But some of what we did in the suspense department can be understood only as part and parcel of the 1930s.

Giannini had been interested in the movie business in California, so when he took over Bank of America in New York that bank became interested in Broadway theaters. When we acquired the bank, we acquired a bunch of bankrupt theaters, formerly the property of the Erlanger family. We owned the Empire, the Fulton, the Morosco, a whole Broadway blockfront. I went to the Schuberts to learn how to run theaters, and they taught me the lesson that you never charge a fixed rent on a theater, you always take a share of the box office. If the production fails, they close it promptly, and you have your theater to rent again. You need the share of profits when the production is a hit— and *Three Men on a Horse* ran a dozen years—to make up for the long stretches when the dark theater brings you no income at all. But it isn't a good business for banks. I remember we sold the Broadway blockfront to the Erlangers' lawyer for fifty thousand dollars and a mortgage, just to get it off our "non-performing" list.

One of the developments of the 1930s was that a bank would turn the loan on a property over to anyone who would just pay the interest, get it back into a performing category. We'd have a piece of real estate we were holding as worth $5 million. If someone expressed an interest, we'd make a deal—Give us a hundred thousand dollars down, deposit with us in advance a year's real estate taxes and interest on the loan, assume the mortgages, and you own it. We'll talk about repayments of the $5 million some other time. If we didn't make deals like that we had to keep lending money to the building, to pay the real estate taxes and the interest on the other mortgages, because there was usually more than one mortgage, and sometimes a prior lien. That sort of deal has been available from many banks with real estate, farm, and oil-producing property loans in the 1980s, too. The people who took those properties in the 1930s did very well out of them, and I wouldn't be surprised to see happy faces on those who are making such deals today.

Shearman & Sterling, our law firm, taught me another important lesson about collateralized loans. Our loans to the Insull holding company in 1929 were backed by stock in Commonwealth Edison and People's Gas in Chicago, worth three times the amount of the loan on the day the money was borrowed, with the provision that if the market value of those securities ever fell below 150 percent of the loan, we could force the sale of the stock to collect our loan. This was one of those Morgan loans Mitchell had made with little in the files except a brief memo saying that Lamont, a Morgan partner, had called and suggested National City should take part of the credit. When market conditions triggered the provision that protected us, the shareholders in these companies went to court and got an injunction forbidding us to sell the stock, on the grounds that the sale would injure their interests. They held us up for seven years, and by the time we came out of the courts and had permission to sell, the stock was worth half the face value of the loan. We had to take a large loss. Thereafter I always avoided these sudden-death provisions that supposedly give the lender access to the collateral when some condition is violated; it's too easy for someone to get an injunction and block your apparent rights.

One of the longest-running attractions in the suspense department was the McCrory Corporation, a chain of stores selling dresses and shoes and general merchandise, which went down the river early in the Depression. They'd run out of cash, and their inventories were worth maybe thirty cents on the dollar. The principal assets they had left were the real estate holdings. Their receivables might be good, but not if you liquidated—people will pay their retail debts if they can still go to the store and buy new shoes, but if there's no more credit after they pay what they now owe, they'll laugh at you. So we stayed with it, lent them additional money so they could continue in business, and eventually we got it all back. That was the most important lesson of all from the 1930s—never rub 'em out unless there's absolutely no other way. Recognize that you can't get blood out of a turnip, take the losses you have to take, then nurture the little plant that's left and make it grow. Of course, the best way to liquidate a bad debt is to get somebody to take over the debtor as a going business.

I remember how surprised I was, five or so years after I retired from Citibank, at the way the banks handled the W. T. Grant chain of stores. When it ran into trouble, they closed it down, turned the business over to a liquidator, paid him a big commission, and in the end got maybe ten cents on the dollar. If they'd turned it over as a going business, even paying somebody to take it on, they'd have collected eighty cents. In all my years with the bank, and I was an aggressive salesman, I can think of only one loan I made—we'll deal with that one later—that produced a significant loss. The reason was that I caught trouble early, and I never panicked, I usually kept my borrowers going, helped them find ways to repay the bank. Sometimes you have to put in a little more to get him over the hurdle; that's all right.

One of the most constructive things the government did in the Depression was a revision of the Federal Reserve Act that allowed the Federal Reserve Banks to insure up to half of a loan. We made the first of these "Section 13-B" loans. There was an iron mine in upstate New York, the Witherbee-Sherman Company in Minesville, near Lake Placid. They'd shut down the mine because there was no demand for the iron ore. That was the only industry in town, so its closing meant everybody went on relief. We went to the government and said, We'll put up half a million dollars for them if you'll guarantee half. We'll put everybody in town back to work, and if the loan goes bad it will cost the government less than the relief bill. We'll stockpile the iron ore, sell it some day. There'd been a blast furnace in Troy, New York, closed down when the iron mine closed; we got that reopened, too.

The reorganization of Witherbee-Sherman was the quickest and coldest ever. Republic had agreed to lease and operate the mine, but only if the lease contract was made senior to the company's defaulted mortgage bonds. We worked it out with them, but we were concerned that some owners of the bonds and their lawyers would object when the matter came before a judge for approval. So we arranged to schedule the reorganization proceeding in Malone, New York, just south of the Canadian border, at nine in the morning on the day after New Year's. We rode with our lawyers and the Witherbee-Sherman officers in a private car of the Lake Champlain & Moriah Railroad, a subsidiary of the company. It was 20 below zero in Malone, and zero in the courtroom, and what with the inconvenience of the date and the locale, nobody came to the hearing but us. The judge invited us to his chambers, where at least there was a fireplace, and I presented the case, that the company really was bankrupt and thus qualified for the reorganization Republic required. The judge agreed, accepted our solution of making the Republic Steel lease senior to the mortgages, declared the plan effective, and accepted our invitation to join us in a whiskey. When the war came, Republic Steel bought the whole company, and all the creditors were paid.

4

Government's Role

If anyone had told me in 1927 that in my forty-three years as a banker I would have to think almost constantly about what some government was doing and what it wanted me to do, I would have thought the fellow was crazy. The Federal Reserve Act had been passed in 1913, but for bankers in New York the important institution was the Federal Reserve Bank of New York, which is owned not by the government but by its member-bank stockholders and in those days paid more attention to us than it did to the Federal Reserve Board in Washington. The strength of the Federal Reserve Bank of New York wasn't something in the statute books, it was the personal force of Benjamin Strong, who was not only a great banker but was also the son-in-law of H. P. Davidson, who ran the Morgan Bank. In those days, the dominant figure on the Federal Reserve Board in Washington was the secretary of the treasury, who was *ex officio* a member of the board—and when I came to work at Farmers Trust the secretary of the treasury was the banker and industrialist Andrew Mellon. He was the boss of the comptroller of the currency, too.

From a banker's point of view, the supervisory authority that really mattered was the clearing house, which made the toughest inspections, because the member banks stood behind each other's checks, and would have to find the funds if anyone defaulted. The clearing house had done the bailouts in 1907 and 1921, when important banks failed but only a few customers lost money.

Somebody like Charlie Mitchell was a much more important man in the 1920s than anyone who worked for a bank regulatory agency. He was chairman and CEO of the biggest bank in the country, soon to be the biggest bank in the world. When Comptroller of the Currency John Pole traveled around the country, he had a berth in a sleeping car like anybody else, and ate in the dining car. When Mitchell traveled, he traveled like a maharajah, in a specially appointed private railway car with its own kitchen and chef, people alerted everywhere the train stopped so they could come and pay him homage. In spring 1929, the Federal Reserve Board warned against stock market speculation and announced plans to tighten money—and Mitchell grandly told the country not to worry, if the Fed tried to make it more difficult for the banks in the boondocks to get money, National City Bank would see that they got what they needed. Mitchell really was an extraordinary salesman. After he was fired from the bank, he became the chairman of Blyth & Company, a Wall Street brokerage and investment banking house. He lived into the 1950s, built Blyth into a major force on the Street, and paid off all his debts, to the penny. But he wasn't the man Citibank or the country needed in the late 1920s; that's for sure.

With its subsidiaries National City Company and Farmers Trust, the National City Bank of New York in 1929 was a true financial department store. People who lived in New York City—for the bank was not allowed to have branches outside New York City—could do virtually all their financial business with City Bank. In addition to the normal deposit-taking and lending business of the bank, we offered people brokerage services, we underwrote new securities (especially bonds, both domestic and foreign), and through the Trust Company we managed money, investing in real estate as well as in financial instruments. When all the markets collapsed in the early 1930s, it was easy to blame the banks, because they were involved in everything, and because of Mitchell, National City was a natural lightning rod.

Looking at what Mitchell and National City did in those years, the only fair yardstick is the standards of the times. Many actions that would make the hair stand up straight on the head of one of today's government regulators were legal and common in those days. Leaders of the Wall Street community participated in pools to drive the price of a stock up or down. If there was a market for a stock or a bond, nobody saw anything reprehensible about offering that piece of paper to that market, whatever the seller's personal views of its value might be. The rule was, let the buyer beware. Most of the people whose activities were later regarded as thoroughly reprehensible went about their business without the slightest sense that anyone might think they were doing anything "wrong." People who are making money by following the ways of the world don't often find it necessary to criticize those ways.

Conflicts of interest are inevitable in the world. Every time a married man looks at a beautiful woman, he has a conflict of interest. The question is whether the conflict is disclosed, understood, and respected. If conflicts are disclosed so that everyone knows where he stands, they need not do harm. When U.S. Steel asked me to go on its board, I called George Humphrey, chairman of National Steel, a long-standing City Bank customer, and asked if he had any objection. To the contrary, he said, he thought it would help me understand his problems better. In the National City Bank of the 1920s, however, conflicts were not disclosed—often they were not understood—with damaging results. For example, National City Company, the broker / dealer subsidiary that underwrote new securities for corporations and municipalities, was also by far the largest trader in City Bank stock, sometimes buying and selling thirty thousand and forty thousand shares a day, steadily pushing up the price, using money borrowed from City Bank itself to make the purchases.

City Bank lent $3 million to St. Louis Public Service as lead bank for a $10 million loan intended to bridge the period between the day the transit company had to pay off a bond issue and the day a new bond issue could be sold. The reason for the loan was simply stated in our files: it was to help National City Company as underwriter to "get the business" of the new bond issue. It "got the business," all right. When St. Louis Public Service couldn't sell the new bonds and went into the bankruptcy courts to seek protection from its creditors, the bank took a loss of $2.3 million on the loan. The bank's involvement with the Insull public utility holding companies and the Van Sweringen railroad and real estate empire was designed to win underwriting contracts for City Company. Sometimes the hand of the investment wing washed that of the bank: $25 million of the receipts from a new issue of common shares in the bank sold in 1927 was assigned to National City Company, which used the money to purchase at face value $25 million of Cuban sugar loans that had been criticized by the bank examiners and would have had to be written down or worse if City Company, which was not examined by anyone, hadn't bought them.

Even by the standards of the time, City Company was often overly

aggressive. When I began calling on potential customers and correspondents in the later 1930s, I kept running into people who had stories about how National City Company salesmen under Mitchell had
pushed bonds that later defaulted. As one of the liquidating trustees of
the City Company, I had to okay the settlement of suits for misrepre-
sentation brought under state laws or common law. Plaintiffs sometimes won these suits even when they didn't have much of a case. I
remember a suit for around $2 million under a Minnesota "blue sky"
statute requiring disclosure in securities sales. After the case was in
but before it went to the jury, the lawyer for the plaintiff offered to
settle for a modest fraction of the amount claimed. The lawyers handling the case for us called and said, "We don't want to settle. We can
tell that this jury is sympathetic to us." Then the judge took the case
away from the jury, on the grounds that the weight of the evidence
was clear, and ruled against us without ever letting the jury vote, and
we had to pay the full amount. Lawyers never give you a warranty
bond, and when they make mistakes it's your problem. Bankers and
businessmen have to pay for their mistakes, and if they make a big
mistake they pay a big price. Many companies and banks made big
mistakes in the 1920s, and paid heavily for them in the 1930s.

What happened in the 1920s, however, does not mean that mixed
banking always leads to such results. Germany and Switzerland have
long had "universal banking," with the banks handling all financial
functions for their customers, both private and corporate, and investing on their own account, too; and there's never been any problem that
I've heard about. Through various subsidiaries, Citibank and a score
of other American banks have been active underwriters in the Eurodollar markets now for two decades, without conflict of interest troubles. There is a unity as well as a conflict of interest here, after all.
Every time a commercial banker advises a borrower, he performs an
investment banking function. The world is capital short, and even after
the rash of mergers and public offerings the investment banking business is still undercapitalized. And the banks need new markets in which
to offer their expertise, for neither lenders nor borrowers will pay the
costs of intermediation by banks when they can make contact through
low-cost brokers.

And, of course, it simply wasn't true that the excesses of the banks
were the cause of the Depression. We didn't even supply the credit
that enabled the brokers to carry their customers' margin accounts:
like today's commercial-paper market, the call-money market on Wall

Street drew funds directly from corporations and institutions, and banks were responsible for less than a fifth of the money advanced. I remember Senator Walter George grumbling while the Banking Act of 1933 was on the floor that "it makes the banks the scapegoats for the Depression. They didn't help, but they didn't *do* it." In 1934, Senator Carter Glass, whose name was on the 1933 Act, tried to get the senate to amend it to permit banks, under close supervision, to return to the underwriting of corporate securities. Then as now, what was really needed was enforcement of the old commonsense laws and rules that prohibited self-dealing and excessive risk-taking with other people's money. Banking legislation from 1933 to this day has been dictated not by what business and consumers want and banks can efficiently provide but by the interests of all the other service-providers who don't want competition from the banks. Still, the climate of the times was to sock it to the banks. I spent much of the spring of 1933 in Washington, with a brief to see what contribution we could make to a mission of limiting the damage.

Our principal contact in Washington was through Larry Haugen, who worked for the National City trust department. He was the son of a retired Republican congressman (whose name was enshrined on the first high-tariff act of the 1920s). Through his father, he knew everybody on the Hill, and he could often get his friends to put in amendments as the bills moved through the committee process. Some bankers (and the American Bankers Association) lived in dread of the pending reform bill, because it would mean the loss of securities commissions at a time when they didn't have many sources of income. At National City, we weren't trying to prevent legislation. Perkins, like Winthrop Aldrich at the Chase Bank, had decided it would be a good thing to separate the stock market and banking enterprises. He was trying to sell off the National City Company before the law was passed to make him do it. (In the end we couldn't sell it, and had to liquidate it.) The substantive issue on which we fought hardest was the exemption of the foreign branches from the new legislation. Those branches had to compete with foreign banks governed by local law, and if we were stuck with the new American regulations in those countries we would have to close up shop. We won this fight, fortunately, then and again in 1935, when Congress passed legislation that enhanced the power of the Federal Reserve System and placed more onerous restrictions on the larger banks. Without these exemptions, we never could have launched Citicorp's international banking enterprise of the 1960s and 1970s.

Like other big-city bankers, I thought deposit insurance was a mistake, because bank liabilities were actuarially an unsound risk, as of course they are—you can predict roughly how many automobile accidents or deaths of sixty-three-year-old males there will be next year, but you can't predict the fraction of the nation's banks that will fail, because that's a function of economic conditions. Some years you have none, other years you have many, and you can't draw on past experiences to set the right insurance premiums. In this argument, as not many people know, the big-city bankers had Franklin Roosevelt on our side, because he didn't want to shore up a lot of country banks that were being run, badly, as little empires for their local owners. But the congressmen in whose districts those banks were located were adamant about the need for deposit insurance, and when it got to be June in Washington and unbearably hot, Roosevelt yielded. In the larger picture, the congressmen were right, because it wasn't fair that little people with a few hundred dollars in the bank and no way to know whether that bank was being run well or not should be the victims of some banker's mismanagement. And you can't have people lining up in bank lobbies because they can't get at the money they need when they need it. Today, though, my side of the argument is right again, because there isn't a good reason to insure deposits up to a hundred thousand dollars, as is now the case. It makes everyone sloppy, including the examiners. When you think about it, the regulators really have to take half the blame for a disaster like Continental-Illinois. Where were the examiners (or the directors, for that matter) when that bank was buying a billion dollars of bum loans from Penn Square with little or no credit analysis? In the end, the government took full responsibility and invested several billion dollars in the bank. At this writing, it looks like $1.7 billion of that will be lost. If deposits were insured only up to about ten thousand dollars, there'd be much more political pressure on the examiners to pay attention.

Probably the most important part of the 1933 legislation, though we did not realize it at the time, was the prohibition on the payment of interest on deposits that remained in the bank for less than thirty days, and the authorization of what came to be called "Reg Q" controls by the Federal Reserve on what banks could pay for time deposits. Interest on demand deposits had been rare in American banking, given only to the biggest and best customers, and the numbers were small. When you added up what the banks paid out in such interest, the numbers just about matched what the experts thought would be the premiums for deposit insurance, and for many bankers the new rule looked like a plus—it would save them what deposit insurance would cost them. But when interest rates began to rise after 1951, the fact that banks could not offer to pay for demand deposits moved a great deal of money out to Treasury bills and commercial paper.

Howard Sheperd, our chairman in the 1950s, said later in the decade that we "shouldn't expect that we can keep getting our inventory for nothing." A couple of years later, Wriston and I (but it was Wriston who invented the techniques) created the negotiable certificate of deposit. This allowed us to pay interest (because the CD matured in thirty days or more) but left the depositor free to claim his money, or something very like it, at any time (because the CD was "negotiable" and could be traded in the market). Even that didn't completely save us, because the Fed could kill our "sale" of CDs by pushing interest rates above the Reg Q ceilings on deposits of whatever duration, as it did in 1966, leaving us close to high and dry for a while.

The legislation we worked on in 1933 was a set of long and complicated bills, touching on a great variety of banking procedures. Even if one agreed with their general purpose, as Perkins mostly did, individual sections could be deeply troubling. And there were two versions, one from the House and one from the Senate. How these two were reconciled, and how the bills were "marked up" in the conference committee, might make a great difference to a large bank like National City, struggling to come out of the shadows. The markups were necessarily done mostly by the staffs of the two banking committees, with only part-time attendance by the congressmen and senators themselves. I was twenty-eight years old, a junior officer of National City Bank, no threat to anyone, and a hard worker. Haugen as our lobbyist arranged for us to have access to the conference room. What we did was to buy a big scrapbook. On facing pages, we pasted the House version and the Senate version, underlining the differences. And down on the bottom of each page we would note which version we favored, and why. The fact was that even the committee staffs, let alone the congressmen, didn't know much about banking. After the first meetings, we came to know each other, we were all smoking cigars together, and they knew we were trying to be helpful, not plotting to sabotage their bill. As each section was called, someone would say

"Okay, George, what do you have in your book about *this* section?" We got a lot of little things changed, just because we had that book and were "in the room."

2

My next major involvement with the law came in a courtroom, not in the halls of Congress, though the lawsuit was based on information unearthed during the Pecora hearings before the House Banking Committee. This was the "Gallin case," a stockholder derivative action against the directors of National City Bank as individuals, for permitting a great range of alleged mistakes in the operation of the bank. There were bad loans, loans to insiders, manipulation of securities, the bookkeeping of the bank, and the "management" fund from which large bonuses and salary increases had been paid in the later 1920s. Chief attorney for the plaintiffs was David Podell. Shearman & Sterling couldn't represent the bank, because many of the actions for which the directors were being sued had been taken with its approval and some of the partners were themselves directors and thus co-defendants. The directors hired John W. Davis, a former Democratic presidential candidate (against Coolidge), to lead the defense with former Judge Joseph Proskauer. Davis's top assistant was Porter Chandler, who would become one of the senior partners at Davis, Polk and a leader of the New York bar. The Davis, Polk fee for the Gallin case was one million dollars. Several of the directors also had their own special counsel. Perkins was now chairman of the bank. As his assistant, I was involved with Walter Pease of Shearman & Sterling in preparing material for Davis and Proskauer and their staff.

The case was tried without a jury, and it was presented by Podell in an unusually gentle fashion. Mitchell and the presidents of the three companies were all called to testify, with others, but Podell did not attempt to impugn their motives or force admissions of wrongdoing. His helpfulness extended to permission for me to stand by Perkins while he was in the witness box and prompt him with answers to Podell's questions. He didn't even make me take an oath.

Nearly all the evidence introduced in the case was by "stipulation," documents that both sides agreed were formally correct, had been prepared for such and such a day and used for such and such a purpose. Having identified the documents, the witnesses were simply asked for their version of why certain loans had been made, why there was a management fund, why officers had been permitted to borrow to carry their purchases of National City stock, and so on. There had been a great deal alleged by the Gallin group in their original complaint that Podell did not bring into his presentation for the plaintiffs. I remember my surprise that he let so many opportunities go to bring out that City Company had lost millions on its own holdings of City Bank stock, which struck me as a very vulnerable point. Each afternoon, after the close of testimony, Davis and Proskauer would meet with us to review what they thought had happened that day and discuss what matters where likely to come up the next day. Then some of the staff lawyers and some of us from the bank would work late into the night. Early the next morning, Davis would join us for an hour or so just before the opening of court, and absolutely master every point we presented to him. I was very impressed with how well he always knew his stuff.

Davis in cross-examination was a master of maneuvering a witness into a position where he could be made to look silly. I remember that the plaintiffs brought on some professor who was supposed to be an expert on corporate salaries to testify that Mitchell's million dollars a year was way out of line. He testified that the head of General Motors got $400,000, the head of AT&T got $350,000—there wasn't any justification for paying Mitchell a million. Davis in cross-examination politely probed the man's qualifications for making such judgments, and insisted on identifying him as an "efficiency expert." That term was, then as now, in some disrepute, and the witness resisted vigorously. He was, he argued, not an efficiency expert but a "management engineer." Finally Davis said sweetly, "I understand. It's the difference between a mortician and an undertaker, isn't it?"

Then, quite suddenly, when we thought he was just gathering speed, Podell announced that he had completed presenting his case. Davis then asked the judge for an adjournment until the next morning. That afternoon, Davis, with Proskauer concurring, recommended to the defendants that they offer no defense at all. He thought he had put a reasonable defense on the record in his own examination of plaintiff's witnesses, and that the directors were probably in better shape at this moment than they would be at the end of the trial if they tried to introduce evidence of their own. Obviously, Podell was holding back his use of some of the documents already filed in the court, waiting until he could do us the most harm. Most of the directors, and some of their counsel, resisted Davis's advice. Davis pointed out that Podell had the record of the Pecora hearings, and he hadn't emphasized much of the damaging material the House committee had published. And there were some questionable things that Podell had not mentioned (the huge losses National City Company had suffered from trading its own stock, for example) and that we had reason to believe he knew. Podell was obviously saving the best part of his case to enter with dramatic effect as part of his cross-examination of defense witnesses, when he need not be polite. Davis proposed not to give him that opportunity.

When some directors continued to resist, Davis suggested that he could demonstrate what concerned him if they would let him stage a mock cross-examination in the conference room. He asked Perkins to be his witness. Davis asked Perkins a string of embarrassing questions growing out of the Pecora record and depositions given by National City officers in other places. This time I did not stand beside Perkins (for Podell might not give us that favor again). Perkins was probably the least vulnerable of the directors, because not only his actions but his instincts were blameless—and after fifteen minutes or so Davis made Perkins look pretty bad. The directors accepted Davis's advice, which was indeed worth the million dollars he had been paid. The next day he told the judge that he and his clients felt Podell had presented the case very fairly, and were willing to stand on the record.

Some months later, the judge ruled for the defendants on all but one of the claims. He said the directors of a bank were entitled to the benefit of any doubts because of their high responsibility, and could not be questioned as to their judgment, however seriously mistaken it might have been, unless they indulged in self-dealing or neglected their duties. The charge against the board that held up on that criterion was the criticism of the accounting procedures used to establish the size of the management fund from which top officers' bonuses were paid. During the time complained of, there had been about one hundred management decisions that increased or decreased the amount to be paid into the management fund. The judge did not criticize the decisions themselves. He said that the board could in fact have accepted every decision management had made. Their error was that they had not examined the decisions, or established a policy to be followed in making them. In effect, they had let the officers who benefited from the fund set their own bonuses by making the accounting judgments themselves. The penalty against the directors in two groups was $1.8 million, divided between directors of the National City Company and directors of the National City Bank.

That afternoon, I remember, Perkins and Gordon Rentschler, the president of the bank, were in Perkins's office when I came in. They were trying to work out by successive approximation how much each of the directors would have to pay. I took a pad and a pencil and did the high-school algebra simultaneous equation that gave the answer, which was something like $82,237 per director. They thought I was a mathematical genius until I modestly explained that it was the advantage of engineering as against liberal arts training: if you studied engineering, it helped you retain your high school algebra. . . . Most of the directors thought they had got off easy, and there was no appeal. For Perkins, however, this was quite a lot of money, and he had to sell securities on the depressed market of 1935 to pay the judgment against him.

A quarter of a century later I was made president of First National City Bank and elected to the board of directors, and one of the first things I learned was that the compensation scheme for the senior officers was again being run as it had been in the Mitchell days, without the necessary directors' control. The officers were still making the accounting decisions that dictated the size of the reported profits. And by then there had been another case with a similar penalty for corporate directors, involving American Tobacco. I called Shearman & Sterling and said, "I guess all your partners who worked on the Gallin case are dead. You'd better see to it that the board appoints an accounting committee before we get sued again." But there are a lot of companies that without referring the matter to the board permit management to decide where to set the rate of depreciation, or whether to capitalize some expense payment, which affects calculated profits and thus profit-sharing plans.

3

I've always agreed with Milton Friedman that the Federal Reserve was more responsible for the Depression than any collection of bankers or businessmen or politicians, but I don't think you can blame any individuals. In 1929 the people at the Fed didn't know what was happening. If they had known, they wouldn't have had any ideas of what to do about it, and if they'd known what to do there wasn't anybody around who could have done it. Benjamin Strong was dead, and his successor George Harrison was not up to the problem. So the Fed let the money supply wind down, which made the deflation progressively worse. But the first law of politics is that government always finds someone else to blame, so by the time we bottomed out the banks had been put in a straitjacket of government rules and regulations. I spent most of my working life in that straitjacket.

We were restricted in where we could have banking offices, in how we could raise the money we lent, in what we could lend it for, in what services we could offer our customers, and even in what we could call the services we did offer. We couldn't, for example, ask people to open a "savings" account, because New York State law restricted the use of the word "savings" to the "savings banks"; instead, we had to call it a "compound interest account." We were slapped down a number of times over the years—when we wanted to acquire the County Trust Company in Westchester, when we bought the Carte Blanche credit card operation from Hilton Hotels and were forced to sell it, when we tried to offer a "commingled investment account" like a mutual fund, not only to our trust customers (for whom this service was unquestionably legal) but also to members of the general public (the Securities Industry Association, on behalf of the non-bank marketers of mutual funds, sued us and won in the Supreme Court). We bought Chubb, an insurance group, and the Fed sent us packing; we bought the consulting firm of Cresap, McCormack & Paget, with the thought that they might help us run the bank and we might help them find customers. But they lost more customers from other banks than we could send them from ours, and in this case we weren't too unhappy when the Fed forced us to divest.

There were of course areas where we worked with the government in the 1930s and thereafter. Roger Steffan had pioneered installment consumer credit at National City in 1926, and went to Washington to help set up the Federal Housing Administration. His argument was that provided a borrower kept his total installment payments below 20 to 25 percent of his disposable income, he paid these debts without hardship. Home mortgages had usually been written in America for a five-year term, for a fixed amount of, say, 60 percent of the value of the house. Steffan said a lender could safely finance 90 percent of the value if the payments were monthly and no more than what the new homeowners would otherwise pay in rent.

City Bank went partners with the Reconstruction Finance Corporation in loans to bring businesses back from the brink, and we made the first loans under Section 13-B of the amended Federal Reserve Act, which permitted the Fed to guarantee half the loan. Perhaps because I had been brought up a Democrat, perhaps because I was working with Perkins, who was on first-name terms with the president, I was less hostile to the New Deal than some others at the bank. I thought the important thing was to get business done. If people sat on their hands, or their capital, the country could never revive. People forget, but it's true, that we had more unemployment in 1939 than we had in 1933. (In those days, people in government work relief programs were counted as still unemployed.)

From the point of view of the bank and its clients, the important fact was that opportunities were being missed. Between the businessmen who thought that the SEC was the end of the world and the university technocrats who thought the country was overgrown and overexpanded, the economy was stagnant. I don't know what would have happened if Britain and France hadn't finally grown so scared of Hitler that they began placing orders for airplanes, which had a multiplier effect in all the industrial towns—you buy the land, you build the plant, you hire the people, they buy groceries. We used to say that each dollar of orders generated five dollars of income for the country. But not many of the business leaders who had survived the Depression were ready to relaunch their boats on this mounting tide. So the job was done in large part by newcomers. Very, very few of the corporate executives of the early 1930s were still significant business leaders at the end of World War II. The world had passed them by, they were old or they were dead, or their businesses went out of existence. We'd been in a fifteen-year tunnel, and while we were in it the economic system and most of the players changed.

During the war, naturally, the bank was plugged into the production part of the nation's defense efforts. The fixed asset vehicle was the Defense Plant Corporation, which insured investments in war-related factories. But the government wisely decided not to insure 100 percent: there had to be a bank ready to take 10 percent of the risk to insure that this was a legitimate business deal. Gordon Rentschler, who became chairman of the bank when Perkins died—and who had started out as a businessman, not a banker—participated in creating this program, and we helped set up many of the early deals. When the war was over, these guarantees were quickly canceled, and after the companies decided whether they wanted to convert these production lines to peacetime goods, the banks had to decide whether they would finance the transition. There were big plants for sale. I remember

International Harvester bought some of them, but Caterpillar wouldn't: they wanted to build their own new facilities, tailored for what they were going to make. Both were sound credits, and we helped both; in retrospect, it turns out Caterpillar was right.

One of the earliest of our Defense Production loans had been to Beech Aircraft, and when the war was over they had large inventories and their contracts were canceled. They wanted a new loan to carry those inventories while they shifted over to civilian production and liquidated their defense operation. The district officers and the credit policy supervisors had disagreed, and the problem came to my desk. The question was the value of Beech's accounts receivable from canceled government contracts—some $38 million. I called the general in charge of air force procurement in Dayton, with whom I'd been doing business, and I said, "My boys want to know about these Beech receivables. Will the government pay Beech?" He said, "There's no problem about that, George—I've had my auditors in there for three months, and 95 percent of the amount claimed is okay, there's maybe a few trips on government expense that we're going to disallow. Don't tell them that, of course, we want to keep the pressures on." So we made the Beech loan, and they became the most successful of the early suppliers to private aviation.

There was also a routine, money-making, instructive activity with the government during the war: we bought their paper, at the weekly Monday auctions. This was to a large extent under allocation. City Bank had about 4 percent of the nation's deposits, so on the average we wound up buying about 4 percent of the new Treasury bills. We paid by creating a deposit to the account of the Treasury on our books. The government would take that money out immediately and spend it . . . and then it would dribble back to us. The fact that we had 4 percent of the nation's deposits meant that our customers did about 4 percent of the nation's business, including that part of the business where the government was the customer. Eventually, we found that our customers' deposits had risen by about 4 percent of the week's Treasury Auction. Because economic activity, while rising, was not moving at anything like that pace, this increase in the nation's bank deposits inflated the currency. Roughly, tax increases paid half the cost of the war and the government borrowed the other half—and what was borrowed was monetized. Between 1939 and 1946 the money supply roughly doubled. The banks' total deposits doubled. So did the cost of living index. So did our average salary. When the war began, we were paying, on the average, about one thousand, eight hundred dollars a year; in 1947 it was three thousand, six hundred dollars.

4

My first public position of anything like an official nature was my membership in 1951–52 on the twelve-man governing body of a hybrid creation called the Voluntary Credit Restraint Program. This was a Korean War phenomenon, a not-quite-impromptu effort to see whether something other than the construction of a huge edifice of rules and regulations and bureaucratic supervision could prevent the return of the inflation that had wracked the country in 1947–48. Banks were awash with funds. (Over half the assets of the U.S. banking system in 1949—$78 billion of $140 billion, to be exact—had been in Treasury securities that could be sold to fund loans, and in 1950, when the Korean War broke out, the Federal Reserve was still buying whatever Treasury paper a bank or anyone else wanted to sell at a price of one hundred cents on the dollar, to keep interest rates low and hold down the government's interest costs. Making loans to businesses, which of course paid higher rates than the government, banks could always find the money for the loan simply by selling paper from their bulging portfolios of government securities.) And nearly all the major borrowers from the banks were companies subject to excess-profits taxes, which could in effect borrow cost-free. The Fed was worried by a rapid buildup of retail inventories financed by bank loans, and also by a projected 29 percent year-on-year increase in business spending for plant and equipment, far beyond the corporate or private cash flow available to support it. Only about a quarter of this planned industrial expansion was part of the war effort (though another quarter was arguably "war related").

What the Fed proposed to do, of course, was slap a ceiling on new lending, bank by bank. At each bank the maximum allowable increase in loans would be set at some percentage of what they had lent the year before. That was the way the British and French controlled credit creation by their banks, and it was the way official minds worked in Washington, too. This seemed folly to me, and to my colleagues on the American Bankers Association credit policies committee, of which I had recently become chairman. Ideally, what the Fed wanted was to limit the extension of credit for "non-essential"—and especially for non-productive—purposes. But blanket controls on lending wouldn't keep the banks from lending to speculators and others whose money did nothing to propel the defense effort. Inevitably, the banks would lend to their best customers, and turn away newcomers, some of whom were exactly the enterprisers the Fed wanted to see encouraged. Meanwhile, the up-and-coming banks with good ideas for productive lending would be held back by the limits, and banks that were simply supporting the status quo would have money to spare. Some of us at the ABA proposed to the Fed that instead of imposing quantitative limits, the government should let qualitative guidelines arise from within the industry.

In late autumn 1950, the Federal Reserve Bank of New York arranged a meeting of representatives of the ABA, the Investment Bankers, the Life Insurance Association, and the Federal Reserve Board. At that meeting, it was decided, somewhat gingerly, to give voluntarism a chance. Some of what we were going to do was obviously questionable under the antitrust laws, but the Defense Production Act had empowered the director of the Office of Defense Mobilization to suspend application of the antitrust laws. Cooperation by all the major lenders was necessary, as Federal Reserve Board chairman Thomas McCabe told the first meeting of our Voluntary Credit Restraint Committee, to stop "shopping around for loans." The guiding committee consisted of four each from the insurance companies, the investment bankers, and the commercial bankers—this last being myself, Carlisle Davis of the State Planters Bank and Trust in Richmond, Virginia, Kenton R. Cravens of Mercantile-Commerce Bank in St. Louis, and Everett D. Reese of the Park National Bank in Newark, Ohio. A few months later, some savings-and-loan executives were added to the group. The committee was chaired by Oliver Powell, one of the governors of the Fed.

We met—every other week, sometimes for two days, during the first few months—to lay down guidelines we distributed in the form of seven "Bulletins," and then to hear appeals by prospective borrowers whose plans had been labeled inflationary by one of the forty-three regional subcommittees formed by the district Federal Reserve Banks. The members of some of the subcommittees, interestingly, were more distinguished than our national body. I was then only a plain vanilla vice-president of National City Bank, but the chairman of the New York region banking subcommittee was George Whitney, chairman of J. P. Morgan, and his vice-chairman was George Champion, who was already a senior vice-president of Chase and known to be on the track for the top job when Winthrop Aldrich retired.

Our first bulletin was an elementary economics lesson: "Any increase in lending at a more rapid rate than production can be increased exerts an inflationary influence . . . Loans which ultimately result in a commensurate increase in production of an essential nature are not inflationary in the long run . . . It is most important, however, that loans for non-essential purposes be curtailed in order to release some of the nation's resources for expansion in more vital areas of production." Even before its publication, this bulletin affected a transaction on my desk at City Bank. I had pretty much written the first draft of the bulletin myself. While it was circulating among the members of the committee, André Meyer of Lazard Frères came into my office to talk with me about a loan from National City Bank to help him buy some Arizona ranch properties from a Scottish trust. It was a perfectly reasonable deal from a banker's point of view, a good credit risk from a good customer. I turned it down, telling Meyer he could take it to Morgan or Chase or anywhere and get it funded, but for reasons I wasn't at liberty to disclose, National City Bank would not make the loan.

Meyer got furious and went to Gordon Rentschler, chairman of City Bank, who called me up to his office to explain. I told him what I couldn't tell Meyer, that I'd just written a communiqué describing precisely this sort of transaction as inflationary and outside the guidelines for voluntary credit restraint, which we were pledging ourselves to exercise. It was the type of loan I had told the Fed would be made under a mandatory quantitative limit, but would not be made if banks were asked to apply reasonable guidelines in distinguishing between inflationary and non-inflationary lending. Rentschler laughed, and said he supposed Meyer would come back someday, as of course he did. When I retired from Citibank, indeed, he asked me to join him at Lazard. I said, "André, I love you. I'm always happy to work *with* you. But I'll never work *for* you." Meyer was a good friend. The only time I had a serious illness, when I had my kidney operation in the early 1960s, the attendants dragged me out of bed in New York Hospital at seven in the morning the day after I'd been through eleven hours on an operating table, to get my system started on its normal pursuits and to protect against possible phlebitis. When I returned to my room at 7:30, I found Meyer and Bobby Lehman of Lehman Brothers waiting for me—they'd heard from their secretaries, who had heard from mine, that I'd been through the operation. Lehman as a trustee of the hospital had unlimited access, and he'd invited Meyer to come with him so they could cheer me up, which they certainly did.

To the surprise of a lot of people, Voluntary Credit Restraint, which Governor Powell described as "the collective horse sense of all kinds of lenders," really made a difference. Banks did use our guidelines, and when they needed protection they did refer loans to the regional committees. And the losers carried appeals to us at the national level, though until quite near the end we never overruled one of our regional groups— at most, we suggested that they look at the question again. But few people disagreed with the rules of thumb we suggested: it was okay to make a loan to build a first television station in an area, but not a competitive television station; appropriate to make a loan to enlarge a mortuary in a town swollen by defense plants, but not a loan to stock a sporting goods store in a suburb; sound practice to lend money to build a dairy or a flour mill, but not money to *buy* a dairy or a flour mill (or a ranch!).

About six months after we published our first bulletin, the staff of the Fed gave us an enthusiastic slap on the back. The program, an evaluative study proclaimed, "has given lending officers new benchmarks to use in their appraisal of loan applications; it has broadened their horizon beyond the fairly limited objective of appraising the creditworthiness of a prospective borrower; it has made them increasingly aware of the importance of credit policy in an economic stablization program; and it has contributed to prudence in lending. Equally important, these have been achieved without shutting off the supply of credit . . . and without imposing upon lending operations a burdensome harness of detailed and specific rules and regulations."

In May 1952, when the tents were officially folded, The *New York Times* editorialized that "the experiment in voluntary cooperative credit controls was a decided success. This suggests that in future we may find it necessary to distinguish between voluntary programs that rest entirely on exhortation and those which are carefully and intelligently organized and executed to produce the desired results." When President Lyndon Johnson revived the name of our program for use by a committee attempting to staunch the flow of dollars to the Eurodollar market in 1965, economists from the New York Fed did a special retrospective study of what we had accomplished, and cautiously concluded (for this sort of thing was and is anathema to economists) that "In general, compliance was believed to have been good."

Of course, we had a lot going for us. About a month into our program, the redoubtable William McChesney Martin became chairman of the Fed, and began to use the central bank's freshly won powers to let interest rates rise, which meant that the price of government securities was allowed to fall. This discouraged banks from lending because it meant that when they went to fund their loans to businesses by selling bonds and notes from their portfolios of government securities, the banks had to take a loss on each sale. Meanwhile, the excesses of the inventory buildup in the second half of 1950 were leaving stores with unsold stock by mid-1951, diminishing their eagerness to borrow. Specific Fed restraints on installment loans, home mortgages, and stock market credit damped the strongest fires. You could also say that we were lucky enough to be killed off before we had time to get sick.

There had been gripes and grumbles from both borrowers and lenders almost from the start. Country banks felt that government agricultural lenders, like the Farm Credit Administration agencies that got in so much trouble thirty years later, were cutting them out of their market because the banks felt bound by the credit restraint program and the government agencies did not. Some small-city banks sold their loans upstream to big-city correspondents, which felt they had to buy, though such purchases were clearly outside the guidelines, or risk losing important accounts. I took that one up with the committee on correspondent bank relations of the Reserve City Bankers, and we got pretty good compliance. Loans to finance companies to support their activities kept rising for six months, because they were drawn against pre-established lines of credit. This wasn't, as I pointed out to a committee meeting, entirely within our control, because the Fed had written separate regulations to control what the banks could do in financing automobile purchases, but the finance companies weren't bound by those regulations. Smaller banks as a result saw their installment lending vanishing into the pockets of General Motors Acceptance Corporation (GMAC) and its rivals. Other observers felt there was too much lending of too high a proportion of sales price for existing housing, and a mess in cattle loans in the West.

But the running sore was borrowing by state and municipal governments. I raised the issue at the very first meeting of the committee, and in May, seven weeks into the program, we got Charles E. Wilson, director of the Office of Defense Mobilization, to send a letter to all governors, mayors, and county finance officers: "On behalf of our government, I ask you to postpone borrowing, no matter how worthy the purpose, if the project is postponable." We didn't feel we could—or should—stop the construction of schools or roads, but we did think we could stop the issuance of bonds for the payment of veterans' bonuses. These bonuses were obviously inflationary, for they put purchasing power into people's hands without adding in the least to the supply of things for them to purchase.

The issue came to a head in the state of West Virginia, where the voters had approved such a bond issue and the legislature had passed the necessary enabling laws. Our investment banking subcommittee in the fifth district looked at the bonds and pronounced them outside the guidelines. The state advertised the issue for bids from investment bankers, anyway. On May 23d, the day the bids were to be opened, there were no bids. Governor Oakley Patteson came to see us. He was entirely honest about it. He thought veterans' bonus bonds were just as inflationary as we thought they were, and a dumb idea, anyway. But both political parties had made the veterans' bonus part of their platforms in the state elections in 1950. I asked him what he thought the veterans would do with the money. "About a third will spend it on women," he said, "and a third will spend it on booze, and the rest I guess will just waste it." We not only affirmed the opinion of the fifth district subcommittee, we called the matter to the attention of all the other investment banking subcommittees to keep the state from shopping the issue.

U.S. Municipal News, the organ of the U.S. Conference of Mayors, wrote a furious editorial: "There does not vest in the Federal Government any legal power to curb the issuance of state and municipal bonds . . . Full and ample responsibility is vested in the appropriate local officials and not in any Federal or private Voluntary Credit Restraint Committee composed of private investment bankers . . . The technique of the Federal Reserve and other Washington agencies concerned will be to 'put the heat' on bond houses and dealers *not to bid* on municipal offerings . . . It is of interest to point out that already a proposed State of West Virginia issue has been sabotaged . . ." Congressman Harley Staggers introduced a bill to put us out of business, and went to see President Truman. Chairman Martin got a memo to Truman first, and Truman responded with a letter to him: "I find it hard to understand why these people can't cooperate with us to keep our inflationary pressures under control." The United Press moved a story that Staggers had been turned down: he "quoted the President as saying that the committee is 'entirely nonpartisan' and made up of the Nation's 'best ecnonomists.' Staggers said he told the President that West Virginians could not see why the National Government opposed a veterans' bonus when it was giving away billions of dollars overseas . . ."

Whatever the propaganda about being able to take the heat in the kitchen, there was a limit to how long Truman was going to subject himself to such temperatures. On March 28th, on the first anniversary of our formation, Martin came before our committee to read a letter from Truman telling us that we were to cease interfering with the issuance of paper by state and municipal authorities. I and several others left the meeting before lunch, and the minutes of the afternoon session report "the consensus of the meeting that there was grave doubt whether the release of such credit restraint might not vitiate the whole Program." Something more politic was found to put in the statement to be published, and Governor Powell announced that another meeting of the committee would be called in "about six weeks," but there never was another meeting.

5

Almost ten years passed before I again held any appointment from the federal government. By then I was president of First National City Bank, which was the second or third largest in the country, and as such I was inevitably a relatively public person. James Saxon, a lawyer and former vice-president of the First National Bank of Chicago, had become comptroller of the currency and Douglas Dillon was secretary of the treasury; this was in the Kennedy administration. Both of them thought the time had come to loosen up considerably on what banks could do, to open new sources of funds, new powers to branch in their own states and abroad, new kinds of business they could enter, new lending patterns. Saxon was much more free than any of his predecessors in chartering new banks and in allowing banks to merge. The comptroller's office is a bank regulating office, with supervision of the National Bank Examiners, but it is also to a minor extent a club, supported by the dues of the nationally chartered banks. Saxon formed an advisory committee of bankers to advise him and asked me chair it.

One can make an awesome list of what Saxon accomplished, often in the teeth of opposition from the Federal Reserve and the banking committees in the House and Senate. He exempted the overnight borrowings of one bank from another (in the so-called Fed Funds market) from the usual restrictions on how much a bank can lend to one borrower, making it possible for the big-city banks to greatly increase the funds they could draw from their correspondent banks. He allowed the opening of permanent "loan production offices" out of town, previously a gray area; he let banks count in their capital for regulatory purposes their undivided profits and the proceeds of sales of capital notes and debentures; he approved the purchase of finance companies, travel agencies, and insurance agencies by banks; he even permitted banks to keep "equity kickers," profit participations, in some of their loans.

More of this than you might think was Saxon's own idea. The fact that you were on his advisory committee did not mean he felt he owed you anything. It was while I was serving on the comptroller's committee that we tried to purchase County Trust and later National Bank of Westchester under the terms of a 1961 state law that had permitted New York banks to branch into adjacent counties. But we needed the approval of the Federal Reserve under the 1935 banking act, and we didn't get it, in part because Jimmy Saxon testified against us. (He thought there would be more competition and the people of Westchester would be better off if we started a branch of our own instead of buying another bank, and he promised to give us quick approval if we applied for the right to branch wherever permitted by the laws of the State of New York—which had not opened many such doors for us. Saxon may have been right in his argument, though we didn't think so at the time. As it worked out, he did us a favor: it cost us a lot less to start from scratch than what we had agreed to pay the Westchester banks, and we became profitable in Westchester very quickly. I once told Saxon that by opposing us in what we wanted to do he'd saved us $50 million.) One of the few things we fought for and got from him was the right of national banks to issue stock options to their officers, like other corporations. I was engaged in recruiting at the business schools, and it was a weight around my neck that other corporations could talk about the possibility of stock options and we couldn't. Though my motives weren't selfish, because I thought of myself as pretty well off, the options First National City gave me in the next few years became the most important wealth I had when I retired.

Some of the things Saxon approved stuck, like the exemption of Fed Funds from loan limits, the acceptance of subordinated debt as bank capital for regulatory purposes, and the right to own finance companies. Some others were knocked down by the courts or Congress, like his approval of our commingled investment fund (a considerable benefit to the public, because we were prepared to go without any sales charge to purchasers of the fund and a management fee of only 0.05 percent, a tenth of what the mutual funds charged). But thanks to Saxon the national charter became a more desirable base for doing banking business than a state charter was, after many years when nationally chartered banks had been at some disadvantage by comparison with state-chartered banks in places like New York, where both flourished (among the state-chartered banks with which I had to compete were Morgan Guaranty, Chemical, and Manufacturers Hanover).

All that moving back and forth between state and federal jurisdiction, which still goes on, has always struck me as nonsense. There really isn't any excuse for the American sort of "dual banking" system, with chartering by either a state or the national comptroller, just as there isn't any excuse for the plethora of regulations that keep banks from competing on equal terms with Sears and Merrill, Lynch and Prudential Insurance and the savings-and-loan associations. As my colleague and successor Walter Wriston wrote, "If you sat up nights designing a system the consumer did not want, you would come up with something very close to today's American banking system." But every time someone tried to make order from the chaos, the competitors of the banks roused their friends in the Congress, sometimes with help from the bankers themselves.

Small-town bankers will talk about the importance of states' rights in banking, for example, but what they really want is to duck out of supervision entirely by playing one regulator off against the others. It's probably true that national chartering for all banks would lead to nationwide branch banking, and I agree that it would be a bad idea for the United States to have only four or five banks like Britain or ten like Canada. But that wouldn't happen, because this is a big country and for many purposes the local bank is going to be much better than the branch of a metropolitan bank. Citibank wouldn't—certainly shouldn't— have the slightest interest in opening a branch in Hannibal, Missouri. Whoever you send to manage it won't be able to find out which are the good loans and which are the bad ones because nobody will tell him, and my cousin's bank there will run him out of town.

In the mid-1960s, I served Secretary of Commerce John Connor as part of a business council giving advice on the negative and increasingly dangerous U.S. balance of payments—a ghost that came back to haunt us in 1986. As just about every aspect of Lyndon Johnson's economic policy was an argument for people with money to send it abroad in loans or investments, there wasn't much an advisory committee could recommend. David Rockefeller was also a member, but he rarely came. He sent an assistant, a very tall young man named Paul Volcker, who pontificated and told everybody what to do. IIe was a brilliant economist, I thought—and like everyone else, I'm full of admiration for what he later accomplished as chairman of the Federal Reserve—but in those days he didn't know much about practical banking.

At the Fed itself, I became in 1967, at about the same time I became chairman of my bank, a member of my first statutory body: the Federal Advisory Council, a committee mandated by the original Federal Reserve Act in 1913. This group, composed of one banker from each of the twelve Federal Reserve districts, meets four times a year to consider questions posed about a week in advance of the meetings by the staff of the Fed. It has a small staff of its own and a permanent secretary, in my day Herbert Prochnow of First Chicago. As a member of the council, I would receive the Fed's questions and call a dozen or so bankers in the district served by the Federal Reserve Bank of New York to ask their views before I went to Washington, so I could speak as more than one man's opinion. Meetings ran two days. The first day, we would sit down with the Fed staff to be briefed on national business conditions and to make sure we understood the ramifications of the questions, and then we would draft our answers, which would go that night to the board of governors. The next day, we met with the board. All or nearly all the governors came to the meetings.

These meetings of the Federal Advisory Council are an important procedure by which bankers can get their views to the attention of the Federal Reserve. There is even a sanction of sorts. If the Advisory Council feels that its views are being ignored, it is not only authorized but ordered to communicate them to the House and Senate banking committees—for the Fed itself, as most people who write about these subjects forget, is an arm of the Congress, to which the Constitution gives exclusive powers to regulate the money supply. And if we feel that the matter is a major question of public policy, we are permitted by law (though not instructed) to publish our comments—and our predecessors did, from 1929 (when the Advisory Council publicly urged the Fed to raise the discount rate to discourage a rash of brokers' loans on Wall Street) to 1948 (when it argued against a rise in reserve requirements or the discount rate). But in my time the board did listen to what we had to say, though of course it didn't invariably act on our advice, and neither we nor our successors to this day went public. The questions the staff submitted to us were always good questions. I came out of the experience of the council with a very high opinion of the quality of the staff at the Fed.

The Advisory Council could be tough on occasion. I have before me the minutes of the last meeting of my term, in November 1969, when the Fed had turned the screws on the banking system to push against the inflation that had resulted from the war in Vietnam and congressional delays in imposing taxes to pay for it. (The timing of this pressure on the banks, incidentally, was not very good: the federal government had just finished a fiscal year in which the accounts actually showed a surplus—we haven't had one since—and the economy was sinking faster than the Fed, or we, realized.) The fifth of the questions we were asked dealt with "the Board's recent proposal that would make commercial paper sold by one-bank holding companies subject to . . . interest-rate ceilings." In reply, we wrote that "the Council believes the recent proposal making commercial paper issued by one-bank holding companies subject to Regulation Q is ill-timed and unnecessary and may be illegal . . ." But the Fed did it anyway, and given the feeling in Congress about one-bank holding companies, there wasn't any point in attempting an appeal.

My time on the council coincided with the heyday of the one-bank holding company, undoubtedly the most important change in the big banks' relations with the government between 1935 and my retirement in spring 1970. Holding companies had long been used by bankers in small communities to unify their various activities, which might include insurance brokerage and real estate work, under a single corporate umbrella. Some individuals who owned a number of separate banks in different places (this was called "chain banking") converted to a corporate holding company for all the reasons individual owners like to incorporate. Then in the 1920s some larger banks began to use the holding-company device as a way to break out of the geographical straitjacket. A. P. Giannini, for example, formed Transamerica Corporation to own Bank of America in New York as well as his established Bank of Italy (which he renamed Bank of America) in California. Transamerica could also own insurance companies, which was an interesting side effect. But before too many bankers could imitate Giannini, the Depression came and everybody became very busy trying to keep his head above water. Giannini himself had to separate Transamerica from Bank of America. The other banks in the Transamerica complex became United California Banks, the forerunner of today's First Interstate Bank Corporation, with subsidiary banks in twelve states (with more coming)—and a bid on the table to purchase Bank of America!

In the 1950s, interest in multi-bank holding companies began to rise, especially as a way to erase geographical barriers, and in 1956 Congress said a firm No: except to the extent that states approved, and with grandfather protection for the half-dozen companies already active, bank holding companies would not be permitted to own banks where a bank would not be permitted to have a branch. But the Bank Holding Company Act of 1956 did not upset the owners of the *one-bank* holding company, partly because Congress was protecting the small-town banker and partly because Congress did not wish to interfere with the dozen or so non-financial corporations like Goodyear and Sears that owned banks in what was, in effect, a holding-company arrangement. In the mid-1960s, Union Bank in Los Angeles and Wachovia Bank in Winston-Salem, North Carolina, reorganized themselves, persuading their stockholders to take shares in a newly formed holding company that would own the bank instead of their existing shares in the bank itself.

Not long after I became chairman, in spring 1967, Walt Wriston brought me a memo written from our legal staff, about all the things the regulators wouldn't let us do as a bank that we could do as a bank holding company. And to the extent that there was any cost imposed by the change, it could be paid for very quickly by transferring the traveler's-check operation from the bank to the holding company. Issued by the bank, the traveler's check looked like a deposit to the Fed, and we had to keep an 18 percent reserve against it at the Fed, where money doesn't earn interest. Once we moved the issuance to the holding company, the traveler's check wouldn't be a deposit anymore, and we could invest all the money.

The story of what we did in those months before December 1970, when Congress changed the law, waits for Chapter 9. We had to be careful what we tried, because the Fed was unhappy and it was clear that Congress would at some point pass some legislation to restrict the freedom of one-bank holding companies. In the end, what we kept was a parcel of legislatively assured rights to operate on a nationwide basis, anywhere in the country, subsidiaries like finance companies and mortgage companies, factors, leasing companies, and others—just about

anything involved with lending money or processing financial transactions, except a deposit-taking bank. And, most importantly, this thirty-
month period when we could think about what businesses we wanted
to do, instead of thinking only about what businesses the government
had already said we could enter, was a time of liberation for everyone
at what had become First National City Corporation, en route to its
final incarnation as, simply, Citicorp.

5
Domestic Matters

One of the earliest and most interesting deals I made at City Bank was not a loan at all. Though I was already working at the bank when this opportunity knocked, it grew out of my assignments at Farmers Trust. When I'd become Perkins's assistant there, I was put into the investment management department for what time Perkins didn't need me, and among the people whose account I handled was William A. Coulter, a man from Greensboro, Pennsylvania, a big Princetonian, who had sold his coal mines and had about $5 million to invest (plus his sister's money, which he controlled). When I started working on his account, we were simply its custodians, but we had given him some good advice—notably, to get out of the stock market in spring 1930, when it recovered most of what it had lost the previous autumn—and he gave us the job of managing the investments. The account paid a good fee, and even after I followed Perkins to the bank I remained in touch with Coulter and his accounts, to help keep him happy.

In 1933, most of Coulter's money was in government bonds, and he was looking to do something entrepreneurial. One day I got a call from a Yale classmate of mine named Alvin Adams, who was president of National Aviation, an investment trust restricted to that adventurous industry. He told me he'd been approached by Ernest Breech, then president of a General Motors subsidiary called North American Aviation (some years later, Breech became president of Ford). One of the lesser revolutions of Roosevelt's first hundred days had been the Air

Mail Act, which was designed to encourage the growth of American aviation, but also to prevent what the New Deal considered antitrust abuses. Among its commandments was that airframe manufacturers should not own airlines—and General Motors, which was then an airframe manufacturer, controlled North American Aviation, which owned about three-quarters of the stock of Western Airlines plus control of Eastern Airlines. Breech was under deadline pressure to sell both of them.

Western was then an infant airline that ran only between San Diego, Los Angeles, and Salt Lake City. But it was part of a coast-to-coast network, making connections with United Airlines at Salt Lake City for flights all the way to New York, via Omaha, Chicago, and Cleveland, among other stops. The planes flew about three thousand feet off the ground, and of course there were no avionics in those days. Flying at night, the pilot aimed for a line of revolving lights maintained across the country. GM had thought it had a sale on Western, to a company called National Parks Airlines that flew between Salt Lake City and Missoula, Montana, but National Parks didn't have enough cash, and under the law General Motors couldn't advance any part of the purchase price. What was the price? I asked. Adams gave me Breech's phone number, and I called. If we could buy it *that day,* Breech said, he'd sell for book value, about two dollars a share, roughly two hundred thousand dollars all together, including the three Boeing airplanes the company owned. I called Coulter in Philadelphia, and told him to hurry up to New York prepared to make a sizable investment.

He did, and that afternoon we sent Breech a cashier's check for his estimate of the purchase price, on the understanding that when the accounts were audited we would adjust in one direction or the other. Breech then said, "Would Mr. Coulter like to buy Eastern Airlines, too?" This was a larger operation, and it would cost about seven hundred thousand dollars on the same basis. In addition, the buyer would have to pick up Eastern's contract with Douglas Aircraft, for a dozen DC-2's at about eighty thousand dollars each. Coulter couldn't do it himself, because the Air Mail Act forbade anyone to own two carriers that carried the mail—but his sister's account was available. On second thought, however, he decided it was too much to take on, and he declined. Breech, incidentally, was unable to sell Eastern by December 31st, and the government gave him an extension on the law's divestiture date. It wasn't until the next spring that he made his deal, with the World War I ace Eddie Rickenbacker, who had put together a group with the help of Laurance Rockefeller and paid something like $4 million. A few years later, Kuhn, Loeb came to Coulter to ask whether he'd be interested in several million dollars for Western—that's how fast some things turned around in the 1930s. I did get involved with Eastern, about twenty years later, when they were in trouble—they owed money to Douglas Aircraft and Boeing and Martin Marietta, and Chase, who were their bankers, had not been able to solve their problem. Boeing asked me to help. With Frank Denton of Mellon Bank, we found a way to consolidate Eastern's debts, stretch out their payments, and work things out.

Adams resigned from the investment fund and moved to the West Coast to be president of Western Airlines. Coulter wanted me to take stock in the company as a kind of commission, but I said, "I have a phobia about these things. I may be involved later, for the bank, and anyway I don't want people to think I have a personal interest in your investment." But I did go to Los Angeles for the dinner party at the Ambassador Hotel that announced the new ownership and management. I was sort of the baby's godfather. I was Adams's baby's godfather, too. I was supposed to turn around right after the dinner and make a night flight on Western to Salt Lake City, so I could take United to New York, but the dinner lasted too long. I missed the plane, and if I hadn't I wouldn't be here today to write memoirs, because the plane crashed on takeoff and killed everybody on board. Some years later, Adams, because he was afraid for his job, blocked a deal we had recommended to Coulter, by which United would have bought out Western at a handsome profit for our client, and I haven't done business with him since.

Over the years, I had many involvements with airlines. We became one of American Airlines' bankers in the 1950s at the suggestion of Mellon Bank. Later in that decade, we became one of the bankers to Swissair, on which there hangs an illustrative tale. My customer in the story was Ernst Schmidheiny, who ran Holderbank, which in addition to its other interests owned about a third of the world's cement business. We had financed a cement plant near Detroit for them, and had other business with them. He knew I was interested in Swissair, which was the only airline in Europe that never had a government subsidy, never lost money, and paid a dividend every year. This is probably still true. Schmidheiny was the non-executive chairman of the airline, and he arranged that on a flight from Zurich to New York I should sit beside the president of the airline to make his acquaintance. He called me the next day. He'd been to Chase, who were his lead bankers in the United States. Swissair was buying more planes, and needed a substantial loan. His usual contact at Chase was out of the bank, and the less senior man who saw him said, "We can't lend you that much ourselves, but we'll take part and make arrangements for the rest." Proud guys like Swissair don't like the idea of someone else hawking their credit around the banking community, and they told Chase they would prefer to arrange the balance themselves. The president called me, and I immediately took the rest of their loan, and became one of their bankers.

We were also bankers for SAS, the Scandinavian Airways System. On one occasion they had asked Morgan, Stanley, the investment bankers, to arrange a financing for them. Morgan, Stanley had gone to Metropolitan Life, which turned them down. SAS was a foreign company, and Met Life couldn't have more than 3 percent of its assets in loans to foreign entities. Moreover, SAS had an ultra-conservative accounting system which depreciated the line's airplanes more rapidly than the ten or twelve years that was the U.S. industry standard, which meant the line's reported net worth and earnings looked comparatively low. Marcus Wallenberg, the most important Swedish banker, was the chairman of SAS, and National City's dealings with him went way back—he had, in fact, been sent by his father to the United States to be trained in banking, and had been part of the 1916 City Bank training class that produced Howard Sheperd and Arthur Forward. We showed Wallenberg's people how to set up an American subsidiary that could borrow from Metropolitan Life outside its 3 percent limit on foreign credits, and how to restate their books to show a twelve-year depreciation schedule. We then took the shorter maturities of the loan, and Metropolitan Life took the rest of it.

I was always happy to see us lending to airlines, because I'd learned back in the 1930s, when we were first beginning to understand about cash flow, that thanks to its large depreciation allowances, an airline can continue to pay its debts for some time even though its P&L may show it losing money. When I was president of the bank in the 1960s, we expanded our airlines financing on a leasing basis, to take advantage of investment tax credits, improve our net yields on the loans, and further strengthen their quality.

Our closest relations in the aviation business, however, were with the complex of companies joined together as United Aircraft—Boeing,

Chance Vought (later LTV), United Airlines, and Pratt & Whitney. The package had been put together originally by Frederick Rentschler, the brother of Gordon Rentschler, who was president of City Bank under both Mitchell and Perkins, and the deal had been taken public originally by National City Company. The offering price had been something like twenty-seven dollars, and the stock had risen immediately; everyone made money. While I was still working as Perkins's assistant, Rentschler sent me up to Hartford to meet his brother and look at United as an important customer. Then the government decided that manufacturers and airlines should not have a common ownership, and United Aircraft, like GM's North American Aviation, had to be broken up. Years later, my friend Harry Gray would re-conglomerate the company under the name United Technologies, which came to include, in addition to United Aircraft and Pratt & Whitney and Sikorsky Helicopter, Carrier Air Conditioning, Otis Elevator, Norden (the bomb-sight makers), Essex Automotive, and a good deal else.

One of the separated subsidiaries, United Airlines, had its headquarters in Chicago, which meant that during my years as a vice-president in the domestic division it was part of my territory. I couldn't serve on its board because the Clayton Act forbade bankers from lending to common carriers if they were on the board (I did serve on the United Aircraft board), but because of the history they were always sort of a favorite among my customers. There's some advantage in *not* being on the board, anyway, when you're lending to people in a dicey business, because if you are on the board you can't be the same sort of Dutch uncle. I once put my neck out for United Airlines. It was in the late 1940s, and they had a periodic cash squeeze, which happens more or less regularly in the airline industry. They had an issue of preferred stock, and they were concerned if they paid the dividend they might be short of cash for other things. By New York State law, if a company passed its preferred dividend its securities would be disqualified for some years to come as an investment for that state's insurance companies. We had confidence in the company. I urged them to make the payment, and said we would take care of any resulting cash-flow problem. They did, and we did, and soon the load factor improved and their cash worries were over . . . for a while.

2

The year 1938 was a watershed year for me. I was married, to Beatriz Braniff y Bermejillo, a Spanish-Mexican descendant of the Irish engineer Thomas Braniff who built the railroad from Vera Cruz to Mexico City. We built a house in New Canaan, where our son George, born in 1939, now lives with his wife and children. And 1938 was also the year Perkins put me on the road as a lending officer, which was not an ideal arrangement for a newly married man, but it was what banking was about in the nation's money center.

"District work," it was called. National City was a national lender, with corporate borrowers throughout the United States, simply because it was one of only a handful of banks, mostly in New York, large enough to handle the credit needs of the nation's biggest corporations. There were few very large regional banks in those days, and even the Chicago banks had lending limits too small to meet the total needs of Chicago-based companies like Sears, International Harvester, Swift, Illinois Central, and Greyhound. And only the New York banks had qualified foreign departments that could help American companies in export-import business, which the Roosevelt administration was especially eager to promote. (Expanding trade through tariff reductions and reciprocal "most favored nation" arrangements was almost a religion with Secretary of State Cordell Hull; he, and sometimes Roosevelt, too, saw it as an essential remedy for the Depression.) By law, of course, all our actual branch banks or owned subsidiaries in the United States had to be in New York City, but we didn't believe in regional or local offices, anyway. One of the most important things the New York banks had to offer was the New York perspective. When I was in charge of the domestic division, I tried to meet every Friday with the men who would be going out of town on calls the next week, so that they could say to the treasurers and chief financial officers and presidents of their accounts that "I was talking the other day with George, and he thinks interest rates will be coming down" or "he thinks credit conditions are deteriorating," or what have you.

Calling officers are successful if the executives upon whom they call regard their visits as a plus for themselves and their companies. It's not likely that a junior officer stationed in a place remote from the bank will be able to offer anything much more than a better price for money. But you make money in banking through steady, long-term relationships, not through one-shot deals. The first job of the calling officer was to keep established relationships shipshape, amicable, and profitable to both sides; and for that you need training.

The man responsible for my training at the beginning was one of Arthur Forward's oldest and most solid assistants, Robert Forgan, who was responsible for the middle-western district, home of some of our biggest credits, the meat packers and the millers, the agricultural machinery-makers, railroads, utilities, electrical equipment-makers, and others. Forgan came from a great golfing family that had become a great banking family, too. His uncle, James B. Forgan, had been president of the First National Bank of Minneapolis and then the First National Bank of Chicago (and Robert's cousin, James's son, would also, some years later, be president of the First National Bank of Chicago). The family name survived on Wall Street into the 1970s in the firm of Glore, Forgan & Company.

Robert's ancestors had founded the golf shop at St. Andrew's in Scotland, which Robert's brother Donald was running at the time when I came to know the Forgans. What many people considered the best golf clubs in the world had been made by the Forgans, and I was amused when I saw that the signature on them—"Robert Forgan"—was absolutely identical to my Robert Forgan's signature. Donald came to the United States for some golf-club manufacturers' competition that year when I was working with his brother, bringing with him a set of clubs made by the St. Andrew's pro Tommy Armour. They won the prize in the competition. I have a recollection, which could be wrong, that these were the first clubs ever made with a wide flange across the bottom of the irons to add weight and distance. Donald gave them to Robert and Robert sold them to me for fifty dollars (Scotsmen, he said, don't need two sets of golf sticks), and I have them still. In fact, I still use the two chippers—"stroke savers," Armour called them. Tony Jacklin, the British golfer who once won the U.S. Open and is now associated with my club in Spain, has offered to buy the set from me, as museum pieces, but I won't sell.

Forgan understood that I was to take his place in the district. He was a considerably older man, only a few years short of retirement. He received me with perfect grace, took me to the midwest with him, introduced me to our customers and our correspondent bankers there, and in general did everything he could to ease the difficulties of breaking in to an unfamiliar job. I was embarrassed then, and I'm sorry in retrospect, that he was never given a vice-presidency. I was, only a little more than a year after I began working with Forgan, who then became, in effect, my assistant.

In the Citibank system, individual lending officers have a great deal of authority. Loans are made on the approval of three lending officers. The maximum amount an officer can approve is a function of his position in the bank. As a vice-president, I could lend five hundred thousand dollars with the concurrence of two other lending officers, neither of whom had to be senior to me. About a year after I got that title I was given a "senior initial," which meant that with the concurrence of two other officers (who did not have to be "senior initials"), I could make or approve loans up to $1 million. With two senior initials on the application, we could lend the limit of the bank, which was one-tenth of capital and surplus. In those days, when banks were more heavily capitalized, that meant a little more than 1 percent of assets. All this was done in New York: nobody in an overseas branch had a senior initial until well into the 1960s, when the accolade was given to our manager in London, and it was not until the Bank Holding Company Act in 1970 that Citibank opened permanent "Loan Production Offices" with senior credit men in other cities in the United States.

My accounts were out-of-town companies, and much of my business was handled on my travels. But I spent most of my time at 55 Wall Street, "on the platform" in the middle of the huge banking floor in plain sight of the people who had come into the bank only to make deposits or cash checks. Few men had private offices in banking in those days; if you had a meeting with several people, you went to one of the conference rooms. I remember that when I started at the bank, there were two men who sat in the center of these platforms at opposite sides of the main floor—Mr. Simonson, who was senior vice-president in charge of domestic lending (and the only senior vice-president in the bank: he was the third-ranking executive), and Mr. Green, who had come to National City with the International Banking Corporation and was in charge of all our foreign business.

Mine was the middle-western district, which extended from the Indiana border to the Rockies. The others were New England, the Middle Atlantic states, the Indiana-Ohio-Michigan district, the South, the southwest (Texas, Arkansas, and Oklahoma) and the West Coast. Roughly, those west of the Mississippi (plus Illinois and Wisconsin) reported to Arthur Forward, and those east of the Mississippi reported to William Lambie, like Forward a senior v.-p. The third senior v.-p. was William Brady, who ran the Metropolitan division—our relations with Wall Street and the New York City-based borrowers, the largest part of the bank. Brady was about to become president when Perkins died and Rentschler became chairman. Each district had a row of desks: the vice-president and his assistants lined up behind him. As vice-president in charge of the middle-western district, I had five assistants, but one or two of them were always out of town making calls. Even without the weekly meeting of the vice-presidents, all of whom could fit easily into a single conference room in those days, we knew what was going on in the bank because it was going on around us. My "rivals" among the vice-presidents (but they were also friends: we weren't nearly as cut-throat as legend has it) were Carl Allen and Howard Laeri. Allen was a very able man who was handling our business in the industrial heartland of Ohio, Indiana, and Michigan. He left the bank a few years later to become president of Campbell Wyant Foundry Company, and when he returned to banking it was as president of the Federal Reserve Bank of Chicago. Laeri was the best lending officer in the New York City division.

It's no criticism of anyone to say that when I came into the district the work was not well organized. That was banking in those days, mostly a matter of personal contacts. Calling officers visited those contacts, establishing (if it was a new man on either side of the relationship) or renewing acquaintance, looking around to see how our business was doing, whether we should recommend a larger line of City Bank credit for this customer, or offer him some additional service at home or abroad, or perhaps scrutinize more carefully what he was doing with our money. Many of these, of course, were what came to be called "Fortune 500" companies, the nation's leading industrial enterprises. Many relationships had a long history. Cyrus McCormick of International Harvester, for example, had sat on the board of City Bank in the 1920s, while Mitchell was chairman. The customers we visited also came to visit us on Wall Street. We had hundreds of millions of dollars in deposits from these companies, and larger credit lines to them. Most were too big to have all their banking relations with one bank, even if hat was the largest in the country, and you knew other calling officers were competing against you wherever you went.

Virtually every company, of course, also had banking relations with local banks in its headquarters city and the cities where its factories were located. Looking around for new customers, which all calling officers did (mostly, in the days when I was starting out, pretty much at random and on their own initiative), you kept up with the local banks in the cities you visited. It was not wise for a calling officer to get on the bad side of a local banker. This was rather directly called to my attention on my first trip to Kansas City, when Jim Kemper, the president of the Commerce Trust Company, asked me to let him know in advance what calls I planned to make in his area. "If I find you've been

around here calling on my customers without telling me," he said con-
versationally, "I'll slit your little throat." It was hard to get business
from Colorado Grain and Elevator in Denver, for example, without the
approval of John Evans of First National Bank there: they had inter-
locking director relations.

Of course you had to be a little bit predatory in visiting places like
Kansas City and St. Louis and Milwaukee—you were making a living.
Sometimes there'd be a company you wanted to solicit, and your correspondent would say, "This is a local business. They don't need an
account in New York." Then I'd sort of walk around the room a little
and decide whether I wanted to make the call. Usually, if you kept a
piece of candy in your pocket for the local banker, he wouldn't resent
you too much. I'd go into Continental Illinois, ask how Armour was
doing, or Motorola, whether there was any business for us there, and
then I would mention that we were going to increase the Greyhound
line of credit, or make a new loan to United Airlines; would Continental like a piece of that? Besides, if they thought you were a smart guy,
they'd want to speak with you anyway. They wanted to know how City
Bank rated some of our mutual credits.

A lot of the work of the district was routine. We had the millers in
Minneapolis, for example. They needed to borrow more than the local
banks could supply within their lending limits. F. H. Peavey Company,
General Mills, Pillsbury, Cargill in Minneapolis, and Norris Grain in
Chicago—we'd give them a line of credit to buy wheat, and they'd pay
us back as they sold the grain or the flour. Those businesses were less
complicated than they are now, when many have "diversified" into
restaurants, cereals, and even toys! Another customer was the Uihlein
family in Milwaukee, which owned Schlitz Brewing, then the country's largest beer company. First Wisconsin was the Schlitz bank, and
they had Uihleins on the board: they influenced that business. There
were meat packers—Wilson, Swift, Armour, Cudahy in Chicago, Morrell and Rath in Iowa. Rath had only one plant, and he was the Tiffany
of the business (which doesn't last forever: in the 1980s, his company
went broke). Mr. Rath knew what he was getting when he sold his
products, and therefore what he could afford to pay for hogs. He usually made a better profit than the big packers, who sold through their
Chicago headquarters and branch offices while buying out in the field,
paying prices that were not as closely related to their sales. The big
packers did better when they decentralized, and made each plant a
profit center handling its own sales. You had to know who the people

were in these companies. The president at Morrell Company in Ottumwa, Iowa, came to work at 6:00 in the morning, and the best time to see him was 7:00. Swift in Chicago was very formal. The financial vice-president and his followers would march into the conference room like the line at the Folies Bergère. They'd tell you what they wanted you to do, and you'd cross yourself and do it.

International Harvester was very formal, too, and I used to hold them up as the example of good corporate-bank relations. They'd request a luncheon, and they'd come to New York with a presentation. Here's our situation, here's what we plan to do this year, here's what we plan to borrow, here's what we plan to do with it. The chairman of Harvester would come, and from the bank there'd be the president, Rentschler, and then Brady, Forward, and myself. Their credit was then tops.

Our railroads were the Harriman roads, Union Pacific and Illinois Central; First National Bank of New York and Morgan had the Hill railroads (Northern Pacific, Great Northern, and the Burlington, plus the Santa Fe), and we couldn't touch them. We had Greyhound Bus and United Airlines. The names come back—Crane Company was an important customer, and later the consumer electrical companies, Magnavox, Admiral, Motorola, Emerson, and Wagner Electric in St. Louis. During my era we obtained the first business we'd ever had from Monsanto in St. Louis, and from Borg-Warner. I remember the treasurer at Borg-Warner greeted me by saying that his company did its banking with Guaranty Trust, didn't need any more banks, he couldn't think of a reason in the world why his company should have an account at City Bank. Then he complained about some account in Brazil that was causing trouble, and nobody had any ideas about what to do, and I said, well, we have branches in Brazil, I think they might be able to help. A friend of mine in St. Louis who was a member of the Borg-Warner board called me up after the next meeting and said, "George, I believe you're going to get some business." We used our international connections often. People would tell us they were thinking of selling in Brazil, and we would say, "Give us a month and we'll line up the people for you to see, set it up for you to meet possible sales representatives, local agents, possible partners"—and then, of course, we'd be the banker.

Also in St. Louis there was American Stove, which made these big iron stoves—they kept the house warm and you did your cooking on top of them, all gone now, of course; the wholesale hardware distributors, Simmons, and Shapleigh, and the wholesale dry goods companies; department stores: May Company and Stix Baer & Fuller had headquarters in St. Louis. And the shoe companies—International Shoe, Brown Shoe. In Kansas City there was H. D. Lee Company—they made blue jeans with prison labor. Abbott Laboratories in Chicago. We had Boss Manufacturing in Illinois, who made work gloves. The farm equipment-makers, of course—International Harvester, Oliver Farm Equipment, Caterpillar Tractor, Le Tourneau. At Caterpillar you'd visit a beautiful research lab but you didn't see much coming out of it. Le Tourneau made the big earthscrapers. He didn't make the tractor itself, just made the attachments. He seemed to have more good ideas than the whole Caterpillar research department.

I recall one visit when I found Le Tourneau on his back in the dirt, watching the scraper. A scraper has very brief moments when it needs extra power. The usual procedure was to bring up a second tractor to push it as it dug into the dirt to get the load. Le Tourneau figured out a way to put an electric generator up front, an old Packard engine from World War II, with an electric motor on the axle of the scraper to give that last needed burst of power. I believe Le Tourneau was the first to do this, and it turned out to be an important idea with other applications. Some of his inventions were Rube Goldberg sorts of things, for example a huge machine he built for King Ranch, to remove mesquite, the rancher's curse. Often he didn't have the cadre of trained engineers who could work out the practical details, which meant that Caterpillar and Deere and Harvester would sometimes take his ideas and engineer them and get the business. Some bankers were scared to lend to Le Tourneau—he was an evangelist, had Holy Roller churches he endowed all over the world, you found them in places like New Zealand. One banker said he was afraid Le Tourneau would wake up some day and give his business to the Lord without paying the banks. But I found him a good customer. Eventually, Westinghouse bought the company.

Sometimes there was a product we could offer that made a difference. One of the best idea people who came to National City with the purchase of Bank of America in New York was Bill Creelman, who developed a system to collect checks quicker, the predecessor of the lock box and cash concentration schemes that have become commonplace bank services. Under Creelman's plan, a customer with multiple operations across the country sent the checks it received to a "concentration bank" we selected in each region, which could collect them quickly. The local banks would process only the checks drawn on themselves and the other banks in their town. The concentration banks kept correspondent accounts with us, and they authorized us to debit their accounts to give our customer immediate access to the collected funds accumulating in their banks. We would tell the customer every morning how much he had on deposit in banks across the country. He could draw against those accounts in various centers around the country, and could transfer the money wherever he needed it, to reduce loans, or pay for a purchase, or what not. This often eliminated as much as two weeks of float between the time the company took in the check in its local office and the time it had "good funds." We used the system with General Foods, and it got us in the door at A&P, which might have a float of $50 million a day, checks taken in at the store cash registers representing money the chain couldn't spend because the checks hadn't cleared. A&P had been a hard sell for us—old man Hartford sat on the Morgan Guaranty board—but this was an offer the company couldn't refuse.

This scheme also won back Standard of Indiana, one of the original Rockefeller oil companies, which had been the largest single depositor in City Bank in the early 1920s. Few people remember that City Bank was the original Rockefeller bank: Chase didn't have any important Standard Oil business until Winthrop Aldrich, who had married into the family, became chairman in the aftermath of the Depression. Mitchell lost the Standard of Indiana account by backing the wrong horse in a proxy fight in 1927. Colonel Robert W. Stewart, chairman of Standard of Indiana, had been implicated in the Teapot Dome scandal of the Harding administration. The Rockefellers then controlled only a small percent of the stock in the company, but they were closely identified with it in the public mind, and when the press took after Stewart the Rockefellers asked him to resign. He refused, and they mounted a challenge to him. Stewart sat on our board, and Mitchell took Stewart's side. When the Rockefellers won the proxy fight, they issued orders that Standard close its account with City Bank and do no more business with us. Rentschler was a friend of John D. Rockefeller, Jr., and in the 1930s managed to get this veto withdrawn. By then Standard had other banking relationships, and we had none of their money or their business—until Creelman's cash concentration arrangement brought them back to the fold.

3

The work of an officer in the out-of-town districts was one of great movement, to say the least. You were a migrant worker. In my earlier, most active years, air travel was still to some extent a stunt. We traveled any considerable distance by train. For a week's work calling on Chicago customers, one left New York Sunday afternoon, on the Twentieth Century Limited, and left Chicago Friday night to return home Saturday morning. Calling officers were on the road one week our of four, under a carefully planned travel schedule that provided coverage of both customers and new business prospects, leaving adequate staff in New York to receive the customers who came to the head office—and, of course, for the followups on the previous trips and the preparation for the next trip.

In a normal week in Chicago one could have fifty contacts, about ten a day, one for each breakfast, lunch, cocktails, and dinner, with three calls in the morning and three in the afternoon. The bank rented space in the Chicago office of Harriman Ripley Company, a New York brokerage firm to which many National City Company securities men had moved after the Glass-Steagall broke the banking business apart. We had a room, telephone, and secretarial service there. I usually stayed at the Chicago Club, the city's blue-ribbon business club and gathering place. If you were calling in the suburbs you would use a Chicago Club limousine to take you around. My competition and counterpart from Chase in those days was George Champion, a top banker who later became president of that bank. He followed the same routine. Once I had the driver who had driven Champion around the week before, and he told me exactly where Champion had gone and whom he'd seen, with some overheard information from conversations in the back of the limousine, and I made a note not to use that driver again, or to let a driver find out what I was doing.

Sometimes I would take a brief break from calls. I played tennis in Chicago with old Solomon Smith of Northern Trust, considered the most conservative bank in the city—its deposits actually rose in the early 1930s, when everybody else's declined. (It is said that Smith carried an umbrella rain or shine. The old ladies from Lake Forest saw Sol Smith going to the commuter train station carrying an umbrella on a sunny day, and they said, "*That's* a good safe bank!") Sometimes customers took me to their homes in the country, or invited me for a weekend, but in general I was on the go from the moment I got off the train until I got back on it. Often enough, the work started even before I arrived in Chicago, and continued after I left, because the "Century" was full of businessmen and bankers, many of whom I knew, and you could do business in the club car. It was there that I dined with Walter Paepke, then head of Container Corporation, a customer of ours, who was starting the Aspen Skiing Corporation, of which I became a founding stockholder. The company was a booming success from the start, and I would have made a small fortune on the stock when it was sold to Twentieth-Century Fox, except that I had already given it to the Metropolitan Opera when I was head of its special gifts drive. The Met, of course, sold it for a fraction of what it later commanded.

When the trip involved visits to places beyond Chicago, normally you took two weeks, up to Milwaukee and the Twin Cities, or to St. Louis and Kansas City, or out to Denver. People who traveled to Los Angeles, of course, always took two weeks on a trip. Longer than two weeks away was discouraged, because you lost touch with head office. Your information became stale, and you couldn't talk intelligently about what was going on in New York, which was, after all, your primary value to the people you went to see. Many trips involved renting a car and driving on not very good roads to visit customers in rural areas. On a trip to Wisconsin, you'd drive out to the countryside to see Kohler and Allis-Chalmers, Johnson's Wax, Kimberley-Clark and the other paper companies. One way or another, I was on the road at least one week out of every four. I can't deny it was hard on families; it was hard on mine. But the first claim I made for my time in the domestic division was that when I came, we were making one hundred man-weeks of calls a year in the out-of-town groups, and when I moved on to the overseas division, we were making a thousand man-weeks of calls a year. This involved a lot more men. But fifty thousand contacts produce ten times as much business as five thousand contacts. You could measure the results of our work by the volume of the bank's out-of-town deposits, which were growing at least $100 million a year by the later years.

Obviously, making calls was useful only if you called on the right people. If you visited a company and then decided you didn't want its business, you wasted everyone's time. And if you visited a company and proposed some business and then had home office turn down the loan application, you created embarrassments for yourself and the bank at the moment, and for your successors later. I made several calls where I was not well received because my host had been through such an experience. We developed the concept of the "approved names"—companies home office had decided it wished to do business with—to guide the calling officers. Some of that came from analyzing annual reports and from Moody's and Standard & Poor's manuals, but calling officers were supposed to make their own contribution. We tried to understand the "power structure" in every city, get to know the fifty or sixty businessmen who really ran the place. Usually, you could get this list just by reading the names of the directors of the local banks.

I wrote a memo for calling officers in 1952 that became a sort of bible in the bank (which is why I have it now: I never kept such papers myself, but Julian McCall, who'd been one of my best men in the southern district and later went on to National City of Cleveland and became chairman and CEO there, kept his copy and sent it to me a year or two ago). Rereading it, I was delighted to see how much of it still applies. On building the list, for example, I noted that

Callers should be alert to make notes regarding large plants *spotted* on trips and look them up on return to New York. Desirable names can also be obtained:

1. By checking lists of securities traded on local stock exchanges—look up any name you don't know;

2. By asking local friends from time to time as to who is "coming along" in their community;

3. By making industry checks—asking what is relative standing of companies in, say, soybean industry—and looking up any unknowns.

Then I added, "It is safest to await a check of our own credit files, etc. before commencing solicitation. This same applies to random acquaintances met on trips [my former assistant had underlined those words on his copy of the memo]. Find out who they work for—make a note—look them up." The "approved list" principle remained, and remains, important.

Whether you were calling on an existing customer, a correspondent bank, or a prospect, there was of course no substitute for preparation. I was insistent about that; I never made a call without mastering—not just skimming, but mastering—all the information the bank had about this business. I wanted appointments in advance, a firm knowledge of the business being visited and our current dealings with it, a prior estimate of what business could come from the encounter. When calling on banks, for example, it was important to know whether they sold our line of traveler's checks, and if they did, what their volume was. Calling on a corporation that did export business, the officer had to know whether it used National City Bank's international financing facilities, which we arranged to have conveniently catalogued in what we called a "foreign facilities book." "Look up the head of the Foreign Department . . . Where the importance of the Department justifies, the Department Head can be invited to New York to spend some time rotating in our departments . . .

"Don't ever," I wrote in the memo, "express the wish that there was 'something we could do' for a customer—it may remind him that he doesn't need the account . . . It is up to us to know why he needs it—what we do—what we have done in the past—in short, we should be well prepared for a new co. Treasurer if he should choose to ask us why he needs his NCB account." And the treasurer, I thought, was probably as high up as my calling officers should seek to go: let the treasurer call his CEO into the meeting himself if he wishes. Sometimes when I went over their plans with my people one of them would say, "I can't call on that company this week, their treasurer's out of town," and I would say, "That's your golden opportunity to meet their assistant treasurer." By being nice to him, you set the bank on the inside track for the time when this fellow becomes treasurer. It makes a hero out of him: when his boss comes back, he sort of drops the word that "I was talking with George Moore of City Bank the other day, and he said . . ." I still know some CEOs I met when they were assistant treasurers.

Every conscientious calling officer keeps picking up evidence of the importance of preparation. If you knew what the company was up to—and up against—you would often hear from the man you were visiting a comment about what a pleasure it was to deal with a banker who understood the company's problems. I was on the board of Northern Pacific, and attended the meetings in St. Paul. Before one meeting I dropped in to see the financial vice-president, and he grumbled about a pair of vice-presidents from Morgan Guaranty who had been in to see him that morning. "I can't figure out these New York banks," he said. "They sent these two fellows all the way out here, and when they came to my office they kept talking about the war and baseball, and I had to be nice to them because that's a big bank. While they were here, I had a call from your Mr. Vancil [who ran the railroad end of our transportation department], and *he* wanted to make some suggestions about the thing that's been on my mind, as you know—the $20 million bond maturity we have next year. Those other bankers didn't even know we had such a note."

Robert Patterson, when he was president of United Airlines, once joked that I was the only person in the country who read his message to his stockholders in the company's annual report. You flatter a man when you show that you've read his annual report and his quarterly statements. After all, your job is to find out what's on his mind. He'll tell you if you know what to ask, but only if you know what to ask. You can also damage a relationship by arriving uninformed. One year I took the man who ran our corporate trust department—did stock transfer work and the like for big companies—out on my rounds in Chicago. I'd sent him a packet of material on the companies we were to visit, but he'd been too busy to read it. We went to Fairbanks, Morse & Company, where the lobby was full of big scales and electrical machinery, and when we got to the offices of Sol Kiddoo, the financial v.-p., my friend from the corporate trust department opened the conversation by asking, "What is it you people make?"

On every call have a point (or points) to make—make them, and get out— but above all give the customer a chance to talk if he is willing—the more *he* talks, the more *he* enjoys your visit. But if he isn't in a talking mood be sure to make a graceful and prompt exit after the day's business has been covered. The NCB sweater will get you into many offices once—but not the second time if you unnecessarily wasted his time. But don't appear to be rushed— always take time to hear him out if he wants to be heard. It costs a lot of money to go to his office—finish the job.

Finally, there was the importance of followup—time-consuming, often wasteful, frequently neglected, and absolutely indispensable. "A follow up well handled is worth two conventional visits! When time is of the essence, don't wait; write or phone or telegraph New York and let the fellows at H.O. handle the follow up. Each District now has a 'follow up sheet' to facilitate, districtwise, knowledge of pending follow ups and also make it possible for supervisory officers to bear these in mind and be helpful where possible." Another part of followup was purely personal. I carried address books, in which I wrote not only the man's name and business address, but the home address and the names of all his family if I had a chance to meet them, and of course the name of his secretary. And I worked at remembering faces. "People we meet often remember us, if we make an impression—and if we don't recognize them next time we meet them we have wasted the contact—possibly offended a potential friend, who can only conclude that we, ourselves, weren't interested enough to remember them."

I always sought an opening that gave me an excuse to write the people with whom I made contact on calls. Once a year I'd make a speech at an American Bankers Association or Reserve City Bankers meeting, and I'd have it printed up and sent to all my customers and potential customers. If people were going to Europe, I'd send them a note about a tailor in London or a hotel in Athens. Or I'd send them answers to business questions that had come up inconclusively at our meeting. The idea was to find something to send him that he would be glad to get; he looks at it, and he says, "This is from that smart young fella who was in here last week." It's even better if you send it through his secretary, demonstrating that you remember her name, too. I've actually heard a secretary say to her boss, "That nice Mr. Moore would like to see you. Can you fit him in today?" My Christmas-card list still has about two thousand names on it, and some of them are secretaries. Of course if I accepted any hospitality when traveling I made sure to reciprocate when the contact passed through New York— take them to the opera, where I had a box.

You don't get quick results with such things, of course, but the bank doesn't need quick results—and if you come to think of it, neither do you. "It often takes years . . . to build yourself into a territory . . . Don't forget that each opportunity you have to do even the most incon-sequential thing for a customer or prospect is a golden opportunity to earn his goodwill—approbation—and possibly to affect his whole atti-tude toward NCB and particularly you."

The first step toward handling followups properly was writing the call memos. They had to be detailed, exact—and prompt. "My own experience is that the best way is to try and find time in the evening or early morning to write them out long hand—they are fresher, shorter and more telegraphic in form—and can be forwarded each night to Head Office so the information will be promptly available. Don't forget to send copies to all interested parties . . ." In the years when I ran domestic division, I tried to read as many call memos as possible. In the end, the volume defeated me, and I had to restrict myself to reports of calls that hit or looked likely to hit some kind of pay dirt. I began to encourage people to write trip summaries: "Carnation's got a loan coming up, here's what we're going to do about it." But you can't run a division properly unless you're reading the important call memos.

These principles apply to any business that sells. And I have yet to find a business that doesn't have to sell to survive.

4

Sometimes accounts fall into your lap. Not too long after I became a vice-president, I was called into Mr. Rentschler's office to meet a man named William G. Woolfolk, who was chairman of United Light & Power, one of the biggest public-utilities holding companies. A new law had ordered such companies to break themselves up, divest most of their operating subsidiaries and set them up as independent entities. (Good law, too, by the way—one part of the New Deal I have no quarrel with. These big public-utility holding companies were like dinosaurs; the head had no way of knowing what was going on down around the tail. It made no sense to have all decisions come to New York or Chicago.) Back in my early days with my little study group, we'd spent a week on United Light & Power, and it all came back to me. Woolfolk was having trouble with his bankers at Chase, who wanted to pick and choose among the companies United was going to spin off. "I want to bring you three kinds of loans," Woolfolk said. "One is the kind of loan anybody would make. Two is the kind of loan somebody would make. Three is the loan nobody will make unless he is making the first two. It's a package deal—if you want our business, you're going to have to take all three." Rentschler gave me a questioning look, and I said, "Yes, indeed, Mr. Rentschler; we'll take that. We want *all* of Mr. Woolfolk's business." We wound up the banker for at least twenty different utilities separated out from United.

About three years later, one of Woolfolk's men came to me with a company called American Natural Gas, which was going to build a pipeline to carry gas from Oklahoma through Missouri to Detroit. They didn't have their federal license yet, and of course they couldn't get a take-out from the insurance companies until after they had the license, but they needed to lay pipe as far as the Missouri River before the ground froze, or the project would take another year. The loan required was $30-$40 million. "This," Woolfolk said, "is one of those class-three loans." We made it, they got the license, the pipeline got the customers, Detroit had the gas, one year earlier. It is still a great company, and still a Citibank customer. When I retired, American Natural Gas chairman Ralph McElvenney and his board of directors came to New York for lunch, and presented me with an attractive silver tray, appropriately inscribed, on which I like to serve cocktails at my home in Spain.

Other pipeline business came our way from one of the most imaginative and successful investment bankers of my day, Francis Kernan, a senior partner of White, Weld & Company. He was a pioneer in the natural gas pipeline business, and he often worked with "Boots" Adams of Phillips Petroleum, another important City Bank customer. Together with a promoter named Ray Fish, they organized Pacific Northwest Natural Gas, to deliver gas from Four Corners, where Colorado, New Mexico, Arizona, and Utah meet, to Western Canada. I invited Bank of America to be partners with us, but their loan committee said Utah was "out of their trade area" and "we need that money in Sacramento." Mellon took the business immediately. That's when I decided that Bank of America wasn't really a big bank, just the biggest little bank in the country. Later, Kernan and Phillips put together the Trans-Canada Pipeline, and we were bankers for that, too, again with Mellon. Trans-Canada Pipeline actually has a clause in its corporate bylaws that Citibank will be the corporation's bank. I was their banker: if you're a man's banker, he comes to you with his problems and you solve them.

There's also business you get—no point in denying it—because you know the people socially. The club car from New Canaan to New York was a useful place for a banker to be in the late afternoon. In some places, there may be just one person you have to know. When I took Howard Sheperd to Texas in the 1940s to introduce him around as the chairman of City Bank, the person he absolutely *had* to see was Amon Carter, who was "Mr. Fort Worth" for many, many years. Carter didn't have a filing cabinet in his office. He had a huge desk, stacked with every letter he'd ever received. He'd say, "Want to show you the letter Roosevelt wrote me," or, "Here's a letter I received from the Queen of England," and he'd just reach into the middle of one of the stacks and pull it out, I could never figure out how. He never sat at that desk, just reached onto it. He gave every VIP visitor a ten-gallon hat. I still wear mine!

Social contacts can also—and this may be even more important—keep you from business you shouldn't want. There was a vice-president at City Bank in the 1930s named George Fraker, who never opened a file, couldn't quote a ratio, but he never took a loss. "Lambie," Perkins would say, referring to another senior officer at City Bank, "has a deserved reputation as a good banker. He shakes his finger at people and masters the numbers, but he often finds out about bad loans only after they've gone bad. Fraker's loans never go bad." Fraker would go to Newport and go cruising on somebody's boat, and while having a drink with someone from Chicago he'd say, "How's Marshall Field doing?" and the fellow from Chicago would say, "Well, they've been having that trouble in the fabrics division, took a big loss on overstocking blankets and towels." Then he'd run into somebody who had a contact with Cannon Mills, and he'd ask him about Marshall Field, too, and he'd hear, "They've been slow pay recently." And he'd come back to the bank and he'd say, "I think we'd better cut back on our lines to Marshall Field." By the time it's shown up in the numbers, Perkins would say, it's happened. I always wanted preparation and I wanted analysis, but when somebody analyzed a statement to death I'd sometimes say, "That's not the whole story . . ." The marketplace often knows what's happening before the numbers show it.

The biggest single block of business that came into the bank in my time in the domestic division arrived via the merger route, when National City Bank acquired First National Bank of New York. First National had been George Baker's bank, J. P. Morgan's sidekick in the days when the trusts were born. It really was the *first* national bank: it held the first charter ever awarded by the comptroller of the currency under the National Bank Act of 1863. First National hadn't exactly come on hard times, but during World War II and the immediate postwar boom, when everybody else was growing like a weed, First National had actually shrunk in size. Not only did it refuse to solicit new business, it was unwilling to accept deposits from just anyone. You had to have the right introductions to have an account at First National. But they did have many top customers, companies that had been on our wish list for years and with whom we'd never been able to develop an important relationship—U.S. Steel, American Can, National Biscuit, the Hill Railroads like Northern Pacific and Great Northern, a string of the companies old J. P. Morgan and George F. Baker had put together in the years before World War I. When I joined the U.S. Steel board, and was put on the audit committee, they mentioned to me there was one holdover tax item: still unresolved from the very early years of the century was the tax status of the fee to the J. P. Morgan group for forming the company—$50 million, in 1900's dollars. . . . The company had taken that as an expense, but the government insisted it was a capital cost.

The senior officers of City Bank, Brady and Lambie, Sheperd and Forward, rode uptown together in a limousine to Grand Central every afternoon. I and others were invited to join them from time to time. I was in the car when the First National merger was discussed. The sellers were insisting that we change our name to "First National City," which Sheperd was reluctant to do. He thought we would be losing our identity. I said, "I've been calling on their companies for years, we can't get them as customers; if all we have to do to get that business is change our name, hell, yes, let's do it." Actually, as it turned out, the name change was a good idea, because there were other National City Banks in the country, but no other First National City. The merger didn't give us much in deposits, and most of the senior officers departed—Alex Nagle, who had been chairman of First National, became vice-chairman of First National City, but he left in a couple of years, and none of our senior officers when I was president and chairman was a transplant in from First National—but we acquired relationships that would be important in our drive to become the biggest as well as the best bank in the world.

6

The Craft of Lending

Speaking from a perspective of sixty years in banking and
in business, I have to say that banking is the surest, safest, easiest
business I have seen or known. I've told people for years that it's a
simple business, perfect for a C student like Moore. If you're not actually
stupid or dishonest it's hard not to make money in banking. But it's
also true that nobody was born a banker, and even more true that you
can't become a banker by taking courses in business school. Lending
money and getting it back is not an art that takes genius, or a science
that takes penetrating study. It's a craft, which you learn by doing, like
playing the piano. I have long thought that Citicorp should have a
degree-granting institute (as General Motors and IBM do) to finish the
training of its younger officers. The reason for setting up such a school
inside the bank is that you can't teach banking effectively unless you
couple theory with practice.

A banker has to be both a salesman and an analyst. If you let the
credit men, the analysts, run the bank, you won't have any customers;
if you let the salesmen run the bank, you go bankrupt. When I was
hiring lending officers, I'd try to assign them where their temperament
wouldn't naturally take them. If a man was a natural salesman, I'd
send him to the credit analysis department, where he'd learn to add
and subtract and be careful. If he seemed to have talent as an analyst,
I'd put him out on the street, to get brushed off by secretaries and
receptionists. He comes back and he says, "I couldn't get in," and you
tell him, "Go back until you do get in." Eventually he learns. I used to

say that a good salesman was worth ten thousand a year, and a good analyst was worth ten thousand a year, but a man who was both a good salesman and a good analyst was worth a hundred thousand a year. If he can say No and sell, too, he's qualified to be a senior executive.

If you're going to run a man through that sort of course, however, he probably should be twenty-eight or less; certainly, if he's much over thirty, his habits will be too deep to change. And some people are hopeless. One day when I was executive vice-president in charge of the domestic division, my secretary said, "There's a young man from the credit department who insists on seeing you." I saw him, and he said he'd been an analyst in the credit department for three years, and he had time on his hands, he wanted to get into lending. I said, "Well, tell me how the bank's doing—our annual report came out the other day." He hadn't read it. I said, "What do you think of business conditions; do you think our economists got it right in that bulletin we put out yesterday?" He hadn't read that, either. I said, "Are you up on the changes in the banking laws? What's our limit on loans for real estate?" We drew a blank again—nobody, he said, had told him to do that reading. I said, "Nobody around here is going to have time to tell you what to do. Why don't you just leave the bank and find another job?"

To be a banker, you need a good head for numbers, and it helps to have a good memory, and you have to be prepared to work some long hours and get along with people some of whom you may not like very much. One of the first lessons Perkins taught me was, "You have to play the ball, not the man." I criticized my people, and I know some of them resented it on occasion, but it was always about something they had done, not about them personally, and they knew it. The fact is that we didn't lose the people we promoted throughout the years when I could be rough on those who worked for me. I can't think of a single guy who ever left me.

Many people think that successful bankers never make a bad loan, but the truth is that nobody ever made a living—or performed a service for his society—by betting on sure things. You have to have a little imagination, and you have to be willing to make mistakes once in a while. The important lesson of banking is that you don't make *big* bad loans or too many bad loans, you don't take a risk you can't afford to be wrong with. Any well-run bank must have losses, but they'll be kept within bounds. One of the training documents prepared under my direction was a brief report of the twenty or thirty biggest mistakes we had made—the bad loans, the Russian branches (see Chapter 7), our largest losses. The people who wrote up those reports usually made it clear that the fellow who'd made the loan or the mistake was a fool, and I would send them back to work on it again, telling them to find the original lending officer's reasons for thinking this would be a good loan, see what it looked like in the environment of the time, *before* anybody knew it was going sour. Ivar Kreuger, the Swedish match king, was the biggest name in Scandinavia and a world financial leader before his empire collapsed; most bankers who lent him money didn't think they were doing anything risky. (As it happened, City Bank had no major involvement with Kreuger, probably because of our close links to the Wallenbergs, who also didn't lend to Kreuger.) While I was president and chairman of Citibank, nobody could get a senior credit initial until he'd read that file. My friend Rainer Gut, who became the head of Credit Suisse a few years ago, told me that one of the things he'd done in his first months was to commission a history of the largest bad loans or credit mistakes his bank ever made, and require that his senior credit officers read that file. He was amused to learn I'd done the same thing.

The fact is that in banking, history does repeat itself. If the officers responsible for Mexico and Brazil and Argentina in the 1970s had known some of the past mistakes Citibank had made through taking excessive sovereign risks, such as the German "standstill agreement" of the 1930s, they wouldn't have made the loans they made. After I left the bank, my successors apparently stopped keeping that bad-debt history current, and stopped requiring that credit officers study it.

Knowing what loans to avoid does not necessarily mean a lending officer has to be hard on his customers. Part of the skill of being a man's partner is knowing how to discourage him. I've often claimed that I never just said No to anybody. If I didn't want to make a loan, after all, what it meant was that I thought the businessman who wanted it was going to get in trouble, make problems not only for the bank but also for himself and his business. He doesn't want that any more than we do. Sometimes I would be able to find a way that he could change his plans so the bank could help him, sometimes I could persuade him not to buy that company or expand that plant. The important thing is that you want him to feel that you've been constructive. He may have a better deal to offer you, some day.

One of our accounts came because I was able to help him restructure a deal that was hopeless when he walked in the door. This was

Kaiser Industries, built by Henry J. Kaiser, who had been a contractor before World War II: his had been one of the seven companies that built Hoover Dam. During the war he'd found a way to build the ships we needed on an assembly line, about ninety days each, and he'd started his Kaiser Aluminum Company and Kaiser Steel and Permanente Cement. When the war was over he'd put together his contracting, steel, aluminum, and cement businesses, and some other ventures, under a holding company he called Kaiser Industries, and he wanted $100 million for the expansion of the group. His bankers were Chase and Mellon, and George Woods of First Boston, one of the best investment bankers of my time (later, he would run the World Bank), was his securities adviser. Woods called, asked if I would see Henry's son Edgar Kaiser, who was president, and his executive vice-president, a very able fellow named Trefethen, who later left Kaiser and started a high-class vineyard in California.

The loan they wanted us to make was for ten years, with no repayment in the first three and a 25 percent "balloon" to be paid off at the end. Chase had accepted these terms, but only on Kaiser's agreement that the market value of the stocks in the underlying companies, which he was offering as security, would always be twice as great as the outstanding balance on the loan. That involved predicting stock market prices ten years out, and Kaiser and Woods didn't see how anyone could safely do that. The penalty for guessing the market wrong would be that Chase could declare the loan in default and force the sale of the shares.

That seemed unfair to me, too, though the fact is that we'd always considered Kaiser a little reckless and his companies a little green for our taste, and we'd never solicited his business. And I didn't like this deal for other reasons. I didn't think Kaiser had the right to ask the banks for a three-year delay before he started making repayments, which meant the banks were giving the holding company a sort of blank check to use its cash flow for other purposes. I said, I might be willing to finance that trip you're going to make to the moon, but I don't want to make the decision until you're ready to go. When you're ready to go, come back. If a man wants a long delay before he has to start repaying his loans, it means he has plans for that money he doesn't want to tell you about. I said City Bank would make the loan for seven years, with repayment in seven equal pieces (no balloon), without imposing any collateral valuation requirement. They accepted the proposal, and we became one of Kaiser's principal lenders, and of course they paid us off. They returned to us two or three times with new programs related to that original loan, and we revised it to suit their needs.

I must say that we never thought Kaiser Industries was a great idea. Some years later, I remember, my friend Jacob Javits called me from the Senate to consult about a bill he wanted to introduce to curb the conglomerates, keep them from gobbling up American industry. I told him not to worry, the marketplace would take care of that, and it did. (For the same reason, I think it's unwise of the Federal Reserve to write regulations slowing down the issuance of junk bonds to finance leveraged buy-outs. Some of those buy-outs are going to come unstuck, the junk bonds will go into default, and the merry-go-round will stop all by itself.) Conglomeration doesn't work very often, because the world changes, and management has to keep a business changing with it. It's hard enough to run just one company. It's impossible to run five of them. General Electric seems to be able to do it, perhaps because it's been dominated for so long by financial men whose expertise really is transferable across a number of areas.

Kaiser Industries had the remarkable distinction of never paying a dividend, ever. Instead, it finally liquidated and distributed the stock of the underlying companies. I remember once returning to New York from Bohemian Grove, a club in the California redwoods for Fortune 500 executives, and sitting on the plane with Jack Parker, a vice-chairman of General Electric, who had been there with me. We were traveling economy class. Up in the front cabin were Edgar Kaiser and six or seven Kaiser executives. He twitted us about our modest accommodations, and my friend from GE said cheerfully, "Those of us who pay dividends, Edgar, can't afford to ride first class." But the company paid its debts, and in fact rewarded some of the people who bought the stock, because the distributions added up to quite a lot more than the price of the holding company before the breakup.

Every once in a while you *can* say a plain No, because your reasons are simple and unanswerable. I remember an enterprising Canadian named Nate Cummings, who had a company then called Consolidated Grocers that grew and grew and grew, finally encompassing Sara Lee bakeries and Hanes hosiery and Samsonite luggage. It's now called Sara Lee, Inc. In the process, he bought many of our customers. One of the first of them was Reid Murdoch in Chicago, and after acquiring them he thought he ought to add us to his list of bankers. He came to City Bank for a line of credit. We looked over his situation and saw that he had some bonds outstanding, and that the bond indenture provided he would never have more than $20 million of bank loans outstanding. He already had lines of credit amounting to more than $20 million, but he was asking us for a $4 million commitment. I said to him, "What good can a line from City Bank do you? I'd be happy to be in your banking picture if you want us to replace some other bank, but you can't use more lines." He said, "You have a point." He came back a year later, when he'd paid off the bonds, we became an important bank for him, and he and I became good friends.

I had a nickname once at the bank (one that I knew about, that is). While I was in the domestic division, someone called me "Three-way-out Moore." I used to say that when I made a loan I wanted at least three ways the borrower could pay me back. One way was from the sources he described when he requested the loan—cash flow, the ordinary operations of the business through the period of the loan, selling the inventory the loan had financed, selling seats on the airplane, and so on. If something went wrong with these cash flows, the second way would be to cut back or eliminate expansion plans: for example, reduce capital expenditures, or stop paying dividends. The third and last was a sale of assets, branches, or subsidiaries or real estate or some piece of the main business. If all three of these roads were open, the loan was unlikely to result in a loss.

2

At my own bank and elsewhere, I was best known as a sponsor of what we called term loans, an advocate for and expert in lending for longer periods than banks had traditionally offered (or, more precisely, than banks had traditionally admitted they offered). Prior to these memoirs, the only writing I ever did for publication in a book was a chapter on "Term Loans and Interim Financing" in *Business Loans of American Commercial Banks,* a textbook edited by Professor Benjamin Hoggart Beckhart of Columbia University. My time as a banker was a period when such lending steadily increased, mostly in the teeth of opposition by theorists, government regulators, and the top management of the big banks. But there was a need for it, and the truth was that under one label or another banks had always made such loans, usually through arrangements that were classified as short-term loans but really provided for an implied roll-over or renewal at maturity. I once had a study done that proved that the apparent increase in term lending at National City was really an illusion—if you added in the fraction of our supposedly short-term loans that had been renewed beyond a year's term, the ratio of term loans to classic loans had been remarkably stable. My basic argument was that banks were more likely to get in trouble by concealing what they were doing (especially from themselves) than by adapting their procedures to serve their market in an open and aboveboard way.

During the 1920s, banks had been big investors in corporate bonds. This was not considered long-term lending either, because long-term lending was by definition illiquid while the bonds were supposed to be part of the bank's liquid assets, salable in the market if the bank needed cash. One of the things that's disturbing about today's "Euromarkets" is that you hear this sort of argument being made again in defense of "securitization," the substitution of bond and commercial-paper sales for bank borrowing by companies, and of supposedly marketable paper for loan contracts in the asset ledgers of the banks. The fact is, of course, that when your bank needs the cash all the other bondholders need cash, too, and the market price of the bonds goes down—if you can sell them at all. And bond issues, as we learned the hard way in the 1930s, are sudden death: they come due, and the debtor can't pay, and the holder finds himself in a bankruptcy process very quickly. When the banks buy bonds they don't do the sort of cash-flow analysis that's routine when they make loans, and the bond indentures rarely contain the restrictive clauses a bank includes in a term-loan agreement.

Investing in bonds certainly was not a good business for the banks when the 1920s became the 1930s: according to a study by the National Bureau of Economic Research, 28 percent of all the corporate bonds issued between 1925 and 1929 defaulted during the Great Depression. Those that survived into the mid-1930s were paying at interest rates much higher than market rates. AA-rated bonds dated 1928 and 1929, for example, carried an average rate of 4.82 percent, and from 1934 to 1947 the posted "prime" rate at the banks was 1.5 percent, with perhaps another twenty-five basis points (a quarter of a percentage point) for longer-term lending on the largest loans. Some of the corporate lending business we did in the later 1930s and early 1940s was to refund such bonds. Where the bond indentures permitted early redemption, companies found it profitable to borrow from the banks and pay off the bonds, and banks, by securing the pledge of the property or cash flow that had backed the bonds, could safely lend them the money. Meanwhile, medium-sized and smaller companies had been locked out of the bond market, more or less accidentally, by the Securities and Exchange Act, which made it illegal to sell unregistered securities, and expensive (as a fraction of the money raised) to register smaller issues.

The banks certainly had the money to lend: from 1935 to 1940, while the Fed was "pushing on the string" of loose money, banks averaged excess reserves of $3.25 billion (up to nearly $7 billion in 1940). It's worth pausing here for a minute to note what a different time that was: the Fed had in effect printed money and given it to the banks to lend or invest, and the banks saw so few loans they wanted to make and so little paper they were willing to buy that they just let it lie there. In those days, the return on Treasury bills was so low, and the cost of trading them was so high, the banks thought themselves better off with idle money than they would be with government securities. We're not likely ever to see those days again, not because there won't be a time when bankers think the interest rates don't cover the risks of lending (though I hope I never see that), but because the cost of buying and selling Treasury paper has become infinitesimally small in an age of computers and computerized communications, when you never even have to send a messenger to pick up and deliver the paper.

Meanwhile, the Banking Act of 1935 had changed the rules of the Federal Reserve to permit the district banks to take any asset they deemed suitable as collateral for loans to member banks at the "discount window." As a practical matter this made term loans more liquid: before 1935 the Federal Reserve banks would "rediscount" only "eligible paper," that is, the most conventional short-term loans, and a bank might have been forced to sell bonds at a loss if it needed cash for a while and had nothing in its vaults but a portfolio of term loans. Now you could borrow against term paper as easily as you could against standard ninety-day loans. And the arrival of deposit insurance had taken some of the bite out of the old warning against "borrowing short and lending long," because there was much less danger of a run on the bank requiring the rapid liquidation of assets. In response to these changes, the comptroller of the currency had eliminated from the lexicon of the National Bank Examiners the old classification of "slow" loans, which had applied automatically to paper that had more than a year to run before repayment. Instead, all loans, of whatever duration, were to be judged by the examiners according to the likelihood of repayment. And the rates on term loans (usually defined as loans contracted to run a year or longer) were of course higher than the rates on the traditional sixty-day and ninety-day commercial loan.

To the extent that we had the numbers, I wrote in my contribution to Beckhart's book, the results seemed to be an expansion of the proportion of admitted term loans from less than 5 percent of the banks' portfolios in 1935 to 11.5 percent in 1940, with even greater growth at the big-city "money center" banks. At the ninety-nine large banks reporting to the National Bureau of Economic Research in 1941, almost a quarter of all loans were terms loans. Big borrowers accounted for two-thirds of this lending, but it was by no means restricted to them. From 1935 on, National City Bank ran a special small-business loan service that offered term loans to the city's lesser entrepreneurs and professionals, and it was a great success. The maximum amount for such a loan was twenty-five thousand dollars, and the maximum term was five years. Over the twenty-one-year period 1935 to 1956, the bank made eighty-three thousand such loans with a total value of $136 million—and took losses that ran less than one-half of 1 percent of that total.

Most bankers were uncomfortable with "cash-flow lending." Old-fashioned credit officers had been brought up with the idea that the proper customer was the one who at least once a year paid off all his debts and was "out of the bank" for a while. They had been taught that when a customer periodically paid off all his borrowings, it demonstrated that he was running his affairs prudently. But if you didn't look at his cash flow, you didn't have any way to know whether he was running his affairs prudently or not—you found out that he wasn't when it turned out he couldn't repay on schedule. And if his cash flow was adequate to service his borrowings, with a good margin of safety, it didn't matter very much to the safety and soundness of the bank that the loan ran longer than one year.

Some bankers were writing ninety-day notes to build a plant or buy an airplane, and arguing that these notes were sound banking because you looked at the paper again every ninety days. But when we made our first term loan, some people at the bank raised their eyebrows. It was to Allied Mills, a company second only to Ralston Purina as a purveyor of animal feeds to build a processing mill. (Allied later became part of Continental Grain as the result of a suggestion I made to Michel Fribourg, who, all by himself, owned Continental Grain.) I felt we had learned from Roger Steffan and his personal loan department, not to mention the FHA mortgages, how to handle self-amortizing loans. We took the first five years, and Bankers Life of Des Moines, which knew the company well, took the longer maturities on the loan, and it was safe as houses—but that didn't matter to some of the old-timers. I was equally happy with the sort of "evergreen" credit we gave to Dow Chemical, a ten-year loan that was automatically renewed in full every year unless the bank gave notice. I could see a dozen ways for Dow to repay us if something went sour. I thought bankers should pay more attention to reality than to theory.

I'm not saying you don't have to be more careful with term lending. You do, for obvious reasons. Predicting what's going to happen to an industry over the course of the next twelve months is hard enough, let alone predicting what will happen to a single company in that industry over a period of five, seven, ten years. You definitely don't want to tie yourself into a declining industry or a declining company. You want assurances of stability, which means that you have to know the history of the company (one rule of thumb is to make sure you have a record of success over a period that goes back at least as far as you're looking forward in the length of the loan). You seldom have pledged assets behind your loan, but you want covenants assuring that the assets you consider vital to the repayment of the loan can't be pledged to anyone else. Remember, a company doesn't always have to be profitable to have the cash flow to pay its debts: the sale of seats on an airliner generates cash flow to pay the lender who financed the purchase of the plane even if the airline, after accounting for the depreciation, is losing money on every flight.

Obviously, you want to see a cash flow with margins sufficient to make the payments on your loan, and the longer the loan, the greater the margin of safety should be. And you want to make arrangements for periodic repayment out of that cash flow, rather than risking the bursting of a big "balloon" at the end. If there's still a big payment to be made at the end of the loan, and you don't have another lender ready in the wings to take you out at that point, it's a demonstration that you made a bigger loan than the cash flow justified; we used to call it "burying the baby." Where the deal is one that involves a commitment fee for a line of credit that may not be used for years (or at all), you have to steel yourself not to think about how profitable it is to collect commitment fees without actually lending out your money, because the day this customer calls on his line of credit may be the day you might not wish to lend him money.

You also, of course, have to keep contact with the borrower. As I wrote in the Beckhart book, "The term lender must live with the term borrower for the entire life of the loan if a successful and mutually agreeable result is to be expected from the lender-borrower relationship. There are few term loans which do not need readjustment during their life." It's organizationally tricky to keep up, because you don't want a loan to be something that's between a company and one guy at the bank, you want to make sure you institutionalize it, send different people to maintain the contacts. But if you think about it a little, keeping up with the borrower is what "relationship" means in banking, and accounts are profitable to a bank not because the spread is a few basis points higher, but because the company does a lot of its business with the bank. If you bind the bank to the borrower more tightly with the term loan, you also bind the borrower more tightly to the bank.

Yes, you have to be tough sometimes. Donald Douglas came to me for help when Douglas Aircraft's cash-flow projections showed a serious shortfall. We had been his bankers for years, and I'd helped him get the contracts that justified the development of the DC-9— we'd held a dinner for three airlines and the insurance companies that would have to help with the financing, and out of that dinner had come enough orders to permit the startup of the project. But he hadn't kept us current on his new problems, and I had to say, "Don, it's close to midnight, and you need more help than a bank can give you. We will help you get the best deal possible." I sent him to Lazard Frères, and they negotiated the necessary merger with McDonnell Aircraft.

Probably the most important discipline enforced by term lending, however, is the need to acquire industry expertise within the bank. Obviously, you can't form an opinion worth having about the longer-range prospects of a company unless you understand where the industry is going, and no one man can master the prospects of twenty industries. When I first went into district work in Chicago, I found that the First National Bank of Chicago divided its lending staff into industry groups, and it was clear to me that their lending officers knew more about the businesses to which they were lending than we did. They paid some price for it: a geographical organization meant that you kept in touch with correspondent and other local banks, and scratched backs with them, while lending by industry groups tempted loan officers to overreach and create what might be dangerous hostilities, losing correspondent relations the industry specialists didn't know or care about.

Even before I became head of the division, I began giving the people in my district assignments to specialize by industry as well as by geography. I'd say, "In addition to Chicago, you're our meat-packing expert." Or, "You've got Minneapolis, we want you to know all about grain." I sent a man every year to the American Petroleum Institute convention, the truckers' convention. You often learn at these conventions who the sleepers are, who the bank might be missing in its calls, who has problems. I remember somebody at the bank said, "We've never liked trucking, George," and I said, "That's cash flow again—depreciation. They can pay off on those trucks even if they're not making money, you know."

More because Chase had built industry divisions for utilities and oil than because of anything I was saying, Brady and Forward allowed us to start hiring specialists. We called the group Special Industries, and we started with oil, utilities, and transportation companies. Robert Hoguet, who had been handling my old district in and around Chicago, became the first head of the new group, and knew just what was wanted. The obvious first necessity was someone in oil and gas to compete with Chase and with First Chicago's brilliant Hugo Anderson (whose son Bob retired in 1986 as CEO of ARCO: I remember Hugo saying to me back in the 1940s, "You know, I've got a bright boy; he just made a million dollars in the oil business"). Energy was a big category, most energy loans were term loans, and to have any judgment about the borrowers, you just had to know the business. Leonard (always "Mc") McCollom at Continental Oil (later Conoco), who was a director at J. P. Morgan, laid it out for me: "Citibank is just a balance sheet lender to the oil industry, George," he said. "Nobody at Citibank seems to understand cash flow from oil wells or know how to lend to a man who's got oil in the ground and wants drilling loans to get it out. Those people go to an 'oil bank.' J. P. Morgan's not big enough to be an oil bank, but you are, and you should gear up for it."

We hired a man named Earl Noble, a driller, but he wasn't a banker and he wasn't happy; he left on his own motion, in 1951. McCollom then recommended a man named Ed Warren, an independent oil producer in Midland, Texas, who was also a driller but made a first-class banker. He headed the oil department for the better part of a decade, until the City Bank men we had fed into it were ready to take over. Then he became head of Cities Service and, eventually, a director of Citibank. William Spencer, who had come to us from Chemical Bank as a lending officer and gone through Warren's training, moved into Warren's chair and later succeeded Wriston as president of the bank when Walt succeeded me as chairman. The Special Industries Group was not officially formed until 1954, after I succeeded Rockefeller in charge of the domestic division, at which time 550 accounts were transferred from the supervision of the geographical divisions into the group. Among those who first made their reputations as bankers in the group was Walter Wriston, who was second-in-command of the transportation district, but had to run it because the commander-in-chief couldn't. A number of accounts that ought to have been in Special Industries remained fiefs of the branches, however, until I became chairman and Walt became president, and a study by Cresap, McCormick & Paget urged that all larger loans be supervised on the basis of specialized expertise. We were glad to follow through on the recommendation.

The creation of the Special Industries group pretty much ended the argument over term lending. Once you had the expertise in place, all the old objections fell of their own weight. Then it became the responsibility of the fellow who ran the group to see to it that the expertise was real.

3

From the beginning, I was impressed with Roger Steffan and his consumer loans, and his theories. He used to say, "The clerk is a better risk than the boss, and the boss is a better risk than the company he works for." If the clerk gets fired, he gets another job, and his cash flow isn't interrupted; if the boss gets fired, it takes him longer to find new employment, though usually he will; if the company goes broke, there's a chance nobody will want to pick it up.

Steffan kept reducing the length of the questionnaire by which we qualified borrowers; when Chase had thirty-two questions people had to answer, we had ten, and Steffan said that was often too many. If a fellow had borrowed from us before and paid it back, and held the job he'd held before, we made the loan 99 percent of the time, whatever the answers were to the other questions. We did keep a "negative file" of people who hadn't paid or had been sued by a creditor, and we took the precaution of mailing our check rather than handing it to the borrower, just to make sure he'd given us a valid address. We had special arrangements with New York Telephone, New York Life, Consolidated Edison, and some of the other large employers that we wouldn't ask any of their people to get co-signers for their loans (which the companies didn't want, because employees sometimes asked customers to co-sign), in return for their providing us with close and accurate information about loan applicants from their records. I'm not sure companies would do that today. Back in the 1930s, long before there were computers, Steffan had his standard questions written out on a punch card, so the clerk interviewing the applicant could simply punch some holes to record the information the bank needed. Then he could do statistical analysis of which questions predicted whether we made the loan. He did the kind of study people now do with computers before anyone had thought of computers.

Probably because I began lending in the 1930s, I always had a special interest in factoring, the kind of lending where the bank takes over fiscal control of the borrower's business. Generally speaking, a factor has to approve everything that affects the business's cash flow— he owns the machinery used in the production process, approves purchases and owns the inventory waiting to be sold, checks the taxes, okays the credit references of the customers, and collects directly, deducting the factor's share of payments on receivables before the borrower sees the cash. Usually, if it's a big enough loan, the factor has a man permanently on the spot and stays closer to the business than lending officers from a bank can possibly do. In the 1930s, there were many companies that didn't have any security to offer other than their receivables. This was a business banks could legally do, under the most restrictive interpretations of Glass-Steagall, but we didn't do it because we didn't know how.

Of course, factoring had a low reputation, because charges were necessarily high and losses were frequent. The usual belief was that customers who didn't have to borrow from a factor wouldn't, that all the good customers went to the banks. After we bought Hubshman Factors I found out that—as I'd suspected—factors had high-quality customers, too. Hubshman had had one customer for years, a manufacturer of neckties who made a million dollars a year on a million dollars of capital. Hubshman kept his books, collected his bills, owned his sewing machines and his inventory and his accounts receivable, made up his tax returns at the end of the year. If he'd had a conventional business operation, borrowing from us like a respectable fellow instead of dealing with factors, he'd have needed $5 million in capital.

The closest credit arrangement to factoring at City Bank was an innovative scheme Forward and I worked out with Sears, Roebuck in 1940. This was an arrangement whereby we bought their receivables with a 10 percent reserve but no recourse. The customer's installment credit agreement said he was borrowing from National City Bank of New York, but his bill came from Sears, and he paid Sears. Once a month we had a settlement statement. Sears paid us interest at prime rate—during the war, about 3 percent—on the money we had advanced over the month. If the total outstandings from customers went up month to month, we added 90 percent of that increase to what they were borrowing from us; if the total went down, they paid us back 90 percent of the reduced amount.

This was the opposite of term lending: our agreement permitted either side to cancel the contract on thirty days' notice, and because people were always paying off their accounts, cancellation would mean that the loans would run down very rapidly. It was an interesting contract. We had to have legal title to the paper, and our loans had to be to the Sears customers—more than three million of them at one point. If the loans had been drawn to make Sears itself the borrower, the totals would have taken us beyond our legal lending limits. In fact, these Sears credit accounts quickly got to be more money than we wanted to lend in this way, so as a policy matter, we put a $100 million ceiling on the outstandings. Sears began to buy the paper back from us and sell it to banks in the cities where it was generated, so that the Philadelphia stores got credits from Philadelphia banks, Detroit stores from Detroit banks, and so forth. Finally they founded their own credit company, which worked on the same principle—the stores sold the paper to the Sears credit company. At first, they funded the credit company with loans from banks, but later they became independent borrowers in the commercial-paper market, where, in fact, they competed with the banks.

The Sears experience gave us a demonstration of how honest people are. They had a fire in their Detroit offices, which destroyed all their credit records. For some months thereafter, when people came in to buy shirts on their credit cards, the sales clerk would hand them a form and say the company was verifying its records. Would they take the form home, check their own records on how much they owed Sears, and mail it in? Customers reconstructed the Sears credit file for the company. In less than a half a year, the stores had good records again, and people paid.

In the course of establishing and monitoring this arrangement, I came to know General Robert Wood, a World War I hero who ran Sears with an iron hand. (Those early years, he also ran America First, the isolationist group that fought every American effort to help the British and French in their war against Hitler, but here he had a partner, Robert Hutchins, president of the University of Chicago and later founder of the Center for the Study of Democratic Institutions in Santa

Barbara.) Every year we had a dinner at the Chicago Club for executives of our best accounts in the district. We always started it with cocktails at 5:30, with a promise that the evening would end at nine, after a dinner speaker who dealt with serious subjects—trends in the money market, foreign-exchange fluctuations, or something of the sort. We had a good attendance because people could come right from work and get home at a decent hour, and I made sure we had interesting speakers. Wood did me the honor of attending these dinners, a special honor since if there was one breed of mankind he was forever denouncing, it was "New York bankers." He used to say I wasn't really a New York banker, I was from Hannibal, Missouri.

When the war came, General Wood went back to service, but he didn't forget Sears. Shortly before the war, Sears had come to us with a request for help in analyzing their prospects if they tried to expand the business into Latin America. They wanted information on retailing in Argentina, Brazil, Chile, Mexico, Venezuela, Peru, and Colombia. We did a study for them—how many houses in each country, how many cars, number of telephones, how many retail stores of what kinds, how much purchasing power. It cost us several hundred thousand dollars, and it made a book about the thickness of the Manhattan telephone directory. We finished it about the time the war broke out. Wood took it with him to Chungking and read it, he told me, cover to cover— nothing else to read in Chungking. On the basis of that study, Sears decided to open stores in most of Latin America (I remember Wood saying, "Not Argentina, George—they have Harrod's there").

We financed Sears's Mexican consumer receivables as we did their American credit accounts, but now there was a currency problem. The accounts were payable in pesos, and they wanted us to advance dollars. Sears took the translation risk—that is, if the pesos bought fewer dollars, they would bear the loss. In those days soon after the war, the interest rate on pesos was 8 percent, and we were advancing dollars to Sears on our prime rate of 3 percent. We told Sears they should hedge the exchange-rate risks, take the difference between the American and Mexican interest rates on the money we were lending them and put it into a reserve account for the day when the peso devalued, but they said Sears couldn't afford that, the profit margins in retailing didn't permit it. A couple of years later, the peso was devalued, as I recall it, from 4.5 to 8 to the dollar. We ran the thing through the calculators that morning, and were ready when the Sears treasurer called. He asked how much it was going to cost them, and I said, "About four million dollars." He said, "General Wood will be *furious*."

I said I couldn't help him now, but I could suggest again that the only prudent way to handle this situation was to hedge from the start. "Tell General Wood," I said, "that if he'd put aside that reserve we suggested originally, Sears would be even. What's happened is that you've overstated your profits and paid taxes on them, and you've paid people bonuses in Mexico that they didn't earn, because you ignored a loss that was building up and that you were always going to have to take." When there's a difference of five percentage points in the interest rates in two countries that trade with each other, that means the market expects a change in the relative value of the currencies. It's not an accident that the $4 million Sears lost in the devaluation was equal to the reserve they'd have put up if they'd assumed they were paying Mexican instead of American interest rates on their peso accounts. That's what arbitrage is all about. Sears lost money on exchange fluctuations in many places because General Wood never hedged currency risks. They were new in this business—more experienced customers like GE and International Harvester *always* hedged foreign-exchange exposure. But Wood was a Missouri boy, like me, and we're stubborn. Eventually, Sears did learn to hedge.

4

Life was sweet for the Moores in those years. We had our home in New Canaan and an apartment at 550 Park Avenue. Young George was at St. Bernard's School. I'd come in from Connecticut with him on Monday morning during the school year, pick him up at school Friday afternoon, and join the club car of the train to New Canaan at the 125th Street station. A lot of the business of New Canaan got done on that club car. I was president of the country club, and we'd have board meetings on the car. Most of the fifty people who ran the town took the same train. That club car was a good place to learn about business conditions, too, and even to make deals. Once not long after the war, John Emery, who had run Military Air Transport Service in the war, and who lived in New Canaan, put together the financing of Emery Air Freight in the club car.

I made steady progress at my bank and in my profession through the years right after the war. Thanks to the years of traveling, I was well known to other bankers around the country, and I was asked to make presentations to important meetings of industry groups, the Reserve City Bankers Association, the American Bankers Association, the Robert Morris Associates (the league of lending officers), and so on. These were pleasant occasions, at places like Greenbriar and Boca Raton and the Phoenix Biltmore, giving me a chance to improve my golf game (not much) as well as make contacts with colleagues. I became chairman of the credit policy committee and the like in all these organizations, which was of course the reason I was one of the four bankers on the Fed's Voluntary Credit Restraint committee. Meanwhile, in 1948–49, as noted, I chaired the survey committee for top management at National City, which was not a public activity but certified inside and outside the bank that I was on a fast track.

Systems inside the bank were beginning to change. Basically, we retained our "senior initial" plan for approving larger loans, but controls were beginning to tighten. Every Monday at 4:00 in the afternoon, the more important lending officers met with Sheperd and Brady, president and chairman, to review loans of five hundred thousand dollars or more made the previous week, in and out of New York, through the branches and the lending officers of both the domestic and overseas divisions. We had been given the folders, a sheet of paper for each loan, the previous Friday night, to give us the weekend to look at them. We sat around a big table, a dozen to twenty of us. The papers would be stacked before Sheperd and he would turn them over one by one. Each had the three credit initials, the name of the company and a list of its other banks, a summary of the company's financials, a statement of the purpose of the loan, and a list of the conditions and the interest rates. Sheperd would go through the loan pages, and anyone could comment. In those days, all the senior credit initials were based in New York, so the man who had primary responsibility for the loan was usually in the room.

This wasn't a system for approving or disapproving loans—these loans had been made, on the signatures of the responsible officers, and the guys who signed for it were on the hook all by themselves. But if Brady said, "Don't you think the rate is a little low on that?" or Sheperd said, "Aren't our shipping loans getting high?" you were careful about what you signed for in the weeks ahead. Brady's question, which still sounds in my ear, was about a ten-year term loan to Inland Steel at 1.5 percent at a time when we could see rates were rising. It was a sudden-death loan, too, with no repayment until the end of the term, just the kind of loan I've always said a banker shouldn't make. The fact was that Forward and I had been banging on that door for years, and finally found a way to get Inland Steel business: we bought it. All I could say in response to Brady's criticism was, "I agree."

These were important meetings for the president and chairman, because they came a day before the board meetings at which they would have to answer directors' questions—and some directors did ask questions—about the bank's lending. And in a system where the lending officers and their immediate superiors committed the bank, which was and still is City's system (for the very good reason that it leaves the maximum authority in the hands of the people who are likely to know most about the situation), these meetings were the most efficient way for the top executives of the bank to influence its lending policies.

You didn't have to be a senior officer of the bank to have a senior initial, the authority to approve a larger loan. I was given my senior initial while I was still a simple vice-president. And the approach was not as nit-picky as the outside observer might think on the basis of my description, because individual loans to the largest customers were not on the table very often. We operated with them on the basis of a "line of credit," which the committee normally reviewed only once a year. A General Motors might have a "global line," some of which would be earmarked England, Germany and Japan, and so on, some of which could be borrowed at the discretion of the lending officers for use anywhere. If an officer made a loan to General Motors within that line, he didn't have to bring it to the committee. But as the bank grew with the economy in the late 1940s and early 1950s, Brady and Sheperd decided they needed someone whose whole job it would be to structure these meetings and follow up on them. That someone could only be Forward—Lambie had retired, and Forward had taken on responsibility for the entirety of the domestic division.

In summer 1951, Forward was taken out of the chain of command in the actual making of loans and given the new title of chairman of the credit policy committee. The new rules required that in certain circumstances, lending officers would have to secure the "concurrence" of the credit policies committee, which would have a small staff of its own and set up meetings somewhat more formal than our Monday-afternoon sessions. If the committee did not concur, an appeal could be taken by the lending officer to the president of the bank. This almost never happened, and decision-making authority continued to reside, correctly, with the lending officers. The words on the memo attached to the loan when it came to the credit committee of the board of directors were, "as reported to and reviewed by the credit policy

committee." Then the minutes of the board would show that the directors "received the report of the credit policy committee on the loans
made last week." But the review of the larger loans and longer term
loans and loans to new borrowers assured that attention was paid where
attention was needed, and the process explains why Citibank has had
a better credit experience than most other very large U.S. banks. The
authority remained close to the customers, but areas of lending that
cause problems got a second look.

Word of Forward's new title and the creation of the committee
that gave him "responsibility and general supervision over all credit
extensions' was conveyed by a letter he sent me at our vocation hotel
in Paris. There followed something of a shock for me and my expectations. I had taken it more or less for granted that I would step into
Forward's shoes when he stepped out of them, but this, he wrote me,
was not to be. Instead, Stillman Rockefeller, who was chief of the New
York branches, would, Forward wrote me, "rotate into the Domestic
Division as my successor . . . Stillman and I had a little talk this morning and both he and Shep [i.e., Howard Sheperd] were anxious for me
to assure you that this move was a rotation and should have no bearing
on [your] immediate status . . . Strictly between ourselves, Stillman
told me that there never had been any question in his mind that you
should follow along immediately behind him, and I know that Shep
feels the same way about it . . ." In short, the powers that were had
decided that Rockefeller not Moore was to stand behind Sheperd and
move into the presidency at the end of 1952, when Brady would retire
as chairman and Sheperd would take his place. If Rockefeller was to
be president, he needed experience beyond the New York City bank,
and he was going to get the domestic-division title to give him some
feathers for his flight to the presidency. Rockefeller was entirely
straightforward about the situation when I returned from Paris, telling
me that he wasn't going to be in the domestic-division job long, that I
should run it more or less as I had for Forward, just keep him informed
of what we were doing. I wouldn't have to wait more than eighteen
months before the job was mine. And he was as good as his word.

Among the others who were disappointed by this turn of events
was Randolph Burgess, who had come to City Bank from the Federal
Reserve in 1939 and was chairman of our executive committee, with
responsibility for the bond accounts, for government relations and public
affairs, economic analysis and investment policy. He left the bank at
the beginning of 1953 to be undersecretary of the treasury under George

Humphrey, for President Eisenhower. Rockefeller was only three years older than I, and City Bank had an absolute rule about retirement at age sixty-five, so his insertion over my head meant that I almost certainly could not be chairman of the bank for more than three years. But I was still going to have fascinating jobs in a fascinating bank, and be paid very well for them, too.

I could work with Rockefeller. He didn't have much of a sense of humor or any great driving force, but he was a solid banker, and, after all, I could supply what he lacked. Brady and Sheperd had decided, I had to assume, that Rockefeller could supply what Moore lacked, everything from a great name in New York and inherited social standing to very heavy specific gravity as a banker. Sheperd's and Forward's old rival William Lambie, I knew, thought I lacked that. Lambie had said once in a place where he knew it would get back to me that the most important thing was never to let a salesman into the boardroom, because he'd convince all the directors to do what they shouldn't do. That's how Charlie Mitchell got the job of chairman, he said, and he saw some of Charlie Mitchell in Moore's aggressiveness.

The guard changed definitively in 1953. Rockefeller became president and Forward as a mark of honor was made the only senior vice-president. (For years under Mitchell and Perkins, my hero William Simonson had been the only senior v.-p.) Howard Laeri in the New York branches, Nathan Lenfestey in operations (a nemesis of mine since the 1948 survey committee work, which he had strongly opposed), and Leo Shaw in the overseas division would join me as executive vice-presidents. Richard Perkins, son of my old mentor, came over from Farmers Trust, still a semi-independent entity, to fill what had been the Burgess job. As the dust settled on the domestic side of our merger with First National, Sheperd decided that the time had come to make the overseas division more than the haven for the weary that it had become.

In 1956, when I was appointed head of the foreign division, it was hinted that I was going to succeed Rockefeller as president of the bank when he became chairman on Sheperd's retirement in 1959. I didn't have much time to think about it then, though, because the winds were blowing from overseas. If I had less than three years in my new job, I had to set my sails quickly.

7

Overseas

It's probably fair to say that I did not have any great respect
for the international end of City Bank during my years in the domestic
division. The official history of the bank says that I referred to it once
as "Siberia," and I probably did. As I read the figures, even on the
overseas division's own books (which made the foreign branches look
lots better than they were), the results of more than fifty years of our
operations overseas, net net net, were red red red. You could even
make the case that Americans weren't much good at international
banking. Among the bad assets we had on our books when I came to
the bank in 1927 was the remains of the $4 million of loans we had
bought at par from the Guaranty Trust in 1921, when the Clearing
House banks joined together to rescue that one of their members from
the unwise loans it had made abroad in connection with its "Edge Act"
foreign trade bank (named for Senator Walter Edge of Florida, whose
law it had been; the Edge Act allowed banks to operate outside their
home state, but only for the purpose of financing international trade).
Lending in remote places, of course, is inherently dangerous. That's
why most banks, at least until modern transportation and communications shrank the distances, relied for international business on their
network of "correspondents" in other countries. National City had been
an exception, but so far as I could see the people who said they were
trying to make a business of our overseas division weren't the people
who could make that business successful.

The chances are good, too, that I communicated these attitudes to the people who worked with me. In 1955, Stillman Rockefeller asked me the name of the best man in the domestic division, and when I told him it was Walt Wriston, who was then running the shipping and transportation district, he said he wanted to take him to manage the desk in New York that supervised our London office. I had a hard time selling the idea to Wriston, and could do it, finally, only by offering him a "repurchase agreement": when and if he grew unhappy in the overseas division, I would take him back, no questions asked. He had good reason not to be happy at the beginning, by the way, because his new colleagues more or less ignored him. The way he put it was, "They don't leave the key out for me at night." One day I had a lunch with International Harvester, partly because the head of Lloyd's Bank was in New York and we were all going to talk about the company's needs in Britain, and I was surprised when Wriston didn't come, though three other people from the overseas division did. Nobody had told him about the lunch . . . But that's another story.

My survey committee in 1948 had not presented its report on the overseas division until June 1950, and we found the thing such a mess that we concentrated on purely procedural recommendations. Most of what a foreign branch did, for example, loans and acceptances and letters of credit and trade finance, could be done only after two signatures had been appended to the paper, "a carry-over of an ancient foreign custom, the origin of which is obscure . . . A staff of authorized signers is maintained to affix signatures." We suggested that forms and procedures be standardized, at least within countries, to achieve a degree of uniformity in, for example, the checks our branches issued to their depositors. "Drafts of Bombay and Calcutta Branches," we noted, "are identical in wording and format but the Bombay draft measures $3\frac{1}{2}$ inches by $7\frac{5}{16}$ inches and the Calcutta draft measures $4\frac{1}{8}$ inches by $9\frac{5}{16}$ inches. The two London Branches use drafts with marked differences in size, wording, and general appearance . . ." We did find in the files a thick manual dictating procedures for the entire overseas division, but one of the things I learned young about manuals is that nobody reads them.

By the time the report on overseas was submitted, the survey committee was old news. And the final revision was completed a week after the Korean War started, so we also suffered from the problem that people were thinking about other things. About the only purpose the document served was to make an enemy of Leo Shaw, chief of the division. The unpleasant fact was that under Shaw, as under his predecessor Jack Durrell, the foreign operation of the bank had simply run down. In 1930, City Bank had eighty-three foreign branches with 29 percent of its total loans, and the overseas division accounted for 30 percent of the total profits; by 1955, we were down to sixty-one branches with 14 percent of the loans, contributing 16 percent of the profits. Even so, City Bank was the largest American banking operation abroad: nobody had gone after the business we had neglected.

Later, after international business had become so prominent a factor in City Bank's world, the public relations department liked to say that we had operated branches in foreign countries since 1901, but that was stretching things a bit. Until the Federal Reserve Act was passed in 1913, nationally chartered banks were not permitted to have foreign branches. (State-chartered banks were: Morgan had been in Europe forever, and Farmers Trust, which was state-chartered, had run a branch in London since before the turn of the century.) Most American money center banks believed that the best way to do international business was to cultivate relationships with big correspondent banks in other countries: you would scratch their backs with your clients going abroad, and they would scratch yours with theirs coming to the United States. But National City had lobbied for the change in the law, and in November, 1914—taking advantage of the fact that the British banks that had dominated this market were distracted by the Great War—we opened our first branch, in Buenos Aires, followed by a second, in Rio, the next spring. A number of American companies active in South America—the Citibank history lists Du Pont, U.S. Steel, W. R. Grace, International Harvester, Armour, and Standard Oil of New York, an impressive roster—were interested in supporting an American bank in South America, and they did.

Meanwhile, City Bank had been acquiring shares in the International Banking Corporation, an existing network of American banking offices abroad. This was a very special company, incorporated by act of the Connecticut legislature in 1901, mostly to open up what were regarded as very promising markets in the Far East following our capture of the Philippines in the war against Spain. (IBC's history is what gave the p.r. people the year 1901.) In 1915, we took control of the chain—which had offices in New York, London, Panama, and San Francisco as well as some seventeen cities in Europe and Asia, financed a great deal of trans-Pacific trade, and was by far the largest American overseas banking venture. With IBC came H. T. S. Green, its British-born manager, who was still in charge of the National City overseas division when I came to the bank. He was also our best money-maker, for the Chinese branches alone in 1930 generated almost a third of the profits of the bank. Of course, in 1930, neither the domestic nor the European economies were in shape to generate profits.

Not long after acquiring IBC, however, National City learned that it was also possible to lose money abroad. Our management had somehow developed an enthusiasm for Russia, where several of our best customers, including International Harvester and Singer Sewing Machine, had factories. Russia had been almost a reserved territory for German banks, and now, of course, thanks to the war, they were out. It looked like a great opportunity. The U.S. government was very supportive, because the Russians needed an agent to manage wartime loans to the czar and then to the Kerensky government from private and public sources in the United States (as J. P. Morgan had managed the British and French loans). We opened in Petrograd (now Leningrad) in 1916, and expanded to Moscow and Vladivostock in 1917. Then, suddenly, it was all over, our branches seized by the Bolsheviks, our managers scrambling to get out of the country by whatever route they could, and almost no records to testify to our claims or our obligations. On my first trip to the Soviet Union, in 1963, I was received by the then prime minister, Anastas Mikoyan, and I gave him the address of our Moscow branch and said I would like to visit it, to see if our manager's hat was still there, as he had left without it. Mikoyan was not amused, and we changed the subject.

The problems that grew out of the Soviet takeover were still with us when I came to the bank in the 1920s—and some were still there when I left in 1970. The United States did not recognize the Soviet government. In terms of our legal position, it was as though bandits had taken possession of a New York branch. Our depositors claimed "breach of contract," and said that we owed them dollars for their ruble deposits in our Russian branches, at the official rate of fifty to the dollar at the date of the breach. We didn't know what their deposits had been, because the Russians had seized the records and kept or destroyed them, but the claimants' documentation indicated about $26 million. If these cases came to trial, our lawyers told us, we were likely to lose them. Fortunately, we had large U.S. dollar balances we had been holding for various Russian governmental entities. We took the position that we were allowed to hold those dollars as a kind of offset for the assets the Russians had taken from us. Our strategy through the 1920s and into the early 1930s, then, was to stall the claimants until they actually got us before a court, and then make some sort of settlement, paying it out of the Russian funds. We had a Russian department in the bank, run by a well-nourished, Russian-speaking, amusing character named George Link, who had worked in that Moscow office. He reported to comptroller Dan Borden, with whom I was working in Perkins's office, so I had some responsibility for him.

In 1933, Roosevelt recognized the Soviets, and the lawyers breathed a sign of relief. Now there was a sovereign government from which the former depositors in our branches could claim reimbursement. We stopped settling the cases, saw them through trial . . . and won. Before we could start celebrating, however, a new problem appeared. In making the arrangements to recognize the Soviet government, Roosevelt's State Department had tried to collect the American governmental loans to Kerensky. Maxim Litvinov, negotiating for the Russians, had offered to assign to the U.S. government his country's claims for deposits in American banks made before the revolution. This clever move cost the Russians nothing, but it might cost us a lot. The U.S. government promptly sued City Bank, claiming to be the owners of the Russian deposits under what came to be called "the Litvinov assignment." We won those cases, too, but the government has deep pockets to pay for lawsuits, and kept finding grounds for appeal. It wasn't until 1983, nearly sixty-six years after the Bolsheviks seized our branches and fifty years after the United States recognized the Soviet government, that the Supreme Court finally threw out the last petition requesting a review of its previous decisions on "the Litvinov assignment." My understanding is that after charging all the settlements, the legal fees and the expenses of the Russian department, there was a little something left over from the Kerensky deposits, which we transferred to "reserve for contingencies."

2

The foreign involvement that had most seriously affected City Bank in its first fifty-five years of overseas lending was a long and complicated relationship with Cuba. Havana had been our third foreign branch (and the first to be purchased rather than launched: City Bank bought the Banco de Habaña). That was 1915, and the war was driving up sugar prices, which eventually hit seventy-five cents a pound. We financed the Cuban sugar industry, supplying what were called "pignoration" loans against 80 percent of the value of sugar-cane crops still in the field, to be paid when the sugar was delivered to the mill; we made loans to sugar processors to buy the cane; we made loans to sugar dealers to hold the sugar they bought from the processors. In theory we weren't lending to the factories, but when the crunch came it turned out we were, because those were the only assets left. We opened a branch in Santiago de Cuba and then other branches elsewhere, and became indeed the central bank of Cuba, with more than 90 percent of all the bank deposits in the country. Central banking was something City Bank did in the 1920s, because when you are the only, or the heavily dominant, bank in a country you have to fulfill central-bank functions. These are important functions, and there is nobody else to do them. We bought what turned out to be the central bank in Santo Domingo and Haiti and Liberia (this last from Firestone). It's always a bad business: you're under constant pressure to make loans to prime ministers and other ministers, and you have to keep telling people to balance their budgets, like Volcker.

Then the sugar price dropped like a stone following the great deflation of 1920, and our collateral was worth much less than our loans. National City Bank wound up the proprietor of about one-fifth of all the sugar-producing facilities on the island of Cuba. In 1921–22, City Bank managers restructured the Cuban sugar industry, forming a holding company called General Sugar that owned and operated four large producing mills—the Vertientes Company, the Camaguey Company, and the San Cristobal and San Isidro properties. Charles Mitchell, who had recently been appointed president of City Bank, made frequent trips to Cuba to see how the work-out was coming. While there, he ran into Gordon Rentschler, whose family owned General Machinery Corporation of Hamilton, Ohio, which had sold the mills their equipment on credit and was trying to collect. Mitchell was greatly impressed with Rentschler's savvy, and persuaded him to supervise the bank's interests in the Cuban sugar business. Rentschler then joined the board of the bank, and in 1929 Mitchell talked him into becoming president. Perkins thought highly of Rentschler—indeed, he wouldn't accept the chairman's job in 1933 until the board agreed to retain Rentschler as president—and Rentschler was always kind to me, setting my compensation generously (Perkins wouldn't touch that question), and introducing me both around the bank and to customers. Especially during the 1930s, Rentschler's talents were very valuable to the bank: businessmen felt he understood their business, which is two-thirds of the game in customer relations. In the sugar story, however, Rentschler's affection for the business was costly to the bank, because in 1927 there were opportunities to sell out at a break-even price. Mitchell and Rentschler, unfortunately, still liked sugar, and sold not to the market but to our own National City Company. This was meaningless.

Sugar prices went south again, actually before the Depression, leaving the holding company with heavy losses. A very able man named Phil Rosenberg ran the sugar mills from New York, making frequent visits. Several of the mills were enormous businesses in themselves— one produced a million tons a year. When sugar prices rose in World War II, Rentschler, having learned his lesson, sold off the City Bank sugar properties, including West Indies Sugar and our Santo Domingo operation, which Gulf & Western later turned into a big resort development called La Romana. We continued to be the bankers for the sugar companies, however, even after their ownership was represented by publicly traded securities. I retained my membership on the Vertientes Camaguey board, which entitled me to take a winter trip to Cuba, ride their private railroad, and stay in their large and comfortable guest house. Rentschler, who had succeeded Perkins as chairman of the bank in 1940, was on a visit to Cuba when he died in 1948. The City Bank branches in Cuba remained large (by Cuban standards) and profitable, with about 20 percent of the country's deposits. Then, in my era as head of the overseas division, shortly before I became president of the bank, Castro came out of the hills, and it was Russia all over again.

By now, we'd made some preparations. We'd set up a system of "code alerts" like the State Department's, with three stages of emergency precaution. We kept duplicate records, moved collateral for loans and foreign currency out of the threatened banks and back to the United States, and in the last moments our people followed certain agreed-upon procedures to destroy currency, traveler's checks, and negotiable drafts. Our contract with our depositors had freed us from liability in the event of a takeover *force majeure,* and Castro took us off the hook anyway by announcing that the new government was grabbing all the assets *and assuming all the liabilities* of the banks. Like the Russians, Castro's people when they expropriated our banks forgot that the Cuban government had deposits with us in New York that we could seize to satisfy our claims for the loss of our capital, our real estate holdings and the accumulated profits we had not been able to transfer to New York. Worse yet, from their point of view, they didn't know that First National City had been the collecting agent for Cuban sugar sales, and that money due the Cuban government was paid routinely to us in New York. We kept collecting and offsetting until Havana realized what was happening and instructed the sugar purchasers to stop paying First National City. By then, we were whole and then some, having in effect collected on a number of bad Cuban loans we had made from New York and had already at least partially written off. The Cuban government sued, and lost.

One bad loan we collected ourselves, in an interesting way. This was to a a freebooter named Jake Lobo, whose purchase of some sugar mills from the Hershey Chocolate Company we had financed at Hershey's insistence, even though we thought him a bad moral risk. Hershey was an old and important and more or less exclusive client, and was going to make the sale; if we had refused, they would have arranged the financing elsewhere, which meant they would have taken some other business elsewhere, too. Lobo, we knew, had been one of Castro's financial backers, hoping to buy peace and quiet, but Castro double-crossed him as he had the Bacardi family (which also had contributed money to the revolutionary cause). Lobo being Lobo, he had double-crossed Castro first, transferring his assets out of Cuba to Tampa—and double-crossed us by putting everything in the name of his daughter after he had personally guaranteed the loan and then declaring that he didn't have the funds to pay off. We took the problem to Shearman and Sterling, our distinguished Wall Street lawyers, but they weren't used to dealing with crooks. Thereupon, we took the problem to the law firm in which Congressman Emmanuel Celler was a partner. They found what Lobo had done in about ten minutes, and did the legal equivalent of hanging him up by this thumbs until he paid off his loan, which he did, all $9 million of it.

We did take one significant loss in Cuba in the end, the only large licking City Bank ever had as the result of something I had done. This was a $25 million loan to help a wholly owned subsidiary of Freeport Sulphur finance a nickel project at Moa Bay on the north shore east of Havana. Most of its $100-million cost was invested in Cuba, where the nickel oxides were extracted from the soil and given a first processing before shipment to a refinery the company had built in Shreveport, Louisiana. Freeport had high hopes for the project, based on anticipated costs. For reasons of accounting and reporting to the stockholders, they didn't want anything on paper, they said, so they refused to guarantee the loan, but they insisted that whatever happened they would see we didn't lose money, they would "see us through." It was unusual but not extraordinary for large corporate borrowers to give these "moral guarantees," providing comfort for us without giving difficult stockholders a footnote they might question at the conclusion of the balance sheet. The loan was to be repaid by cash flow from the sale of the refined nickel, and it looked safe, because the company had other sources of partially processed metal to substitute if the Cuban mine for any reason went sour. We could have insisted on political risk insurance from the U.S. government, but the Cuban government had never signed the agreement the Commerce Department required. I think Batista wanted the investment in Cuba badly enough that if we had made a condition of our loan he would have approved the risk-insurance papers. But Freeport didn't want us to make requests of Battista in connection with this project, and I mistakenly didn't demand it. This violated the principles of "three-way-out Moore," and we paid for it. Because I trusted Freeport, I proceeded on the loan without either government or corporate guarantee. So did Bankers Trust and Mellon and some others.

At about the time Moa Bay began operations, Castro took over, and confiscated the plant. We expected that Freeport would shift to another source of nickel "mat" for its Shreveport facility. Instead, the company abandoned the project, denying its moral obligation to the lenders. We seized the Shreveport plant and sold it for about $10 million to someone who converted it to other uses, and we threatened to sue for the remainder, but eventually we took a derisory $1 million settlement and wrote off the rest. In hindsight, I think that was wrong: we should have sued, and although we had only a "moral guarantee" from the company, I think we would have won, because the company had showed the loan as a liability on its consolidated report for tax purposes, and had taken a tax loss for the parent on the Moa Bay investment. Meanwhile, it was an expensive reinforcement of J. P. Morgan's great lesson—when he tried to teach it, the House of Representatives committee thought he was pulling their leg—that you lend to a man not on his balance sheet but on his character. From that day to this, Citibank has refused to do business with Freeport Sulphur. They've been around a few times to ask my successors if they could do business again with Citibank, and every time they've been turned down. In my sixty years as a banker, it's the only case I have ever known where a top company just walked away from an obligation.

3

We had troubles, too, in the Far East. I remember from my early years with the bank a problem involving Marshal Chang Hsueh-liang, the warlord who controlled Manchuria at the time of the Japanese invasion. He also controlled a bank in Mukden, which had correspondent deposits in our three Manchurian branches. Shortly before Japan's Kwantung Army seized Mukden, General Chang ordered the transfer of $10 million from the accounts of those banks to the account in New York of a business he controlled. When the Japanese went over the books of his bank, they became highly annoyed, and demanded the return of the money. All the papers had been proper in the transfer of funds from General Chang's bank, and of course we had to refuse. We did, however, put a hold on his account in New York. He sued for his money, and the Japanese government sued us in Tokyo (where we had a branch) to recapture the money. Our lawyers told us we would probably lose both cases. We suggested to the litigants that they each take half of the $10 million and go away, but they refused. Finally we worked out a deal: we threw additional money into the pot—my recollection is a figure something like $1 million—and the two sides then split 50/50. We had a sizable loss just from making a routine cable money transfer.

As noted earlier, the Chinese banks we had bought with International Banking Corporation were very profitable, and unlike our other banks. As I understood it, all banks in China hired compradors, guys with knives in their hands, who arranged the actual loans to local businessmen and guaranteed their repayment. Our mostly British and Scottish staff in the banks (IBC's secret had been that it hired the British to compete with the British) were not people who found it easy to tell Chinese apart. As was not uncommon in those days, we also operated on both sides of the battle line between the Chinese and the Japanese, but when war came between the United States and Japan we were of course closed down. After the war we thought we could reopen, but the people we sent to our old branches soon reported back that Mao and the Communists were going to take over the country. When the Maoists seized the banks, they tried to hold our managers hostage for the payment of the U.S. dollar assets of the people who had done business with us, but most of them escaped, some by land routes to Malaysia and Burma. One senior man, however, Fred Harnden, remained in the early 1950s. He was ill, and we wanted to get him out at any cost.

Through various intermediaries, we negotiated our officer's release for a ransom of $250,000, to be paid upon his safe delivery in Hong Kong. A deposit for this purpose was placed in Hong Kong and Shanghai Bank. Then we had an amusing phone call from Hong Kong. The Chinese Communists were in a purist phase, in which they didn't want to soil their hands with "capitalist currencies." They were demanding to be paid for their ransom in yuan, and they were specifying how many yuan they wanted, at their own arbitrary and overvalued exchange rate, which was 20 percent above the actual market rate in Hong Kong. So Hong Kong and Shanghai Bank with our total approval wrote the letter of credit in yuan, and refunded $50,000 to us.

I did not visit China until 1981, when I went in part as a tourist and in part on a piece of work for W. R. Grace & Company, for which I have been director and (it amounts to the same thing) director emeritus for almost as long as I can remember. I was eleven years beyond my time as chairman of Citibank, and there was nothing in my papers to identify me with the bank. But as we were leaving the Peking Hotel, the very courteous waiter who had served us our meals in the dining room bade farewell with the comment that he hoped I would return, and that my bank would some day reopen its offices in China. I guess he was more than just a waiter.

Our Japanese offices have been, of course, much more important to the bank, and I have had fine relations with the Japanese banking sector since my days in the domestic division, when I became friendly with Gengo Suzuki, who was the senior representative of the Bank of Japan and the Ministry of Finance in the United States. One day he came to me and asked whether I could help the Japanese banks achieve a prime rating in the London acceptance market. This was the early 1950s, and the Japanese economic miracle was already apparent, but before the London dealers would trade paper representing the credit of a Japanese bank they required an endorsement by an American or European bank. I thought it was clear that acceptances by top Japanese banks were as good as any in the world, and arranged that the next day City Bank in London would tell the London bill brokers that we stood prepared to buy Japanese bank paper, without endorsement, at prime. The rest of the market followed suit, and everyone in Japan, of course, knew about it.

Many years later, Yoshizane Iwasa was retiring from the chairmanship of Fuji Bank the same year I retired from Citibank, and to honor the two of us, Fuji suggested a group of joint ventures. We formed what we called "the F study," with equal membership from both banks, and our successors carried out its recommendations. The results included a merchant bank active in Hong Kong, a consumer credit company, and a leasing company, all profitable. There were also two failures—we couldn't sell the services of a business consulting firm we established together, and we couldn't introduce factoring to Japan, because Japanese banks often do the kind of close supervision only factors do in America, and will carry customers who are in trouble longer than American banks will. Iwasa gave three retirement parties for me in Tokyo—one in his home (which is of course unheard of for a Japanese), one at a geisha house for senior Citibank officers in Tokyo, and one at his bank.

But our Tokyo office was very well plugged in as far as back as the 1930s, and we heard from them the September before Pearl Harbor that the Japanese government was sending special ambassadors to Washington to discuss what Japan would have to do to cancel Roosevelt's boycott of oil and steel sales. They would propose, our sources said, a final offer to limit the extension of Japan's "co-prosperity sphere." If that offer was refused, there would be war. Then in October we heard form the same people that the offer *had* been refused. We ordered most Americans home from our Japanese branches, including all wives and children, and sent over Tom Davies and two other men who were bachelors and knew the risks they were running. They were interned throughout the war. Someone also went to see the State Department and inquire what we should do about our extensive staffs in Manila, Hong Kong, and Singapore. The department told us not to worry about those people, that all three of those cities were within the perimeter the United States planned to hold if war broke out. I still don't know whether they were ignorant or whether they misled us. We had a hundred people very uncomfortably interned for four years at the University of Manila, and nearly all of them could have been safe in their beds at home in the United States, if the State Department had leveled with us.

Our other major venture in the Far East was in Hong Kong, where we had, when I took over, a single bank we had purchased in the IBC package. Its manager Hank Sperry was Mr. Hong Kong; he knew all about the Crown Colony, and he was full of reasons why he would never recommend that we try to expand our operations. He's my prime example of why it's not good to have a guy in one place too long: he hadn't seen how Hong Kong had changed. Coming from far away, we could see (but he couldn't) that there was a heaven-made match of the entrepreneurial spirit of Hong Kong and the entrepreneurial spirit of Citibank. He retired. Eventually our operation in Hong Kong grew to more than one hundred offices, some entirely our own, some shared with local and Japanese partners, with profits that exceed $20 million a year.

There were some dark days in the 1950s, when it seemed that the Communist armies, having eaten the mainland, would come and bite off Hong Kong, too—certainly, there was no way the British could have stopped them. A number of foreign banks, including Chase, abandoned the Crown Colony at that time, but we decided to ride out the storm—we'd been seized before, after all, by experts. This had great values later, because the Hong Kong authorities refused to give new licenses to the banks that had cut and run when the colony was in trouble, and the only way David Rockefeller got Chase back in was to buy the "franchise" of the Nederlandische Handelsbank, which was disposing of its foreign branches. We'd had the opportunity to buy that Hong Kong branch ourselves, for the entirety of the Dutch bank's overseas division had been offered to us, but we felt we didn't need more offices in Hong Kong or Tokyo, so we merely cherry-picked the Canadian subsidiary as a way to get into one of the most severely protected markets in the world. We probably should have thought the matter through differently, and taken the Dutch Hong Kong operation as a way to keep Chase out, but our minds didn't work that way in those days. It wasn't what you might call a carefully considered decision, anyway: we had lunch with the Dutch bankers, and turned down their more extensive offer on the spot.

I wouldn't want to leave the impression that we were always out to do our competitors in the eye—only sometimes. I saved American Express from an acceptability problem in the early 1960s, when a New Jersey con man swindled them out of millions of dollars with fake salad oil warehouse receipts, and partly because the story was so funny and so discreditable there was a worldwide crisis of confidence in their traveler's checks. That was a business in which we were competing with them as hard as we could; we were second and they were first, by a big margin. I found out about their disaster in a peculiar way. I was in South Africa, eating in a restaurant outside Cape Town, and

Howard Clark of American Express was at the next table. He was called to the telephone, and came back visibly upset: he'd just heard the news. Chase was their bank—the securities arm of Chase had owned American Express back in the 1920s—but when Clark's people went to David Rockefeller for help, he just looked out the window.

A month later, Clark and Peck Owen, chairman of Amex, came to me in New York and told me they were finding it difficult to get their checks honored in some foreign cities. I said, This is ridiculous. We called our branches around the world and said, Call everybody in your town, tell them we'll pay off whatever American Express traveler's checks they acquire; and of course we never had to take any.

4

I had been indirectly involved with the overseas division for some years. Many of our customers in the domestic division also did an international business with the bank, and the existence of our overseas network was one of the selling arguments we used with American corporations. Personally, having married into a Spanish-Mexican family and become fluent (if not without accent) in the language, I had a continuing interest in Latin American business and development. I was still a domestic lender when I coined the phrase that is my continuing and I hope permanent contribution to the worldwide dialogue of development. I was in Buenos Aires as part of the group that inaugurated Braniff Airways service from the United States to Argentina, and we were given an audience with President Juan Perón, who was running what had been one of the world's most prosperous economies into a brick wall of theory, government interference, and stupidity. Perón said to Thomas Braniff, "We would like more investors like you in our country." Braniff spoke no Spanish, and asked me to reply. "Capital," I said, "goes where it's invited and stays where it's well treated."

The idea that I might take some supervisory responsibility in the international area did not arise, however, until 1956, when Sheperd and Rockefeller asked me to make a study of our stagnant overseas division and come up with some recommendations to improve its performance. I thought we were doing an inadequate job everywhere, but especially on the European continent. We'd been a force in Europe before the war: a favorite story at the bank told of Von Runstedt's arrival at the head of the panzers in Brussels, where he stopped at our old branch at the head of the Grande Place, routed out our nervous manager Gordon Morier, and said to him, "I would like you to make arrangements to transfer my Shanghai account in your bank to this branch, for I expect to be here some time. I'll send my orderly for you tonight; we are taking a castle for my use, and I understand these Belgians are good cooks." But we had (we thought cleverly) sold off our branches before America joined the war and the Nazis could seize them, which meant that when the war was over we didn't have the automatic right to return that some of our competitors did. We had not returned to Belgium, Italy, and Spain, and our return to France had been in the form of an office on which we hung the old shingle of International Banking Corporation, though the branch had borne the name of National City Bank before the war, when it was for a while the largest foreign bank in Paris.

Meanwhile, the Marshall Plan had come and gone, the Treaty of Rome was under negotiation and would produce the Common Market, nearly all the governments were conservative or "Christian Democrat," and the Communist threat had receded everywhere. Currencies were still convertible into dollars, and into each other, only under severe restrictions in each country and through the bureaucracy of the European Payments Union between countries. But much of that was going to go (the EPU had only two more years to live). American companies were selling to Europe, buying in Europe, producing in Europe in increasing numbers—and being served by European banks. There were immense business opportunities in Europe, and we were doing nothing to grab them. And if we'd wanted to grab them, we didn't have the hands to do the work.

Our overseas team was experienced and knowledgeable, but it was overaged, tired, and demoralized. In those days, employees of the overseas division could retire at full pension at age fifty-five. Most of our branches were in tropical climates, at a time of steamer travel, before airlines and air conditioning, and the theory was that overseas service aged men prematurely, which it probably did. I came back with a report that said we needed new offices everywhere (but especially in Europe), new strategies for our branches in Latin America and the Far East, and new men. In brief, my message was, "Hey, fellas—there's a whole new world out there. The war's over. City Bank hasn't recognized it. Fortunately, nobody else has, either."

About two weeks after I filed this report I was summoned to Sheperd's office at about a quarter to twelve. Rockefeller was there. Sheperd said, "George, we like your report. You are in charge of the foreign department, effective at 1:00 this afternoon. We have a board of direc-

tors meeting in a few minutes, at which I am going to announce Leo
Shaw's immediate retirement, and I would like to report that you are
replacing him." I wasn't entirely surprised, and I accepted. I'd been in
the domestic division for fifteen years. I was getting to the point where
I thought I knew all the answers, and that's the time to get out. Sheperd added, "Leo thinks you will foul up, but we don't. Go ahead and
do what you've said has to be done."

What I knew I did not want to do was run the division day-to-day:
I needed time to develop strategies and make plans. So I went in to see
Pete Mitchell, who had been Shaw's number two, told him that I was
going to be Shaw's replacement, that I wanted him to move into Shaw's
corner office and really run the division for me, making the decisions
on credit and administrative matters. Shaw had spoken unkindly of
me, but Pete was a nice, nice guy, and also a professional, a good credit
man and administrator. He took all the daily burden off my shoulders,
and the fact that he was in charge (which wasn't all that different from
the way the department had run under Shaw) reassured a lot of officers who needed reassurance. He retired a year and a half or two years
later, which allowed me to move Walt Wriston into the number-two
slot, from which he naturally advanced to the executive vice-presidency in the overseas division when I became president.

The first thing I asked Pete to do was to call a meeting of all the
senior officers in New York, for my very first afternoon on the job. It
was the saddest thing you ever saw, a bunch of vice-presidents sitting
around looking out the window and waiting for retirement. They were
long on experience and on loyalty to Shaw, but it was obvious that they
weren't going to generate ideas. And nobody new had come in in years.

As my survey committee report had indicated and my 1956 report
had said straight out, the problem with the organization of the overseas division was that the branches had too much procedural auton-
omy and too little freedom to make banking decisions. (Or personnel
decisions: we had a crazy system whereby if Bombay hired an
untouchable to clean the toilets we had to open a personnel file on
her in New York; I put a stop to that.) If I could commit the bank in
the Middle West, within limits, the man on the spot should have the
power to commit the bank in Hong Kong—again, within limits. At the
same time, the branches should be following a policy coordinated from
New York, so that we were offering the same quality of service to our
American customers all over the world, and winning local business,
where the local authorities would permit, by giving an American-quality

service. Among my more embarrassing moments at the bank was the telephone call I received when International Harvester learned that General Motors was borrowing from our bank in Manila for two percentage points less than the branch was charging them—after I had promised that they would have our best rate everywhere in the world. That's the sort of thing I meant when I complained about our failures in policy coordination.

The men who worked in the foreign branches didn't know each other. They came home independently once every three years, went back to their home towns on leave, maybe took a week at headquarters. I held a three-day conference at the Westchester Country Club for all the managers of our foreign branches. It was the first time they'd met each other. At that meeting, which was such a novelty that the bank mentioned it in the annual report to shareholders the next spring, they spent all their time talking about the reports New York demanded and what a burden they were, and about their compensation and perquisites, why the Texaco man's wife had a fur coat and theirs didn't. I gave them a pep talk, told them, "Remember, you're an ambassador. You're a guest. You have to conduct yourself so that people are glad you're there, feel you're making a contribution to the country, helping its development." They weren't much interested in that.

To be fair to them, most of their contact with New York didn't give them much encouragement. It was all nit-picking about whether they had the right to pay that much money for a nanny for the children, or whether they were buying the right car. When the boss came, they were supposed to genuflect and make sure he had a good time for the day or two he stayed. I honored William Brady and respected him, but when he was chairman of the bank he expected to travel like the King of England. The manager in Peru told me the story: Brady was coming for a day and a half, told him to make appointments with the President of the Republic and the finance minister, arrange a dinner with the local business leaders, set up a trip to see the ruins, leave some shopping time for him and his wife, and make sure she had social engagements with the wives while he was busy. Then the plane was five hours late, Brady said he was tired and cancelled the appointment with the president (the manager was able to reinstate it for the next day), canceled the dinner with the business leaders, ran around doing the sight-seeing and the shopping.

The manager, who'd had some business and personnel problems he'd hoped to talk over while the chairman was in town, got fifteen minutes with Brady in the car back to the airport. Brady said, "Put it in a letter to me, will you, and I'll think about it when I get back to New York." I learned from that. When I visited, and for the next fourteen years I spent almost a third of my time visiting around the world, I took a minimum of three days in a city. My purpose was not to meet the high and mighty (though I did some of that) or to enjoy the tourism (though I had a good time, too) but to meet my people and get to know their problems.

I was prepared to help the overseas managers with their personal situation, too. In a few places we bought houses for managers of Citibank branches, so they could live as well as the Shell managers and the British merchant bankers, who had always lived in company-owned housing. We paid any added taxes to which an officer was subjected because he was working abroad. We helped finance American schools in many cities. But the major difference was that we put the benefits associated with overseas assignment into a formula, to minimize the number of individual letters and individual deals. Everyone got a bonus for overseas work, running from 10 percent in the desirable places like Paris to 30 percent in the difficult places like Calcutta and Monrovia, plus so much housing allowance and travel allowance and school allowance. When I became president of the bank, I saw to it that foreign assignment was never an exile, but an important step up the ladder. My successors have carried on with that, too. It's still true under John Reed that you only have to do one good job at Citibank, anywhere in the world, and you're jet-propelled.

What was obvious from my conferences and my travels was that the bank needed, as I told Sheperd, "people, people, people." I went to Europe and took a trip with Harvey Gerry, who ran the Paris branch. He'd been a U.S. consul before he was a banker, and like me he'd come to City Bank with the Farmers Trust acquisition. We went to Brussels and Milan and Frankfurt together. I said I wanted to open branches in all three, and then in Geneva, and then elsewhere. He said he agreed, we should do it one a year. I said, We're going to do it all next year (which in fact we couldn't do, however hard we tried), and, by the way, I have a job for you in New York, you're leaving Europe. He took early retirement about a year later. In my two years and eight months, we changed the managers of two-thirds of our foreign branches, and we began the long, slow process of opening new branches, which always required the approval of both the overseas government and our own, neither of which was in a hurry.

My own reason for hurry was simple: every year you delayed could cost a fortune. Not everybody recognized that, because you almost never saw much of a profit out of the first year of a new branch—you were lucky if you got back your expenses. But if you were right, you might be making $5 million a year out of that branch in the tenth year. What you were losing if you delayed wasn't the trivial profits of the first year (if any) but a year's worth of.that five million. Of course, we made good use of the time it took to get the approvals and rent the space and furnish it. We'd let our customers elsewhere in the world know we were going into, say, Amsterdam, keep them informed of our progress, and ballyhoo the party on opening day. By the time we opened our doors, we had business lines up; it wasn't uncommon for a new branch to do two hundred transactions of some size the first day.

To carry out our plans, we needed literally hundreds and hundreds of people. I raided the domestic division for officers, and hunted not very successfully through the British merchant banks. In 1958, Cal Calhoun and I went to the World Bank meeting in New Delhi, and on our way stopped in Ceylon. There was a crowd of bankers at the airport, but it turned out they had come not to welcome us but to bid farewell to John Exter, who had once been an adviser to the Central Bank in Colombo before becoming vice-president of the Federal Reserve Bank of New York, where in effect he ran a correspondent banking business for the larger banks of the Third World, and some European countries, too. That was business City Bank had done before the war. Fortunately, in those days the Fed paid much less than City Bank, and I was able to hire him to do that work for us. He was a brilliant, cynical man with a sardonic wit, the original gold bug, better with ideas than with people—but he brought us Al Costanzo, who was then deputy manager of the International Monetary Fund, having made his reputation by reorganizing the Greek central bank, and Costanzo was a superb administrator. Costanzo supervised the growth of our South American operation, then succeeded Wriston as executive vice-president of the overseas division and retired as a vice-chairman of the bank. He in turn brought us Jack Clark, who had worked for Costanzo at the IMF, and who became his number two at Citibank and eventually succeeded him as head of international banking. But all that derived from Exter.

After a while, we began to get people from the foreign branches themselves. The first time I realized we could do this was at the party opening our new branch in Amsterdam, in the early 1960s. The place was full of these very attractive young Dutch bankers and their wives, and a couple of them asked me, as president of Citibank, whether they would get a chance to work outside the Netherlands. Their country had lost its colonies, cutting off their opportunities to travel and work in exotic places. They said they'd heard that our youngsters from Oyster Bay and Yale only wanted to work in Paris and London (which was true enough) and they'd be delighted to go to Dakar and Jakarta and Asunción. We did that. We established a rule that any officer in any branch was eligible for assignment away from his home country. If he accepted the assignment, he became part of the overseas staff, eligible for all perquisites and premiums; if he didn't, he remained on the local payroll. Today, most officers in foreign branches who are not nationals of the host country are not Americans, either: they're Citibankers born outside the United States. And people we brought up in the foreign branches are moving into commanding positions in corporate headquarters. John Reed's successor as chairman may well be a foreigner—it's already happened, after all, at Dow Chemical and IBM, and we are as international as they are.

But mostly we recruited from the colleges and the business schools. We'd had a training program back in the 1910s, as Sheperd well knew—he had been one of the students the first year, 1916 (and Arthur Forward and Marcus Wallenberg had been among his classmates). That training program had been associated with the acquisition of IBC and the bank's expansion internationally, and Sheperd, though he advanced to his presidency through the New York City branches, had done a turn in the 1930s as the number-two man in overseas. We revived the program, and also made a deal at the Harvard Business School, where we had never recruited, partly because Charles Williams, chairman of the banking department, had negative feelings about us—we didn't pay enough, didn't offer interesting work, didn't advance young people quickly enough.

We told Williams we were going to hire fifty to a hundred people a year for the overseas division, and they'd have fascinating work, good pay, and a chance to move ahead fast. He agreed to recommend his top students and let us put on a dog-and-pony show for up to one hundred first-year students: cocktails and dinner from six to nine, with the four top officers of the bank in attendance, and then the next day the personnel department would stay around and interview people for summer jobs. Eventually, he even gave us the names of some of the best graduates of a few years back, so we could check around through their friends who were already working for us, and find out whether they were happy in their work. Once we had Harvard on our side, of course, the other business schools came clamoring, too. The great accomplishment of my superintendency at Citibank was the massive improvement in the caliber of our people; but that's a story for Chapter 9.

We also made mistakes, of course, as I had warned Sheperd we would, and one of them was expensive. Among the players in our new Brussels office was a foreign-exchange trader who put the bank into a position of making a giant bet against the devaluation of the pound, even though his orders were not to take any positions in foreign currencies beyond those necessary to do the daily business of the bank in Belgium. The way he did this was to make sales of pounds for delivery in the next few weeks (at fairly high prices, because the devaluation that the market expected was not supposed t' be around the corner), and buy pounds for delivery some months away (at prices that were depressed by the general belief of the market that devaluation lay ahead, as indeed it did). Every night, on a quick glance, he went home with a balanced book—that is, he owed as many pounds as he had promised to buy, he had no net position, and he was obeying the rules.

But in fact there was a "gap." If the pound stayed weak, the discount on the contracts for delivery in several months, where he stood to lose money as the price went down, would grow more than the discount in the contracts for delivery in the near term—long foreign-exchange contracts, like long bonds, fluctuate more than short contracts or bands. To keep the appearance of a balanced book, and not take losses, he had to increase his wagers, every day. Our manager in Brussels knew something unusual was happening, and he called in the auditors. The auditors, as auditors will, looked to the rules rather than to what was actually afoot, and saw only that the great volume of short-term trades between our Brussels branch and certain American banks had left us with lines above the authorized limits for those banks. He suggested that we raise our credit limits, which was done.

By the time the tale was told, the difference in discounts in the gap was $8 million, which meant that we owned and owed many hundreds of millions of dollars of forward pounds. Everybody in town knew about it except Wriston and Moore. When we got the bad news, Wriston went to the chief trader at the Bank of England (which had made most of the sales to our Brussels man on the longer contracts), and said, "Why didn't you tell us?" To which he made the reasonable reply, "Why should I tell you what's happening in your own bank?" He made us a proposition: the bank would take our whole position, close it all out at today's rates (which no private player could have afforded to do, because the transaction would have been so large), and we would pay them our $8-million loss.

I'm still unhappy about the end result of this episode in people terms, because the monkey got put on the back of the manger in Brussels, who had really done everything a manager should be asked to do: the blame should have fallen on the senior officers in London and New York, who were paid to know better. It's very hard to supervise foreign-exchange traders. I used to say that there are four kinds of people you can't treat rationally—opera singers, good cooks, beautiful women, and foreign-exchange traders. Our Brussels manager was summoned home and pretty much stripped of his epaulettes, and a few years later he resigned. I apologize to him. Once on an airplane, when we were traveling together from a board meeting, Fred Donner, then head of General Motors, said to me, "You know, in businesses as large as ours, you don't notice zeros. Two billion dollars is just another number. Man says he wants to buy twenty million pounds of copper, you don't ask him why, you just initial it." That's true.

5

We had begun doing business with Spain in 1950, when they were importing grain from Cargill and other grain dealers, $25 million to $50 million at a clip, and we would advance them the money on a schedule keyed to payments they would be receiving from abroad on contracts already signed. It was all a close call, but they were careful. I used to say that I preferred a poor man who knows where his money is to a rich man who just spends it. The credits were for the Istituto de Moneda, a branch of the Bank of Spain. They had zero reserves: the Republican government had shipped all the gold to Russia (or, some said, Mexico) during the Civil War, and the Russians (or the Mexicans) had just kept it.

In 1959, Spain wanted to join the World Bank and the International Monetary Fund, but those institutions then as now were insistent on seeing the stabilization plans of nations with troubled economies that wanted to do business with official international lenders. Alan Temple, our chief economist, and I sat down with two ministers from the Spanish government during the IMF / Bank meetings, and made some suggestions to them. At the end of the week, back in New York,

I received a call from the Spanish consul—the ministers would like to see me again over the weekend, before they went home. We arranged that they and Temple would come to my home in New Canaan on Sunday, which they did (I remember that the consul drove them out but sat in the car through the whole meeting). Part of Spain's problem was the total lack of reserves: they didn't have the cash required to buy the stock in the bank and make the deposit at the Fund required for membership. I worked with the ministers on how to handle that problem, and we were part of the group of bankers that lent them the money to meet the requirements. A few years ago the Bank of Spain had a one-hundredth anniversary party, and central bankers came to it from all over the world. I was the only private banker there. The Marques de Tejada, governor of the Bank of Spain, announced my presence, and said I was there because without my help the Bank would not have been there.

Spain was a lesson to me and, I hope, to Citibank. It had been IBC's European success story. The two branches in Spain were big banks, the third or fourth biggest in the country. We stuck with them through the Civil War—for a while we had branches on both sides. (Our manager in Barcelona was named José Antonio Primo de Rivera, which was the name of the man who had been the Fascist dictator before the Republican revolution, and the peasant soldiers of the Republic came by and lined him against the wall every so often, but he always succeeded in convincing them he was another fellow.) When war broke out in the rest of Europe, New York decided to close down the Spanish branches, give them to Banco Hispano Americano if they would take over the liabilities. The head of their foreign department was a banker named Andres Moreno, and he cabled an offer to City Bank—Hispano Americano would carry out the deal as agreed, but he recommended that we keep our corporate shell alive, with one peseta in deposits and a single employee (whom they would supply, without cost to us). That would allow us to resume business after the war without getting anyone's approval. New York rejected the offer with the offensive comment that "we won't want to come back." Hispano Americano formally took over our banks on Friday, December 5th, 1941, two days before Pearl Harbor, and in New York everybody congratulated the overseas division for getting out of Spain in time, because it was generally believed that Franco would come in on the side of the Axis. But Franco was too smart for that.

In 1950, the United States made a deal with Franco to open military bases in Spain, and we applied to reopen our branches, hoping to get some of the business that would flow from the camps. The Spanish authorities approved the application, assuming it was some sort of quid pro quo for the large expenditures Americans were making in Spain as part of the military deal. But the Fed refused our application. We were told that an assistant secretary of defense who had been a director of Bankers Trust, and didn't want to help City Bank, said to the Fed that Defense wanted to deal with Spanish banks for public relations reasons. Once the Spanish banks had that business, they didn't want to lose it, and we couldn't get in. The Bank of Spain said our applications would have to be approved by the Consejo Bancaria, something more or less like the Federal Advisory Council in the United States, and they finally refused approval.

When I was president in the 1960s I brought Stillman Rockefeller a proposal to buy the Banco Internacional de Commercio, then a fairly small operation with two branches. But Rockefeller said, "George, you've got a Spanish wife, you're prejudiced, biased for Spain, turn this over to someone else." And Wriston wasn't interested. Finally, in 1978, Spain opened up to foreign banks and we got a chance to own a branch again; and in 1983 the government virtually gave us (it wasn't worth much) the Banco de Levante, with seventy branches and more problems than branches. We renamed it Citibank Espaãna, and it flourishes. My estimate of the potential earnings we lost by that foolish telegram to Moreno in 1941, based on the growth of our profits elsewhere in Europe, runs up as high as half a billion dollars.

The moral of this story is that you should never close a foreign office if you can possibly keep it open. Leave a shell, a token, to keep your options open and your franchise available, just in case. City Bank did just that in a domestic situation, when we sold the operations of the IBC Edge Act bank in California to Wells Fargo in 1931, but kept the shell in being, paying a few dollars a year in state franchise taxes, and keeping a nominal time deposit of $300,000 in the company. One day while I was executive vice-president in charge of the overseas division, the then controller came to me to tell me he was closing down this San Francisco "bank" that did no business and cost us tax money. I told him he didn't have the authority to do that, it was a policy decision. We then made a study and decided that although our San Francisco correspondents would complain, we should reactivate the business. After all, Bank of America had an Edge Act in New York, which occupied the splendid old Lee & Higginson banking floor on Broad Street and employed more than a thousand people. That Edge Act two decades later became the nucleus for the very large Citicorp presence on the West Coast. Yes, the law limits you to a trade-related "foreign" business at an Edge Act branch, but every company has people who travel abroad and need a little advice about business conditions there and maybe some traveler's checks . . .

Expansion into Latin America was an uphill battle. I remember one rather amusing incident when I brought to Sheperd for submission to the board of directors proposals to open two new City Bank branches, one in South Africa and one in Paraguay. IBC had been in South Africa years before, but had been chased out by Barclay's; this was to be a second try. Paraguay was virgin territory. Its banking business, such as it was, had been monopolized by the Bank of London and South America ("Bolsa"), which took two weeks to clear a Paraguayan check through its Buenos Aires offices. Sheperd looked over my proposals and said, "George, I like South Africa, that's a real country and a great banking market—but why do you want to go to Paraguay? That's a backward place." I said, "Yes, boss, but there are three thousand banking offices in South Africa, and we'll have to fight to make a profit. In Paraguay, banking services are very poor, competition doesn't exist, Bolsa is giving dreadful service. I want to do both."

We did. It took three years before we made a penny in South Africa, but the Paraguay branch earned back its capital in less than three years, and by the fifth year it was one of the more profitable smaller branches of the bank. We had half the total deposits in the country by then, and most of them didn't come from Bolsa: it was money that came out of the mattresses, very helpful to the country.

Our South African experience has been complicated and not always pleasant. The dinner I gave in Johannesberg to celebrate the opening of our branch was well attended by representatives of the South African government, but they were present with their own agenda. The finance minister responded to my toast by telling me City Bank was not welcome in South Africa, and they had accepted our application for a license only because they could see no legal way to refuse it. Barclay's local management not only pressured South African and British companies not to do business with us, but tried to interfere in our normal relations with U.S. companies. I finally became fed up, and told our London office to inform Barclay's senior management that we were angry enough about our treatment in South Africa to retaliate against them in the Caribbean and Panama, where we had the domi-

nant position and could make life hard for them. London said the South
African managers had been acting on their own initiative, which may
have been true, and that they would stop their antisocial behavior,
which they did.

In later years, we got on good terms with the South African government, but came under the gun from church groups in the United
States for our operations there. We had always ignored apartheid, and
had African employees in all our branches. We took the position in
meetings, and still do, that the foreign policy of the United States is
conducted by the president with the advice of the Congress, not by
banks. If the government wanted us out of South Africa, all it had to
do was say so; in the absence of such guidance, we did business where
we found it. People who wished to influence American activities in
South Africa should take their case to Washington, not to New York. I
will say that what is happening in South Africa has become more and
more distasteful, but it's the international political community, not the
international economic community, that must decide what is to be done
about it.

Some of our trouble with governments came not in exotic places
with tropical climates and socialist regimes but right next door, in
Canada. It was unfair as could be. The Canadians would not let us
open a branch or buy a bank in Canada, but they could operate virtually as they pleased in the United States, open agencies in any state
they wished, lend out all their deposits (from foreign accounts) without holding back anything to keep as interest-free reserves at the Federal Reserve, and pay depositors whatever interest rates they wished,
regardless of U.S. government controls.

While I was in charge of the overseas division, we had a cable one
day from the Venezuelan central bank asking us to quote our best rate
for the renewal of a $40-million time deposit they had in City Bank.
The most the Fed would let us pay was 3 percent, and that's what we
quoted. The next cable read, "Regret. Please pay $40 million to the
New York agency of the Bank of Nova Scotia." The following day at
our money committee meeting, Halsey Cook, our Wall Street district
vice-president, reported that our broker loans were down by $40 mil-
lion because Harris, Upham had paid us off with a transfer from the
Bank of Nova Scotia. The Canadian agency could afford to pay Venezuela more than we could and charge Harris, Upham less because it
didn't have to keep a reserve at the Fed. A study by the New York
Clearing House in the 1950s showed that the Canadian branches and

agencies had more money out in brokers' loans in New York than all the New York Banks combined.

Then the Netherlandische Bank decided to abandon international banking, and among the assets they put up for sale was the Mercantile Bank in Canada, with about $10 million in capital and $100 million in deposits. We bought it gleefully—and then the Canadian government changed the rules, passing a new foreign-banking law that would keep us from expanding. Canadian banks were allowed to have deposits totaling fifty times their capital, while we were restricted to less than twenty times ours and we weren't permitted to increase our capital. We complained about the discrimination in Washington, and we were ignored: every U.S. government is a patsy for Canada. When we tried to expand within the laws, doing business with Canadian companies that used our services in the United States, we found that their banks were telling them that if they borrowed from City Bank for their Canadian operations, their usual lines of credit would be canceled. That would be illegal in the United States under the antitrust laws, but it wasn't illegal in Canada.

Nevertheless, we rapidly grew to the limits the government had placed on us, because we were less stuffy than the big Canadian banks, more willing to lend to middle-sized Canadian companies, without as much paperwork, and without the clubby atmosphere that meant that if one Canadian bank turned you down you were dead everywhere. The government finally decided we served a purpose, and agreed to let us expand and increase our capital—on the condition (the sort of thing you expect in a banana republic, but the Canadians do it even better) that we sell stock in the bank *to Canadian nationals only*. We had $10 million of capital and surplus; they authorized another $10 million, to be sold only to Canadians, and later another addition on the same terms until City Bank's share was reduced to 25 percent. We did that, at a considerable profit, and Mercantile flourished until the early 1980s, when declines in energy and farm prices, and the collapse of a real estate boom, and worries about Latin loans, combined to put the entire Canadian banking enterprise in trouble. Mercantile had to be bailed out. By then, the banking laws had changed. Canadian branches in the United States no longer had their old advantages over the natives, and Citibank had its own separate Canadian branch, about as big as Mercantile—which, of course, did not need help from the Canadian government. There is some justice in the world.

Another branch that was troublesome to open and much resented by some local colleagues was our first Swiss branch, in Geneva. David Rockefeller specifically warned us against it, saying we would lose our valuable correspondent contacts in Switzerland, and when we opened we had a mixed reception. Alfred Schaefer of Union Bank of Switzerland, the original gnome of Zurich, told us we would never be accepted in Switzerland, but the chairman of his own bank, my friend Ernst Schmidheiny, made the first deposit in the branch. The government restricted us at first to twenty employees, on the grounds that the labor market was tight and without the restriction we would create a wage spiral in the banking business. So we farmed the clerical, secretarial, and bank operations work to outside services, and hired nothing but bankers. Eventually, they let the restrictions drop. Shortly after we opened our doors, David Rockefeller applied for a Swiss charter for Chase. Someone once once explained Chase's strategy in international banking in a single sentence: "They wait to see what Moore's doing, then they copy it."

6

This is what happened. The history is true and important. Moreover, it is most of what we knew while we were building this new world. Our policy at City Bank was to grow and make money, not to change the international economy. And we did make money—we went from net red to profits in the hundreds of millions of dollars a year. But we also had a profound influence on how the world economy developed. We pioneered new *kinds* of international banking, which led to new money flows and new relations among economies and societies. Questions that seemed just practical when we were working on them— should we have branches abroad or acquire affiliates? should we fund the bank in the United States or develop the new "Euro-markets?— really had deeper meanings that our answers brought to light over time. The official historians of Citibank described me and the people I brought to the overseas division as "change agents." We were that, all right. We changed more than we knew.

8

The International Focus: Banking and Money, Debt and Development

When I first went to Mexico in the 1930s, National City Bank was the third largest in the country. Banco Nacional had about $400 million in deposits, Banco di Commercio had about $200 million, and we had about $170 million. When I was making trips there in the 1950s—which was fairly often—Mexico was one of the few stars in our foreign constellation, and National City was still a ponderable factor in that nation's economy. We were in fact the *only* foreign company allowed to operate a bank in Mexico. Our exclusivity traced back to the 1920s, when all the other foreign-owned banks in Mexico cut and ran to escape Obregón's revolution, and we remained. So when they wrote the new banking laws, they specified that National City Bank could continue to operate in Mexico but no other foreign bank would be permitted.

This was a valuable franchise after World War II, for Mexico's economy grew rapidly, and so did the opportunities of our seven Mexican branches. Our people complained when I visited that we in New York were holding them down. They couldn't increase their deposits because the Mexican government insisted on a minimum ratio of capital to deposits, they were bumping the ceiling, and New York was refusing to commit additional capital, even though the branches were profitable. As the law stood in the 1950s, we could even have opened new branches, and grown geographically as well as financially. But Stillman Rockefeller didn't really like Mexico, and he held us down on capital. By the time New York wanted to encourage our Mexican business, the laws and policies had changed, and we were stuck with what we had. Today, Citibank branches account for less than 2 percent of Mexican deposits. On the other hand, thanks to the 1928 law, we are now the only privately owned bank in Mexico, not just the only foreign bank, for all the Mexican-owned banks were nationalized in 1982.

Since 1981, there has been much agitation about Mexican debt, and a lot of hand-wringing about the inability of Mexican borrowers to pay back the dollars they owe. National City in my time didn't have and couldn't have had this problem, because few borrowers in Mexico owed dollars. They owed pesos. Our Mexican branches were not permitted by law to have dollar-denominated deposits, and neither they nor head office made many dollar-denominated loans to foreigners. When our American customers arranged credit to help Mexican importers of their merchandise, we lent pesos to the Mexicans, and bought the foreign exchange on the spot market to pay the American manufacturer, leaving us with a peso-denominated asset that would be collected in pesos. It was possible for New York to lend dollars to a Mexican company operating in Mexico (as we did to the Mexican subsidiary of Sears), but such loans would be decided upon and booked in New York rather than in Mexico, and as a practical matter they were made only when the borrower had a source of dollar earnings outside Mexico to use in repaying the loan.

The initial capital we put into the Mexican branches was dollars, most of which we used to buy the property in which the branches operated, but thereafter we expected these banks to live as Mexican banks. They might have dollar holdings as a result of their foreign-exchange trading, but like Mexican banks they had to report such holdings to the Mexican central bank every day. I remember one occasion when the Mexican government devalued the peso after the close of the business day, and slipped a note under the doors of our branches to say that the central bank had taken over our "excess position" in dollars at the closing rate that afternoon, to keep us from making a profit on the newly increased exchange value of the dollar.

City Bank was virtuous as well as wise in expanding its foreign branches: they were good for the host country, for the United States, for the local and American and other businesses that used the facilities, and for us. Money came out of the mattresses and into the economy when a branch of an American bank opened, and many foreigners became more interested in doing business in a country where there was a branch of an American bank. There's hardly a business that went to Mexico or Brazil in my time that we didn't have a catalytic influence on. Nothing did more to promote American *and* European *and* Japanese investment in Mexico and other Latin American countries than the comforting and constantly useful presence of an American bank.

We found local agents to help exporters sell their products. We lent the local currency to enable their customers to buy, and handled the foreign-exchange transaction so they could take their receipts and profits home in dollars. We introduced them to the right people and protected them from the wrong people when they decided to become manufacturers in Mexico and Brazil. We helped them find partners, if they wanted partners. We saw to it that their timing was right. Sears was going to Brazil for the first time, buying a piece of property in São Paulo, paying for it with cruzeiros they were acquiring from Continental Illinois. Someone at Sears called me, and asked if I had any suggestions. I said, "God, no—our people say there's going to be a devaluation tomorrow." Continental Illinois had no way to know that: they didn't have anybody in Brazil in those days. The cruzeiros they were selling Sears, in fact, they had bought from us.

Those were our roles in a number of countries around the world, and at bottom that's still what an international bank does. Even today, a man is unwise to do business in Brazil or the Philippines, for example, without consulting Citibank. The Brazilian-American Chamber of Commerce in 1970 began making an annual award to the Brazilian and the American who had done the most that year to further relations between the two nations. The first awards went to planning minister Delfim Netto and myself.

Branches help each other. Every one we opened became a source of information for companies in other countries. For years we sent out periodic newsletters, with information about economic developments in foreign countries, gathered at our branches. While I was still a lending officer in the domestic division, we formalized these newsletters into what we called the Foreign Information Service, a loose-leaf book with tabs for each country, so that the bulletins would be filed where they could be found. Once the jet plane made it possible for people from the overseas branches to be in and out of New York, these reports included branch officers' schedules of visits, so those doing export or import business with a country where we had a branch could take a trip to New York instead of a trip abroad to get their information from the horse's mouth. Sometimes these foreign branch officers traveled with calling officers on their U.S. calls. At the end of each year we sent customers a new book, with last year's summary sheets in place. You couldn't get that book or those bulletins unless you were a customer of City Bank; it was a great sales tool for us.

While we were building City Bank's overseas division there was a standing dispute in the banking world between people who wanted to expand by branching and people who wanted to expand by acquiring existing banks. We favored branches rather than acquisitions. When you buy a bank abroad, you often find the owner has all his relatives working for him. The bookkeeping is not easy to understand; the auditors have trouble figuring out what you bought. There are often loans to the owner and his relatives. When your new partners come to New York, you have to take them out to the best restaurants and to the opera. (Of course, this can happen to you with domestic customers, too. I remember that during the 1939 New York World's Fair, when City Bank gave guest tickets to visitors and their families, Heber J. Grant, the head of the Mormon Church, came to New York. Perkins asked him if he was going to the fair, and offered him a pass to the club there. We asked how many were in his family, and he said, "Thirty-eight," and our controller almost jumped out the window when I called, for the passes cost us ten dollars each.) In many countries a domestically chartered subsidiary could do more kinds of business than the local government would permit for a branch of a foreign bank. But those extra powers didn't give us enough to be worth the inflexibility and the nuisance.

And we were right. No question about it. Branches were better than subsidiaries. Our competitors had little choice. Arriving later than we did, they found it difficult to get permission to open branches, and often had to acquire a local institution (usually paying more than it was worth) to establish their presence. What I learned only after the local banks had been picked over by those competitors was that opening branches and buying local banks are not mutually exclusive. We do both in a score of countries these days, including Spain, where Citicorp in 1983 took over the troubled Banco Levante, all eighty offices of it, changed its name to Citibank España but keeps it separate from our branch. The branch does mostly an internationally oriented business to Fortune 500 companies and European equivalents, and the subsidiary does a local business. The governments like it that way, too. Before we learned this lesson, however, we lost some opportunities. We let Chase acquire the Mercantile, the best bank in Venezuela, which had been offered to us, and we failed to acquire Banco d'Italia, Giannini's old bank in Italy, at a stage in the Italian economic miracle when it was worth more than its numbers.

In the end, we learned, and acquired a number of foreign banks— Trinkhaus in Germany, for example, which Citicorp sold off a few years ago, unwisely in my view. As noted, we got into Canada through buying Mercantile from the Dutch. In 1965, we bought half of Grindlay's Bank, a substantial merchant banking business with offices in Asia, the Middle East, and Africa. This started out as an informal lunch at the bank, where Wriston and I entertained Toby Aldington, CEO of Grindlay's, which was owned by Lloyd's, one of the then five (now four) big British "clearing banks." I asked Aldington what his game plan was for Grindlay's, and he said he was on his way to a meeting with David Rockefeller at Chase that afternoon. He was doing business in relatively high-risk developing countries, and he had only $50 million of capital against $1.5 billion of deposits. Lloyd's had agreed to let him increase the capital by selling 50 percent of the common stock, at book value. This would be double the capital of the bank. He was going to Chase to offer them the stock.

We told Lord Aldington that City Bank would be interested in half of Grindlay's on that basis. Why was he going to Chase? Well, he said, they had thought of us but decided we wouldn't really want what he was offering. In most of Grindlay's locations, there was a City Bank branch already in place across the street or around the corner. We said he was wrong. His customers were Dunlop, Shell Oil, Imperial Chemical; ours included Firestone, Esso, and Du Pont. His bank, because it had absorbed the State Bank of India, had 15 percent of the rupee deposits in the country, and despite our sixty-five years there we had perhaps 1 percent of the rupee deposits. His customers needed dollars, and ours needed rupees. We more or less made the deal at lunch, a 50 percent interest for 50 percent of book value, and Aldington called Rockefeller to cancel his appointment. It's possible that before reading these pages, David never knew why Lord Aldington had made an appointment with him, or why he canceled it.

Lord Aldington came on the City Bank board, where he was a wise counselor, but the Lloyd's partnership was not happy. They didn't see eye to eye with us on a number of matters, lacked our aggressive attitudes, and in general held us back. There was a movement in City Bank to sell back the half-share to Lloyd's, but we hung on and finally we were able to buy Lloyd's interest. Then we sold Grindlay's to a bank in Australia. This was after my retirement, and I wouldn't have done it—I think: I'm not in touch with the Citibank game plan these days, and if they think they can cover the same bases with our own offices I'm not in a position to quarrel about it.

2

It was during my time at the bank that dollar lending to overseas customers first became a significant part of our activities. Everyone around the world was short of dollars, wanted dollars, regardless of the risks to both lender and borrower. Governments borrowed dollars themselves, and encouraged companies to borrow dollars as a way to fund their domestic investments. When governments borrowed, the central bank often booked the loan in its own currency, which helped the country's reported balance-of-payments figures; for the international statisticians, the loan became another mysterious entry in the "errors and omissions" column. Dollar-denominated loans to local enterprises, which the borrower would put into the local central back for conversion to the local currency, provided foreign reserves to the country. Sometimes, but much more frequently after my days at the bank, a country would borrow abroad rather than print money or borrow at home to cover its government budget deficit—something the United States has in effect been doing, it should be noted, all through the 1980s. When the OPEC bubble appeared in 1973–74, of course, most countries had to borrow dollars to buy oil, because the oil producers wouldn't sell in other currencies (until 1976 the Saudis did take pounds sterling, but even then they preferred dollars, and after 1976 it was no-dollars-no-oil).

Usually, dollar loans were not made by the branches, because they weren't allowed to have dollar deposits. Dollar loans were made from New York. But of course the branches were invaluable sources of information on the credit-worthiness of foreign borrowers and foreign countries. New York might make the loan to, say, Mexico's Gruppo Alfa, but only with the assistance of the Mexican branches. The availability of dollar loans from headquarters was valuable to the branches in their dealings with their Mexican customers. They had two violins to play, pesos and dollars; their local competitors had only pesos, and their international competitors had only dollars.

Branches lending in pesos or pounds or Swiss francs raised their own funds in those currencies and could, within limits, make their own decisions. As time went on, and the dollar markets abroad expanded, a branch might also make a contribution to funding dollar loans to the country where it was located, or to other countries. It became routine for London to find dollars for loans anywhere in the world. By my last years in the bank, in fact, there was nothing unusual about a transaction that brought dollars back from Europe to meet our domestic funding requirements. But all the books on dollar funding and dollar lending had to be kept in New York, because that affected the bank worldwide, and there was a limit to the decision-making authority that could be left in the field.

The "Eurodollar" market was a strange invention. It was started after World War II, I've been told, by the Russians, who wanted to keep their reserves denominated in dollars but were reluctant to have their money where the Americans could block it. This wouldn't have been the first time the U.S. government had stopped payment on foreigners' checks. During World War II, we had frozen the accounts of the Swiss banks in the United States when they wouldn't identify the actual depositor (because we feared the money might be German). Then, in the mid-1950s, there came the development of the European Payments Union, with $350 million in Marshall Plan money set aside to serve as the backup for trading denominated in a "currency unit" that happened to be defined as having the same value as the dollar. In 1956, Arab deposits in the United States were frozen briefly as part of the American reaction to the British-French-Israeli invasion of Suez, which gave the Saudis a reason to want to hold their dollars elsewhere, and the next year the British made the pound even more inconvertible than it had been before, which gave the dollar another boost. There were certain advantages for American banks in doing a dollar business abroad as against keeping it all in the United States. You could use all the money—there were no reserve requirements for deposits on the books of foreign banks and foreign branches. You didn't have to pay deposit insurance premiums. And when you needed dollars, you could bid for them—the Fed's Regulation Q controls over interest rates didn't apply abroad.

Then the Kennedy administration, not intending the consequences it achieved, made the Eurodollar market irresistible for American banks by putting an "interest equalization tax" on dollars lent from the United States to foreign borrowers. The administration couldn't tax loans made abroad, however, whatever the currency, because the United States government can't write laws that apply outside its jurisdiction (though sometimes we try—anti-trust, insider trading, and corrupt-practices acts come to mind). And if they had tried to tax American banks on their dollar loans regardless of where they were made, the upshot of it would have been that foreign banks would have done all the dollar business overseas. This was a truly free market. My good friend Milton Gilbert when he was chief economist for the Bank for International Settlements in Basle used to grumble about the way banks got around regulation in the Euromarkets, and to suggest that the central banks find a way to control the Eurodollar market. I said that if they did that, the market would move to the moon!

In looking at these dollar loans to foreigners, I had one advantage over my successors at the bank: I remembered the German standstill agreement of the 1930s. Dollar loans, after all, were not something invented in the 1950s. During World War I, the people and the government of the United States had made large loans to the Allied powers, building up the famous "war debt," which a lot of Americans foolishly believed would make everybody in the United States rich when the foreigners paid it back. And during the 1920s, it became obvious even to the French that there could never be a peaceful and prosperous Europe without the recovery of the German economy (which was necessary, too, so the Germans could pay their "war reparations" to France, enabling the French to pay their war debt to the United States: it all sounds peculiar now, but it was taken very seriously then). A series of plans—the Dawes Plan, the Young Plan (which also formed the Bank for International Settlements)—envisioned dollar loans to German enterprise to help rebuild that economy and take the World War I debt monkey off everyone's back, losers and winners alike.

National City, as the largest American bank active in Europe, was inevitably the largest lender to German companies and municipalities, and those loans were in dollars. This was in the days of the Weimar Republic, before Hitler. With other American banks, we also provided a great deal of "trade credits," loans that enabled manufacturers and vendors in our country and in Germany to sell to each other. Many of these loans were in the form of "banker's acceptances," which meant that we had accepted the promise of the German importer's bank to pay us in dollars for goods one of our customers was shipping to Germany. The German bank would get its dollars by selling gold, then the universal means of settling debts between currencies. In the great crisis of 1931, the world joined together to preserve the rapidly declining gold stock of the Reichsbank, the German central bank, and one of the contributions of the commercial banks was an agreed-upon "standstill," which would permit the Germans to continue to owe dollars. The essence of the situation was that our debtors in Germany were not broke, they could pay their bills—but only in marks, which were no use to us. Germany lacked the reserves of gold or foreign currency to repay the dollars we had loaned. There were large amounts involved—for City Bank in 1933, about $95 million (counting $7 million or so we had acquired when we bought the New York Bank of America). This was more than the bank's reduced capital of $77.5 million, after Perkins's "clean-up."

When Hitler came, the Reichsmark was declared "inconvertible." We had been able to get some dollars out in 1932, and the debt subject to "standstill" in 1934, when Perkins took a trip to Germany to see first-hand what was happening, was about $43 million. Unlike some visitors to Germany in 1934 (Geoffrey Crowther, editor of the *Economist* and later of the *Times* of London, was deeply enthusiastic about how the German people were rallying around their führer), Perkins thought Germany a bad sovereign risk. Schacht, the head of the German central bank, who wanted to pay the debt, offered a way out. Foreigners traveling in Germany needed marks, and were not allowed to buy them abroad and take them in. So foreign banks were allowed to sell "travel marks" to foreigners inside Germany, and the foreigners, of course, paid for these travel marks with dollars and pounds and convertible French or Swiss francs. As there was an oversupply of marks to be sold for foreign currency, the "travel mark" sold at a 30 percent discount from the official exchange rate, which meant that we had to take a bookkeeping loss every time were converted some of our German assets by these means. Perkins ordered our Berlin branch to go full speed ahead selling travel marks, and by the time World War II broke out we had disposed of most of our German assets.

That was half a century ago, and it seems longer. Today virtually every country with paved roads wants to earn foreign exchange through tourism, and it's an impossibly strange idea that a nation would deliberately and directly allocate the foreign-currency earnings of its tourist industry. (I'm sure that if Hitler hadn't been economically illiterate, and had known what Schacht was doing, he'd have killed the plan.) One great lesson from the standstill agreement, however, remains valid today and will be valid forever: when you make a cross-currency loan—when you lend in dollars to people who do business and have their assets and cash flow in pesos or cruzeiros or dinar—you are lending not to the private borrower or even the state agency that signs the loan papers, but to the central bank of that country. Our Mexican and Brazilian branches, lending in pesos and cruzeiros to local business or even to the government, and funding their loans with local peso and cruzeiro deposits, had a diversified portfolio, and could judge the risks of each loan individually. Lending to some of the same borrowers in dollars from head office did not provide a diversified portfolio, because only the central bank could provide the dollars to repay us.

For these reasons, while I was president and chairman of the bank, we had a "sovereign risk" limit on dollar loans to borrowers in foreign countries (private and public combined). We set the same limit here that we had on loans to a big borrower in the United States—10 percent of our capital. The exceptions were for Britain and Germany and Japan (where the limit was 20 percent). These limits did not apply to self-liquidating trade loans guaranteed by our Ex-Im (Export-Import) Bank, or loans to local subsidiaries of multinational companies with their own source of dollars, when they would agree to guarantee the credit. (In other words, a dollar loan to General Motors Brazil guaranteed by General Motors could be charged against the bank's total exposure to General Motors rather than Brazil's sovereign limit.) Usually, the experienced international companies borrowed in local currency, not in dollars, with a parent company guarantee. This guarantee was often informal: if you put it in writing, the local government could say the subsidiary didn't have enough capital to stand on its own feet.

My successors faced problems that were different from mine, for I retired before OPEC unbalanced the economic world, and I don't criticize them. The banks were not the villains of the piece in the 1970s when they so dramatically expanded their loans to the developing countries—they were the heroes, for without those loans those countries and the international trading system might have collapsed. Despite all the gloom, many of those loans are going to work out, for reasons we shall discuss in Chapter 12. I'd have few worries, for example, about loans to Brazil. U.S. Steel tells me they can produce steel ingots in Brazil for two hundred dollars a ton less than it costs here, and my friends in the timber business tell me that Brazil can ship wood pulp at three hundred dollars a ton or less, when it costs five hundred dollars in Norway and Finland, and more than that in the United States

and Canada. Brazil will earn its way out of its debt. Even the least
likely debtors may do much better than anyone expects. I've seen real
basket cases not just get out of their baskets and walk, but dance away
from their troubles. Spain was considered weak in 1960, when it joined
the IMF and first adopted sensible economic policies; then, after swal-
lowing its bitter pill, the country grew for seventeen years at an average rate of better than 8.6 percent a year. The problems of development
are not difficult if you've got hard-working people, capital, and trade,
and you encourage foreign investment, as Spain always has.

3

Lending to developing countries is like going out onto a big swamp.
There are soft places out there, and if you don't have the right team,
you're going to sink. Like any money, the proceeds of a loan can be
completely wasted, or spent in ways that do nothing to generate the
income that will be necessary to pay it back. I remember that sometime in the mid-1960s, when we were disbursing dollar loans to Mexico, I saw a jump in the dollars Mexican depositors had on account
with us, and with other banks as reported weekly by the Federal Reserve.
These days we would call that sort of thing "capital flight," but we
didn't have such fancy terms then. I remember talking once with my
old friend Rodrigo Gomez, the president of the Bank of Mexico, about
the possibility that Mexico might impose exchange controls. "Ah,
George," he said, "we can't. The border is too long and the people are
too crooked."

It's important not to be sloppy, both for lenders and for borrowers.
When the central bank has approved dollar borrowings by its companies and agencies—and it should be remembered that in the years
since World War II the United States is the *only* country where companies have always been permitted to borrow foreign currencies without the approval of the central bank—it's incumbent upon that central
bank to help assure that the money is used productively. No question
there have been more failures than there should have been, and also
that the information the banks had from the developing countries was
too late and insufficiently accurate. But year after year City Bank made
30 percent and more on the capital allocated to overseas banking and
overseas lending, because where the risks are greater the rewards are
greater, too. And it was always a less risky activity for us, because we
had our own banks on the spot, and so we had a better chance to know
what was going on.

Remember, too, that this is no a parlor game, or a way for a bunch of bankers sitting around offices to make a lot of money. There is no political or human question in the world more important than the economic development of places like Latin America, Africa, the Pacific rim, and the Indian subcontinent. Most of the people in the world live there, and they live badly. Since we brought them the blessings of public health, their numbers have been growing at a rate of 2 to 3 percent a year, which means that there are twice as many people in these countries every thirty years. Badly as they live now, they will live even worse unless their economies can grow at a rate of 3 percent or more—and most of them expect to and are entitled to live better than they do today. The rule of thumb is that you have to invest five dollars for every dollar of growth in your annual production, and these people don't have the margin that permits them to save enough themselves. So they have to tap other people's savings, they have to recruit loans and investments from foreigners, or their children's lives will be no better than theirs and quite possibly worse. It's also true that confidence begins at home, and that in successfully developing economies it usually turns out that three-quarters of the new investment is locally financed. But even a Brazil, which has the best record of confidence and local investment, needs foreign capital.

Everybody knows all this, but many learned discussions about "international debt" these days seem to forget that what we're talking about is development, just as the learned discussions at the UN and in the universities in the 1960s and 1970s forgot when they talked about development that the only way to increase a nation's GNP is by attracting foreign loans and investments. The United Nations would hold two-week meetings of UNCTAD, its Council on Trade and Development, without anyone ever mentioning anything so vulgar as paying back debts or compensating investors. In those days, I was a member of an "advisory board" for the School of International Affairs at Columbia University, where professors came and presented papers that built mushy towers of political rhetoric without ever connecting those towers to the real ground of human production and consumption. Once when the government reduced the funding for these studies, the School of International Affairs came to me and asked whether I could intervene in Washington to help them get their grants back, and was very surprised when I said, "No." It isn't only Third World governments that waste their money.

I became specifically involved in Latin American economic development in 1962, when a delegation of Latin business leaders stopped in New York on their way to a meeting of the Pan American Union in Washington, and asked to meet with Rockefeller and Wriston and me. There were about fifteen of them, and they brought us a message. Latin America was on fire. Our government was talking about that fire, but doing nothing effective to put it out. These Latins felt that the United States had a variety of policies that nobody coordinated. State had one, Treasury another, Commerce yet another, the Ex-Im Bank still another; the military had its own agenda, and the White House lived in another world entirely. In the private sector, there was the U.S. Chamber of Commerce and the International Chamber of Commerce, the Conference Board, the Committee for Economic Development, the Pan American Society, and others. Latins were forever being invited to meetings to tell their story, and the only thing that would happen afterward was that they would be invited to another meeting. It was late in the day. If American businessmen didn't pull some sort of policy together from this chaos, and bring the government along, we were going to have to deal with the consequences of an explosion to our south.

They were right. Our group in New York agreed to center our activities dealing with Latin America under the umbrella of a single organization, which we decided to call the Council for Latin America. The other private-sector organizations concerned with Latin America would be told, politely but firmly, that American business would deal with these matters *only* through this council. David Rockefeller agreed to be its chairman. I agreed to accept the post of president of CICYP, the International Council for Commerce and Production, an organization that was in being but not in doing, though it had branches in all the larger South American countries. (The Council for Latin America became the U.S. member of CICYP.) We went to see President Kennedy, and told him that we wanted to coordinate our activities with his Alliance for Progress. He was all for that, and asked Averell Harriman, who was then undersecretary of state, to bring us into the process of formulating U.S. aid policies for the area. After Kennedy was assassinated, Lyndon Johnson confirmed the council and CICYP as central to his Latin-American planning.

The idea of CICYP was that American business speaking with one voice could effectively influence policy in Latin America. There is, after all, no mystery about how you get foreigners to invest in your country. You give them a business opportunity, a stable rule of law affecting property and economic activity, fair taxes, labor laws that encourage people to do a day's work for a day's pay, and a fiscal policy that gives some reason to believe that inflation will not destroy the value of financial assets. That's what local investors need, too, and it's almost always true that foreign investment is most successful where local investment is available and also prospers. Often, the great service performed by a foreign investors is that his project generates local investment of five or ten times as much as what he puts in himself.

It's also desirable to have rules that permit investors to repatriate their profits, but most commentators put too much weight on that. Businessmen don't normally regard their investment in a developing country as a one-shot that has to be recouped as quickly as possible. Abroad as at home, they are hoping that the seeds they plant will grow, which usually means reinvesting profits and even adding to the initial capitalization. Of course, if they think there's a danger that they'll be expropriated or their assets will be blocked, they'll keep looking for a way out. But if you give them a reasonably free market to work in, and an environment that produces success, they won't keep looking around for exits. It's also useful if officials don't have their hands out for bribes.

If Ford came down and said this to, say, General Perón, the first thought he and his statist advisers and the military would have would be, Never mind Ford, we can make a deal with Chrysler. But if CICYP came down and advised that these were the ground rules for investment, Perón would know that he'd have to shape up or do without. That didn't mean we expected to go south and give governments orders. I'd been dealing with Latins long enough to know you can't do that. In fact, you can't even say No to them, just as they can't say No to you. Instead, you say, Mañana, and when Mañana comes you say Mañana again. No party to the negotiations has ever said No, it's just that when the other fellow calls he gets a busy signal. During my time at CICYP, Bolivia defaulted on obligations to the owners of the pipeline running to Argentina. They had some projects pending with the World Bank, which had a minor involvement in the pipeline. The Bank simply put the papers in the bottom drawer until they took care of the pipeline debt. Peru had the same experience when dealing with some foreign investors; the Peruvians came to me and complained that nobody ever returned their phone calls. That's the mañana game.

At best, CICYP was a catalyst, bringing in money from others, making the Alliance for Progress more effective. There was more to be done. Senator Jacob Javits invited me to breakfast in the Senate dining room and said to me, in effect, "The time has come for you business-men to put your money where your mouth is." He was a leading mem-ber of a group called the "NATO Parliamentarians," who met in hopes of coordinating their countries' policies in various areas. They'd had a meeting on Latin America, and had decided to lean on the business communities of the NATO countries to form what Jack named "Adela"—an acronym for "Atlantic Development Group for Latin America." This would be a merchant bank to provide venture capital to new or grow-ing Latin American business. Because its stockholders would be some of the biggest businesses in the world, it would have standing and publicity, and its success would serve as an inducement and a model for other investors. Javits put together a "core group" including Henry Ford, Tom Watson of IBM, myself, Pete Collado of Exxon, and Giov-anni Agnelli of Fiat.

Our first stop was Europe, with an American delegation that included me, Javits, Collado, Arthur Dean of the law firm of Sullivan & Cromwell, Gil Jones for IBM, and Walter McKee for Henry Ford. We met in Paris at the offices of the Banque de Paris et des Pays-Bas, with about a hundred bankers and industrialists from all over Europe. Jean Reyre, the tough-minded boss of Paribas, in effect threw a glove in my face, asking me why I thought ADELA could get anything accomplished. I was tired, having come right off the overnight flight to the meeting, and not in a mood to be badgered. I said forcefully that I wasn't in the habit of working this hard, living with all the inconve-nience this meeting offered, in order to invest a lousy half-million dol-lars of Citibank money. If Citibank, Esso, Ford, IBM, and Fiat were ready to put up half a million dollars each and participate in the over-sight of a venture capital project, others should pay attention. If the day came when companies like these couldn't successfully supervise development projects, we might as well go out of business. We were used to problems. Most of those at the meeting signed up, put in money, and joined the board. So did a number of Canadian banks and com-panies, and some Japanese. But not the French—de Gaulle turned it down.

I thought it would be best not to have an American at the head of ADELA, and I asked Marcus Wallenberg to be chairman. He said he was very busy. As it happened, City Bank was then working with Wal-lenberg's Enskilda Bank of Stockholm on a whole bunch of problems. I had just got Metropolitan Life to finance Boeings for SAS, of which Wallenberg was chairman, and we were helping his Grangesberg min-

ing company build a railroad as well as a mine and a company town in
Liberia, there were problems with a paper mill and a shipping company and an expansion of L. M. Ericsson. I said that if Wallenberg
couldn't help me in Latin America, I'd be out to lunch when he wanted
help elsewhere in the world. He accepted the job, and he kept his
bargain: he came to the meetings and met with the heads of state, and
as an aristocrat, a Swede, and a most successful businessman, he was
very effective. He wasn't, of course, the active head of the organization. That was Ernst Keller, who had run the W. R. Grace operation in
Peru before going off more or less on his own and compiling an admirable history of starting successful businesses in Latin America. Ted
Seiler of the Swiss bank Corporation introduced us to him.

As I write these words, more than two decades later, ADELA is
about to be buried, and the word on the street is that it was a failure.
A number of the original sponsors were called on in the 1970s to throw
in additional capital to keep the scheme afloat, and they resented it.
Now that the organization is essentially dead, they resent it even more.
But the fact is that in its first ten years Adela was a great success. It
lent or invested about $200 million, for projects that drew a total
investment of $2 billion, at least half of it local and some small part of
it from official lenders like the International Finance Corporation of
the World Bank, the Inter-American Development Bank, the U.S.
Export-Import bank, and some others. Few if any of these projects
would have been created without the startup help of ADELA and its
direct subsidiary Adelatech. A few of them were gold mines, most
notably, perhaps, the Brazilian mass-market shoemaker Alpargatas,
which ADELA launched and eventually sold off to Brazilian investors
at a handsome profit. Though Keller kept his head office in Peru, his
projects were significant in all the larger South American countries,
especially Argentina, Brazil, Mexico, and Venezuela, where he started
branch offices. In all of them, he proved our principle: it was possible
to invest and make money in Latin American ventures. With help from
Wallenberg and from CICYP, Keller was especially effective at getting
laws and attitudes changed to make countries more hospitable to foreign investment.

What happened was partly that both CICYP and ADELA simply
ran down with the passage of time. I could persuade the Edgar Kaisers
and Henry Fords to come, bring with me David Rockefeller, Bob Tyson
of U.S. Steel, Jack Javits; but as time went on there was nobody strongly
involved who had my clout, and soon the only people who went to the

meetings were the professional meeting-goers—and Moore, who had retired from Citicorp. But the board was always too big—we might get fifty people at a meeting, which meant that the meeting became an excuse to go to an exotic place and eat in good restaurants and see exotic things. Nobody supervised Keller. When you asked him a hard question, he gave you a blizzard of facts from which you could never make even a snowman's worth of real information. He was a good businessman, and had an eye for new ventures, but he wasn't a banker at all and he began doing a banking business.

With the top banks and Exxon and Ford behind it, ADELA's credit was absolutely top-drawer, and he could borrow money cheap. By lending it on at a considerable spread over his cost, he made enough money to support what became no fewer than twelve offices with five hundred employees. I found he was making loans the local Citibank branches had turned down. He was borrowing short to lend long: if rates rose, as they did, he was going to be squeezed. And he wasn't diversified: he had more than the total capital of ADELA in Peru alone. I gave speeches at board meetings, but there weren't many bankers on the board, and to businessmen without banking background, Keller's figures and "facts" looked good. There was a succession of chairmen after Wallenberg, but none could control the staff. Earl McLaughlin, chairman of the Royal Bank of Canada, a tough banker by any standards, undertook the job, but he couldn't plug all the holes. I went around and passed the hat for ADELA one last time—especially with Al Costanzo of Citibank—but ADELA's sun had set.

PICA—The Private Investment Company for Asia— was modeled on ADELA, which should be evidence enough that he ADELA concept looked triumphant for a number of years. Its strongest advocates were the Japanese bankers and industrialists who participated in ADELA, especially Yoshizane Iwasa of Fuji Bank, the dean of Japanese banking, and at the beginning there was even some thought of bringing Keller in as a consultant to help get it started. The idea was the same— a professionally managed merchant bank to promote and assist private investment in Asia. The execution, however, was never entirely satisfactory. The Japanese took the lead (this was their back yard, as Latin America was ours), but were even less willing to supply the personnel, didn't want to look aggressive. Where we had Wallenberg and Keller, however, they wound up with an old British Empire hand who was not, in fact, competent to run the enterprise. Headquarters was in Singapore, but, as with Keller, offices sprouted everywhere.

I left the PICA board at about the same time that I left ADELA, but they brought me back in the early 1980s to be part of an advisory group that would meet once a year with the executive committee. The only meeting I attended was one in Madrid in 1982, where I was impressed by the directors' attention to detail. My old friend Tadayoshi Yamada, for example, a vice-president of Nippon Steel, criticized the management for failing to maintain a "square" foreign-exchange position and risking PICA's assets in what came out to be (though it wasn't intended to be) currency speculation. The manager explained rather superciliously that these foreign-exchange things were complicated, when you were dealing in so many currencies it was difficult to keep a square position in all of them, and Yamada interrupted him: "At Nippon Steel we deal in more currencies than you do, and we square our position every night. I was not giving you a suggestion, I was giving you an order." PICA changed its procedures.

But when Marcos got in trouble, it developed that PICA had committed more than 150 percent of its capital to loans in the Philippines, where the proceeds from even the few good ones were blocked. And there were bad loans elsewhere. The board called in Lazard Frères, whose partner Stanley Osborne had been chairman of PICA's board in earlier years (he retired about the time I did), and the bankers finally recommended an unhappy solution, selling off the assets to a strong Australian banking conglomerate on a basis that yielded the original shareholders about thirty cents on the dollar originally invested.

There are cheerful, useful, and sad lessons to be drawn from the ADELA and PICA experiences. The cheerful lesson is that venture-capital firms can successfully operate even in contexts as inhospitable as Latin America in the late 1960s and 1970s, when statist attitudes toward economic development were in full flower. PICA was remarkably successful: all but a dozen of its two hundred investments made money—but bad banking loans put it under. That was the useful lesson, that venturing and banking are very different businesses and should not be mixed—less because the dangerous ventures will drag down the bank, which is what most commentators think, than because the inability of ventures to understand banking will saddle the organization with too many unacceptable banking risks. The sad lesson was that "consortium" banking is not viable: big boards of directors and diffuse authority make losses worse and prevent timely profit-taking. Everybody's business is nobody's business. Nearly all the private consortium banks that seemed to flourish in the 1970s are now in process of liquidation. My hunch is that the Australians will make PICA successful again, because they'll run it as an enterprise, which was the original intention.

4

All international banking was handicapped in my years as president of City Bank by the accelerating collapse of the monetary "regime" established in the Bretton Woods Conference of 1944. This meeting created the International Monetary Fund and the World Bank, and thought it had also created an international organization for world trade, but that one never got out of committee in the Congress. What it really created was a world currency system in which the dollar was linked to gold and all other currencies were linked to the dollar. Having raised the price of gold in the second year of Franklin Roosevelt's New Deal, and having collected in gold for much of what it supplied to the Allied powers as the arsenal of democracy in the early years of World War II, the United States at the end of the war owned about two-thirds of the world's monetary gold and kept it in vaults at Fort Knox. Americans had been prohibited from owning, buying, or selling gold coins or bullion since 1933 (legally, you couldn't own gold even if you kept it abroad), but the United States had remained on a sort of gold standard because the law required a "cover" in gold of 25 percent of their face value for the Federal Reserve notes that were nearly all the paper currency of the country. (U.S. one-dollar bills were issued by the Treasury itself, and were not backed by gold: they were "silver certificates," and until the 1970s they were "payable in silver to the bearer on demand." Then the price of silver rose, and the one-dollar bills, too, became Federal Reserve paper notes that could not be converted to a metallic base.) The theory was that given a choice of holding their reserves in gold (which paid no interest) or holding them in dollars (which were earning assets), the nations of the world would take the paper and let the metal stay in the United States.

The Bretton Woods arrangements assumed that the United States would always follow non-inflationary policies, but we had paid for World War II by inflating the currency, limiting price and wage increases through controls, and leaving the future to worry about the long-term effects on the value of money. We were likely to do that again. Any time the business cycle turned down, we were likely to go once again to high government deficits and cheap money—and then who would want to hold dollars as a reserve? More than that, as time passed and world trade increased but the world's stock of monetary gold remained the same, a fixed price for gold was going to leave insufficient backing for the world's money, whether it was dollars or pounds or Swiss francs (the notion that it might be German marks or Japanese yen would have been farfetched for ten years after the war).

Having been at City Bank in the days of Bernie Duis, moreover, I had a deep suspicion of these "pegged" currency rates. Duis liked to say in the 1930s that a peg was the easiest thing to break—you just leaned on it a little harder. In the early 1930s, he took a boat around the Pacific, selling yen at every stop. By the rules of the game in those days, the people who bought that yen could trade it in for pieces of the Japanese stock of gold. The Bank of Japan was very upset; the Japanese government complained to Charles Mitchell; but eventually the Japanese devalued their currency—that is, they raised the yen price of gold. I thought Bretton Woods was likely to produce similar stories before its tale was told.

If the international monetary system was to work, we needed a steady rise in the price of gold, to support additional trade and keep the dollar / gold ratio abreast of inflation. The system we had was certain to self-destruct. With the dollar as an international currency, the growth of trade would mean that more and more dollars would be needed. We would have to run a deficit in our balance of payments, either by importing more than we exported (which seemed very unlikely in the 1950s) or by foreign aid, or stationing armies abroad, or investing in other countries. Eventually, people and governments abroad would grow uncomfortable about acquiring all those dollars, and would want to trade them in for gold. As the American gold stock shrank, the rush away from the dollar could snowball, with incalculable consequences. But if the price of gold kept rising (at a rate less than the Treasury-bills rate, so that foreigners who decided to hold gold rather than dollar investments would still be losing income by the decision), Bretton Woods could be made to work.

I can't pretend that I thought market forces would push gold up when the governments stopped holding it down. *Nobody* thought that. In several of my speeches on the subject in the 1960s, I made reference to studies in London indicating that as an industrial metal, gold was not likely to sell for more than eight dollars an ounce. But that wasn't the question—the question was the monetary use of gold, and for that purpose the price had to be higher. I was entirely clear that paper money would never be an acceptable substitute for gold, and for a long time I stood alone among the bankers of my time, who all agreed with the experts that if people would stop being barbarians there wouldn't be any call for the barbarous relic.

The Sunday after his election in 1968, President-elect Nixon called me in my New York apartment at about 10:00 in the morning to talk about the price of gold. I told him the United States simply could not keep selling gold at thirty-five dollars an ounce. He asked if he could send Arthur Burns to see me. My chief economist Alan Temple and I gave him our reasons, and I thought he agreed with us. But a week later he called to say we'd been turned down—Joe Fowler, Johnson's Treasury secretary, wouldn't hear of it. So we muddled along until the crisis came in 1971, and Nixon had to "close the gold window" to keep the entire hoard from leaking away and to force the rest of the world to allow us to devalue.

Some months before, I had advised my old friend Aristotle Onassis to buy gold, which he did, at the pegged price of thirty-five dollars an ounce. He bought about $100 million worth. And soon after the central banks announced their first quick fix to the problems of Bretton Woods— an agreement not to increase or diminish the total stock of monetary gold—the price did rise, to forty to forty-two dollars, as I had told Onassis it would.

Then the Swiss National Bank told the private Swiss banks that it would not permit them to value gold in their vaults at more than the official price of thirty-five dollars an ounce, and they sold enough of it to push the price down, actually below what Onassis had paid. He panicked, and without consulting me he sold out at a small loss. I would have counseled that he hang on, not because I expected the private market to go up by ten, then twenty times (think: Onassis would have made more than a *billion* dollars if he had stayed with that purchase!), but because I thought the governments would have no choice but to buy gold at increasing prices for their own purposes of economic management. As I said to an interviewer from *U.S. News and World Report* in January 1968, "The main reason people want gold is that they hope to make a profit on a higher gold price. Once the price was raised, who would expect another change for many, many years? After the gold price was raised, prudence would suggest getting out of gold and into dollars, to earn a return on your money."

My earliest speeches on these subjects go back to 1958, but my period of greatest interest in monetary systems was the 1960s, specifically from 1965 through 1968, when I served as chairman of the Commission on International Monetary Relations of the International Chamber of Commerce. My friend Arthur Watson, head of IBM International, was then chairman of the ICC. The great drive of the governments through this period was the creation of a Special Drawing Right in the International Monetary Fund, a kind of "paper gold" that would be an administered world currency. Such a currency, I said somewhat skeptically to a Montreal meeting of my commission, "must find its place alongside [gold and reserve currencies] without impairing their usefulness or bringing Gresham's Law into operation." What I was sure of was that gold itself could not soon be forced out of the system, whatever international meetings might decide. "Until we can depend on governments to impose on their countries the discipline of necessary monetary and fiscal restraint to provide stability," I told *U.S. News and World Report,* "or until nations are willing to transfer their wealth to support the economic needs of their neighbors, it seems to me that the world's economic system needs the discipline of gold."

I had the best advice, from all sides. On my staff at the bank I had John Exter, whom I had recruited from the Federal Reserve Bank of New York (where he had been in charge of relations with central banks in other countries). Exter was one of the original gold bugs, and believed that the paper money system would collapse in an inflationary heap some day, with great harm to world trade and private fortunes. I met often with Dr. Jelle Zjilstra, a deeply courteous and serious, fatherly man who was governor of the Netherlands National Bank and chairman of the Bank for International Settlements in Basel. He argued for making the Bretton Woods system work, at almost any cost. After one of my speeches another central banker, the Italian Guido Carli, told me that talk like that was going to wreck the world monetary system. I thought, If a speech by Moore can wreck the system, it must be in even sorrier shape than I had thought. But the man who most influenced my thinking was "The Economic Adviser" of the Bank for International Settlements (B.I.S.), a wonderfully irascible American economist named Milton Gilbert, who wrote an annual report for his bank that was a compendium of the world's wisdom on international money. Whenever I went to Europe I would try to find a way to visit in Basel, and dine with Milton in his dark, old-fashioned German house above the Rhine in the old section of the city.

It was Gilbert who most perfectly stated (in an unpublished paper of which he sent me a copy) the case for a rise in gold prices: "It is an illusion to think that the United States has been losing its gold reserves to defend the dollar; it has only been subsidizing an outdated price of gold . . . The simple economics of the matter is that the United States all these years has only been prepared to pay the 1934 price for gold and in consequence it has not gotten any. If it similarly insisted on paying only the 1934 price for coffee, diamonds, steel, Chevrolets, champagne, bus drivers, civil servants or trips to outer space, it would not get any of those either." And the United States *had* to have gold: "It may seem that I have some special prejudice for countries holding gold as against other reserve assets. Not at all! I do not mind in the least if Russia or China hold no gold reserves—or even France or the Netherlands. I am quite willing to allow them the sovereign right to make their own choice of reserve policy. I only insist that the United States hold its reserves in gold—because there is nothing else for the reserve currency country of the system." My speeches for the International Chamber of Commerce sounded so learned and secure because I had help in writing them from Gilbert's assistant, an equally brilliant young man named Alexandre Lamfalussy, who took over Gilbert's post when he retired in the late 1970s, and who is now executive director of the bank.

B.I.S. is one of the world's most interesting institutions. It was formed in the early 1930s as part of the Young Plan to resolve the German war debts (hence the word "settlements"), but was almost immediately overwhelmed by the Depression. It survived because it was a useful adjunct to nationalist economic policies, providing a place where the world's central bankers could meet, see what they agreed upon, and do business with each other. When it was begun, the thought was that the central banks of the major trading nations would own the stock themselves, but the Congress would not allow the Federal Reserve to participate, and the shares set aside for the United States were acquired by the First National Bank of New York, mostly because Leon Fraser, chairman of First National, had been active in the negotiations and considered the new institution very important. This meant that we wound up with them when we acquired First National in 1955. Some other shares in the original allocation had not been taken up by governments, and were sold privately. They traded on the Paris Bourse, and were one of the great investments of the postwar period, because B.I.S. was profitable and paid good dividends—and because the bank's own reserves were gold. In fact, B.I.S. shares were a legal way for Americans in effect to own gold, though nobody realized it. City Bank made nothing on the shares we took over from First National, because the Federal Reserve in effect expropriated them from us, paying us only what First National had paid a quarter of a century before.

Because it is run by a relatively informal governing board of a dozen central banks, B.I.S. is the court of first resort when there are international economic crises, and supplies the bridging loans until the IMF and the national governments can drag up their ponderous procedures. It saved the pound in 1967 and 1976, the dollar in 1968 and 1979, Mexico in 1982. The United Nations has always hated it, because only the industrial nations are represented (one of the sections of Bretton Woods that was ignored not only privately but in the end officially, despite treaty obligations, was a clause prohibiting IMF members from participating in the work of the B.I.S.). But when people like Bill Martin, former chairman of the Federal Reserve, talk about the need for a world central bank, I tell them we already have one, and a very good one, in Basel.

As a banker in the 1960s, I did not believe that floating exchange rates could be a good idea. Businessmen and bankers needed to know when they entered into their contracts how much they would receive, in the currency they used in their own business, on the day the payments fell due. If currency prices were constantly fluctuating, businessmen and bankers would have to buy expensive insurance to make sure they were really doing their own business and not just speculating on foreign-exchange movements. Trade would slow and the world's goods would become unnecessarily expensive. But that was a time before satellite communication made messages between countries virtually cost-free, and computers with very large scale integration made it possible to process transactions of tens of millions of dollars, all but instantaneously, for a few pennies. Today businessmen and bankers can "hedge" their foreign-exchange "exposure" easily and inexpensively, in futures and forwards markets, through swaps and options and even more exotic instruments.

I am not as optimistic as my partner Walter Wriston that in what he calls an "information standard," free markets will compel governments to follow wise policies. Just as it was easy for bankers to believe that "sovereign countries don't go bankrupt," it's easy for the sovereign countries to sustain unwise policies for some time, borrowing on their sovereign credit and digging themselves deeper and deeper into the hole as the Latins did in the late 1970s and early 1980s, before reality catches up with them. The United States has been doing something of the sort itself in recent years. In time—not tomorrow, but some few years down the road—we will pay, with a new burst of inflation and new declines in the values of the dollar internationally, for the great surge of money the Federal Reserve has generated since 1982. The price the market sets for the dollar is not entirely a matter of economics, because so many people around the world feel safer when they can have their wealth stored in the United States. But eventually economic reality asserts itself. And then, of course, the dollar will come back again, and overshoot again, unjustified premiums following unjustified discounts.

The markets are *not* quick to punish folly, and there remains room for the IMF and the B.I.S. to exercise that "firm surveillance" of the member nations' economic policies that we agreed to accept in 1962, and again in 1976, and in 1979, and in the economic summit meeting in 1986. But these "committees of ten" or "committees of five" the governments keep setting up don't do their work and never will. Though I have my own "dream" monetary system, which I am saving for the last chapter, I no longer worry about fixed vs floating rates, or the precise nature of the best monetary "regime." Markets may not be the *answer,* because markets break windows before they settle down, but markets are certainly the *process* through which answers will be found.

9

President and Chairman

Retirement at age sixty-five was and is an inflexible rule at Citibank, and everyone knew that the guard would be changing on November 1st, 1959, when chairman Howard Sheperd reached that milestone. It was also part of the tradition of the bank that the president succeeded, which meant that Stillman Rockefeller would become chairman. It wasn't even too much of a surprise, I think, when the board announced after its meeting September 29th, 1959, that I would be the new president. I was supposed to have one rival for the job—Howard Laeri, who ran the metropolitan division of the bank—but my range of experience was broader than his. The future of the bank did not lie in its Wall Street business, but in the national and international roles that the domestic and overseas divisions had expanded under my leadership.

I stopped by Howard's office the day after the announcement had been made, to tell him that I thought the only reason I had been preferred was the accident of my assignments, that I would have been proud to serve under him if he had won the nod, and I hoped he would be willing to work with me. Howard was one of the best all-round commercial bankers in the bank, and the very best customer-relations man, and he deserved to be president; and if Rockefeller hadn't been inserted into the line of succession he would have been president at some time in this period. Instead, he moved into my place to run domestic division when I became president, and his final title at the bank was vice-chairman. Through the next decade, on those occasions when the two top men were out of New York, Howard was often the man we left in command.

My time as president and chairman of Citibank was a period of great growth. At the end of calendar 1959, as I was becoming president, the First National City Bank had $8.3 billion in assets, and for that year our profits were $68 million. At the end of calendar 1969, my last full year before retirement, the total assets of First National City Corporation were $23 billion, and for that year our profits were $119 million. We had about eighteen thousand employees when I became president, and about thirty-four thousand when I retired as chairman. Obviously, I didn't "do it"—no individual can do things like that. And I didn't drive my people to do it, either: you can't get results like those by giving orders. If you don't have thousands of people doing it their own imaginative way, this sort of growth won't happen. What we did can be placed under four headings:

1. Most simply, we got the ship in motion. We created a planning and budgeting process. We identified the potential of the overseas business, and the people we hired and promoted realized that potential.

2. We identified the financial-services concept—that there was more in the life of our institution than just being a bank. To facilitate our entry into other financial services, and to give us the added stability of funding by the public sale of securities, we created the holding company, First National City Corporation, later Citicorp.

3. We constantly expanded our personnel programs, our procedures for finding, training, and promoting personnel. Without the capable people these procedures developed, none of our goals would have been attainable.

4. We made Citibank an "institution" with a clear-cut plan everybody understood and worked to achieve, as contrasted to an organization that had been to a large extent the wishes and judgment of a few people who had headed it from time to time. Citibank will never be a personal bank again!

The results speak for themselves, and they have been sustained. They can be credited to a plan, a good plan, people capable of carrying it out—and a decision-making process, an administrative structure, that draws on the capabilities and imagination of many good people. For them, and for Citibank, the best is yet to come.

My mentor James H. Perkins, chairman of
City Bank from 1933 to 1940.
Pirie MacDonald photo

The new management team in 1959: Dick Perkins (chairman of the executive committee),
Stillman Rockefeller, and me.

President of the bank, in 1960; note the pins on the map, designating branches.

At a dinner for President and Mrs. Macapagal of the Philippines, in 1964. *Tommy Weber photo*

2

As the by-laws read in those days, the chairman was the "chief executive officer" of the bank, responsible for policy, and presided at the meetings of the board of directors, which were then held twice a month. The president was the "chief administrative officer" and ran the bank day-to-day, "with the advice and concurrence of the chairman." Neither of us, of course, made loans—the bank had already got far beyond the Charles Mitchell days—but we both sat in on the Monday afternoon meeting of the senior credit officers, because we had to present the reports on the larger new loans to the board of directors' meetings on Tuesdays. Under the law, bank directors themselves are held responsible for the bank's lending policies, and under certain circumstances for specific loans. (Some eminent leaders of American business were publicly thrown off the board of Continental Illinois by the Federal Deposit Insurance Corporation because they had failed to keep the bank from buying all those bad loans from Penn Square Bank of Oklahoma City.) Our lawyers had ruled that if the directors approved the bank's lending procedures, and examined the larger loans themselves with an eye to changing policies or people when something was wrong, they would meet their responsibilities.

A page or two of description of each of the larger loans was placed in each director's "black book" before the board meeting (many of them came in half an hour or so before the meeting to look through the book ahead of time). While I had to be ready to answer questions about all the loans, it was rare that anyone actually queried an individual loan. Similarly, the board received once a month a report on the trust department, with the "approved list" of securities in which we invested our trust accounts (I was pleased to see that the format I had established for Perkins in 1933 was still in use). Directors were often interested to learn that their companies' stock hadn't made the list, but it was unusual for anyone to ask a question.

The centerpiece of each meeting was the president's report on what was going on at the bank, with a request for approval of those few matters that required board approval. In practice, this is trickier than it sounds, and I was green. Fortunately, I already knew almost all the men on the board. At my first meeting, I mentioned a problem that was on my desk that I thought the board should know about. Mike Haider, chairman of what is now called Exxon, asked me for my recommendation, and I said I hadn't yet decided what I thought should be done. With a smile—I was grateful for that smile—Haider suggested that in the future I bring matters to the attention of the board only when I was prepared to make a recommendation. The board of a properly run corporation meets to consider and screen management recommendations and decisions—not to make them.

And they meet also, of course, to keep an eye on the books. As a banker, I've sat often on the audit committees of the corporations where I am a director, and I'm always conscious of that dotted line on the organization chart that connects the comptroller directly to the board. After the auditors make their report, the board asks the corporate officers to leave, and asks the auditor if there's anything he'd like to say but felt he could not say in the presence of management, and also if there was any piece of information he wanted and could not get. My desire to make sure that this procedure is always followed may trace to the special situation of the senior officer of a bank, because the authors of the National Bank Act were very suspicious people. The law *requires* that every major officer of a bank must take two consecutive weeks of vacation every year, which gives time for any check-kiting scheme or misappropriation of customer funds to come to the surface.

To my surprise, I found myself with a major problem on my hands my first day as president. After the board meeting, Charles Allen, president of National Cash Register (now NCR), pulled me aside and told me that his company and IBM and RCA and GE and Burroughs were far advanced in their work with the American Bankers Association to develop a magnetic ink character recognition (MICR) system that would make it possible to process checks through a computer. The ABA had already adopted this process as the industry standard, and our operations people were being pigheaded about going their own way in a joint project they had with ITT. This was a sort of Rube Goldberg machine ITT had first proposed to us in 1951, which involved placing each check in a plastic envelope that would be treated essentially as a punched card and then move through the bookkeeping system of the bank untouched by human hands. The machine had been scheduled for delivery to us in 1954, but the schedule had kept slipping, and in 1959 it was still "on the way." By the terms of our contract with ITT, however, our right to cancel expired December 31st, 1959. Otherwise we would have to make a large immediate payment, around $25 million, and irrevocably commit to purchasing equipment that might ultimately cost as much as $100 million. That equipment, Allen said, was never going to work anyway—and even if it did work, it would not be of use to us, because every other bank in the country was going to use the MICR system.

I discussed this with Rockefeller, and we agreed on the need for a task force to look into the matter, very fast. I appointed a committee of nine, to be chaired by Alan Temple, vice-chairman in charge of our economics and public relations departments, because he outranked George Guerdan, our chief of operations, who had been godfather of the ITT project. Guerdan was on the committee, of course. We gave them two weeks to come back with a recommendation. The recommendation was to get out of the project immediately, with Guerdan the only dissenter. He had the chance to speak his piece at a meeting of the bank's policy committee that Rockefeller summoned for the day after we received the report, but again the decision to cancel was unanimous, except for Guerdan. We moved Guerdan to another part of the bank, appointing his assistant Carl Desch to succeed him as chief operating officer, and we told our lawyers to prepare the appropriate documents to cancel the ITT contract.

All hell broke loose. Harold Geneen, chairman of ITT, had had close relations with the bank over the years (his predecessor Sosthenes Behn had been for years a director of City Bank, and our Dick Perkins was still a director of ITT). Geneen wrote me a five-page letter, denouncing me as, among other things, stupid and irresponsible. He said I was violating not only the spirit but the letter of our agreement with ITT, and that I was condemning the bank to a future of ruinous operating costs that could be avoided with his wonderful machine. He sent a copy of that letter to every member of the City Bank board, too— the only time anything like that has ever happened. Only one other bank had bought the system, the Valley National of Phoenix, Arizona, and they cancelled soon after we did. ITT abandoned the project and, as Allen had predicted, magnetic check processing came into being shortly afterwards. This decision not only got us off a dead horse but also saved ITT many millions of dollars—but it was some years before Geneen would talk to me again. We are now "friends."

I had already intervened once in the march toward computerization, and would have one further role to play. My first action had been partly social. While working with ITT on the check-processing machinery in the mid-1950s, we had solicited help from IBM on the job of automating other parts of the bank's bookkeeping. The IBM salesmen who came to the meeting said they couldn't see how their standard equipment would be useful for our needs. Period. GE and

RCA might be interested in building special machinery for banks, but IBM had bigger fish to fry, mostly governmental. We weren't likely to be important enough customers for them to design special equipment for us.

As it happened, Tom Watson, Sr., who was still chairman of the IBM board, rode the club car form New Canaan to New York, and I often sat next to him. I told him about the brush-off his people had given us, and I told him also that I thought they were making a mistake. "Hell," I said, "we handle two million checks seven times a day, and that's more paper than any other business handles, and anything you design that works for us will work for all the other banks, too." Tom Watson was probably the best salesman that ever was, and you didn't have to draw diagrams for him. My friends at IBM told me that he came into the office that morning, summoned the senior officers, chewed them out, and ordered into being a bank-equipment department which eventually became one of the big profit centers of the company. In 1960, Rockefeller and I made arrangements to put a senior executive from IBM on the City Bank board. But then, late in the decade, we ourselves became manufacturers of equipment for bank operations, through a California subsidiary we called Transactions Technologies, Inc., with sales getting up into the half-billion-dollar-a-year range. If we were going to be competitors of IBM, of course, they couldn't sit on our board, and they left.

Before that happened, however, I had another computer involvement. When banking machinery became generally available from different suppliers in the early 1960s, each company had its own separate system: check-processing equipment could be used only with computers by the same manufacturer, and even the printers were "compatible" only with one company's processing units. We refused to buy any of it, and made our refusal a matter of general knowledge in the banking business. We insisted that we would buy only equipment that was compatible with that of other manufacturers, so we would never find ourselves at the mercy of single suppliers. Other big banks took the same position. Soon the computer companies found a way to make their components generally compatible with each other.

It's not an unusual problem. When you travel, you find that if you want to use your electrical equipment you need portable transformers and a whole bunch of differently shaped plugs. because the nations of the world never got together to standardize what ought to be standard. I complained about this once to somebody in that business, and he said I was right, but now, after everything was in the walls, it would cost about a trillion dollars worldwide to make the changes. Television is the worst example, with 545-line American systems and 625-line European systems, 50-cycles per second, 60-cycles per second, tape recorders with Beta formats and VHS formats, and a new Japanese telecasting system direct form satellites that would be much better than anything we have now held back because the world can't agree. Of course, it's presumptuous for an American to complain: we still haven't accepted the metric standard used everywhere else in the world—and then we wonder why our manufacturers, designing their equipment in feet and inches, having trouble competing abroad!

3

You can't give orders in a place like Citibank. If people don't agree with you, they say, "That's one of Moore's crazy ideas," and nobody does anything. "If you can't persuade people you're right," Perkins used to say, "then either you're wrong in your idea or you're the wrong man for the job." What you had to do, Perkins said, was make reasonable suggestions to reasonable people; it takes time to convince your associates that you're reasonable, but after that you never have any trouble. "You can always tell," he said, "by how they turn around to leave. If they stand there and wait for you to explain what you want, they won't do it anyway."

There are only eight or nine people you can have reporting directly to you when you're president. My nine were the chiefs of the overseas and domestic divisions, the special industries group, the trust and investment section, the bond department, the operations department, the economics department, advertising and public relations, and personnel. I kept three secretaries busy when I was president of Citibank (one for correspondence, one for appointments, one for files), but I never had an "assistant" doing the sort of job I had done for Perkins. I never thought I was smart enough to handle second-rate people: I felt about them the way the bullfighter feels about a second-rate bull— he's dangerous because you can't predict which way he'll turn if anything distracts his attention. When I appointed as chairman of the credit policy committee a capable traditional banker named George Scott, who had run Texas and the Southwest for me in the domestic division, he said with some surprise, "But, George, I've been opposing you on a lot of things." I said, "That's right: what I need most is good men to oppose me when they think I'm wrong." My ambition at the bank was to have a top cadre composed entirely of first-rate people, and then I wanted to deal with them myself. Most of them I saw every day. Nobody came between me and these nine: my door was open to them all day long. If I had a customer in with me, I was happy to have him meet my division chiefs, and vice versa. I didn't have any secrets.

In fact, I didn't have much time to see customers when I was president. What I wanted to do was use my needle all day to get things done. Rockefeller used to complain that I was out of town too much, at meetings of CICYP in Latin America or the Borg-Warner board in Chicago, and he was right, but if I hadn't done that I'd have been a different man. (And I did turn down some attractive invitations, two of which I still regret—Johnson's Wax, one of the most successful marketing organizations I ever encountered, and Perkin-Elmer, run by my New Canaan neighbor Dick Perkin, one of the nation's most imaginative and profitable high-tech companies.) I thought then and I think now that the bank benefited by my outside involvements, which also gave me additional chances to find out how our people were doing around the world. And, of course, I stayed on top of what had to be done at the bank. To succeed, you have to run your job, you can't let your job run you.

What I had to face early on was that even if I was perfect at persuading those eight or nine men who reported directly to me, I still couldn't say with any confidence that I was running the bank or knew what was going on. The fact is that there's only one way a president really influences what happens in anything as gigantic as Citibank: through its budget. And the only way you get a budget that makes sense is through a realistic plan. Unless you have a plan, everything you do is just a transaction. These things are reciprocal. A budget without a plan doesn't get you anywhere, and a plan without an appropriation in your budget is a New Year's resolution. My first five years as president of Citibank were a long and ultimately successful struggle to introduce real planning and real budgeting into what was in the numbers the second-largest bank in New York and the third-largest bank in the world but in fact had been to a large extent a very personal, almost seat-of-the-pants operation.

When I started talking PLANNING the whole bank put their tongue in their cheeks. The fact was that we didn't have anybody at the bank who knew how to plan. I had to bring in a planner named Owen, then a junior financial man at General Electric (still the best source of planners, because it always has an oversupply of financial men) to be our director of planning. (Some years later, when I was on the board of Union Pacific, that company brought in a team of finance people from GE to reorganize the operation and help make it much more than just a railroad, and today the CEO of Union Pacific, Bill Cook, is the GE man we hired.) Owen found he was talking to the wall, nobody listened. We kept writing memos and calling meetings, which people had to attend, because I was the president of the bank. In fairness to Stillman Rockefeller, who was not enthusiastic about planning and would have preferred to run the bank the way Sheperd ran it, he let me do it. He thought planning was just one of Moore's hobbyhorses, but he backed me when I needed backing.

Citibank's budgets came out more or less all right from the beginning, less because we were geniuses than because the bank had wide diversification and good balance and built on "congenerations" between key divisions. The domestic retail division produced more deposits than were required for the borrowing needs of its customers. The corporate division was in exactly the opposite situation. When interest rates moved above budget, the branch division gained from improved earnings on the funds it had in the bank's "money pool," and the corporate division was hurt. Retail and wholesale businesses balanced each other. When business was so-so in the industrial countries, the bank made money in the commodity-oriented countries. The usual result was a balancing out of experience against budget, which made us look like bigger heroes than we were.

Of course, it takes time to see the benefits of planning on the bottom line. A plan usually takes ten years to deliver what it promises. It's like a new aircraft at Boeing—from the moment management takes its first look at the drawings to the day the first plane flies off the runway for delivery to a customer, it's about ten years. In Citibank it took us five years to get rid of planners who set unachievable goals and of line people who couldn't realize achievable goals. Setting up a new overseas branch, you have to send someone to Taiwan to survey the opportunities, find the right place, make the initial contacts. Then you need approvals from the local government and approvals from the Federal Reserve. Then you send a man to start the branch, and you often send the wrong man the first time. You send other people, they have to make a game plan, find customers, and by the time you have a worthwhile profit center in Taipei, it's usually ten years from the date when you first wrote a branch for that country into your plan. A lot of the things I planned came through only after I was gone, and Walt

Wriston got the credit. But that wasn't unfair, either, because he'd been the source of many of my ideas.

From the beginning, we set a goal for the organization: we wanted earnings growth at a rate of 15 percent a year. The end of the first year, we thought we'd made it, but when you added up the numbers we had only 12 percent growth. We had five divisions. Four of them had met our target, but the fifth, the bond department, which constituted a substantial part of our balance sheet and relied on our capital funds for support, didn't have a growth factor and pulled us down. This was all wrong. The department that handled our reserve funds should be a profit center, probably the most profitable part of the bank— after all, money was our raw material, we should know what to do with it better than anyone else. One solution was that the bank should become a dealer in U.S. Treasury securities. It was important for us to know about this market, anyway; we should use that knowledge to buy and sell government paper for our own account and make trading profits as well as the investment earnings on our holdings. Later we found ways beyond simple trading to make money on our money, and today, what with swaps and arbitrage, the Treasury function is the most profitable in the bank.

That was a base my committee had failed to touch in 1948, and it was our mistake. Apart from questions of our own profitability, we really had an increasing need to be dealers in Treasury paper, because many of our biggest customers kept some of their short-term funds in Treasuries, we had a duty to advise them, and you never really understand a market unless you're a player in it. The difference between market-makers and outsiders was especially striking in the Treasuries market, where the big players were recognized by the Federal Reserve as "primary dealers" and did some of their trading with the Fed itself. This meant they knew first-hand what the Fed was doing, which is of course the key to that market. The quid pro quo that the recognized dealers gave the Fed was that they kept the Fed's trading desk informed about everything *they* did in the governments market. That's still the way this game plays, and it's fair: you can't have both privacy and recognition.

I already knew something about this market, because City Bank had been one of the founders of Discount Corporation of America, together with Chase and some of the other larger banks. We owned 20 percent of that firm, which was one of the largest dealers in government paper, and as president of the bank I became a member of the

Discount Corporation board. The banks had started Discount at a time when they were still under attack for their conduct in the securities markets in the 1920s, and while the Glass-Steagall Act had specifically permitted banks to be dealers in Treasuries, a lot of bankers were more comfortable with a situation where they lent money to the governments dealers (safe loans, because they were collateralized by government securities), and let the dealers take the trading risks. The head of our bond department, Leo Kane, opposed our entry into the governments market, and said repeatedly that we'd lose money if we tried it. He sat on the policy committee of the bank, and voted against the recommendation that we not only enter the market but seek status as a primary dealer. Fortunately, Kane was retiring. We went out and hired John Larkin, who had been the chief trader for the Fed itself and knew where all the bodies were buried, and of course we made money. Lots of it.

Our decision to enter the Treasuries market as a dealer had an amusing sequel. Once it became clear that this trading was going to be an important source of profits for us, I grew uncomfortable about sitting on the board of a firm that was, after all, one of our competitors. It took a few months, but finally we arranged to sell off our shares in Discount Corporation. The day before we were to make the announcement, I received a call from a young man in the U.S. Attorney's office, to inform me that he was about to file suit in federal court to compel the First National City Bank of New York to divest itself of its Discount Corp. holdings, on antitrust grounds. I told him rather enthusiastically that I couldn't agree with him more, and that in fact we had already sold off our shares—the announcement was to be made the next day. He said that was as might be, but his office had put a lot of work into this case, and they were going to prosecute it anyway. I said he could do whatever he liked, but he was likely to look a little foolish when it developed we had already done what they wanted us to do. Needless to say, the U.S. Attorney never brought the case.

Among the most instructive moments in those meetings when we were first wrestling with the nature of planning were those when people tried to teach me why something couldn't be done. The head of the trust department, for example, said the best he could hope for in his division was 8 percent growth and 8 percent improvement in profits. I told him that those results were "unacceptable." He said, "What do you mean by 'unacceptable'?" I said, "I mean that if that's the best you can do, I'll have to find someone else to run the division." I couldn't understand why he couldn't do better.

Finally I asked his deputy, a tall, cool drink of water named Tom Theobald (who now runs the so-called "investment bank" on which Citibank rests so much of its hopes for the future), and he said there were two problems: the fees from corporations for running their pension trusts were too low, we lost money on that business, and there was an impossibly low statutory fee imposed by New York State law on personal trusts. His boss interrupted to say that the statutory fees were a matter of law, nothing we could do about it, and that we didn't dare raise our pension management charges to the corporations because most companies involved kept huge balances with us and would pull their money out of the bank as well as out of the trust department if we tried to charge them more. Exxon, which had one of the largest of the pension funds we managed, had $50 million on deposit at the bank on an average day. Our people went to Exxon and they said, "You're doing a good job with our account; we expect to pay for what we got." We almost doubled the pension management fees and we didn't lose but one account. The state maximum fee on individual trusts had been set thirty-two years before. We went to the State Fiduciary Association and the other trust companies joined us in asking the legislature for relief. We didn't have to lobby: the banking committees in the legislature said, "You never asked us." The statutory fees were raised, the trust division met our profit goals the following year.

Part of the resistance to the idea of planning grew from the argument that banks just couldn't control their own destiny enough to plan intelligently. Their options were limited. The mutual savings banks, the finance companies, the factors, the commercial-paper dealers had taken away our most profitable businesses. It was hard and unprofitable to sell personal trust accounts to small investors against the competition of a mutual fund, which wasn't expected to give people personal attention. My position was that all this was nobody's fault but our own: all that business had been in the banks at one time and another, and we'd opted out. One way or another, we must get it back. Our objective, I said (inside the bank and at meetings of bankers and others) should be "to perform every useful financial service, anywhere in the world, which we were permitted by law to perform and which we believed we could perform at a profit."

In my time as president, I think I can claim we made a start.

Between 1960 and 1967, we opened eighty-five new foreign branches—fifty-four in Latin America and the Caribbean (my area of special interest), fifteen in Europe, fourteen in the Far East, and two in the Middle East. And that doesn't count ninety-three offices of subsidiaries and affiliates in twenty-one foreign countries. Domestically, we finally got the New York State legislature to let us move into the counties adjacent to New York City, we acquired Hubshman Factors, we went into the credit-card business in a big way, we formed the holding company that could buy and operate finance companies, we began to offer Commingled Investment Accounts that were directly competitive with mutual funds, and we put out negotiable certificates of deposit to sell to investors who were the natural buyers of commercial paper. The Securities Industries Association sued us on our investment account, and won in the Supreme Court, I still don't understand why. We never did figure out a way to acquire a savings institution until some big ones dropped in our laps in the early 1980s, long after my departure, when the Federal Home Loan Bank Board badly needed help to keep the doors open at big savings-and-loan associations in California, Illinois, Florida, and then the District of Columbia.

The center of our planning process was that plans had to rise from the field rather than be imposed from the top. I knew what I wanted for the bottom line, but in the nature of things I couldn't know the way to get there. The process began early each year. Each branch and each department prepared a five-year plan of work—not a wish list, but a structured proposal, positive steps to be taken, offices to be opened and shut, jobs to be added and eliminated, business to be solicited and won, money to be spent and money to be earned. These budgets would then be consolidated, ultimately into divisional budgets by late summer, questioned at every level by supervisors assisted by staff personnel from the planning group. The divisional budgets would come to the top executive level in formal budget meetings starting in September; and Rockerfeller and I and our comptroller would put aside everything else for the better part of two months. That was the one time when my door was closed: when we were sitting in budget and planning meetings we didn't make other appointments, we didn't answer telephone calls; it was almost like a religious retreat. In November, the plan went to the board, and in theory it was approved before the first of the year, though sometimes discussion at the board level dragged on until January.

There were always a lot of tricky decisions, some of which were still being re-examined annually when I retired, and probably are today. The language gets fancier with the passage of time—it is now sophisticated to say that one place "books" the loan while the other place "funds" it—but the principle and the problems are the same. Then there are the "cost centers" that must be charged against other people's budgets—from something so simple as the annual meeting and the p.r. department to something so complicated as the centralized check-clearing machinery and demand-deposit accounting. When you include all the aspects of foreign exchange and differing tax systems and worldwide relations with companies handled primarily from one office—it gets to be mind-boggling. But it has to be done. And it was done. And it is done.

Some years later, I realized that what we had going for us was the freedom that the plan gave to the man in the field. He didn't have to come to senior management for day-to-day approval of his decisions. He already had the okay to open a new branch, or to start a chain of "money shops" (small loan offices) in England. So long as he stayed within his budget, he could go ahead without all those prayer meetings. Before we had effective planning, he was forever coming to New York, because he needed approvals. Some people worried that planning would centralize decisions too much, but the area manager or department head is not at the mercy of central office in the planning process. In reality, it all starts with him. Before the plan is approved, he gets a chance to see whether his recommendation has been accepted, and if it hasn't been, he can get a full hearing.

There may have been some backsliding in these areas—as I go around the world and talk to Citibankers, I get some feeling that unnecessary layers of supervision were allowed to creep into the organization of the bank in the 1970s and 1980s—but planning is still the name of the game. Over and over again, when I've dropped in on Citibank branches in Switzerland or Argentina or Hong Kong or Mexico, the manager has given me a slide presentation to show me his plan for this year and next year and the year after, his market penetration, his profits, all concise and logical and full of facts and numbers, and reasons why it's going to work.

Of course, you have to be ready to adjust. Any plan can have errors in it. But if the plan is right today, you should be able to stay within its basic outlines tomorrow. The one sure thing in the world is change, but the purpose of the plan is to manage change. We soon learned that a realistic plan cannot be extended as far as five years, because you can't manage change that far ahead. In the last two years of a five-year plan, you're pouring stardust—but for the first three years, if you plan is right, you're pouring concrete. Every month in every division the supervisor gets his results, and whether they're over or under budget. If they are on budget, all is okay and nothing must be done. But if they're under budget, all the lights go on. You can't change that budget during the year, you have to live with it. The question becomes, What can you do to get back on budget? You can't fire people, because that requires severance pay. It doesn't help the current year's budget, though it might help on next. But a good plan has some immediately postponable things in it. We had been taking the back cover of *Fortune* for every one of what were then twelve issues a year: we knew our image wouldn't go to hell if we missed three issues of *Fortune*. Or we could postpone refurbishing the twenty-ninth floor, make plans to repaint the front porch next year. This goes on all through the bank, and the totals become significant.

If you're really hard-pressed, you can sell an asset at a profit to make things look as though they've come out right, of course. To say the least, this isn't a long-range solution, but it happens even in the best-run companies. As they say, you can't get hurt taking a profit!

4

To make our plans a reality, we needed people, people, people. Also the raw material of our business, which was money. And, ultimately, some new lines of business.

Those are the three areas that absorbed my time during my eleven years as one of the two chief officers of the bank.

I had started the crusade for new people when I became the head of the overseas division, and when I became president I intensified and systematized it. I could see that some day we were going to have a thousand offices, and you need a lot of people to run a thousand offices. It's not the building you built on Park Avenue or the pipeline you financed that makes the bank—it's the leadership and follow-through and understanding of the people who work there. That's the excitement of being president, too, to see a raw kid from Terre Haute, Indiana, who comes in, and you meet him again ten years later and find he's become a banker. Our problem was that banks had a reputation as a dull place to work, where people didn't get paid very well, and the reputation wasn't entirely unjustified. When I began traveling to the Harvard Business School I heard from just about all the MBAs I was trying to recruit that they thought they'd get lost in a big bank. I said, "Look, we are going to hire one hundred college graduates next year, their names are going to be on my desk, and I'll know about them. I guarantee you won't get lost." We made City Bank a popular place for MBAs to go, and many of those we recruited then hold top jobs today.

One recruiting technique was to invite college seniors and MBA candidates to come for summer jobs before graduation, so they could see how they liked us, evaluate our promises, while we got a better estimate of them. We had to revise our previous summer job arrangements. Traditionally, summer employees were a pain in the neck. The boys usually came in as a result of pressure from friends or customers, some of whom just wanted to get rid of their sons for the summer. For the bank it was a double pain, because while their compensation was small enough, they occupied a desk and they wasted the time of everyone they talked to. Someone got the brilliant idea that the personnel department assemble during the year a number of projects that had seemed worthwhile to pursue but not sufficiently important to justify taking full-time employees from their other work. I remember a few such projects. The Long Island branch division had never really made a house-to-house checkup, asking housewives whether they used a bank, if so for what, if not why not, and so on. One summer we put a couple of college charmers on the street in Manhasset. They came back with some useful ideas for the division to consider. We sent two summer interns to Hong Kong to come to an opinion on whether that would be a good place for consumer lending. One year, we paired up two students who had been editors of the Harvard *Crimson* and the *Dartmouth*, and asked them to write the first draft for a history of City Bank. They took much of their information from the *New York Times* files and got most of it wrong, so we had them back at Christmastime and again for a second summer, gave them a list of fifty or so retirees to interview, and they got it right, finally, they captured the real characters while they were still living, which was very helpful a dozen years later to the authors of the official history of the bank, recently published.

Even after we had changed a lot of the realities at the bank, our recruiting suffered from foot-dragging in the personnel department, which had been a barony of the bank. I had a standing order in at Yale for anyone who showed brilliance and energy and initiative, and one day the Yale placement officer called me to introduce what he considered one of the best prospects he'd ever seen, a young man who had a wife and two children and had finished near the top of his class and earned two major Y's (what in lesser schools might be called varsity letters), though he had had to work his way through. I met with him and sent him up to personnel to fill out the forms and take the medical exams. He came back and I said, "How'd it go?" He said, "Fine, but your personnel director told me he thought I was crazy to come to work for City Bank, which wouldn't pay me enough to live on with a wife and two children." The man who said that was at best suffering from lack of imagination, in that it never occurred to him that to hire the right fellow I might be willing to bust the salary scale. I asked the young man how he had replied, and he said, "I told him that my wife was a qualified secretary, and that whenever we had a family budget problem, she went out and got a job, and could do it again." I thought that was a good response. We did hire this fellow, and he wound up with a good career, but in investment banking rather than commercial banking.

If we didn't get the people we liked fresh out of business school, we kept trying. We knew that on the average, Harvard MBAs change jobs once in their first five years. We asked the men who came to work for us whom they considered the special stars of their own class, asked them to keep track of what those fellows were doing, were they happy. Maybe this is the place, sort of in the middle of a paragraph in the middle of a chapter, to admit that when I use the male pronouns in writing about my personnel policies, it's not habit but truth. The record shows, I can't deny it, that the first woman vice-president of Citibank was appointed after my retirement. I was prejudiced. I thought women were emotional, they wouldn't stay with you, you wasted a lot of time training them and then they had a baby or their husband got assigned to work somewhere and they followed him, and . . . but there's no point listing all the wrong arguments I believed in those days. When I was a young man there was a song about "What can I say, dear, after I say I'm sorry," and I'll have to leave it at that.

Once people were at the bank, I worked hard to keep an eye on how they were doing. Every day I was in the office, I had a half-hour meeting, usually 9:15 to 9:45, with Bob Feagles, my personnel man, who's now running one of the Aetna companies. Every company needs a system to effectively evaluate the organization, and see that promising people get the right training, are properly deployed, and move ahead as needed and qualified. Different companies have different systems. We developed one that worked, but the truth is that any system is better than no system. I am sure that what Citibank uses today is more sophisticated, and possibly even more effective than mine, but mine was right for the time. And there had been no system when I recognized the need.

We started at the bottom. Each employee was rated in what we called Personnel Book I, first during his training program, as T–1 (very promising), T–2 (okay, good enough for later evaluation), and T–3 (N.G., below what we expected). If we found that department heads were keeping T–3 trainees, we inquired as to why. Thereafter the staff was rated according to three basic banking qualifications—credit analysis (leading to credit judgment), understanding of the mechanical, legal, and paperwork functions of the bank (handling the everyday work flow), and ability to sell, to get new business, and to handle existing business imaginatively. There was also a fourth quality rated— administrative ability—but at the earlier levels the employees usually had no experience handling people and could not be rated in that category.

Again, we gave ratings of 1, 2, or 3. One meant superior to the requirements of the job *then occupied,* 2 meant good enough, 3 meant substandard. If the employee had not had experience in this area (like the younger staff on personnel management), the rating was a noncommital 0.

On the organization sheet for the branch or department to which the employee was assigned—say, the credit department—the supervisors put numbers for everyone. I might see the numbers 1, 1, 3, 0 beside a man's name. That meant he was ahead of his required skills in credit, and in operations, but deficient in selling and customer relations, and had no administrative experience. Conclusions: this man should be assigned to the new business department, required to go on the streets, selling the bank's services. If the employee was rated 1, 1, 1, 0, he was ready for promotion. If the supervisor wasn't doing what the system indicated he should do, *his* supervisor told him so, and if his failures persisted, he would be given a different job, not requiring personnel administration.

It was a rule that the ratings had to be done by a supervisor not more than two steps senior to the person being rated. Anyone further removed from the staff member than that would not know enough about him to make the ratings properly.

In addition, each employee had what we called a "potential" rating. A blue line under his name meant he could ultimately be a senior officer, a vice-president. A red underline meant he could eventually aspire to being a branch manager or a department head, and a green line marked the names of people who would not become more than junior officers.

My chief personnel officer saw to it that the system was maintained, the ratings reviewed by the regional officers at least annually, either from the field or on the supervisor's periodic visits to New York. From the way the supervisors handled the personnel system, we could get a feel for *their* ability in the vitally important work of personnel development.

At our meetings, Feagles would give me statistical data drawn from the system. We had 121 blue potentials, all in all. Of those 121, thirty-five were in South America, twenty in Brazil alone. (Brazil was the nursery of leaders for Citibank, a garden for training bankers. It's a place where the central bank changes the rules every day; where your customers go broke because they can't handle the foreign exchange or the inflation; where labor unions shut you down every other hour, and you have different unions in different towns. Every problem known to the banking business, you find in Brazil—so if a guy can run a bank in Brazil, he can run a bank anywhere.) But we had only fifteen blue potentials in all of Asia, where our development prospects looked better than in Latin America generally. I could say to Feagles, "In the course of the next year, let's transfer ten blue potentials from South America to Asia." In this way, over the years, we could see to it that our talent was deployed where we needed it most.

The next step in the system was to identify the top twenty-five administrative jobs. Those jobs were outlined on separate pages in Personnel Book II, which set forth the incumbent, his age and so forth, and his personal record, and then listed below at least five possible candidates for this job—name, where now working, age, when he would be qualified to take the job in question (now, in two years, longer). At least two of the candidates had to be from a different department of the bank, to insure cross-fertilization. There was no rule against a good man being listed for more than one position. Some might be qualified candidates for three or four top jobs.

There was also a Book III, called the "production" book, which kept track of the development of the blue potentials. There was a page for each man, with a photo so we would know him when he saw him around the office. The information would include vital statistics, personal record, and a training plan, which might include sending the man to the Harvard advanced management program for a year, or an overseas training trip.

All these books were maintained in multiple copies, so all division supervisors would have an overview of the personnel resources in his own part of the bank. Book IV, however, had only two copies, for the president and chairman. That was the list of "gold potentials," the candidates for the top posts, our own jobs, vice-chairman, executive vice-president. That book was kept under lock and key, and of course the conclusions in it changed from time to time, as we observed the performance of our stars.

Of course, this is not the only possible system. It was ours. It's still paying dividends. And I know it's still viable, because they instituted it at Commerce Union in Nashville, and they tell me they are very pleased with the results. Other systems will work, too, provided they meet three goals:

    1. to have always, in house, qualified people to carry out your plan;

    2. to assure that everyone is given the best possible training experience to reach his or her potential;

    3. to assure that everyone gets a chance for the jobs, and that the best person is selected.

5

I tried to meet as many of the younger people as I could. Stillman Rockefeller as president had started a custom of occasional morning coffees with the trainees, and I made it a daily occurrence, at nine in the morning every day I was in the bank, with a somewhat wider range of communicants, from trainees through officers of the bank in town from foreign posts, and visitors from foreign banks and governments taking a study tour of National City Bank. Personnel would give me brief biographies of each of them the night before. It was a small group, four or five, and we met for only fifteen minutes or so, enough time for a cup of coffee and a Danish, but it's interesting what an impression it made. Over and over again, I've been at an international meeting somewhere, or visiting a major correspondent bank, and a finance minister or a bank president will come up to me and say, "You wouldn't remember me, Mr. Moore, but I was a trainee [or a 'guest observer'] at City Bank in the 1960s and I had coffee with you in your conference room . . ."

When I traveled, I made it a point to meet with some of our younger officers, just the two of us, the only rule being that I was interested in comments and criticisms on the bank's policies, but not in anything about persons or personalities. Once a manager in Brazil talked about a mistake head office had made there by telling me how much he had opposed it but the head of the division in New York wouldn't listen, and I interrupted him to say, "Young man, I came here to cut through seven layers of supervision to find out what you and people like you think of policies and procedures, not what you think of people. The decision you're complaining about, I made myself. You boss was on your side, and I overruled him, but he was loyal enough not to tell you that." Among the lessons Perkins has taught me is that you always criticize policies, never people.

Another rule was that I never let anybody threaten me, tell me that if we didn't give him a raise or a bigger staff or change our policy to please him he was going to quit. Perkins had also taught me that. He once said to somebody, "If you tell me there are changes we ought to make, I can talk about whether we ought to make them. But if you tell me there are things I have to do or you'll quit, you leave me nothing to talk about but you." My answer on the few occasions when people threatened that they'd quit unless this was done or that was done was to say, "I accept your resignation." Later, I'd meet them again and they'd say, "You fired me"—and I'd reply, "I did *not*. You resigned."

I expected people to be willing to move. One of the more interesting experiences I had as president of Citibank was a trip to Australia in 1966 to see what could be done to open that market for the bank. We'd sent a man there, and he'd reported back that despite the sympathy of finance minister Sir Wilkins McMahon, who later became a good friend, there was absolutely no way in. I refused to believe him. I traveled with my niece, Monica Davidson, who had been to school in Canada with a girl from Sydney (a Miss Walton) and had written her to say we were coming. When we got off the plane, the Waltons were waiting for us and I invited them to the reception laid on for us that night. It turned out that Mr. Walton was a retailer, had been a partner of Sears in Australia, and had bought Sears out. We didn't talk business, but a few weeks later Walton came to New York. We sent flowers to his hotel and arranged to take him and his wife to the opera later in his stay, and then one afternoon I got a call from him. His mission in New York was to sell a half interest in the credit company that financed his sales, and he'd thought he had a deal arranged with Chase. But it had turned out that David Rockefeller was out of town, and nobody at

Chase was empowered to sign off until Rockefeller got back. This deal won us the first significant American presence in Australia.

Now I needed a man to go to Australia. I called in my first choice, and he wanted to know, What's the salary, where do I live, how often will I get home—and finally I said, "Forget it." The next man I called in was Tom Theobald, who had been so helpful in the trust department. He was very enthusiastic, and I asked him why—his wife was going to have a baby, and it was a long way away. He said that where he was, he had so many bosses he didn't have any chance to make important decisions. In Sydney, he'd learn whether he was any good or not. That was the right answer.

Over the years, we've lost more people than any other bank has trained. I expected that. I used to tell these fellows that training at Citibank was like accumulating capital, and what they were learning would greatly increase the marketability of their services. But that applies only to younger officers, who have been at the bank perhaps ten years or so. Once a man rises to senior level, he becomes dependent on the team, he gets in the habit of pushing buttons to make things happen. If you put him in some other organization, he'll push the buttons, and nothing will happen. Able as they are, neither Wriston nor Reed would have been able to accomplish much at Bank of America, unless they had brought with them a bunch of Citibank officers. And it doesn't detract from their performance at Citicorp to say that they were heroes in large part because of the team they found when they took office—a team that wasn't there in 1960.

Even today, after the departure of scores of officers in 1986–87, the bank continues to be deep, deep, deep in personnel. There's a club in London of former Citibankers, with more than a hundred members. They asked me to give a talk to them in fall 1985, and I was delighted. Sixteen years and more after my retirement, a lot of them still come and talk to me about their lives, their careers, what they should do next. They know I was interested in each of them as a person. I could be tough with people, and I won't deny that sometimes I didn't listen when I should have listened, but there were hundreds of men who worked for City Bank when I was president who felt that I knew that they were alive and that their little hearts were beating at the bank— and they were right, and that matters.

6

Not all my interventions in personnel questions were well regarded. One of them, in fact, made the worst uproar of my time running the bank. This was an assignment in 1964 to the Alexander Proudfoot Company of Chicago, to reorganize the paper flow at the bank. The background was that ever since the bank had moved its headquarters to 399 Park Avenue in 1960 we had been getting nibbled to death with unanticipated expenses, especially personnel expenses. I knew from my contacts at the American Bankers Association and from the Federal Reserve reports on bank expenses that we were spending more, sometimes much more, than other large banks. Among my customers who had benefited from "Proudfoot Scheduling Installations" was Caterpillar Tractor, and they gave the firm their highest recommendation. From my work on the survey committee in 1948, from reports by our trainees (one of whom came back to me with a story about asking why a certain form had to be filled out and being told that "Mr. Simonson had asked for it in 1927")—and just from my own casual observation—I knew we needed a good strong shaking up. Proudfoot's usual procedure was to bill for a fraction off what the client saved in payroll expense in the first year of the new system, but we decided we would rather pay a flat fee. Rockefeller approved the contract, and Proudfoot's people went to work in our areas of highest clerical payroll: collections, bookkeeping, commercial credit, foreign tellers.

Even when paid a flat fee, Proudfoot demanded an unusual degree of control over personnel. They assigned people to jobs, chose "coordinators" at various levels, and cut staffing levels. After their preliminary study, they indicated to me that they thought they could save us 30 percent of our clerical payroll costs by eliminating an inherited mess of paper-shuffling. And the fact is that in the first departments they tackled they did save more than 25 percent. They broke a few windows and they stepped on a lot of toes, and they infuriated the old-time supervisors who were being forced to do just what they had said couldn't be done. The rank-and-file clerks were unhappy, too, because they could no longer hide behind an uncontrolled, unscheduled system where the work flowed as fast as they made if flow and nobody could measure their performance. Some of the affected supervisors hatched a conspiracy to get rid of Proudfoot, and when I went down to Buenos Aires for a CICYP meeting at the end of February, 1965, they requested an audience with Rockefeller. They told him I was wrecking the "City

Bank Spirit," and if somebody didn't put a stop to it, I was going to ruin the bank. Various CIO unions had been trying to organize the bank for years and now, they warned, the unions might win. There were organizers all over the place, they said, and there was going to be a mass meeting at a ballroom in one of those Lexington Avenue hotels . . .

The first I heard of any of this was a query from Senator Javits, who was with me at the meeting in Buenos Aires. He was always wired in to what was happening in the financial community in New York, and he'd been on the phone with one of his sources. He warned me I seemed to be in trouble, going so far as to say, "Are you sure your job is safe?" (Javits was a good, good, friend. Once at an editorial board luncheon at the *New York Times*, one of the editors asked me how a deep blue conservative like myself could be so close to a flaming liberal like Jack Javits, and I said that every time there was a cause I cared about—development in the underdeveloped world, a sound monetary system, government economic policies, some elbow room for bankers to operate—I found Javits fighting at my side, and I didn't care what the rest of his politics might be.) Since nobody had been in touch with me, I ignored the whole thing. In fact, I didn't call or telex the bank for several days, until a piece of business was called to my attention which needed a quick response from me—and even then I sent my response not to Rockefeller or Laori or even Wriston but to Tommy Wilcox. This provoked an inter office airmail letter from Rockefeller:

> Dear George:
> We were concerned about your strange silence until Wilcox got your Dowling cable this morning.
> Those of us who are here have been devoting our main effort on the labor front.
> On the unanimous feeling of everyone here, backed up by the opinion of our advisers, Proudfoot's work was terminated at the end of February. Having accomplished the major portion of their objective, there was more to be lost than gained in having them around. Their presence and their activities had become the rallying point and the battle cry.
> To show how jittery the staff was, the grapevine noticed your absence, had you resigning, had you fired, had you joining Proudfoot, had you taking over the Fair, had you as Secretary of the Treasury. Those rumors have all been dispelled . . .

In short, Rockefeller had panicked. As far as I could find out when I returned, the famous organizing meeting in the hotel ballroom had been attended by twenty-five paid organizers and seven City Bank

employees. In the end, I think that the truncated Proudfoot reorganization served its purpose, because the departments they didn't get
around to visiting realized they had to pull up their socks. And soon it
would be necessary to reorganize the entire bank, to adjust our operations to the computer. The man who did that job, John Reed, would
get sufficient velocity from it to propel him all the way to the chairman's slot after Walt Wriston retired.

7

Among our most serious banking problems during my time as
president and chairman was the need to find the money our customers
wanted to borrow. We were repeatedly squeezed. It was a new problem
in my time at the bank. In the 1930s, there had been a great shortage
of borrowers; during the war the government had seen to it that there
was plenty of money around for the defense industries that had to be
financed, and after the war the banks were full of the government
bonds the Federal Reserve System had helped them buy as part of the
process by which we borrowed to pay for the war. Even then, those of
us working the districts were conscious of the importance of getting
corporate customers to leave deposits with the bank as well as borrow
from it, and one of the measurements of the success of a regional
department or a special industries group was its ability to increase the
deposits credited to its customers.

An obvious way to increase the money the bank has for lending is
to move out geographically, adding new branches and new depositors.
That was how Bank of America, which was chartered to operate through
the whole state of California, became the biggest bank in the world in
the 1960s and 1970s—by opening more than a thousand branches. It
is as far from northern California to the Mexican border as it is from
Maine to Florida. The Bank of America had a huge market at its door-
step and for years they were the only California bank that exploited
this huge potential. But we were restricted by law, first to the five
counties of New York City and then to those five plus the immediately
adjacent suburban counties, and before we could move into those we
had to jump hurdles at the Federal Reserve and the comptroller's office.
We did the best we could—we opened thirty-six branches in Nassau
and Westchester Counties between 1960 and 1966, not to mention
another forty-three branches in the boroughs of New York City. But
the yield in terms of lendable deposits was relatively small.

It was clear that if we couldn't get more money to lend, we were eventually going to be suffocated. We had constantly before us the lesson of First National Bank, which depended on a handful of giant customers for much of the money they had to lend. That was why First National Bank shrank in size during the boom years of the 1940s and 1950s, and had to come to us to merge. We had always looked for ways to give service for the money companies left with us. I remember Sheperd saying at a meeting as early as the mid-1950s, "We can't expect people to give us our inventory for nothing; we're going to have to pay for it." Thus for example, City Bank invented the "lock box," the system by which customers paid their bills to a post-office box that would be opened by the bank rather than by the company that had sent the bills, so the money could be credited to the company's account before the bookkeepers went through the process of canceling out the payer's indebtedness.

But companies still didn't want to leave a lot of money lying around idle, especially as the U.S. inflation rate in the 1950s lurched up toward 3 percent a year, high enough in people's minds in those days that Jack Kennedy ran against Richard Nixon in part with the challenge that the Eisenhower administration had weakened the country by failing to control inflation. And the Glass-Steagall law of 1933, written by congressmen who thought (wrongly) that banks had collapsed because they paid too much interest for demand deposits, prohibited us from paying anything at all for money that had been left in the bank for less than thirty days. Companies that would once have carried high balances in their checking accounts, then, began routinely to transfer the money out to short-term Treasury bills, or to the purchase of interest-bearing "commercial paper" issued by other large companies to meet their short-term borrowing needs. We had a double whammy: companies that used to leave spare cash in the bank were taking it out, and companies that had financed their short-term financial needs with bank loans were borrowing directly from our ex-depositors.

Banks had for years issued "certificates of deposit" for a given term—thirty, sixty, ninety days, six months, one year. Those could pay interest under the law, and though the Federal Reserve System controlled the maximum we could pay, it usually kept that rate above the market rate for money. Corporate treasurers with money to hold for more than thirty days were usually, not always, willing to lend it to the banks by purchasing CDs rather than lend it directly to other corporations by purchasing commercial paper. Banks were considered safer. But the issuers of commercial paper had a gimmick. Informally—but anyone who didn't live up to these informal arrangements would be dead in the market in the future—they promised the buyer of the paper that if for any reason he needed cash while the paper was still outstanding, the issuer would buy it back for the face value. And we couldn't make such promises.

Sheperd and Wriston found a way around this problem. We would issue a *negotiable* certificate of deposit, which the owner could sell to someone else if he needed his funds sooner than he had expected. We tried this first in Europe, and it didn't work; Swiss Bank Corporation, which had bought our first negotiable CD for a million dollars, found that there was nobody ready to pay them for it when they wanted to sell. So when we introduced the plan to the United States, we very carefully arranged with Discount Corporation, where I was still on the board, that their traders would make a market in bank CDs parallel to the market they already made in Treasury bills and notes. Today this negotiable certificate of deposit is almost as important as straight checking-account deposits as a source of funds to the very big banks.

In the early days of our plan, we didn't need new capital for the bank, because Howard Sheperd, believing as old-fashioned bankers did that a bank can *never* have too much capital, had sold a lot of stock through rights issues in the early 1950s. This held down our earnings-per-share for the better part of a decade, but by 1963 the bank was growing so fast that our "capital ratio" was falling below what the examiners liked to see, and we went to market. The vehicle was a $200 million issue of convertible debentures (much more money then than it would be today). The advantage of the convertible debenture was that interest rates on the bonds were lower (because there was also a play on the stock), and the dilution of our stockholders' equity would presumably be postponed until we had begun to earn enough on the new capital to pay it.

Our underwriter was First Boston. The terms were a coupon of $3\frac{3}{4}$ percent, with conversion to common shares at a price of seventy dollars a share, about 20 percent above the then market price. But the day before the issue was to be brought to market, disaster struck, in the form of the foreign-exchange losses in our Brussels branch. Our lawyers and First Boston's lawyers agreed that this $8-million loss was "material" and would have to be reported. The issue had to be postponed and re-priced, to offer a sweeter 4 percent coupon and a lower conversion price of $66.75. Oddly, we probably wound up making money on this, because the higher coupon meant that holders of the debentures delayed converting them to stock somewhat longer than they otherwise would have done. Our dividends rose every year that I was president and chairman (and still do), but with the improved coupon on the bond (4 percent vs. 3¾ percent) it took an additional eighteen months before the dividend on the stock into which the bond was convertible exceeded the interest we were paying on the bond. Because the 4 percent interest payment on the debenture was tax-deductible to the bank, while dividend payments are after taxes, our bottom line showed greater retained earnings than it would have showed if we'd been able to keep the original pricing of 3¾ percent and the bond had been converted earlier.

Then, as a last straw, on the morning of the day we were to go to our directors for approval of the new arrangements, James Coggeshall of First Boston arrived at my office at nine in the morning to tell me that two days after the scheduled sale day for our issue, his firm would be in the market selling bank bonds again, this time as the lead underwriter on a similar issue for Chase. I was flabbergasted by his total unconcern about the obvious conflict, arising from the fact that the same customers of his firm would be interested in both issues and would seek advice on which to prefer. I told him that if he insisted on his "right" to manage both issues, we would exercise our "right" to remove his firm from the leadership of our syndicate, and proceed with the five firms now listed in the second "bracket." Moreover, I said I had to know by 10:00, because we had a board meeting. He excused himself, went to a conference room and made a phone call, and returned to say that his firm was dropping out of the Chase issue. The next day I had a call from George Woods, who had recently retired as chairman of First Boston, to apologize for his former firm's behavior.

While I waited for Coggeshall to change his mind, incidentally, I had a visit from André Meyer of Lazard Frères, who had scented something in the wind. He generously offered to underwrite the issue for us on what were really better terms than First Boston's, for First Boston had as usual included in its contract some protections for themselves. The obligation they were undertaking was to purchase and sell to the public that part of the convertible bonds issue not purchased by our existing stockholders (who had rights to buy first). So there would be some time between the day the issue first went on sale to stockholders and the day when they had to accept their commitment. Their contract, as is usual, provided for "escape clauses": if there were a major change in the condition of the bank, or in the economy, they didn't have to make their purchases. Meyer said he would waive that escape clause, agreeing that Lazard Frères would immediately put the money for their commitment into our account at the Federal Reserve, no questions asked. But when Coggeshall withdrew his previous suggestion that First Boston would do the Chase deal, too, I felt bound by our previous arrangements. Then, of course, Meyer and Lazard did the Chase deal . . .

But we never got away from our funding problems, all the rest of my time at the bank. The one meeting I attended every day I was in New York was that of the money committee, and the most elaborate of our communications arrangements after headquarters was moved from 55 Wall Street to 399 Park Avenue was the closed-circuit television system that allowed midtown and Wall Street economists and market specialists to see each other during this mid-morning meeting, where we exchanged information about what our biggest customers were going to take from or pay into the bank that day, and what funds we would need to meet their demands and maintain our legally required reserves at the Fed. It was our policy that when the president or the chairman was out of New York, the other sent a letter at least every week, and more often twice a week, to describe what was happening at the bank. I have a stack of these letters, to me and from me, and there's scarcely one that doesn't express concern or relief about "the money position."

Although we had the negotiable CD in our armament, the Fed could determine whether or not we could use it. The top interest rate we could offer was subject to control by the Fed, without right of appeal. In 1966 and again in 1969, the Fed in effect stood us against the wall by keeping the rates we could offer below what the market was paying for commercial paper and even Treasury bills, which meant that the money simply ran out of the bank. To square our books on Wednesdays, when the Fed added up our reserve position for the week, we often had to borrow from the Fed itself, at the "discount window." This left us to a degree at the government's mercy, because the Fed insisted that access to the discount window was a privilege, not a right. What saved us was the availability of Eurodollars. There was no control over the interest rates we could pay for funds abroad (it never would have occurred to anybody in the 1930s when the banking legislation was being written that an American bank would be borrowing dollars abroad). It cut into our profits to buy money abroad, but over the long run we would have been hurt worse if we had been unable to meet the needs of our good long-term borrowers.

Soon after my retirement, the Fed needed help from the banks to handle the crisis in the commercial-paper market that followed upon the collapse of Penn Central, and the compromise that was worked out established a category of large certificates of deposit—over $100,000—that would not be subject to interest-rate controls. Thereafter, Citibank never had to worry that money would actually be unobtainable. For my successors, the daily problem was not the availability but the price of money. You sleep a little better at night, but it may be even harder to make a living.

8

What all of this said to Wriston and me, finally, was that we were in the wrong business. Banking as a separate line of commerce, to use the phrase Chairman Paul Volcker of the Federal Reserve Board likes, had only a limited future. What we had to do was find ways to employ the status and resources of the bank to satisfy the financial needs and wants of our customers, whether those ways were called banking or not. General Electric in those days had an in-house think tank called Tempo, and we went to them for a study of the future of our sort of business. The Tempo academics' basic statement to us was that we didn't want to be a bank; we wanted to be a financial-service institution—and, especially, we wanted to be in the information business. Computers, Tempo said, were going to be like automobiles in their contribution to the economy. In the early 1960s, when they did their study, information-processing by computers accounted for only about 1 percent of the U.S. GNP, like automobiles in the early years of the century. But just as economic activity associated with automobiles (gasoline, road-building, garages, and so on) doubled every few years, until the car accounted for 15 percent of the economy, computers and the activities associated with them (new services, software creation, and so on) would double every few years and reach 20 percent of the economy, half for hardware, half for software. Banking, when you came right down to it, was an information business.

The problem was that our banking charter gave us only certain limited powers, and even those had been further circumscribed by legislation or regulation. National City Bank had owned Farmers Trust since 1929, and Farmers Trust *was* our trust department. We had no employees in that department who weren't on the Farmers Trust pay-roll. But when we moved to absorb the Farmers Trust entity into Citi-bank in 1960, we triggered an investigation by the Justice Department, where some lawyers felt that under the doctrine of "potential compe-tition" we should be forced to divest ourselves of Farmers Trust and build our own brand-new separate trust department. The government probably could have done that too, but cooler heads prevailed in Wash-ington, and I didn't even hear that we had been in that danger until some years later. In 1966, we bought the Carte Blanche credit card from Conrad Hilton through the agency of André Meyer and Lazard Frères. Then the Justice Department scared us out of keeping it, and we sold it to Avco, at a profit, again through Meyer and later we bought it back through him, too.)

The solution, which emerged in discussions among Rockefeller and Wriston and myself, was the creation of a holding company that would own the bank and also own other corporations not limited by banking charters. We had to be a little tentative about this, because the history of the National City Company in the 1920s was far from glorious—as I knew full well, having served as pallbearer—and because there was some question of what the law did in fact allow. Congress in 1956 had passed an act restricting the businesses that could be pur-sued by a *multi-bank* holding company, but it had made exceptions for a *one-bank* holding company, essentially to sustain the small-town banker, whose living might come as much from his insurance or real estate agency as it did from his little bank. Well, City Bank was one bank. We could become part of a one-bank holding company. We still wouldn't want to step over the line of Glass-Steagall, much as I might think that law should be repealed—Congress had unquestionably intended in that act to prevent the formation of new National City Companies to act as securities underwriters.

In 1967, we took our policy committee to Nassau for a special three-day meeting to discuss the future organization of our financial-services institution. That meeting gave us the go-ahead, and then we were further encouraged by a speech George Mitchell, the vice-chairman of the Federal Reserve Board (a college professor but a man who really understood banking), made at the annual summer School of Banking at the University of Wisconsin. The time had come, Mitchell said, to allow banks to offer new services to the public, both because they would provide these services less expensively and perhaps better than other suppliers, and because there was a growing need for banks to acquire income sources other than the spread between what they paid for their money and what they could charge for it when they made loans. That was why we needed a holding company.

In 1968, to paraphrase the charming comment by historians Harold van B. Cleveland and Thomas F. Huertas, the bank gave birth to its own parent. We were not quite the first: Wachovia in North Carolina and Union Bank in Los Angeles had formed one-bank holding companies into which they had folded control of their bank and their other activities, but we were by far the biggest and most prominent pilgrim on this new path. Almost immediately, the regulators and the securities-industry organizations and the small bankers moved to apply to one-bank holding companies most of the rules written into the 1956 act to control multi-bank holding companies. I stood and fought, but couldn't see it through: my retirement was inflexibly scheduled for the last board meeting in April, 1970, and the amendments to the act were still pending when I left. The bill that finally passed on New Year's Eve, 1970, gave the Federal Reserve Board complete authority to define those businesses "incidental to banking" that bank holding companies, one or many, would be permitted to own. We were denied the chance to acquire the Chubb insurance group, our acquisition of a management consulting firm was reversed, and we were put out of the travel-agency business. But we kept finance companies and factoring and leasing, and the chance to develop and sell computer software (which was what the Tempo study had said we should want most), and many other things that Wriston and Reed later brought to fruition.

As noted earlier, my accession to the chairman's post in June, 1967, had been accompanied by a change in the by-laws that left the bank without a chief executive officer—and a change in custom that left Rockefeller on the board after his retirement, presumably so he could continue to keep an eye on that Moore, who some thought was inclined to be a little brave. I noted in my diary that the action had been "ungracious, undeserved and unnecessary"—and then Walt and I went about our business. We both said we never read the by-laws anyway; and we had been working together, after all, for more than fifteen years. Neither of us paid too much attention to Stillman Rockefeller. In a letter to Wriston, who was on vacation in summer 1968, I noted "one for the book. JSR called up and asked to come down a couple of days ago, with his usual warm friendly attitude. He expressed his desire to be helpful without interfering and ended up asking if I couldn't put him on the list to get internal memoranda so . . . he wouldn't look as dumb as he otherwise looks when he doesn't know what is going on. In my usual cooperative way I smiled, repeated our desire to keep him as well informed as possible, but emphasized the problems of selectivity as to what to tell him. I said I would talk to you, that we obviously wanted to keep all the directors as well informed as possible!"

When it came my turn to pass the baton in 1970, I made a motion to return the by-laws to their previous condition, which was passed without discussion; and Rockefeller and I both left the board. What his feelings were, I do not know. I felt nothing but pride in my forty-four years of work for Citibank, and in the great, professionalized institution I was leaving behind in the place where, as Rockefeller had seen fit to remind me, there had once been only a collection of personal fiefdoms.

10
Civic Duties, Civic Pleasures

My introduction to the world of the great New York charitable institutions came when I was an assistant to James Perkins and represented him at meetings of the board of the American Museum of Natural History. That's still a great museum, of course, and a noble pile running four blocks on Central Park West, but it doesn't have quite the standing in the world that it had in the 1920s and 1930s. Then the man who had been its spiritual leader, Theodore Roosevelt (his statue on horseback stands on the front steps), was a live memory in the minds of the leaders of the community, not, as now, just another name in the history books. The eminence of the board of this museum in the 1920s and early 1930s may be judged by the membership of the finance committee: Perkins, J. P. Morgan, George Baker of First National Bank, and Felix Warburg of Kuhn, Loeb.

When that committee met, a young man learned something. I remember one investment meeting early in my time with Perkins when the principals were accompanied by assistants. This was a period when the railroads were visiting the bankruptcy courts and their bonds were selling for a quarter or less of their face value. One of the directors wanted to know about some Great Northern bonds the museum owned, 7 percent-bonds due in 2027. I knew a little about them from the manuals, and I was about to speak when Perkins put his hand on my arm. Across the room, a little mousy guy from Morgan got up and said, "These are secured by trackage from Tacoma to Seattle . . ." He went on, giving details of the traffic on the line, the income he estimated the railroad derived from it, something like $98,327 per mile per year, and the legal status of the mortgage, giving it as his opinion that the bonds, having gone through the previous reorganization, were unquestionably an underlying lien and would survive any future reorganization. He concluded by saying, "I think it's safe to hold, Mr. Baker." As the meeting broke up, Perkins told me that this man was John Oldham, who was J. P. Morgan's railroad expert, had participated in a number of railroad reorganizations, and was probably the world's leading expert on railroad securities. I learned a lesson—don't talk except the niceties until you know who's in the room, even at a dinner party!

With people of that eminence, the finance committee didn't meet often, and sometimes Perkins would send me around to the offices of the other members to gain their consent for something he as treasurer wished to do with the museum's investments. Once, I remember, someone had left the museum a minority interest in a hat factory in Rhode Island, and Perkins wanted to sell it. The best offer we could get from the majority holders was about half the book value of the stock, and Perkins asked me to poll the committee. Morgan thought the price was low, and we should keep the stock until a more optimistic buyer came along. Baker agreed with Morgan. Warburg agreed with Perkins that we should sell. For some reason, I remember Warburg vividly, a man with a bald head and a moustache, sitting at his little antique desk with no papers on it—only an ashtray and a pen with a feather top in a silver dish full of lead shot. "There are," he said, "only two kinds of investment I will make or retain. One is where I have control and it's important enough to get my best attention. The other is where someone I have confidence in has control and is giving it his best attention. Neither is true in this case. I don't like the price, either, but you tell me Mr. Perkins doesn't think we can do better. I can see the committee needs a reason." Morgan and Baker withdrew their objection and we sold the stock to the majority owners.

It was valuable to me as a youngster to meet with such men, and, frankly, I always thought in later years that in terms of personal contacts and what I learned, I got as much as I gave from my work on non-profit boards. It wasn't a Citibank tradition. Neither James Stillman nor Charles Mitchell had been especially public-spirited, and between Perkins and myself none of the presidents or chairmen—not Rentschler, Brady, Sheperd, nor Rockefeller—had been significant figures in New York outside the bank itself. Rockefeller used to say to me, "You spend too damned much time out of the bank, George. You spread yourself too thin, and neglect the bank." I did spend perhaps a quarter of my time outside the bank during the years I was president and chairman, in addition to my traveling. I was president of the Metropolitan Opera and chairman of the special gifts committee that raised the larger contributions for the performing arts center at Lincoln Center—endless lunches; and I was vice-president of New York Hospital, chairman of the finance committee of the 1964–65 World's Fair, one of the organizers of the Bedford-Stuyvesant Restoration Committee, and a founding member of an economic development council for Mayor John Lindsay and of an export promotion committee for Presidents John F. Kennedy and Lyndon Johnson; and all through that time, though I didn't hold any title, I was running the Spanish Institute in New York out of a back pocket in my office. Plus I had accepted a number of Yale responsibilities—I chaired the endowment fund for the engineering school, and my class reunion committee, and for a while I was treasurer of the class. Of the three secretaries I kept busy, at least one spent most of her time on my non-profit work. But I thought I did a better job for the bank by mixing with the world. Besides, if you've got my temperament, you're always full of ideas about how people ought to be running things. You'd better keep your mouth shut, or better yet, stay away, because if you can't keep quiet—and I can't— you end up running them yourself.

Actually, the first time I joined a board on my own, I was motivated in part by self-interest. Perkins had been active with Columbia-Presbyterian Hospital, and he told me while I was still a junior assistant that one of the things I should plan to do in New York was to establish a connection with a hospital, because then I could be sure that if I or anyone in my family got sick we'd be well taken care of. Soon after World War II, I worked on a number of pipeline deals with Frank Kernan, senior partner in White, Weld & Company who was president of New York Hospital, and I asked him whether he thought there was some work I could do for the hospital. The next thing I knew, I was a member of his board of governors, and I became fascinated by the institution itself.

New York Hospital is a mini-city in its own not very efficient 1920s skyscrapers on the East River in mid-Manhattan. The Cornell-New York Hospital complex has three functions—it takes care of patients (New York Hospital), it teaches doctors and nurses (Cornell University Medical School), and performs important medical research (at both). The founders of the hospital in 1772 talked about the three functions more than two hundred years ago: on the two-hundredth anniversary we had a party at Trinity Church, where the original papers for the hospital were drawn up, and some members of the board got into powdered wigs and costumes for the occasion and read the speeches that had been made that first day and preserved in the hospital's record books. I think all hospitals should have university affiliations. I've been active at the Lahey Clinic in Boston, which also takes care of me, and when James Killian was chancellor of MIT and had a stomach operation the same time I did, the two of us conspired together a little to see if these two institutions could be joined in some way, developing a medical school at MIT to create—instantly—a major new medical center. "We're right in the door of medicine," Killian said, referring to MIT's work in biology and genetics. But his successor at MIT was not enthusiastic and never followed through.

Obviously, laymen can't run hospitals and shouldn't try, but a board member who's asking the right questions can keep the administrators thinking about what's important. At a hospital like New York, there are a number of decisions that have to be made where a businessman's experience is essential. It's an endowed institution, and it has to have an investment policy. It raises funds on a regular basis, and must have plans and procedures for soliciting contributions. It has to decide on building and modernizing facilities, which involves guessing the near-term course of the economy and what may happen to government policy and government appropriations. In our age of technological change, it needs a steady stream of new equipment, and thinks it needs even more than it does need. It has labor relations problems.

I'm still on the investment and real estate committees of the hospital. I come to New York for some of the board meetings, try to help them get contributions from VIPs I know who have reciprocated generously for the excellent care the hospital has given them and their families. Such gifts are anonymous, of course, as a practical matter: once news of a large gift gets out, the giver is relentlessly badgered by all the world's other good causes. Among my personal reasons for gratitude to New York Hospital is the excellent treatment I received on the one occasion in my adult life when I became seriously ill, with a nasty kind of sharp-pointed kidney stone, in winter 1959. I had so many tubes coming out of me after the operation that I looked like a petrochemical plant. (Today, by the way, such an operation might not be necessary, because there is a remarkable new machine that uses sonic waves to break up kidney stones inside the kidney so they can be passed nature's way.) When I was recovered sufficiently to leave the hospital, the doctors sent me to Puerto Rico to rest before returning to work at the bank. And it was during those weeks at Dorado Beach in Puerto Rico that I met Charon Crosson, the daughter of the political editor of the New York *Daily News*, whom I married in 1967, who became the mother of Tina and Steve and Pia, and who has kept me lots younger than anyone else I know whose passport says he is as old as I am.

2

My introduction to the opera came through the great soprano Lucrezia Bori, who was Spanish from Valencia (though her ancestry was Italian, and her name was really Lucrezia Borgia). She had already retired from the stage when I met her, but she was still significantly involved with the Met, as the only singer ever elected to its board and one of the company's most important fund-raisers. She was one of the three people most widely credited with saving the company when it almost went broke in 1935, the others being Mrs. August Belmont (who had also once been a stage professional, as the actress Eleanor Robson, thirty years before) and Cornelius Bliss, heir to one of the country's great textile fortunes and one of the first professional philanthropists—with whom, by the way, Miss Bori's name was romantically (but quietly) linked. Bori arranged for my family to have a Met subscription of a pair of good seats in the Grand Tier, which was not so easy in the old opera house, where so many seats had only partial or blocked views. We went to parties at Miss Bori's house and met some of the artists.

One day in 1958, I received a summons to the chairman's office at the bank, and when I arrived I found Sheperd sitting with Anthony Bliss, Cornelius's son, a tall, rather gray lawyer, who had recently become president of the Met. The company's treasurer hadn't been coming to meetings or attending to the Met's problems (oddly, it was Sloan Colt, who had originally hired me into Farmers Trust, and was then very busy running Bankers Trust). Miss Bori, who was still active on the board, had suggested to Bliss that a young man she knew (I was older than Bliss, but young to her) was a rising figure at Citibank and might be persuaded to take the job. Bliss as a courtesy had gone to Sheperd to inquire whether the bank would have any objection to my becoming a board member and treasurer at the Met, and Sheperd said the bank would have no objection if I agreed, which I did.

I soon found that the Met's financial planning was poor and its books difficult to understand. The tradition of the Metropolitan had been that it did not solicit charity. Between World War I and the Depression, the opera company had made money every year. This bookkeeping had been somewhat artificial, because the opera house itself was the property of a small group of boxholders (who never had to pay admission: they "owned" their box and could occupy it or give the seats to friends or sell them for any and every performance). The producing company got the use of the theater free and kept all the receipts from the sale of all the seats other than those in the boxes. In the 1930s, the cost of running this expensive property (which paid real estate taxes, as a private enterprise) was considerably greater than the box-office price of the seats the boxholders kept for themselves, even if all the seats had been sold. Part of the financial crisis of the opera company in the Depression had been the inability or unwillingness of the boxholders to pay for the repairs to the house that were necessary if the fire department was to permit performances to continue. In 1939, a new Metropolitan Opera Association had been formed to own the opera house as well as produce the operas, and except for an odd year here and there that company had always been dependent on contributions, many of them from the general public that bought the tickets in New York or heard the broadcasts all over the country.

In 1958, when I joined the board, the general manager of the Met was Rudolf Bing, a sharp Viennese who had run the Glyndebourne Opera in England and founded the Edinburgh Festival before coming to the Met in 1950. Bing had worked out a general arrangement with the board that he would find the money for new productions and we would give him a budget large enough to pay the costs of the rest of the season. Ideally, the revenue side of that budget would be met by ticket sales (the Met virtually sold out its 3,800 seats for seven performances a week even in a theater built in 1883 where many of the seats were "partial view" or blocked by posts), plus a little extra money from concessions, broadcast rights, recording royalties, tour performances, and so forth. But that ideal had grown increasingly difficult to realize as the European recovery bid up the prices for opera singers and the stage and musical unions raised the costs of presenting a performance. Meanwhile, we had an old theater in very bad shape: two firemen were permanently stationed in the building at every performance in hopes of catching problems early if the antiquated wiring shorted somewhere in the thick walls. We couldn't air-condition it to make it rentable in the summer months, and we couldn't introduce any of the stage innovations that were revitalizing serious musical theater elsewhere, especially in Germany.

All that was going to be history, rather soon. By the time I joined the Met board, thirty years of argument had ended and the die had been cast to build a new opera house. We had joined with the New York Philharmonic and the Rockefeller family (the John D. branch, not the William branch from which my colleague Stillman was descended) to create the Lincoln Center for the Performing Arts, in which the Met would have the largest building—as a gift, incidentally: we wouldn't have to raise the money to build it, and we would be able to keep as an endowment all the money we received by leasing or selling the Broadway site of the old opera house. Once we moved, of course, we would be responsible for all maintenance and upkeep expenses on the new building, plus 30 percent of the common costs of the Lincoln Center group of buildings.

Bing and Bliss were not delighted by Lincoln Center, because the Met would have to share the plaza with the New York City Center and its New York City Opera, which would present performances around the corner, as it were, at a much lower price. As a result, Lincoln Center had not been able to tap some of the Met's most generous contributors, who had been counted on to help defray that supposed $28 million (in the end, it was almost $50 million) cost of the new opera house. But the project had the unstinting support of the forward-looking members of the board—Colonel Joseph Hartfield, the very small, very brilliant lawyer who was senior partner of White & Case, Bankers Trust's law firm; C. D. Jackson of Time, Inc.; and John W. Drye, a well-named Texas lawyer who ran not only the firm of Kelly, Drye in New York but also the Juilliard Foundation, which sponsored the Juilliard School of Music (one of the partners in Lincoln Center) and had a long history of involvement with the Met from the will of the first Juilliard. Not long after I became treasurer of the Met (and soon after I became president of Citibank), I accepted appointment by John D. Rockefeller III as chairman of the committee that was to raise the "major grants" from corporations and foundations for the building of Lincoln Center.

Board members can know the financial condition of an opera company only if management makes it clear to them. For most of the year, an opera company that sells its seats by subscription has money in the bank and seems to be in good health even if it isn't. The performances for which tickets have been sold by subscription are owed to the subscriber just as much as magazine issues or newspapers are owed to their subscribers, and an opera company should spend the income from subscription sales only as the performances are given, just as a magazine should take its subscription sales income onto its books only as the issues are put in the mail. If they haven't paid attention to what's going on, the board of an opera company might be personally liable to the subscribers, to refund their money or put on some sort of performance on the subscription evenings, should the company go bust.

Accounting for a new production is not an open-and-shut case, either. No doubt the sets and costumes are an asset of the company, can be carried on the books as an investment and depreciated with time. But opera productions are more like goodwill than like, say, machine tools. If the company needs money, it's not likely to get much by selling its old sets and costumes. Meanwhile, a new production costs a lot of additional money for rehearsals and so on. Today the Met tries to include these startup costs in the new production budget, and asks the contributor who gives the production to pay those, too. But sometimes you have to load it onto operating costs. Management can get away with paying a lot of its bills late, because people are reluctant to sue an opera company. Finally, management can keep some big bills in the desk, and can keep the true financial position hidden for a good while, if they desire.

Wonders of misinformation can be communicated when you have an operation as large and as expensive as the Met, with a budget that ran into eight figures even in my uninflationary time, with tour revenues as well as subscriptions to play with and various pieces of ancillary income. The praise I must give Rudolf Bing is that even in those first days, when I was a stranger to the procedures of opera accounting, he was always straight and honest with me about what was going on in the house. He was also a good businessman, who hated to waste money. But when he thought ahead, he thought in terms of artistic planning more than financial planning—and once the house was committed to the artistic plan, of course, the budget was locked in. Bing often gave me a hard time. He understandably thought that my role, duty, was to find the money necessary for him to do what he thought was artistically necessary. But when he concluded that he had got as much as was there, he always cut back as necessary, and lived within the available means.

The crisis at the Met came after we moved to Lincoln Center in 1966 and found we had created an octopus of operating costs. Of all people, I shouldn't have been surprised, for only a few years before I had lived through the costly experience of moving the bank from Wall Street to our new building at 399 Park Avenue and learning that *everything* cost more than we had expected. Every item of overhead goes up when you triple the floor space. Cleaning costs rise astronomically. Somehow the old furniture doesn't look right, and you buy new. Things you never think about until you live with them rise up to bite you—in the old building, for example, many people didn't have their own telephones, but in the new one they handed out telephones like hors d'oeuvres, so the phone bill doubled and tripled. As John Drye of the Met board said a few years later when the Juilliard School got into financial trouble following its move from a sort of high-school building uptown near Columbia University to the stunning modernity of its new home in Lincoln Center, "When you go from a hovel to a palace your expenses increase."

In theory, the extra expenses of the new opera house would be matched by extra receipts and by operating efficiencies. The new house didn't have more seats than the old one, but the distribution was different—there were more high-priced seats in the orchestra and the Grand Tier, fewer low-priced seats in the Family Circle. In fact, even the sell-out first season in the new building was disastrous. There were special difficulties on which one could put the blame: management had planned (and we had okayed) seven new productions for the first season, which turned out to be more than the company could handle without horrendous overtime. The opening-night opera, the world premiere of Samuel Barber's *Anthony and Cleopatra,* was the heaviest production its librettist-director-designer Franco Zeffirelli had ever tried to mount. It made much use of the stage turntable, and the turntable broke down because of a design flaw, which meant Franco had to improvise some of his staging with two or three hundred people waiting around, getting paid, to see what he decided to do. The musicians were threatening to strike and refusing to prepare any performances except opening night, which meant that the schedule for the early weeks had to be drastically and expensively rearranged, even though the orchestra finally settled without a strike. But it soon became clear that the costs of running the opera company in Lincoln Center were going to be higher than anyone had anticipated.

Looking back, it is clear that nobody gave sufficient thought to the future operating problems of the cultural organizations that were to be involved in Lincoln Center. They were delighted with the thought of new homes for the Met, the New York Philharmonic, the City Center, the Juilliard School. They didn't want to ask how much it would cost to live and perform in these new, rich, enlarged quarters.

If we had thought it through, we might have seen that there was one possible source of additional revenue to sustain the performing companies: the revival of what had been an economically dead area on the West Side of New York City. It has been suggested that the city could have dedicated to the performing institutions of the center some portion of the extra tax revenues it would derive from new construction and improved use of the nearby buildings, but this was New York en route to deep financial trouble, and not about to give away income. At the start, however, it would have been possible to take for the benefit of the center, under the urban renewal laws, more land than the new theaters and school and library occupied, and dedicate the revenue it would yield to help pay for the performances. Today various projects are pending to permit the center to sell its "air rights" to builders who could improve the zoning envelope on their land by purchasing the center's worthless "right" to build much taller buildings where the theaters now stand. It's second-best, but it might be worthwhile.

As treasurer, I had to report to the board in fall 1966, only a couple of months after the huge party that had marked our first night in the new quarters, that the Met was in serious financial trouble. My report was not well understood. There were only a few directors who were what I would call economically literate and understood budgets. And this small group did not include Bliss, who was a lawyer by trade. As a result, the financial problem was made to take a back seat to the decision about whether or not to continue Metropolitan Opera support of a national company that had been launched the year before to offer low-cost opera productions with young artists in smaller cities around the country. I had always been against it—my line, which became a kind of joke on the board, was that "The Met is not in business to perform opera in East Lansing"—and now it seemed to me we could not possibly afford the million dollars a year the company was budgeted to lose. But this had been Tony Bliss's baby, and he fought to save it, arguing that money could be raised for the national company, especially from Mrs. DeWitt Wallace of *Readers Digest,* one of our most generous patrons, that wouldn't be available to the parent company. I thought this was nonsense, and said so. On the vote, the national company lost. Director John Drye, my wisest counselor, said, "It's been my experience that you can't run two losing businesses at the same time." That remark ended the discussion.

Bliss withdrew, and I became president of the Met. For the next half-dozen years, I met regularly with Bing and his assistant managers and with a fund-raising committee headed by Mrs. Lewis Douglas— Peggy Douglas, a great tough-minded lady who loved the opera and was in a position to put the arm on some of the richest people in America. Which she did. Robert C. Devine of *Readers Digest* explained our needs to Mrs. Wallace. There were other stalwarts, too, notably Nin Ryan, the daughter of Otto Kahn (who had been president of the opera from 1903 to 1931), Lil Phipps, the lawyers Lowell Wadmond and Chuck Spofford, a very big-league fellow, and my board chairmen, first Lauder Greenway and then William Rockefeller. Meanwhile, I was in touch several times a week with artistic administrator Bob Herman and general administrator Herman Krawitz, both intensely loyal to Bing and the opera company, and very capable. We cut down on the number of new productions the Met would attempt and on the lavishness of some of them, we cut the bureaucracy and the number of stagehands, we drew up a budget and a plan that would allow the company to live on its receipts and the contributions we thought we could raise. Announcing my election as president to the annual meeting of the Association the next spring, chairman Lauder Greenway said that I was the man "who had got the train back on the rails."

And on the budget Bing had, he gave New York the greatest singers in the world, year after year. He was of course responsible for artistic decisions. I'm sure that every so often I brought him artistic suggestions that others had made to me, not pretending to know whether they were good ideas or not. But the only time I interfered seriously with his planning was while I was still treasurer, and I had dinner with Onassis and Maria Callas, who gave me to understand, subtly, that she would be willing to sing again at the Met. Contrary to myth, Bing and Callas liked each other very much, personally—Bing's assistant John Gutman, a German near his own age who was perhaps his closest friend in the administration, once explained that it was because they were both dog-lovers: Callas came to her first stage rehearsal at the Met with her little poodle, who peed on the stage tree, and instead of complaining about it Bing told her sympathetically that his little dachshund would probably have done the same thing. When I told Bing what Callas had said, he authorized me to explore further, and the result was her return to the Met (from which she had departed in an apparent rage in 1958), to sing two unforgettable Toscas in 1965. As Bing once said, there was a magnetic power in the woman: when she walked on stage, or into a room, you never paid attention to anyone else.

I was also with Callas when she and Tebaldi had their much-photographed kiss-and-make-up scene in Tebaldi's dressing room at the Met during a performance in 1971 (this was a publicity event completely: the two artists had not been fighting). And I was with her when she taught her master classes in the Juilliard Theatre, a gem of a small opera house built into the Juilliard School. (This should have been, if the people planning Lincoln Center had understood what they were doing, an auxiliary theater where the Met could perform eighteenth-century opera and chamber opera; instead, it cannot be used for anything but school events, because the unions have said that once tickets are sold for an attraction in the Juilliard Theatre they will demand that the school use union instead of student technicians and stage-hands for free student performances, too.) Callas sat on a high stool beside the rehearsal pianist while the poor students tried to get the audience to pay attention to them rather than to their teacher. But they all learned from her. So did Juilliard president Peter Mennin, who had gratefully accepted Callas's offer to teach without a fee, just her expenses at the Plaza—which by the time she was done ordering champagne and caviar for all her friends ran several times what Mennin would have paid her to teach the classes.

Bliss remained on the Met board after I became president, and was often a focus of dissent. He still wanted a national company, and he criticized our handling of our labor relations. He wanted us to do much more with ballet (he had married a dancer from the Met's ballet company). Most of the time, he had a potent ally in Mrs. August Belmont, a grand lady, who with Bori's help had founded the Metropolitan Opera Guild to help the Met in the 1930s, and who was still its mother hen. The Guild published a magazine, produced and sold souvenirs, ran a ticket service for members, and gave parties. At the end of the season, it gave us a check for something like a quarter of a million dollars. "You were formed to support the Met," I told Mrs. Belmont and the Guild people on the Met board. "Today you have the retail franchise for the Met, and I can't give you that franchise for the two, three hundred thousand dollars a year the guild contributes. I have to raise ten million, and I need at least a million from you." Everyone said I was guilty of disrespect, but the next year we got a million dollars from the Guild. Mrs. Douglas suggested to me that I should drop Bliss from the list of nominees to the board, because otherwise he would bide his time until he could get back in control, but I told her I always need people around who oppose and question me—otherwise I make too many mistakes. After my retirement, Bliss did return, first as a working salaried president of the Met and then as general manager.

After we pulled through the 1967 crisis, my personal involvement with the management of the Met dropped to a less time-consuming level. But one thing I had to do myself: find a successor to Bing, who turned seventy in 1971, and after twenty years had grown a little bored with the day-to-day grind of the opera house. He wanted us to make Herman and Krawitz joint general managers, but the feeling on the board was that the house should have a cleaning when Bing left, with a new management and a new approach. Bing was not happy about this, naturally, but he was a complete professional, and when in fact we chose his successor and the man arrived for a year of observation prior to taking over, he received absolute cooperation from everyone on Bing's staff.

Our search was extensive. The first choice was Peter Mennin, president of the Juilliard School, a composer himself, a good fund-raiser and a man of suave charm. He wanted the job, too, but the day I approached him was the day the Ford Foundation had agreed to give his school $25 million to fund a development program he had worked out himself. He couldn't run out on that. We talked with Julius Rudel, the conductor who was also general manager of the New York City Opera, and with Leonard Bernstein. A couple of us on the committee went to Milan to check out Massimo Bogianckino, the "superintendent" at La Scala (later the general manager of the Paris Opera and then mayor of the city of Florence), but we decided that the experience of running an Italian theater, with its heavy municipal subsidies and incessant politics, was not really relevant to what we needed in New York. Maria Callas had indicated to me that she would be interested in moving on to opera management, and I brought the idea to the board, adding that of course we would have to hire a first-rate administrator to do all the things Maria obviously couldn't do; the board didn't think much of the idea, and neither, to tell you the truth, did I. Bing's contract was up in spring 1970; we extended it for two more years. Then in spring 1971, I had a call from Lord Drogheda, chairman of the *Financial Times* publishing company and my opposite number at the Royal Opera House, Covent Garden. He knew just the man for the Met, he said—Goeran Gentele, the chief of the Stockholm Opera. "You keep talking about opera as musical theater," he said. "Here's a man who's a stage director, but he's also a musician, he plays instruments. And he knows how to live with a budget, because they've always been poor in Stockholm."

By then I had retired from Citibank, and was spending most of my time with my family at my home in Sotogrande, on the Costa del Sol not far from Gibraltar. I called the president of the Stockholm Opera, a member of the Wallenberg clan, who gave a rueful consent for me to approach Gentele, whom I then called and asked if he and his wife could come visit with me in Spain for a weekend. They did, and both Charon and I were enchanted. Gentele spoke perfect English and what he said made sense. If he became general manager of the Met, he said, he would try to set up a troika at its top—himself as artistic director for all but musical matters, a major conductor as music director, and a skilled administrator to run the business functions. He was extremely presentable, and his actress wife Marit was if anything more presentable.

I had of course kept the Met's nominating committee informed, and now I called board chairman Lauder Greenway and asked him to get the committee together. They and other key board members (including Bliss) concurred that Gentele was the right choice, and he accepted. Charon and I flew home, and we arranged a dinner for the entire board and Gentele at my home in New Canaan, on three days' notice. After dinner, the board formally met and offered Gentele the job, to start two years later, one season for him to arrange his departure from Stockholm and a second to live at the Met and prepare to take over from Bing. Among the relatively few people Gentele knew in New York was Schuyler Chapin, scion of the Chapin family after which one of the city's most famous private girls' schools is named. Chapin had worked in arts administration all his life, including a term as Leonard Bernstein's administrative assistant and some years of running the Lincoln Center summer festival. Gentele wanted Chapin to be his administrator, and of course we agreed.

The transition year with Bing went more smoothly than anyone had expected—a tribute to Bing, Herman, and Krawitz, who would all be departing. Gentele approved retaining Herman's and Krawitz's assistants, Charles Riecker and Michael Bronson, to fill their shoes. He engaged the Czech conductor Rafael Kubelik, who had been music director of Covent Garden and was conductor of the Bavarian Broadcasting symphony, to be the musician in his troika. He retained as director of press relations Francis Robinson, a bon vivant theatrical press agent with a plummy voice and fine Southern accent who had become a serious scholar of opera and an expert on Caruso during a generation at the Met. He signed off on the union contracts before the 1972 summer vacation, assuring us a peace on the labor relations front we had not enjoyed for more than a decade. We were all looking forward to Gentele's first season, 1972–73, which was to open with *Carmen*, himself as stage director and Leonard Bernstein conducting. Among Gentele's lesser plans was a week in July for himself and his wife and their daughters with Charon and me and our little ones at Sotogrande. But one of his daughters had a boyfriend in Sardinia, and she persuaded him to take the family vacation on that island, where the cruel fates had waiting for him a truck driving a mountain road in the wrong lane, crushing the Genteles' car, killing him and two of his daughters and leaving the third seriously injured.

I was at the Pan Am terminal in Kennedy Airport in New York when they paged me with the incredible news. I have rarely been so sick with sadness.

Bing reached me that evening with condolences and with an offer to return temporarily and keep the company going. I thanked him but said I thought we had to move on. The board would not have stood still for Bing's return. We had to give Chapin his chance, and we named him acting general manager. He was soon upset about the "acting" label, and with some reluctance, for his first season was not impressive for system, organization, or financial results, we gave him the full title. It was, of course, a season Bing had planned, and one could not hold Chapin responsible for the artistic results, which most people whose judgment I respected considered mediocre. Chapin reconstituted the troika by asking the British stage director John Dexter to become administrator in that area, and hired the American conductor James Levine, who was still under thirty but had made a deep impression at his debut in Bing's last season, to fill in for Kubelik, who spent little time in New York—and was, indeed, preparing to abandon ship the next season. I had relatively few dealings with Chapin. The people who came to me with their problems and from whom I drew the information I needed were Riecker and Bronson. I felt comfortable with them, and they appeared comfortable with me. I wasn't comfortable with Chapin, who seemed to believe his dignity required that he keep his distance from someone who was, in a sense, his employer. He hired his own personal p.r. man, separate from the Met's.

Gentele's death was a great loss to the Metropolitan, where he might well have revivified the stage presentations of opera, and to me personally. Sometimes I think that if he had lived we would have kept our home in New Canaan and spent much of the season here instead of in Spain. He was great fun to be with, and it would have been exciting to share his plans. Instead, I was stuck with a general manager whose greatest concern seemed to be his own image, and who could not be relied upon and probably did not know the real facts about the company's deteriorating financial condition. Time after time William Rockefeller and I met with him to tell him that he had to live within his budget, and time after time he told us that he was doing so—only to tell us a month or two later that he had found additional expenses or that revenues had fallen below expectations, and really we were losing a million dollars or two million dollars more than expected.

Chapin was a born number-two man. A good number-two man is indispensable in any organization, but he needs someone to stop him once a day or he wrecks the place. Chapin ran through proceeds of the sale of our property on the site of the old Met and spent the biggest legacy the Met ever received, from the will of Martha Baird Rockefeller, in not much more than two years. He has told his side of this story in his memoirs, in which he berates us (but William Rockefeller much more than me) for our failure to understand that he really did have things under control, and that he really did have a plan. The reason we didn't understand is that whatever plans he thought he had didn't show results. If he had met his figures as Bing had, or at least kept us informed that he had money problems, the awful indignities to which he feels he was subjected would never have occurred.

The way out was to bring back Tony Bliss. He also was not much of a businessman, but he had the capacity to raise the money the company lost, and he led the drive for the $100 million endowment which has given the opera a more comfortable climate. The other great fundraisers of the Bliss years were Frank Taplin, a Cleveland lawyer and energy magnate, who was a superb pianist and looked at the Met with a musician's eye, and James Marcus, a Goldman Sachs partner with a passion for opera, who is at this writing the company's chairman. I can't claim credit for Taplin, who was not only on the board when I came but one of my fiercest antagonists in the fight over the future of the touring company, but Marcus was someone I recruited for the board while I was president. Though Bliss and I didn't see eye-to-eye and still don't, I say admiringly that the Met is a better opera house and a better place for his contributions to the company. I have remained on the board as an honorary director, and I keep up with both the numbers and—when I'm in New York—the performances. It's still a very great opera house, and it still has financial problems. When Bruce Crawford, an opera loyalist, left his post as c.e.o. of the advertising agency Batten Barton Durstine & Osborne to become the Met's general manager in 1985, he inherited as I had in 1967 the results of Bliss's business failings but also an improving artistic situation built on the talents of conductor and artistic director James Levine, whose future with the company Bliss had assured contractually. I went to one of the early meetings at which Crawford presented his money problems and his production plans, congratulated him on his start at the job of handling the Met's difficulties, and received from him the warming comment that he was trying to do what I had done under not entirely different circumstances in 1967.

3

The greatest public prominence I ever had in the eyes of the ordinary newspaper-reader was the moment of my departure from the post of chairman of the finance committee of the New York World's Fair of 1964–65. This was the last hurrah of Robert Moses, the great builder of bridges and parks and roads and beaches in New York State. It was to be in Flushing Meadow, on the same site as the 1939–40 World's Fair, about a dozen miles from midtown New York. Moses didn't have the money to get it started, and he came to me in 1961—we had known each other around town—to ask me to be chairman of the finance committee and arrange help from the banks. Fairs, as Moses' veteran aide-de-camp Tom Deegan persuasively argued, are usually good for business. I put together a consortium of ten banks, each of which bought a million dollars of debentures from the fair and eventually wrote it all off. Around three million of that ten, I later learned, had gone into setting up a fund to pay Moses' salary during the years the fair was being planned and operated, and then his six-figure pension for the rest of his life.

After it was all over, I went through the history of that fair with Billy Rose, whose career had achieved lift-off from the impetus of his work on the 1939 World's Fair, and he ticked off the mistakes. First, fairs should be popularly priced: they're for ordinary people. Moses priced the tickets, and everything else at the fair, much too high. They were charging three dollars for an itty-bitty hamburger in 1964—you

With James Saxon, Kennedy's innova-tive comptroller of the currency, in 1965.

On the opposite page: Playing tennis against Jacob Javits, 1965.

With William Renchard, president of Chemical Bank, who joined me in resigning from the New York World's Fair in 1965.   *NYT Pictures, Don Charles photo*

With David Rockefeller at a CICYP meeting in 1966.

With Generalissimo Franco in 1966.   *M. Santos Yubero*

Receiving an honorary Doctor of Laws degree at Wagner College, fall 1967.

Speaking at the Vatican, at the 1967 meeting of Pro Deo, an organization devoted to the development needs of Latin America. *Attualità Fotografica*

With Yoshizane Iwasa of Fuji Bank, at a meeting of the Private Investment Company for Asia in 1967. *B&G International photos*

GSM, Walter Wriston, and Carl Desch (far right) at a stockholders' meeting in 1968.

**With Enrique Monjo at the dedication of the great bas relief in the lobby of City Bank head-
quarters, 1968.** *Sancho Fotografo*

Maria Callas and Giuseppe di Stefano visiting Sotogrande in 1973.

With Charon and Anna Moffo.

President Nixon, Juan Carlos of Spain, and me in 1974.

The two new generations of Moores: my son Steve, my grandson George B., my daughter Pia, my granddaughter Tanya, my daughter Tina.

Charon and Pia in 1976.
Hispania Press

Dinner at the Waldorf in honor of the King of Spain, sponsored jointly by the Spanish Institute and the Spanish-American Chamber of Commerce.   *Hispania Press*

Onassis party with gypsies and Jacqueline Onassis, at Sotogrande.

With Giovanni Agnelli of Fiat at the party for my eightieth birthday, in London.

The three male Moores at the birthday party.

With Antonio Navarro Rubio, governor of the Bank of Spain, at the birthday party in Madrid.

Son George, Jr., his wife Kathy, and my grandchildren George and Tanya.
Allan Mitchell photo

The house and golf course at Sotogrande.

can get a Coke in Disneyland today for less than Moses charged at the
World's Fair in 1964. Transportation added to the cost: Moses wouldn't
let the aerial railroad run to the gate, because he'd made a deal with
Greyhound that wouldn't generate the necessary revenue unless lots
of people got on the rubber-wheeled open passenger carts or buses
at the entrance. People went, felt cheated, and told their friends
not to go.

Fairs need a midway, with lively, even vulgar, entertainment. At
a successful fair—New York in 1939, Montreal, Seattle—a third of the
attendance comes after six o'clock. And there wasn't any real midway
in 1964–65: Moses was seventy years old and bored with entertainment, especially vulgar entertainment—he kept saying, "I don't want
Sally Rand out there," which was, I suppose, a great tribute to Sally
Rand, that her fan dance was remembered a quarter of a century later.
We had only about 10 percent of our attendance after six o'clock, which
devastated the restaurants.

Worst of all, over the long run, the 1964–65 fair was all temporary
structures. A fair doesn't make sense economically unless it leaves a
legacy of permanent buildings, a university, concert halls, a convention center, a museum, a park. It costs almost as much to tear down
the temporary stuff as it did to put the buildings up in the first place.
What you want when it's over is a university, theaters, office and convention space, and so on. The first fair left the Triborough Bridge and
Grand Central Parkway, an aquatic stadium, an ice-skating rink, and
a museum, as well as a park in what had been marshland. The second
left one small stadium in a city that already has a number of small
stadiums (though it has come in handy for the national tennis cham-
pionships), a helicopter pad where nobody wants to land a helicopter,
an inferior science museum, and some rusting symbolic structures
that don't even have a roof.

Because he was in a hurry, Moses planned his fair for a year that
had been approved by the Bureau of International Expositions for some
fair in Europe. This meant that instead of having an official exhibition
from the French government, say, he had to make do with something
put together by some perfume-makers and wine merchants; he got
nothing from the Soviet Union and only a commercial show from Britain. The BIE would have given him 1965–66, but he demanded 1964–
65, and the first of those broke the rules. He told the world he didn't
get official status because he needed two years rather than one to recoup
his $700-million costs, but it wasn't true.

And he made two deals that meant anyone who got involved with his fair was sure to lose money. The first was with unions, and provided that everything on the site would be deemed "under construction" for the life of the fair. That meant everyone was subject to construction union rules—for the whole fair. You couldn't turn on your own lights—you needed somebody from the electricians' union. If a toilet leaked, you had to bring in a union plumber and his helper on an eight-hour call. We took the license to be the fair's bank—he promised us a certain level of deposits from the concessionaires and exhibitors, and we never had them—and then we learned that we wouldn't even be allowed to drive our own truck onto the property; it had to be one of the construction companies' trucks. The other deal was with Governor Nelson Rockefeller and the state legislature, and provided that there would not be any independent outside auditing of the books. The auditors would have access only to such information as Moses made available to them. I found out about this outrage when the city rebelled against it, and threatened to withhold a subsidy payment unless Moses gave access to their auditors. They complained to me as chairman of the finance committee that there was a million-dollar item in the accounts labeled "incidentals," and Moses wouldn't break it down. I'm sure he didn't keep it himself, but he refused to recognize that other people had a legitimate reason to know what he had done with it.

At the close of the first year, I told Moses I felt I had to give a full financial report to the directors—a very large group that met only once a year (it was an honorary post). He said, "Sure. Go ahead." In my report, I noted that the fair had already spent the complete advance-sale receipts for the second season, and that the finance committee was unable to learn where some of the money had gone. Moses was muttering "son of a bitch" under his breath. Then he got up and said, "Since our finance chairman has no confidence in the future of the fair, and in its president, he should get to hell out." I said, "Since the president has politely questioned my confidence, I'd like to say that I'm prepared to match my confidence against his. I raised ten million dollars for this fair, I put in a branch of Citibank—which has been a loser because the fair never generated the deposits Mr. Moses promised would be kept there—and when exhibitors needed financial help, at Mr. Moses' request we made loans, many of which have gone bad. Meanwhile, Mr. President, you took three million dollars of that first ten to guarantee your pension plan. Nothing illegal about it, indeed it seems to have been prudent, but it doesn't say much for your confidence."

The other commercial bankers quit the board with me, which is why my picture was on the front pages and on TV, but all the big investment bankers—Kuhn, Loeb; First Boston; Dillon Read—went down the line with Moses in the vote on the board. Moses was the head of the Triborough Bridge and Tunnel Authority; they were forever selling bond issues to the public, and he had told the underwriters that anyone who didn't back him against Moore at the board meeting could be sure he would never see another TBTA issue, ever again.

New York is a much better place because Robert Moses lived. Few men in my lifetime made a contribution to rival his. But you had to watch out, and forget about the appeals to public service, when you did business with him. Not long before he died, we had lunch together at his request, and he asked me if I was still mad at him, to which I said I'd never been really mad at him. We didn't talk about the fair.

4

To be president and chairman of Citibank in the 1960s was an experience different from that any of my predecessors had (though I was spared the trauma of my successor Walt Wriston, who had to deal with the near-bankruptcy of the city in 1975 and the Latin borrowers in 1982). Bankers were suddenly expected to find places in the vanguard of social "change." To some extent, surprisingly, we did. I helped form, for example, the Economic Development Council that worked with Mayor John Lindsay in trying to design job opportunities for black and Hispanic New Yorkers. And I found both residential and commercial mortgage money for the Bedford-Stuyvesant Development and Services Corporation, which was, as I liked to put it, seeking to make an infrastructure for an underdeveloped country of a quarter of a million people who happened to live in New York City. The director of the parallel community organization, the Bedford-Stuyvesant Restoration Corporation, was Franklin Thomas, who is now president of the Ford Foundation. I was so impressed with him at Bed-Stuy board meetings that we later invited him onto the board of Citicorp, where he served with distinction. The secret of the Bed-Stuy project was the close involvement of the people on the spot, who wanted *restoration*, not the sort of slash-and-burn-and-build approach most government agencies followed under the name of "urban renewal." In 1985, the corporation held a celebratory dinner and gave the founding fathers a handsome portrait bust of Bobby Kennedy as an award for our help.

It had been Senator Robert Kennedy who brought me into the Bed-Stuy group, through his very able assistant Eli Jacobs. Later, I helped Kennedy by organizing a lunch at the bank for about fifty business leaders from around the country, to meet him and hear what he had to say. That was the only time I met Bobby, but I did know his brother Jack and got on with him well, though I wasn't always enamored of his public policies. The fact was that City Bank were bankers to the family, though it was a closely guarded secret. I remember a lunch at the White House for a group of businessmen involved in Latin American development, at which President Kennedy introduced me with the comment that "George's bank handles my family's accounts— I get my income checks from him every month." I said to him later, "Mr. President, we have twenty-five thousand employees in our bank, and only about six of us know we are the bankers for your family. We six have been under the most extreme orders never under any circumstances to mention that relationship to anyone. And now you've told all these businessmen about it." It was during the Kennedy administration that some wag in the foreign service said that the government of the United States is the only vessel ever made that leaks from the top.

The one organization I can say I created is the Spanish Institute, which essentially ran out of my office in Citibank (we kept the addressograph cards and sent out all the mail) for more than ten years. It started with my first wife's going to lectures and social events at the French Institute, (for which Archer Huntington had provided a splendid building at 32 East 60th Street,) and as a Spaniard asking why there wasn't any equivalent Spanish Institute for New Yorkers with an interest in Spain. Americans don't know anything like as much as they should know about how important Spain has been in the history of this continent. Salvador de Madariaga's great books *The Rise of the Spanish American Empire* and *The Fall of the Spanish American Empire* never received the attention they deserved, and there hasn't been a significant followup. But George Washington knew how important Spanish help was in the American Revolution, and the remains of Spanish influence in California are much more significant than red tile roofs and Hispanic names. Our fate as a nation has long been entwined with the fates of our Spanish-speaking neighbors in this hemisphere. We had a Hispanic Society, way uptown at Broadway and 156th Street, also in a building endowed by Huntington, who cared even more for Spain, which he had explored in carriage and on burro as a young man in the nineteenth century, than he did for France. Huntington's was one of the great railroad families, the Rockefellers' partner in developing the oilfields of California; one of his brothers built the Huntington Library, a wonderful repository of English art and literature, in Pasadena. The Hispanic Society, however, was a scholarly establishment, a library more than a museum, with limited public access, and Huntington was afraid to do anything that would expand its functions. In the early 1950s, when I began nosing about to determine the prospects of a Spanish Institute, the community interested in Spain was sharply divided between the people who were on Franco's side and the emigré and intellectual community for whom the Spanish Republic was still a live cause. Huntington was concerned that if he opened the Hispanic Society to concerts and social occasions, which was what we wanted, there would be political turmoil.

We rented a room in the French Institute building, which gave us access to the auditorium there. Now we had housing for a secretary, a sort of meeting place for people from Spain when they came to New York, and a location for lectures and concerts. The partners in the venture included Lucrezia Bori and Angier Biddle Duke (who had been working with a social organization called Amigos de España), Theodore Rousseau, curator of European paintings at the Metropolitan Museum (who had a house on the Costa Brava), the lawyer Edward Tinker, and the sculptor Melvina Hoffman. Our first affair was a concert by the great guitarist Andres Segovia at the home of Dr. Ramon Castroviejo, a prominent ophthalmologist who was another of the founders, and whose wife Cynthia was our first, highly capable, president. We used as our symbol on our stationery a statue of a conquistador that now stands in University City in Madrid, sculpted by Huntington's wife, who worked under her maiden name of Anna Hyatt. I wrote the memo describing what the institute would be, and said its purpose was "to promote friendship and understanding between the *people* of Spain and the people of the United States." The Spanish government then sponsored and subsidized a chain of Spanish Institutes across Latin America, but we decided not to accept money or official support: we were non-political and independent in every way.

When Huntington died, his wife's nephew Hyatt Mayor, the great print curator of the Metropolitan Museum, became head of the Hispanic Society, and joined the board of the Spanish Institute. And he made me a trustee of the Hispanic Society, with the thought that long-term something could be done to bring the two institutions closer together. (Being a trustee of the Hispanic Society is more of a responsibility than these things usually are, because the old man in his will provided that if the society ever overspent the income he had provided for it, the trustees would be personally liable. Fortunately, that's never been a problem. When Mayor died, I became president of the society myself, which I learned recently took me off the hook should the budget be overspent, because the president isn't a trustee. In 1986, the Hispanic Society gave me a medal to recognize my twenty-five years on the board, with a citation noting—I was surprised myself—that I had never missed a meeting.) Mayor opened up the society to a larger public, hiring Ted Beardsley, a scholar who is also a skilled arts administrator, to make the institution more of a museum that people could visit and less a scholarly enclave. But Broadway and 156th Street was awfully far uptown for concerts and social events. By the terms of Huntington's will we could not move the collection (or allow the older exhibits, those acquired before his death, to be shown anywhere outside that building). The Spanish Institute, which by 1960 had grown to five hundred individual members and twenty-five corporate members, still had to find its own home.

About the time I became involved with David Rockefeller in the launching of the Council for Latin America, there was a story in the papers that three of the great mansions occupying the southwest corner of Park Avenue and 69th Street had been sold to a developer, who was going to put a big apartment house on the site. These handsome buildings had been built by the great New York architectural firm of McKim, Mead & White for descendants of the Moses Taylor who originally built City Bank, and one of them had been occupied by Eben Pyne, who was president of City Bank Farmers Trust in the 1950s. The Marquesa de Cuevas (whose husband had a ballet company bearing his name) lived across the street from these mansions, read the newspaper stories, and was furious that her view would be ruined. She was Rockefeller's aunt, the daughter of John D.'s sister. She called the Chase trust department and told them to buy the buildings for her, which they did. I suggested to David Rockefeller that he should ask his aunt whether he could have the corner building for our council, with the two lower floors to be used by the institute. He countered with the proposal that *I* do it (he always had trouble handling her, he said!), so I called the Marquesa, and she invited me to tea and promptly agreed to my plan. Then Rockefeller objected that if the institute had the two lower floors it would get all the visibility, leaving the Council for Latin America obscure. I called the Marquesa again to ask if by any chance she would also give us the smaller building next door, for the exclusive use of the institute. Her response was to say, "Can you use that third building, too?" (We couldn't, and it became Automation House, home of a sociological study group that holds conferences there.) Rockefeller and I then founded a separate Institute of Latin American Affairs to fill the corner building, and the Spanish Institute acquired exclusive use of its magnificent home at 684 Park Avenue.

I raised a million dollars in 1963 to put the Pyne house in shape, mostly from foundations (McMicking, Tinker, Hastings, and Bori), partly from corporations that did business in Spain and were members of the institute. Owen Cheatham of Georgia Pacific made a generous contribution, as did John D. Rockefeller III, with a nice comment about how helpful I had been to him in Lincoln Center. David Rockefeller supplied me with a president for the institute (I'd asked him to take me off the hook, because "everybody says the institute is a George S. Moore subsidiary"), and also with a quarter-million-dollar loan to finish the job when the costs ran that much over what the president he had supplied had said they would be.

Over the years, Franco became a fading issue (though I don't think anyone on either side imagined how easily Spain would make the transition to a monarchical democracy), we had glamorous visits from the King and Queen of Spain (he lent me his own ribbon of the Grand Cross of Isabela la Catolica, with which I had been honored by his country, when he found that I had left mine in Spain and thus couldn't wear it to the party), and the Spanish Institute in its elegant home became one of the major cultural centers of the city. Jack Javits's nephew Eric has become the president and raised enough money, some of it through an annual dinner at the Waldorf, to start the institute on the road to an endowment. There is still one piece of unfinished business associated with the Pyne mansion, however. During the course of the reconstruction, a grand marble fireplace, an English antique, disappeared from the building. I have been told it now stands in Getty's English country house. Among the items on my agenda for the next few years is a conversation with Getty to try and get that fireplace back where it belongs.

In 1979, the Spanish Institute gave me their gold medal for my contribution to Spanish-U.S. relations, but my real reward has been a kind of immortality. Among the people who stopped by when the Spanish

Institute was just a room in the French Institute, back in the 1950s, was the Catalan sculptor Enrique Monjo, an unimposing little man who asked shyly if we could find him a place to give an exhibition. We did that, and I had him to dinner and took him to the opera. He was grateful and said he wanted to do a bust of me, and I said I was too busy. A day or two later I had a call from Ted Rousseau of the Metropolitan Museum, one of our founding fathers. He said, "I hear you declined to pose for Monjo. You're wrong. Bankers are a dime a dozen, but this is the best sculptor since Rodin." Monjo worked on me in the studio of Melvina Hoffman, another founder of the Spanish Institute, who had a converted stable on the East Side and had done a bust of Tom Watson of IBM that was much admired. When mine was finished, she said to me, "I spent one hundred hours with Watson, he spent four hours with you, and yours is better, catches your strength. Monjo is a sculptor; next to him, I'm a photographer."

I was involved with Monjo for the rest of his life. I commissioned from him the medal marking the 150th anniversary of the founding of Citibank, and the great mural relief at the back of the entrance hall of our new building at 399 Park Avenue, which is a panorama of America's contribution to the twentieth century. (I now own his maquettes, the casts for some of the various models Monjo made as he was developing the final design. Some years after I retired, an old-timer at the bank called me to tell me they had found those casts in a warehouse and had no use for them and were going to throw them away, until somebody remembered I had taken a personal interest, and did I want them?) At the dedication, Tom Hoving, president of the Metropolitan Museum, made me promise that when we tore down 399 Park Avenue we would give that great relief to the museum. Monjo worked on it a full year and said it was the most important thing he had ever done. "I was born in 1900," he said to an interviewer. "This is my century, and it is also, whether people like it or not, America's century." I've thought about that interview while writing these memoirs, because this is my century, too.

When we built our house in Sotogrande in 1968, Monjo made us a beautiful statue of a lovely girl to perch at the end of the swimming pool, and he did a wonderful portrait of Charon in white marble. After he died, his widow gave me some of the small clay models he made in developing the designs for some of his works, and these are behind glass in our living room. He liked my head (he said it was "Roman"), and used it twice in major works. One is in the chapel next to the mayor's office in the Barcelona City Hall, celebrating the Black Virgin of Monserrat. This is the legend of the church that burned down to the ground, leaving only the wooden statue of the Virgin, which was blackened by the smoke but miraculously did not burn. (In his admirable book on Spain, James Michener gets this story interestingly wrong; he says the Virgin is black to illustrate the absence of racial prejudice among the Spanish . . .) The statue shows a crowd of dignitaries awed by the miracle, and the mayor of Barcelona is Moore. (The *real* mayor, who had commissioned the piece, is present on the side as a simple soldier.) My other appearance in Monjo's work is on the south portal of the Washington Cathedral, where I am among the characters in the life of Christ, as the banker Nicodemus. I helped Monjo get the commission to sculpt these portals, and he wrote to tell me that he couldn't portray me as a saint but he was sending me a book about Nicodemus, the richest banker in Jerusalem, who spoke up at the trial of Christ to say that he knew this young man's parents and knew that he was a fine young man. (Before Monjo could portray a living person as part of the fabric of the cathedral, he needed the approval of the archbishop, who agreed. Monjo told me it was the best reference I ever had, even better than being known as a name at Lloyd's.) It gives me a stake in the survival of Washington, D.C.: as long as the city is there, people will be looking at George Moore as Nicodemus.

I will give a copy of this book to the library of the Monjo Museum in his birthplace Villasar, near Barcelona. Monjo had a copy of his portrait bust of me cast for the front room of that museum, with the legend, "Honor to George S. Moore, *gran Espanista,* who pushed ahead the creation of this museum." In the centuries to come, when visitors to the museum ask, "Who was this Moore?", perhaps one of the curators will have looked at the book and will be able to tell them about the C-student from Hannibal, Missouri, who built a great bank but also cared about other things.

11

Retirement: The Active Years

On April 23, 1970, at the conclusion of the monthly board of directors meeting immediately following my sixty-fifth birthday, I formally retired from the bank and the holding company, gave up my limousine and my wonderful chauffeur Willie Washington, said goodbye to my three secretaries and wished them well in their new positions. I had already received not only the ritual public tributes but also a most unexpected and cherished comment at the last stockholders' meeting I ran, from Lewis Gilbert, one of the fiercest of the gadfly lawyers who haunted such meetings in my time and made executives' lives uncomfortable in the name of promoting stockholders' interest: "In the many years at which I have watched [Mr. Moore] preside," he said, "I have never found he was presided unfairly; he has been a most patient Chairman, as well as a great banker, and he has united two talents." He then moved a standing vote of acclamation, and everyone in the room rose and applauded. The night after that last board meeting they put icing on the cake, staging a black-tie party at 399 Park in my honor and in honor of vice-chairman Dick Perkins, who was also retiring. They gave me a sliver money-clip.

I proceeded to fill it. At my retirement, I think my net worth was about half a million dollars; by my seventieth birthday, I had multiplied it, and I've never looked back.

People who retire at age sixty-five, I think, had better organize their lives to keep busy, and keep earning. We live longer these days, and no matter how good your pension looks on the day you walk out the door, it won't carry you through the inflation years of the money cycle in anything like the style to which you've grown accustomed. My pension from Citicorp was in most people's terms a lot of money. But in the first ten years after my retirement, the price level rose by 100 percent. If I hadn't had anything to live on except that pension, I'd have long since been out in front of the cathedral with a tin cup in my hand. I'd always earned more than I'd been able to spend, and at sixty-five I wasn't equipped to live any other way.

Obviously, few people have my opportunities. With a wife thirty-three years younger than I and small children around the house, I had a commitment to staying young. I had the physical constitution to do it, too. And while I had retired from Citicorp, I remained a member of the board of U.S. Steel, W. R. Grace, Union Pacific, and Mercantile Stores, among others. Mercantile, which I consider probably the best-run group of department stores in the country, is controlled by the Milliken family, whose principal business is a private textile company, which I consider probably the best of its kind in the country. The Millikens had told me before my retirement that they would like more of my time when I left the bank, to advise Mercantile on financial matters, and I was happy to comply. Then I became a limited partner in White, Weld, a long-established Wall Street investment house, with a brief to help them make deals. And I went on the board of Onassis's Olympic Airways, which meant I could commute across the Atlantic to Spain without charge, a big help in the time when I was first internationalizing my "retirement" career. Meanwhile, people who wished to speak with me could still find me through Citicorp, which continued its long-standing generous tradition of giving retired top officials an office (and a secretary) in the headquarters building.

Among my early international roles was membership on the board of King Ranch España and its sister company Rancho Adaroche, in Morocco. Rancho Adaroche was a venture in partnership with King Hassan. Citibank had been bankers for King Ranch in Texas for longer than anyone remembered—James Stillman's family was Texan and somehow related there—and I had made my first visit to the Klebergs and their fantastic establishment in 1948. The ranch is near the Mexican border, and its work force consisted almost entirely of the descendants of wetbacks, so called because they had arrived by swimming across the Rio Grande, plus no small number of more recent immigrants. Spanish was the language of the ranch in 1948. The writ of the immigration department did not run on King Ranch—when I first visited, in fact, nobody's writ ran except that of the Kleberg family. The sheriff stayed off the property; the ranch protected its own.

The aim of King Ranch España was to propagate the famous Santa Gertrudis cattle in Spain. They bought a property near the Portuguese border, but they also needed a feed lot and showplace nearer to a metropolitan center, and their manager Michael Hughes and I found them a ranch just north of Seville. But the Klebergs didn't like that property, felt that the roads were inadequate, and Hughes and I wound up buying it from them. That was the origin of the ranch I now own three hours' drive from my retirement home, where I have cattle and pigs and I've begun to breed and raise Angora goats, who can live on that dry land, and whose wool commands a premium on the Spanish market.

Kleberg's Moroccan venture was started at the request of that country, which spends hundreds of millions of dollars a year to import meat and would have excellent other uses for that hard currency. King Ranch was to supply the breeding stock and to manage the ranch, and Morocco was to provide the property. We brought over fifty pure-bred Santa Gertrudis bulls (and a few cows, too), and crossed them with a thousand Moroccan cattle, which were pretty poor specimens. But King Ranch knew what it was doing. The Santa Gertrudis, a combination of the Brahman cattle and the Spanish Rio Tinto cattle that was first fixed at King Ranch, was the first new breed in cattle since the Hereford in England in 1910. Established breeding practices would have given Morocco a herd of Santa Gertrudis 87 percent pure—and thus by world definition "pure-bred" with four crosses of the King Ranch bulls and cows that were the progeny of previous crosses. But the Moroccan government didn't live up to some of its partnership promises. We had difficulty getting to the king to complain. Whenever we had an appointment, the minister of agriculture managed to see that it was canceled and that we had to talk with him. Finally, I learned that the only way to be sure of seeing the king was to play golf with him. We played a foursome that included the "chief of the Royal Household" and the King's golf pro, Claude Harmon. These outings gave me the only reason I've ever found to want to be a king. When you're a king, you concede your putt when your ball lands on the green, and then you stand around and wait for everyone else to putt out.

King Ranch finally abandoned this venture, but the king continued to invite me to his birthday party every year. Fortunately, Spiro Agnew, then vice-president of the United States, was visiting in Spain

Chapel of the Black Virgin in Barcelona City Hall, with GSM as medieval mayor of Barcelona, at left.

The cattle ranch, Fuente del Berro at Castilblanco de los Arroyos, Province of Seville.

on the occasion of the King's birthday in 1971, and though I had never met the man before (and have never seen him since), I had a first obligation to play golf with the vice-president of the United States in Sotogrande, to whom we had loaned our house at the request of the U.S. ambassador. I therefore begged off the king's party that year and wasn't there when some generals trying to upset the government of Morocco sprayed the luncheon area with machine-gun fire and killed seventy-five guests. Those at the table where I had sat in previous years were killed. Spiro Agnew saved my life, which I've always taken as a good deed to be marked to his credit.

Perhaps my closest associations in retirement have been Finnish, especially with the Ehrnrooth family. Its head, Goran (George, in Finnish) is exactly my age, born the same day of the same year. I advise the family on the international activities of the Finnish companies in which they are interested, in banking, paper, shipping and technology. In Spain, I've helped them with decisions relating to the Tampella paper mill in Barcelona. An extra dividend from my involvement with the Ehrnrooths is an annual invitation for myself and my wife to visit them in the lovely country to which their ancestors migrated five hundred years ago. These brave, capable, hard-working people have learned how to live with dignity and in freedom next to the Russians. That doesn't mean, of course, though some of the European Socialist parties seem to think it does, that "Finlandization" is a viable option for other countries. If the Russians had the same veto powers in Europe as they have in Finland, they wouldn't be as polite as they are to the Finns.

Since 1978, I've been a "name" at Lloyd's, and part of syndicates managed by Roberts & Hiscox. Lloyd's a very interesting institution. Brokers deal with customers seeking insurance coverage, and bring each "risk" to the underwriting floor with a premium they think will be acceptable to the underwriters. The latter consider the risk, accept whatever position they wish to take, or pass it by. If the insurance is not placed, the broker has to go back to his customer and propose a higher rate, or different conditions in the contract. When the insurance is fully placed, the insured party gets a policy with a lot of signed rubber stampings, one for each underwriter participating. Each syndicate is fully responsible, without limit, for its agreed share of the risk. To become a "name" at Lloyd's, you have to establish a minimum financial responsibility, and provide a bank letter of credit on which your agent (in my case Roberts & Hiscox) can draw immediately if there is a loss in excess of the premiums collected. A new "name" must appear before members of the "committee" of Lloyd's and acknowledge that all his worldly goods are "on the line," if necessary, to pay his obligations.

Each underwriting syndicate operates on a year-to-year basis, and each year is "closed out" two years later, by which time nearly all claims should be in and the result of the insuring activity should be calculable, leaving some reserve for unsettled claims. The syndicate is then dissolved, distributing the profits (the excess of premiums over losses) or the losses (vice versa); and the risk of any subsequent claims is assumed by a successor syndicate usually composed of the same members. Lloyd's itself as an organization carefully supervises this process, and keeps a large reserve fund, provided by all members from their premium receipts, to draw on in the event that any individual syndicate fails to honor its share of a policy. Reinsurance can be arranged by syndicates, and by the "names," to limit their otherwise unlimited liability. Some "irregularities" in the last few years have produced rule changes that require underwriters to disclose what contracts they have placed with reinsurance companies they control themselves, and prohibit brokers from acting also as underwriters.

During the second World War, American insurance companies threw cabbage at Lloyd's, questioning how the syndicates would pay on claims if Hitler took over England. The reply by Lloyd's was to set up an American reserve fund invested in bank deposits and U.S. securities. The fund was originally established at City Bank, while Hiscox's father was the chairman of the "committee" at Lloyd's (its governing body), which is how I came to know the firm. They still ask my advice (and others') on where to invest their dollars. So far, all my syndicates have shown a profit, some years larger than others, but the first reason to be a "name" at Lloyd's is the honor of it, the world's knowledge that you have met all the responsibility requirements and passed a strenuous interview. It beats any "gold card" or "platinum card" any consumer-credit organization ever issued. In 1987, my wife Charon also became a "name" at Lloyd's.

In addition to these activities, I've been a consultant. Walt Wriston in effect gave me my start in that capacity the day I retired. He called me and said, "I have George Livanos in my office. He just bought a fertilizer company in Spain and he needs help." Wriston knew about my home in Spain, of course, and knew I planned to spend a lot of time there. (I'd bought land in Sotogrande, on the Costa del Sol near Gibraltar, and two years before my retirement my wife saw it and liked it, and we built a house in an international community being developed around a Robert Trent Jones golf course.) Wriston also knew that I was reasonably well informed about the world of chemicals and chemicals companies, have kept up with them since the days when I studied them at the Sheffield School in Yale. Livanos was part of one of the great Greek shipowning families with whom Citibank had done business for generations. He came to my office and described the situation, and we worked out an arrangement for me to become a director of his Spanish enterprise—and take two Spanish friends with me onto the board of the company.

The company was callled Cros, and it was the second-largest fertilizer manufacturer and distributor in Spain, based in Barcelona. Livanos had gone in with a partner, an Italian capitalist named DeNora, who had patents on an important process for the manufacture of chlorine. Part of the attraction of the company was some valuable real estate it owned in Majorca and elsewhere in Spain. One of the first things we learned was that we didn't *really* control Cros. We were a minority on a board of Catalan capitalists. (One of the cant lines for visitors is that Catalans own Spain, Basques run it, Andalusians do the work, and Madrilenos do the talking, the politicking, and the banking.) These Catalans were somber, uncommunicative fellows, descendants of the Phoenician traders who landed on Spanish shores before the Romans. They listened politely to what we said—but nothing happened, and the business did not prosper. The one thing they did that we had recommended was acquire the Exxon ammonia plant in Malaga, which reduced the cost of their feedstock. We hired Arthur Anderson to investigate and write a report, which they did, and we distributed it, and still nothing happened. We threatened to use the muscle of our control, but our Spanish lawyers told us that would not be "possible."

Finally someone told Francisco Gimenez Torres, my attorney in Spain and my close friend since the days when he was governor of the Bank of Spain, that the problem was that nobody was "going to let some Greek shipowner run the corporate jewel of Catalonia." We then recommended that Livanos sell out, and Banco Santander, whose president Emilio Botin is widely considered the best banker in Spain, took him out at a profit. But Livanos asked me to continue with him as an adviser, which of course I was happy to do—at Citibank we had always considered him one of the wisest and strongest of the shipowners.

In fact, by contrast with some of our competitors, we at Citibank had good experiences with the shipowners who borrowed from us: men like Livanos, Niarchos, Onassis, Goulandris, Embiricos, Costa Lemos knew the business, covered themselves by negotiating charters before they contracted to buy their ships, and they always kept large cash reserves for troubled times. We did business also with the brilliant banker-turned-shipowner Y.K. Pao and with the best of the Scandinavian shippers, men like the Danish magnate Maersk Moller and Nils Waring of Willemsen Lines, a top Norwegian shipowner. Waring gave me a dinner once in Oslo, and every year his company sent me a case of aquavit that had been around the world ten times in its ships, which was supposed to make it better.

My closest relationship in this community, however, was with Aristotle Onassis (whose first wife was Livanos's sister). Onassis had come to City Bank soon after World War II asking us to finance his purchase of government surplus "T-2" tankers used during the war and no longer needed by the navy. Men like Onassis and Niarchos and Livanos had been successful in the dry-cargo business, but it was the oil companies that made them multi-millionaires. The oil companies after the war needed most of their cash flow and credit for exploration and the construction of refineries, and they were willing to let the shipowners provide the necessary transportation. They gave contracts that paid out the cost of the tankers in five years. With that assurance, we and Metropolitan Life handled the loans Onassis needed to make his purchases. He was the perfect customer, completely straightforward with us. We were his bankers from the beginning to the end, and we are still the bankers to his heirs.

Onassis's usual contact in the bank was Wriston, but I saw something of him socially—especially during his relationship with Maria Callas, with whom I had opera in common, and after I married Charon, who greatly enjoyed both of them. Onassis stood godfather to our oldest daughter, Tina. When he was in New York we would often meet him and Maria at his corner table at El Morocco at 11:00 or midnight. He would order champagne, and it would keep coming. I would go home to get some sleep after an hour or so, and Charon and Ari and Maria would remain through the early morning hours. Then, of course, Onassis would sleep late. We kept opposite hours. But I always enjoyed his company. Despite all the ignorant comment to the contrary, he was a cultured gentleman from a well-to-do family. He spoke seven languages well, and I never heard him use a four-letter word. He knew music and art, and cared for them.

It's also true, of course, that Onassis liked the good life, wanted to own the best of everything and be surrounded by important, intelligent, attractive people. Those are not unreasonable desires. He could afford to assemble such a community around him, but the reason they accepted his invitations was that when they came he made them happy. Except perhaps for some of his rivals, everyone liked him. I know I did. I will say that I thought his breakup with Callas was unfortunate. She was, of course, independently wealthy from her singing and the royalties on her recordings, and he added to her income by giving her the revenues of one of his leased tankers, but their separation wrecked her life. She kept up her spirits. I remember two visits she made to Sotogrande with the tenor Giuseppe di Stefano, the first with Pepe's wife and daughter, the second without them. Di Stefano and I played golf together, Maria riding around in the cart, and on the sixteenth hole he cut loose with a rendition of "O Sole Mio" that could be heard, I was told, in the clubhouse. That night we sat in our living room and played his old recording of Neapolitan songs (which had made him more money, he said, than all his opera recordings put together), and he sang the English translations for us softly below the sound of the loudspeakers. But Maria never got over Onassis. I always said that when he died, she died. She had been scheduled to visit us again in Sotogrande during the week after her death.

While I was authorizing loans, and even when I was president of the bank, I was very careful about accepting hospitality from borrowers, and my contacts with Onassis through that period were pretty much restricted to an occasional meal at his New York home or a restaurant, or on his yacht when it was anchored in the Hudson River. I remember one particularly happy dinner on the *Christina* with Callas and Prince Rainier and Princess Grace of Monaco, among others. After I became chairman, and was out of the line of direct customer relationships, Charon and I spent weeks on Scorpio, his island in the Ionian Sea. Though he put me on the board of his Olympic Airways, I was a friend more than a "consultant"—but I was a friend whose business judgement he wanted to have from time to time. He made his own decisions, and, obviously, he was usually right.

Onassis liked to tell his story. He always insisted, for example, that his father had cut him off as a rebuke for spending the family's money on ransom when the father was being held in a Turkish jail and threatened with execution. He went to Argentina to make a new start in life, he said, and got a job in a hotel working on the switchboard, which gave him access, he liked to say, to the information he needed to start trading on the exchange and in the commodity markets. In the 1950s, he acquired a controlling interest in the Societé des Bains de Mer, which owns the famous casino, the Hôtel de Paris, and much real estate in Monte Carlo. The story goes that he had tried to arrange for space in Monaco for his worldwide office, and some flunky in the company said he wasn't welcome. Resourceful and tough, as usual, he went to Paris, where shares of the Societé trade on the Bourse, acquired working control of the company, and returned to fire the flunky and make the arrangements for the space he needed.

I met Prince Rainier of Monaco and Princess Grace on the Onassis yacht on several occasions, and relations seemed amicable, but in the end, as the world later learned, Rainier became unhappy with Onassis's control of the largest source of income in his principality. He thought he was entitled to a larger share. I've been told that among those to whom he complained was a New Yorker lawyer, who advised him that as the sovereign of Monaco he could simply expropriate the company. I am told Rainier feared that the French government would object, but the lawyer went to Paris and got a shrug of the shoulders from the authorities there, and on his advice Rainier took over the company, paying Onassis only what he had paid for the shares some years before. In hindsight I should have advised Onassis to make a deal with Rainier for the joint development of Monaco real estate. But I didn't volunteer advice to Onassis as a normal matter: when he wanted to know what you thought, he asked you.

One day in early summer 1972, I got a call from Onassis. He was being offered a tin property in South Africa, and wanted to know whether he should buy it—would I come on the trip and help him? I said I didn't know anything about tin mines, but I'd get him someone who did. The Citibank mining department recommended an engineer, Armine Banfield of Behre Dolbear & Co., and we all went off to Johannesburg on Olympic Airways, a dozen of us. In Johannesburg we met with the Standard Bank people who were pushing the sale to collect a loan, and went out to what was then South-West Africa (now Namibia) to look at the mine. Banfield didn't like any part of it. He said, "There's no question there's as much tin in that valley as there is in the rest of the world, that whole river bed is tin, but it's not profitable to mine it, at least not yet." The lowest profitable concentration of tin ore is 7 percent, and that's about what they had. But the samples that had been shown to Onassis were 1.5 percent. They had been, as my engineer delicately put it, "hand-selected." Eventually, the South African who was trying to sell the property wound up in jail.

The day Onassis died I received a phone call from his daughter Christina in Paris. "I need help," she said. "Can you come?" I flew to Paris on the next plane. Onassis's last months had been terrible, and he had been unable to make business decisions. So the first thing Christina inherited was a backlog of things to be done. We sat in a room in Paris the day after her father died and she resolved a number of important pending and neglected matters. The sale of Olympic Airways to the Greek government had been pending; she concluded the deal. Onassis had contracted with Japanese and French shipyards for new tankers. Christina had sat in on the meetings at which the deals were made, and knew that to finance these ships she would have to borrow money, which she did not want to do. She knew the contracts had termination clauses, and she exercised them. Then we went to the little chapel out in the hospital where he had died, for a service with a handful of close associates and friends.

As part of the reorganization of her affairs, Christina asked me to serve as trustee for the shares in Victory Carriers, which owns the Onassis U.S.-flag carriers and Olympic Towers across 51st Street from St. Patrick's Cathedral and Rockefeller Center in New York. Board meetings of Victory Carriers are among the more likely reasons for me to take trips across the ocean, though of course when I come I always find a number of others things to do, too. Christina has inherited her father's business acumen. She can take pride in the fact that she has maintained the strength and managerial efficiency of the Onassis group, now led by Stelios Papadimitriou and Captain Paul Ioannidis, and has increased the activities of the Alexander Onassis Foundation founded by her father. At the Foundation, she is helped by Nicolas Cokkinis, now retired, who was Onassis's chief financial officer for many years, and often visits with us in Sotogrande. My wife and I share her joy in her daughter, knowing how much the certainty of succession meant to Ari Onassis.

People always ask me why Onassis married Jackie Kennedy, and the fact is that I can't explain it, even to myself. The best answer I know is that he always wanted important people around him, and he wanted only the best, and I guess the world considered Jackie Kennedy the world's most eligible widow. It wasn't a good idea, and I know the marriage did not bring him happiness.

2

In 1973, Charon and I pulled up stakes, gave the New Canaan house to my son George, and made a permanent residence of our home in Sotogrande, with its lovely view to the Mediterranean. The developer of this grand residential community was Joe McMicking, a San Franciscan who had married into the Zobel family in Manila, proprietors of Ayala, the largest business enterprise in the Philippines. He had long been a client of Citibank's Philippine branch, and I had been an investor in Sotogrande from the beginning. Now, of course, I became a participant. We needed a school for our children and the only English-language school in the area, the Iberian School in Estepona up the coast, promptly went broke. I took two of the teachers and started an International School, which I eventually moved to Sotogrande, to the cloistered building that housed the administrative offices of the development company. Because the international community of the Costa del Sol still has an essentially English focus, most of the children go on to boarding school. So when my children were old enough for high school, we took an apartment in Madrid, so they could go to the schools there. But I'm still chairman of the Sotogrande school. In fact, at this writing I'm trying to arrange a complicated deal that would allow us to expand and include an occupation-oriented community college on the property as a help to the local working-class Spanish community. As with everything I do in Sotogrande, I'm working on it with Dr. Werner Kreidl, a research chemist from Vienna who is the leading citizen of those parts.

From my first visit in 1952, I have always liked Spain and had close business and social relations there. City Bank was Spain's leading bank, and through the Spanish Institute I met the leaders of the Spanish cultural world who passed through New York. When Prince Juan Carlos and his wife first visited New York, I organized at the request of the Spanish government a dinner with a number of leading American businessmen. That afternoon, the prince came to my office and asked whether he should make a speech at the dinner, and I told him that his audience would be very disappointed if he didn't. Then he asked me whether he should take questions, and I said that was up to him. What sort of questions, he inquired, was he likely to get? I ran down a list of what he was likely to be asked, from his attitudes toward foreign investment to the future of American bases to the likelihood of a communist takeover after Franco died. He answered them one by one, and quite effectively, I thought. That night he was pleased to find that nearly all the questions he was asked were those I had told him he was likely to receive—and I was delighted to find that in the few hours between our conversation and the dinner he had thought further on all these subjects, and his answers were even more precise and politically wise than his first replies. Some years later, I was host for the banquet at the Waldorf for the king and his queen on the occasion of their first official visit.

In 1963, I was awarded the Grand Cross of Isabela Catolica for my part in developing Spain's economic plan, and the ministry of finance arranged an audience for me with General Franco. When he found I could communicate in Spanish, he kept me an hour, and asked me when I thought Spain might be ready to join the Common Market. I said I thought that decision was ten years away (I had the number understated: it was twenty years away). He then volunteered some advice about Vietnam for me to take back to President Kennedy. The way to prosecute a war against guerrillas, he said, illustrating from his own experiences in Spanish Morocco, was to hold the forts and make a show of strength in daytime, allowing the rebels freedom to control the countryside at night. "The real estate," he said, is worthless, provided nobody can challenge your control in daylight. If any individual gets too strong, you can find out who his enemies are and pay one of them to wipe him out. He said we should follow that tactic in Vietnam, controlling a few towns and strategic areas, and not try to control "the back country."

The plan that Franco instituted when his country joined the IMF is one of the great successes of the postwar period. It was an austere plan. (During our discussion, after he had invited questions, I asked Franco if there was any truth to the rumor that his cabinet had voted 20 to 2 against the plan he had put before them, and he had then declared it adopted; and he smiled and said, Yes, the story was true. I asked why he had overruled his advisers, many of whom were more knowledgeable than he in economic matters, and he said that it was because Spain since the war had been "left out of the world"—it had been denied entrance into the United Nations, the Marshall Plan, the OECD, the World Bank, and so on. This was the first invitation Spain had received, and he could not turn it down. If his advisers had lived through his experiences, they would have voted his way. He had, he added, given them a chance to change their minds: after telling them that he was going to meet the IMF conditions, he adjourned the meeting for a day, and when the cabinet reassembled the next day he called for another vote, which was unanimously in favor of the plan.

The first year under the stabilization plan was very hard. I visited Spain that year, and there were few people sipping sherry on the Castellana. But the government balanced its budgets, Spain lived with the tough conditions of the plan, and as we have learned elsewhere the pain from a truly tough plan lasts much less long, because the recovery is quicker and stronger. Unfortunately, few governments have the strength Franco had to impose so tough a plan so quickly. In the eighteen years from 1961, Spain's real growth in GNP, adjusted for inflation, was 8.6 percent compounded, better than anywhere except Japan, Brazil, and Iran. Average disposable income rose from some five hundred dollars per capita to nearly three thousand. But that sort of statement is very abstract. I can illustrate what it means with a homely example: when I first visited Sotogrande and stayed with Nicholas Biddle, one of the first homeowners in the development, the workmen who were building the houses arrived each day for their jobs on bicycles or packed into trucks. Then they had motorbikes. Today the development continues, and each workman comes in his own little car.

Over the thirteen years that Spain has been my primary residence, I've had a lot of business interests there. I sat on the Cros board for Livanos, and on the board of Altos Hornos, the U.S. Steel Spanish affiliate; consulted with Sevillana Electric about the best place to buy coal; and helped Pepsi-Cola purchase the half of Yago Sangria it didn't already own. I've helped Monsanto sell off its unprofitable polystyrene company to a Spanish investor. I helped Venezuelan friends buy the Pepsi-Cola bottling plant for the Costa del Sol, and at one point I went into (and then out of) a Spanish kosher-wine business with Pedro Domecq (this business left me with a number of cases of very good wine that happens to be kosher, that is being bottled with my name on it). I've been a consultant to Abengoa, a manufacturer of electrical controls of various kinds. I've been a stockholder and promoter of the development called Puerto Sotogrande, on the Mediterranean near our house, where we will probably have a berth for our boat, which Christina Onassis generously gave me some years ago. I'm one of a group of golfers / investors who bought the superb Robert Trent Jones course in the hills above Sotogrande, and are now selling off homesites around the course. On a much smaller scale, I owned and ran Sotogrande's sole travel agency (because nobody seemed to want to start one: I think I've now found someone to buy a majority share in it and keep it humming).

Among the major relationships of my supposed retirement has been one with Gustavo and Ricardo Cisneros, whose father was a Citibank customer before them. The foundation of the family fortune was an enormous success with the Venezuelan Pepsi-Cola franchise—Venezuela is I think the only country where the two compete that Pepsi outsells Coke by nine to one. Then they branched out to television, computers, retailing, and so on. I've advised them on their holdings in the United States, which include Spaldings, a large bottling company, and pieces of two bank holding companies. When First Boston suggested to them that Galerias Preciados, the second-largest department store chain in Spain, was available at an attractive price, they naturally asked my advice.

It's an interesting story. A quarter of a century ago, this was the premier Spanish retailer, the Bergdorf or Saks of Spain. It was started by a man named Fernandez, who also at one point lent some money to a nephew to start his own department store chain, which he called El Corte Ingles. Fernandez died, and none of his successors knew how to run the business. In fairly short order, though it didn't have the quality locations of Galerias, Corte Ingles became the biggest and best department store group in Spain.

Looking for American expertise, the estate sold 30 percent of Galerias to Federated Stores in America, and Federated sent a group over from Bloomingdale's, one of its leading stores, to straighten things out. They didn't help at all: what worked at Bloomingdales didn't fly in Spain. The Americans then sold their share to Banco Urquijo, a Spanish merchant bank with which City Bank had close relations. Bankers can't run department stores either, and the bank traded it to the rickety empire of Ruiz Mateos. The Mateos group came apart when the new Socialist government took a look at its books, and then the government owned Galerias Preciados. There were some sixty stores that did about $500 million of business a year, and between the stores themselves and the companies that supplied their needs you could see more than twenty thousand jobs. The government couldn't run the stores (its losses were climbing toward $100 million a year), but, obviously, couldn't close them down: Spain needed a number-two retailer. No one in Spain was prepared to pick up the unavoidable losses of the years, at least two and perhaps as many as five, that would be necessary to turn it around, which meant that the price was low in relation to the assets involved.

Galerias was in bad shape. Some merchandise on the shelves was four years old. Morale was non-existent. When we did a survey of our employees, 80 percent of them thought Galerias Preciados was a bad place to shop. We've spent a lot of money on these stores, clearing out the old merchandise at a loss and filling the racks with new and more stylish goods, improving the appearance of the buildings with every-thing from new paint to new fixtures, installing a better inventory-control system. We also have a crackerjack new manager from the Cisneros retail enterprise in Venezuela, Humberto Gonzalez. I'm con-fident of our success. There's lots of room for department stores to expand in Spain, because Spanish retailing has been dominated by small shops. In most developed countries, the chain department and variety stores do about 30 percent of the retail business, but in Spain it's only 8 percent. We don't have to go very far toward the European average to make Galerias Preciados profitable.

Perhaps the most ambitious of my activities in Spain has been a non-profit cause, the development of the port in the Bay of Algeciras ajoining Gibraltar, which is physically the best (and only) deep-water port in Europe and strategically the best location in the Mediterranean area. I'd been talking to people about developing the Bay of Algeciras for about fifteen years. When the Socialist government decided to explore this project seriously in 1985, they asked my advice—and I recom-mended that they get Bechtel to prepare a feasibility study and Citi-bank to examine the financing prospects. The president of Andalucía has been to the United States to talk over the prospects with experts in America, and the project has been given a lot of attention in the local newspaper and on television. As I write in late 1986, the Bechtel and Citibank feasibility reports are about completed.

There is, of course, a long way to go. The government of Spain will have to spend huge sums on infrastructure to bring the roads and rail lines of Andalucía up to the necessary standard. I'm told that to get a container from Algeciras in the southwest to Saragossa in the north-east, it's about as fast and as cheap today to send it by boat to Copen-hagen and truck it back through the good highways of Europe to northern Spain. But if you put in an efficient, modern oil transfer port in Algeciras, appropriately served, you can cut the buyer's cost sub-stantially by comparison with taking the giant tankers to Rotterdam. There's no question Spain can get the financing—long-term money from the European Development Bank and the commercial market.

My model is the Port of New York and New Jersey Authority, which I had some small part in supporting, back in the 1930s. It runs the docks, the airports, the tunnels and bridges in and over the Hudson River. The governors of New York and New Jersey have to agree on all major appointments, and the two state legislatures have the power to tell the Authority what to do, but these people rarely meet, and a strong administrator can run the show. In Spain, the problem is that the area is in the State of Cadiz, whose governor has to approve, and he's protecting the business of the port at Cadiz. Now the generals exert special control over what is called the military district of Gibraltar: when I built my house in Sotogrande I needed permission from the military governor, and you can't fly a private plane over Spanish territory within some dozens of miles of Gibraltar without a special license from the Spanish military. If the Authority were created, civilians would set the rules for the military. And the port technicians would, as they do in New York, acquire the power to develop the port and to finance it without constantly seeking the approval of all the ministers and the local political leaders.

Behind a lot of the bickering, however, is the fact that carrying out some of these plans will require the cooperation of Spain and Gibraltar. The airport the new Authority should operate would be half in Spain and half in Gibraltar. My belief is that collaboration with Spain on such a major project would alter the political attitudes of the Gibraltarians considerably.

Some of my old-guard Spanish friends are surprised that I can (or that I want to) work with the Andalucian government. Some Spanish businessmen have gone into hibernation since Filipe Gonzales became prime minister. They don't have the relationships they used to have with the ministers, and many have lost what entrepreneurial spirit they had. But I saw American businessmen make that mistake in the days of Franklin Roosevelt, to the point where not many of those who were leaders before 1932 were still leaders in the 1940s. I see happening in Spain today what happened in America—the rise of a new generation of businessmen who understand the new situation and know how to thrive in it. This Socialist government has done more than any previous Spanish government to solve the problems business has had in Spain. Inflation is down from 28 percent to 8 percent, Spain's credit is high in the banking world, there are liberal labor laws that permit managers to manage. And the wide acceptance of the role of King

Juan Carlos, which he has played so correctly and courageously, has given everyone confidence in the country's fundamental political stability. All Spanish governments since the war have invited foreign capital to Spain; this one has truly made it welcome when it arrives.

3

I'm retired from Citicorp, but of course I still wear the Citicorp sweater, and I always will. The banking business I can do in retirement, then, is limited somewhat by the fact that I can't, and wouldn't want to, be in a situation where I was seriously competing with Citibank. This does, it turns out, leave me a lot of leeway.

The one American commercial bank with which I became associated was Commerce Union of Nashville, run by an old friend named William Earthman, whom I had known since my days on various American Bankers Association credit committees in the 1950s. Earthman asked me to be a board member and "honorary chairman," and make myself available as an "adviser." I used my contacts in Japan, for example, to help persuade Nissan Motors and Bridgestone Tire to locate in Tennessee. And I think I can claim some credit for the fact that Commerce Union after I came on board made Latin American loans primarily in the form of trade cedits and on a short-term basis, and avoided involvement with Jake Butcher's United American banks both before and after they went under. The bank's loan portfolio and bond holdings have steadily improved, and our return on assets is up over 1 percent, probably the best in Tennessee. Moreover, the stock price has multiplied, which makes me especially happy because I've taken my fees in stock.

My closest Spanish banking connection was with Juan Llado Urrutia, who built the Urquijo family's Banco Urquijo into one of the biggest and best merchant banks in Spain. He was a dedicated friend to City Bank, used to say we had saved his life—when the Republicans took over in Barcelona, he hid in the City Bank vaults until arrangements could be made to spirit him away. I ran into him at the World Bank meetings in Copenhagen in 1970. His bank needed an international program, and I became a consultant. I recommended that he start an operation in London to handle Spanish–UK foreign trade and Spanish–UK financial transactions. We opened our London bank for business in April, 1973, and promptly in July received Authorized-Bank status from the Bank of England. Since Banco Hispano Americano acquired the shares of Banco Urquijo it hadn't already owned, a few years back, we've been called Banco Hispano Americano, Ltd. I was chairman of the board and Kenneth Mendenhall, a capable former Citibanker, American but with two decades of experience in the London market, was managing director. I moved on to be honorary chairman in June, 1986, and José Maria Amusategui, number-two at Banco Hispano Americano in Madrid, became chairman.

Early in 1987, all outside directors retired to permit the bank to be run as an integral part of the Spanish operation.

Like any bank of its kind, Buhal (as we call it) issues letters of credit, acts as the principal market maker for pesetas, and managers or places prominently in the syndicate distributing all bond issues sold by the Spanish government or Spanish industry. For example, we may sell a German tour operator forward pesetas. He is selling trips to German tourists, and making arrangements with Spanish hotels, charter buses, and the like, for business sometimes as long as six months in advance. The Spanish vendors can quote him a price in pesetas, but he has to quote his customers a price in marks. He doesn't want to run the risk of exchange-rate movements between now and the time the German tourists begin traveling, and the Spanish hotels and charter-bus people don't want to take the risk of foreign exchange, either. So we take it at the bank. Meanwhile, sellers of machine tools and refrigeration equipment to Spain who are going to collect pesetas can lock in a price for those pesetas in their own currency before proceeding with the contract. Banco Hispano Americano, Ltd., made few mistakes (and no large mistakes: we had, for example, no significant loans to Latin LDCs), and had always made a handsome profit.

In 1986, I turned the crank on yet another bank of which I was to be chairman and chief executive officer: a partnership with Credit Suisse to form a subsidiary for them (though I will have an ownership share) on the rock of Gibraltar. I can see the rock from my front porch in Sotogrande, and now that the border crossing is easy many Gibraltarians, as they call themselves, have become our neighbors. Through my brother-in-law John Crosson, my wife and I have made good friends there—the governor, Sir Peter Terry, and his wife; Prime Minister Hassan and his wife, businessman Joe Gaggero and his wife (he was photographed in *Town and Country* as "the man who owns a piece of the rock"); and my lawyer Alfred Vasquez, speaker of the Gibraltar Parliament, among others.

There are few significant international banks in Gibraltar, only Barclay's and more recently Lloyds Hambro's, and the Hong Kong and

Shanghai Bank, and clearly there's room for more, with the growing offshore banking needs of multinational companies. Our purpose is to provide a tax-efficient residence where top-quality service and confidentiality can be given to the multiplying billions of homeless dollars in today's world. Credit Suisse agreed to finance this bank, and we are partners in the venture. The charter for our Gibraltar Trust Bank came through in February 1987; I've rented premises and hired a managing director, Keith Risk, an admirable young English banker whom I found in the deep personnel pocket at Citibank in London. Lord Keith, formerly head of Rolls Royce, is among my directors, and John Crosson is a valued consultant. I've got a lot riding on this one—not so much the money (though of course I'd like the bank to make money) as my reputation. I'm facing the fact that this may be the last bank I ever start! It's five times more important than the money for me to be sure Moore doesn't blow it on his final venture.

12

The Best Is Yet to Come

For those who believe as I do that the most important record of your life is not the clippings or the bank accounts or even the memoirs but the friends you made in your time, the crown of my story is the eightieth-birthday party given for me in London in April, 1985. People flew in for the occasion from all over Europe and several places in the United States; there were some funny stories told about men sitting next to each other in the airplanes who hadn't previously met, greatly enjoyed their airborne conversation, and then one inquired of the other what brought him to London and they both learned they were going to George Moore's birthday party.

My hosts were my friends at Credit Suisse and its London subsidiary—CEO Rainer Gut, Michael von Clemm, and Jack Hennessy. Among the fifty other names on the list before me are those of Herman Abs, chairman of Deutsche Bank; Giovanni Agnelli of Fiat; John Loudon, former CEO of the Shell group; Lord Aldington; Peter Ardron, the senior general manager of Barclay's; Ernst Brutsche, the CEO of Midland Bank; Dominic Cadbury of Cadbury-Schweppes; Paul Christian, the general manager of Swiss Reinsurance; the Venezuelan industrialist Ricardo Cisneros; the golf champion Henry Cotton; J. Dewey Daane, a former governor of the Federal Reserve System; Jan Ekman, president of Svenska Handelsbanken; the Finnish businessman Goran Ehrnrooth (also celebrating his eightieth birthday); Killian Hennessy of Hennessy-Moët & Chandon; Lord Keith of Castleacre; Ian MacGregor, the chairman of the National Coal Board in England;

David Mulford, Deputy Secretary of the Treasury; Jaime Ortiz-Patino of the Bolivian tin family; Stanley Osborne of Lazard Frères in New York; Karl Otto Poehl, governor of the Bundesbank; Gengo Suzuki of Associated Japanese Bank; my old friend Francisco Gimenez Torres from Spain; Henry F. Tiarks, former chairman of Schroder's in London; my sons George and Stevens, forty-six and fourteen, respectively; and many others whose names are as dear to me as these. These are very busy men. Their willingness to put aside their work (and their Easter week!) to entertain me on my birthday was as great a thrill as I have ever know, or can imagine.

And then, a month later, not to be outdone, my Spanish friends from banking and business and government gave me a very similar party in Madrid, at the resplendent Nuevo Club. The master of ceremonies was the vice-president of Spain, Juan Antonio Garcia Diez, and among the guests were the Duke of Badajoz, brother-in-law of the king; Rafael Escuredo Rodriguez, the former president of the Junta de Andalucia; Antonio Garrigues Walker, who had been ambassador to the United States; the industrialist Javier Benjumea and Juan Luis de Burgos; several past governors of the Bank of Spain; and an important group of CEOs of Spanish banks. The men who started the ball rolling were the bankers Alejandro Fernandez de Araoz and Juan Llado, Jr. I made a speech in Spanish and it went down very well.

Over the years I have compiled a list of what I enjoy calling the Moore awards, my private accolades to businessmen who have accomplished greatly in my time. This list, too, is headed by Hermann Abs, who brilliantly exploited the possibilities of the German "universal bank" to acquire major positions for the bank in companies like Mercedes Benz, until he could take his bank abroad from a base so solid no intelligent risk could frighten him. As a merchant bank with broad placing power as well as the world's deepest pockets of its own capital, Deutsche Bank, much as I hate to admit it, is well ahead of Citibank in the new worldwide securities markets.

Agnelli's name is another high on the list. He brilliantly used the influence he had on government as his country's largest private employer to make Fiat a leading worldwide auto company under almost impossible political, environmental, and economic conditions.

And of course one must pay tribute to Japan as a society for what has been accomplished from the rubble of World War II, in no small part under the leadership of friends like Yoshizane Iwasa, Japan's top commercial banker of my day, still in the background at Fuji Bank after his formal retirement, and still making his individual contribution to the Japanese miracle.

One hears less of the Indian accomplishment, but it is perhaps as remarkable as the Japanese, because it was done in the teeth of unwise governments and unwise policies. The leader here was my old friend J. R. D. ("Jeh") Tata, who inherited an industrial empire and made it stronger while supporting schools and hospitals and other charitable institutions. India is a continent, not a country, with as many people as Europe, a potential merchant of truly vast dimensions.

Among the Americans I would like to honor, I think pride of place goes to Henry Ford II, if only because he's had such bad publicity in recent years from his former employee Lee Iacocca. I know, in ways a banker's confidentiality still would not let me disclose, how close the Ford Motor Company was to desperate financial trouble in 1948, when Henry took over his grandfather's business. The brilliant team of "whiz kids" he installed to make it the secure number two of the world's automakers included not only Iacocca but Robert McNamara, who later ran the Defense Department and then the World Bank, Arjay Miller, who built the Stanford Business School into an equal rival of Harvard's, and many others. Yes, he wasn't always polite when he dismissed people, he was a crown prince with a third-generation golden spoon in his mouth, and there were nights when he partied hard. But he worked hard the next morning, and made the right decisions.

This is not to take anything away from Iacocca, who may well be the best automobile chief executive of our day. I know of no one else who could have done what he did for Chrysler, pull it out of virtual collapse, redesign the product line, rebuild the organization and its financial strength. What he forgot in his bitterness about Henry Ford was the fact that he learned everything he knows about turning around a troubled auto company from Ford—and the same could be said about the team of talented Ford people who went with him to Chrysler.

Another man who triumphed against the odds was Peter Grace, whose inheritance was an obsolete Latin American trading company. When he became CEO of W. R. Grace he found a conglomerate nearly every part of which was going downhill. We knew all about Grace. His father and grandfather had been on the City Bank board, and when he succeeded he was our youngest director; when he retired from the Citicorp board in 1985, he had been a director for thirty-four years. Howard Sheperd did not have a high regard for Grace. Peter went to Sheperd one day after some years of this and said, "You don't trust me and I don't get good treatment around here. I think we'll both be more comfortable if we drop this family relationship."

Sheperd said, "You're not wrong, but let's give it one more chance. I'll ask one of my best men to make a report." So he went to Moore, even though I had just become executive v.-p. in the overseas division, and I came back and said Grace was making magic. He was getting out of all the bad businesses—the shipping and the airline Grace shared with Pan Am, the plantations and the trading company and the bank—and putting the company into chemicals and other growth industries. Sheperd accepted my report, the City Bank–Grace relationship was put on track; and, I suppose not surprisingly, Peter put me on his board, where I still serve.

Another outstanding chief executive and good friend was Jim Duncan, who built and ran Massey-Ferguson for thirty years, with time off to serve as minister of industry in Canada during the war. In Duncan's time, this tractor manufacturer was one of the strongest companies in a strong industry. Corporate politics eased Duncan out while he was still in his prime, and the result was perhaps the greatest possible tribute to him: in other hands, the company went over the cliff.

Charlie Thomas, who built Monsanto from a little chemicals company to a giant, was the last of the Ohio gang that produced Alfred P. Sloan and Charles Kettering of General Motors, Tom Watson of IBM, John H. Patterson of National Cash Register. He was one of those rare men who knew what goes on in the molecules as well as in the market, a scientist, not just a businessman, and was one of the architects of the atom bomb in the Manhattan Project. Later he became an enthusiast for solar energy, and I was among his converts—I have no doubt that scientists will get the efficiency of the solar cell up to 35 percent if not more, at which point direct energy from the sun will become not just competitive but triumphant against the stored energy from the sun we use in the form of fossil fuels. Some of the credit for Thomas should go also to Edgar Queeny, who had the sense to hire Thomas to run his fledgling company. Queeny also, not seeking credit, made large contributions of both money and time to the cause of wildlife preservation. He also taught me a banking lesson when he showed me a letter one of my predecessors had written to his father, denying a loan to the fledgling Monsanto. The letter said the company's capital was too thin, its debt was too high, it was illiquid, and didn't seem likely to improve. Queeny's father had kept it, because the analysis was right—

just the prediction was wrong. The lesson was to avoid unnecessary predictions, and to bet on people, not numbers.

I want to speak flowers of Morgan-Guaranty, and of the men who ran it in my time, especially the lawyer Henry Alexander, who put the two banks together and ran them, and his successor John Meyer, whom I knew from the beginning because he had represented J. P. Morgan at meetings where I represented Perkins. Morgan had few deposits— the way Morgan had been run, you had to be a very important fellow to keep your account there. Guaranty was a successful business bank in New York and had plenty of deposits, but it lacked effective leadership. William Potter had been brought in to clean it up and keep it clean after its debacle in foreign lending in 1921 and had run it essentially as a trustee. Alexander saw the opportunities of the merger. But what made J. P. Morgan such a great bank was not any individual; it was all the brainpower in that one building. City Bank was a diversified institution, with plenty of balance wheels to keep it moving—a base of deposits which through my time meant cheap money to lend, consumer business, loans to smaller companies in the New York market, and so on. Morgan as a corporate bank have to buy much of the money they lend, work with restricted lists of customers, and play the money markets just right. They have made fewer mistakes, and though they had no natural advantages at all they put the rest of us to shame in their return on assets and return on equity, year after year.

Republic of New York is the outstanding bank built since World War II in the United States, and that's the work of one man, Edmond Safra. One of the strange stories of recent years was American Express buying Safra's private banking business in Europe but not Republic Bank in the United States (because the law doesn't allow American Express as a multi-purpose financial holding company to own a full-service bank in the United States). That was like buying half the horse, and perhaps the wrong half. Safra understood the precious-metals markets, which other bankers didn't, but he also understood how to avoid the sort of loans that get you in trouble. I say bankers should never make big mistakes; Safra rarely makes even little mistakes.

I've watched the Solvay family in Belgium for sixty years, through good times and bad. To an almost unique degree, that company had adjusted to the times: whenever there's been a change in the petrochemical business, they've been ahead of the learning curve. Ian MacGregor built American Metals Climax and then ran the London end of Lazard brilliantly for André Meyer; I wasn't surprised when it turned out that he saved the British government from what looked like bottomless pits of losses at British Steel and at the National Coal Board. Owen Cheatham took the small Georgia Plywood Company and by developing a broad-based forest-products complex made his Georgia-Pacific a leader of an industry that had been dominated by Weyerhauser. And of course there was Tom Watson, Jr., at IBM, inheriting a company that was in some danger of falling behind, and moving straight ahead from the era of punch cards to the era of computers to create the greatest industrial empire of our time. While admiring IBM, one should also, however, remember Digital Equipment Corporation, which came from nowhere after giants like GE and RCA abandoned the computer field and now offers the leader at continuing challenge in some of its most important markets.

Of the giants of my time, the one I worked with most closely was Walter Wriston, my successor at Citibank in every job I had from 1956 through to the end. We had come together when I got disgusted with the quality of people the personnel office was sending me as candidates for fast-track jobs in our expanding domestic division in the late 1940s, and our director of personnel assured me those were the best we had. I asked to see the files of all the college graduates we'd hired in the last few years. Wriston was then working for the controller's office, counting assets in the branches. His file jumped out of the stack, clearly a brilliant man, son of the president of Brown University, who had come to banking after a brief stint as a foreign service officer, by a big margin the best prospect in the bank. I asked the personnel director why he hadn't told me about Wriston, and he said sort of shamefacedly that he'd promised the controller he wouldn't. That's the way the bank ran in those days. It was crazy to believe you could hold a man of Wriston's quality very long in the job they had given him.

Walt was a big, imaginative guy, with absolute confidence in himself. Without my telling him, he was conscious of all the things I'd been talking about in my reports. He was a fountain of new ideas to expand our services and increase our profits. And he had a sense of how things worked: when Sheperd said we couldn't expect to continue to get our inventory free from depositors, it was Wriston who worked out the system of the negotiable certificate of deposit and the arrangements with Discount Corporation to trade in them. He was ahead of me in understanding the importance of governmental relations, and he became a much bigger man in Washington and in the newspapers than I had every been. I couldn't see the P&L in all that public relations and politics, but he did, and he was right. I should also say, I think, that at all times, even when it was costly to him in the politics of the bank, Wriston was entirely loyal to me. Shortly after Rockefeller had changed the by-laws to make trouble between the two of us, I learned from Carl Desch, secretary of the board and the man in charge of protocol, that Wriston had told him I was always to be listed first and he was to be listed second. Walter himself never told me.

Walt also remembered little things. When we were opening our international banking office at 399 Park Avenue, one of the things we wanted was a very impressive rug in the lobby. Walt remembered that when he was in the controller's office one of the things he counted at the Canal Street branch was a magnificent Persian rug that the bank had taken when a fifty thousand dollar loan went sour to some fellow in Iran. We'd written the rug down to one dollar, spent thousands of dollars to fumigate and store it, and it had been in a vault on Canal Street for sixteen years. It made a superb centerpiece for the decoration of the new banking room. There's a banking lesson here, by the way—that it's a mistake to write anything down to zero. When you do that, you forget about it; so long as you carry it on the books, even at one dollar, someone looks at it once in a while.

Of course, there are lions around the throne of great men. At Citibank Walt had the services of first-class men he and I and Rockefeller had moved ahead over the years. William Spencer, one of our wisest lenders, who had been the first banker (as distinguished from oil man) to head our petroleum group, became the head of the Special Industries division and then bravely undertook the job of running the operating departments when they were troubled and needed reorganization: he was president under Wriston after I retired. Ed Palmer, another banking professional, was liked and admired by the whole community of those who did business with the bank, whether they liked the rest of us or not; George Scott, one of our best lending officers, ran our credit policies committee without a flaw; Richard Perkins, my old mentor's son, came to Farmers Trust from Harris, Upham as an investments adviser, ably represented the bank on a number of boards, and successfully supervised our trust operations while vice-chairman. Alan Temple, a former newpaperman with the *New York Times,* was our enlightening economist and with his other hand supervised our public and governmental relations. For me in the years before my retirement, there were three great ladies who put up with the incessant drive and vagaries of Moore as chairman—Erna Tebben, who handled my correspondence, and could type two hundred words a minute without making a mistake; Ruth Anders, who made my appointments; and Eva Popper, who kept track of my cultural and charitable and governmental work—and also, incidentally, wrote the first drafts of my statement to the stockholders in the annual report.

My friendship with Walt Wriston yielded an additional benefit in the form of acquaintance with his father Henry, former president of Brown University, the most brilliant man I've ever met. I asked him once what he would want if he could have one wish in the world, and he didn't mention money or fame or good health; he said, "One more waking hour every day." I laughed, and told him that I already had three hours a day on him, for I slept only five and he slept eight. But I too wanted more than anything else one more hour a day. In 1975, on the occasion of his eighty-fifth birthday, Henry Wriston published a brief essay on retirement in the *New York Times*. "If every job you ever had brought rewards," he wrote, "retirement can bring fresh zest and joy to new activities . . . It is in the mind that great events occur. If you dull the mind the world will be drab. If your mind grows, as it should, retirement is exciting." And so I started a second career with a good example.

2

The central facts of economic life in my time have been the proliferation of technologies and the decline in the value of money. Not long after World War II, I was at an American Bankers Association convention in Detroit with Randolph Burgess, our vice-chairman, who was president of the ABA that year. A woman asked him whether he thought there would be more inflation. He said, "Inflation is a perpetual phenomenon. The only question is, how much, and in what period of time." I was interested in inflation from the start of my banking career. During the depth of the debt deflation of 1931, Perkins and Robert Lovett of Kuhn, Loeb commissioned a paper from the economist Frank Graham on the German experience of the 1920s, and after Roosevelt began his course of deliberately inflating the currency (raising the price of gold because his economic advisers had told him that would raise the price of wheat, too), they commissioned another academic paper on banking under conditions of severe inflation. I still have them. Those studies showed three protections against inflation—copper coins (Germans in the 1920s didn't have gold: that had gone for reparations), the forest industry (manufacturing plants get abandoned and rust, but the trees keep growing 2 percent, 3 percent a year), and banks (because their inventory keeps rising as the money supply expands, and they don't have to pay much for it).

If you always keep in mind the dangers of inflation, you can buy insurance against it cheap, because except when the experience is recent the people with whom you are dealing don't think their money is about to lose its value. In 1940 we were negotiating a long-term ore contract with Republic Steel to sell iron ore from the upstate New York mine we had reopened, with that loan partly guaranteed by the Fed under one of the New Deal programs. I asked the steel company to write in an additional royalty per ton of ore once the market price of pig iron got above a certain figure. Pig iron was then selling for about ten dollars a ton. I asked them what figure they considered so ridiculous as a price for iron that they wouldn't worry about it, and they said, thirty dollars. The deal we made was sixty-five cents a ton plus 7.5 cents of every two dollars the price rose above thirty dollars, which Republic's negotiator accepted irritably with the comment that it didn't make any difference to his side whether the clause was there or not. During the war, pig iron went to seventy dollars a ton, and the contract became so expensive for them that they had to buy the mine itself, at a good price.

Similarly, when we were going to move uptown from Wall Street, the site we decided we liked was 399 Park Avenue. (This decision followed some maneuvering—we negotiated with Bill Zeckendorf and the New York Central Railroad for a while to put the new City Bank world headquarters in the air space over the back of Grand Central Station, where eventually they built the Pan Am building.) We had sometime earlier bought that land for the Astor Trust, an English entity that we managed, at a price of about $4 million. We had then leased it for ninety-nine years at six hundred thousand dollars a year to John Jacob Astor, an American Astor not part of the trust, to build what he planned to call Astor Place. This was to be something of a family monument as well as an office building, and the life insurance companies that were asked to write the mortgage felt the architecture was too "artistic"; it didn't fill the cubage allowed by the city's zoning code. They wouldn't write the mortgage unless Astor personally guaranteed it. He backed away, and offered to give us the cost of the hole if we would take over his lease. In part at my urging, Rockefeller hung tough, insisting that we had to have an option to own the property, if at any time we were prepared to capitalize the $600,000 annual lease on a 5 percent basis, paying $12 million for the land. These were delicate negotiations, because the terms were satisfactory to Lord Astor in England (the Bill Astor who had been at the next desk when I started at Farmers Trust), but there were minor children in the trust, too, and we had to get the surrogate's court to approve the ultimate deal.

Similarly, when we decided to move back downtown some of the operations we had taken with us to 399 (notably check processing and foreign exchange), we built a special facility at 110 Wall Street. The land on which we built was owned by Columbia University. I insisted that we had to have an option to buy both the building and the property, and I was told that Columbia never sells. We were to pay a big rental, and I asked from them, as I had asked from the Astors, an option to buy the land at a reasonable capitalization. To Uris, the builders and operators who had built the structure, I said, "How much would you hope to make on this transaction? Would you be happy with a five-million-dollar profit?" Yes, indeed. Eventually, we exercised the options for both land and buildings.

I've always been a hard-money man. Over the centuries, people have been betrayed by paper money. On one of my early trips to Mexico, I was at a bar with a Mexican couple, and when the bartender put silver coins before me as my change, the wife said, "George, do you mind?", reached into her purse, substituted paper pesos for the silver pesos, and put the coins in her bag. I said, "How long have you been doing that?" She said, "Since I was a little girl; my father taught me." That woman didn't have to worry about the peso at 480 to the dollar—she had her silver. I was one of the early gold bugs, because I think gold eventually holds its value. Valued at market, two-thirds of the reserves of the central banks today are in gold, and though they say to the contrary, they wouldn't have it any other way. It's the only way they can protect their national monetary reserves against the inevitable inflation.

Of course, gold is a commodity, and like any commodity its price is controlled by the costs of production. My friends in the mining business told me early in the 1980s that the range for an ounce of gold was three hundred dollars to four hundred dollars. Below $300, some marginal mines go out of production and gold becomes scarce until the price goes back up; above $400, additional mines come on-stream and supply eventually pushes the price back down. Those figures, of course, assumed constant dollars at what was then the dollar's value; inflation, or just the decline of the dollar in relation to other currencies, would move the price up, at least temporarily. In 1986, for example, the Japanese bought gold heavily, allegedly because they wanted to coin millions of medals honoring Emperor Hirohito, actually because gold would retain its value in terms of yen when the dollar declined. And then the price stayed up over four hundred dollars, even though with the declining rand the cost of production in dollar terms diminished in South Africa, because of political concerns about whether that country would be able to maintain its output.

I no longer think gold is the answer to the international monetary dilemna, though I still don't want anybody giving me the International Monetary Fund's SDRs or the Common Market's ECUs. Those are paper money like any other. My dream is for what I call a "Geostable," a "currency" that would maintain a stable purchasing power everywhere in the world. Local currencies would be adjusted daily to the Geostable by computers to assure that stable purchasing power everywhere. Businessmen could make their trade deals and investment arrangements in the Geostable, with assurance that their plans would not be ruined by what are from their point of view completely meaningless and incalculable currency fluctuations. It's a dream, perhaps an impossible dream, though I'm not the only person working on it (a decade ago, the French monetary theorist Jacques Riboud proposed the idea of a "Eurostable," to perform the same functions within the Common Market). Certain dreams, however, are *necessary* dreams, and those are the ones that are most likely to come true.

For investment purposes, gold doesn't have the appeal of earning assets that also retain their value in times of inflation, especially timber properties and farmland. I remember Tom Watson telling me once on the New Canaan train that the family had made as much on their Indiana farms as they had on their IBM stock. The most certain, stable value in the world is farmland. I am told that twenty million acres a year are taken out of production, worldwide, by the growth of cities, the construction of factories, and so on, and there's an increase in population every year. The productivity of the land keeps going up. When I was traveling in the 1940s and 1950s, black land in Iowa and Illinois sold for one thousand dollars to one thousand five hundred dollars an acre. In 1980, it was five thousand dollars an acre or more, but in 1986 it was back near where it had been a generation ago— down more than 50 percent not just in dollars, but in the number of bushels of corn and other crops it will yield. And there are more sellers than buyers. That land is black gold, and it's better than metal, for you can eat what it produces.

3

I'm not a man of the market; I am better at judging long-term trends and values. When I try to play markets short-term, I usually get burnt. I've been taught my lessons by experts. In my time, one of the fabled traders on the floor of the New York Stock Exchange was my friend "Duke" Wellington. One day I suggested to him that Schenley shares were cheap. They were then selling at about thirty dollars a share, and I estimated that just the whiskey in the warehouses was worth around fifty-six dollars a share. Wellington shook his head and said, "Yes, George, but the specialists have a big sheaf of sell orders on Schenley, the market wants to sell it, and it's going to go down. You're right, it's worth more, but I'll wait until the buying trend is up, regardless of price." That's not the way my mind works: I don't share consensus views, and I'm impatient. Sometimes I take short-term losses, and I give the wrong short-term advice. But since the 1930s, I have not often been wrong in my long-term judgments.

One of the reasons may be that I've picked up a few easily applied rules of thumb. Investments can be in truth very complicated, and it can give you a headache to figure them out. I takes twenty pages to compare the relative values of Shell Oil / Royal Dutch as against Exxon, because in 1901 Shell / Royal Dutch made a favorable tax arrangement with the British and Dutch authorities. They are not taxed on foreign earnings brought home for working capital *and dividends,* and they are not restricted by foreign-exchange controls when they use their resources for investment around the world. But most things are much simpler.

My friend Harry Helmsley tells me that when he looks at hotels to buy, his staff gives him long memos to read, but that he can check the value pretty well himself—on the back of an envelope. His formula is that a hotel is worth one thousand dollars a room times the average daily rental of the rooms based on 90 percent occupancy. If it's a thousand-room hotel with an average daily rental of eighty dollars, and they average nine hundred rooms rented each night, that means $80 million. This rough formula tells him whether all the price factors are in line—cost of land, construction, number of rooms, occupancy, and room rates. If I was looking at a bank, and I knew that the assets were good, the rough yardstick used to be that it was worth about 5 percent of its demand deposits plus 2½ percent of its time deposits, plus its trust and other fee income capitalized at 10 percent, with a plus or minus for the real value of the premises. If you get it for that, you won't be far in the woods.

Bob Kleberg of King Ranch used to say that farm or grazing land is worth twice the value of the animals it will feed.

In the oil patch, the rule of thumb is that reserves in the ground are worth the present value of five years' production.

Stocks should be worth the multiple of their present earnings that equals the average rate of growth of those earnings over, say, the last five years. If the earnings have grown and seem likely to continue growing by 12 percent a year, the stock is worth twelve times current earnings; 15 percent a year, fifteen times current earnings. That may not work between now and next Christmas, but it should over the years. Nobody can calculate the length of the lags, which is why few "experts" I've known have made money on their expertise. The lags can be long—in gold, it took thirty years—but market judgment eventually catches up with reality.

Over the years, yields on money should average about 10 percent on equity investments, 8 percent on preferred stock, 6 percent on bonds, and 5 percent on bank loans. When you get too far from those numbers, there's going to be trouble. Those 20 percent rates in the markets in the 1970s and early 1980s, for example, were blown high by what I called "the OPEC bubble." It was painful while it lasted, but the bubble is now being liquidated. Over the years, even if you're as good as IBM you can't make more than 15 percent on equity. It's hard for a company paying 15 percent interest on its debt to stay alive, much less grow. When rates drop, of course, the benefits are great. Another rough yardstick says that when interest rates fall one percentage point, gross national product will rise one-half of 1 percent. When the OPEC bubble burst, as it had to burst (in 1983, I made a speech predicting that the real danger to the banks before the end of the decade would be not the loans to Latin American but the loans to the Middle East, based as they were on artificially inflated oil prices), prosperity returned to America. There is a law of compensating forces, and what goes up will come down. I don't see an apocalypse ahead, but one of the things mankind was told a long time ago was that lean years follow fat years before the fat years return again. It's wise to look ahead.

So I'm a "contrarian." Opinion makes markets; if you accept the consensus view of the world, you accept the current market. Someone once asked J. P. Morgan why the market had gone down, and he said it was because there were more sellers than buyers. I like something more predictable than that. I bought into Harry Helmsley's real estate fund because in effect you were buying a piece of five million square feet of office space at fifty cents a foot, and it had to be worth more than that.

Yes, I make mistakes, too. I got hooked into a mining venture in Alaska and Canada because the promoters and I underestimated what it would cost to start in effect a whole city up in the tundra (and perhaps overestimated the value of the metals that would come out of the mines). I've been too trusting in my judgment of some of the people with whom I've done business. But generally speaking my rules of thumb haven't let me down. And I find that most of the successful people I meet have similar rules to help them make their decisions.

4

Nobody can predict the future. During the World Bank meetings in Toronto in 1982, six of us financial leaders, all supposedly well-informed, met for dinner and talked about what was going to happen in the rest of the 1980s. Finally, after we had pontificated, Dr. Jelle Zijlstra, head of the Netherlands central bank and chairman of the Bank for International Settlements, interrupted our conversation. He said, "We are confidently predicting the 1980s. Let's look back and see how well we anticipated the 1970s, how accurately we foresaw what turned out to be the five most important economic happenings of the decade. How many of you predicted that gold would go to over eight hundred dollars an ounce? Raise your hands!" Nobody did. "How many saw oil rising to forty dollars a barrel? Raise your hands!" Nobody did. "How many expected the prime rate in the United States to reach 21 percent? Raise your hands!" Nobody did. "How many expected inflation to reach 12 percent?" "How many expected the U.S. dollar to be devalued 30 percent?" Still, of course, no hands. "Now gentlemen," he concluded, "please continue predicting the 1980s."

Many things can go wrong. The Greek islands, where we spent a month of the summer of 1986, can't afford to keep grazing sheep on land that's so easily destroyed by an animal that pulls up the roots of the grass. (And it doesn't have to happen. Between my two visits to George Livanos's island, he acquired a desalination plant to multiply his fresh-water resources, and planted trees on the hillside. In a few years, the island went from a brown bump in the blue sea to an oasis of greenery.) The world obviously cannot afford the waste of lives and wealth in wars. It's discouraging to see that the great powers cannot even agree on the need to stop shipping arms to the small countries that fight the small wars that can so easily get out of hand. You can't look at the world today and not see that some fraction of what is being spent on arms would quickly clean up all the LDC loans and allow those countries to return to the path of economic growth, which their people so desperately need. By an accepted rule of thumb, it takes about five dollars of capital investment to produce one dollar of increased gross national product in these countries. Those numbers mean the problem is manageable, but to date in the 1980s there has been virtually no new net investment in Latin America, and the national product in real terms has actually declined in many countries, despite continued rapid population growth.

The debt of the LDCs is a serious problem, and in its early phases it was not properly handled. The statistics from these countries were two years late, which meant that the banks did not know how deep in they were getting—and in many cases did not want to know, because they thought they were making good profits. The banks performed a great function when the recycled the OPEC profits, but six months of that should have been enough—thereafter, the international institutions and the governments should have assumed the burdens. And there's no doubt some of the money that was lent was stolen or wasted. At City Bank, we always figured that the real trade figures for almost any of these countries were several hundred million dollars better than what was reported, because pervasive exchange controls gave businessman a good reason to overinvoice the price of imports (giving them an excuse to be sending foreign exchange out of the country) and underinvoice the price of exports (reducing the nation's apparent earnings abroad). In the future, banks in dealing with these countries will undoubtedly return to the sort of trade financing they did before the days of the OPEC bubble. That's what banks do best. And it doesn't hurt the LDCs to borrow that way: money is money, and when imports can be financed there's more local money available for longer-term investment.

To clean up the weight of current debt, I have suggested that the International Monetary Fund issue what the British call "consols," bonds that pay interest but never pay off the principal. The interest rate on these bonds would be below what the borrowers are now paying, which means that the debt would, in effect, sell at a discount. Banks could agree to swap their third-world debt for these consols, taking some loss on the discount; and the borrowers could receive the benefit of lower rates, which they need to build their infrastructure and industrialize.

Another promising road, already being followed in a small way, is the swapping of debt for equity. Chile has led the way, making arrangements so that business firms which buy the country's dollar debt in the market for such paper, where it sells at a considerable discount, can trade it in at almost the face value of the paper *in pesos* to invest in Chilean enterprises. Mexico has done a few tentative individual deals on this basis, most recently at this writing one with Nissan Motors, which will finance its investment with Mexican bonds that can be bought just now for something less than sixty cents on the dollar.

These countries need something like $20 billion a year of new investment—not $20 billion over three years, as the "Baker Initiative" suggested, but $20 billion a year. Of course, they have to help by making a climate more conducive to investment. I have recently been asked to join a "council of presidents" of CICYP, which argues that someone is attempting the intelligent step of re-activating that potentially useful organization, which could help the governments (including ours) direct their efforts toward increasing private initiatives. The danger is that the poor countries will lose that aggressive hope that has carried them through tragedy for so many years. I remember almost thirty years ago visiting India for the first World Bank / IMF meeting to be held outside the United States, and being granted (together with my chairman, Howard Sheperd) an audience with Nehru. We warned him that his plans were too ambitious, he was trying to do twice as much as India could achieve. He didn't seem to be listening.

The next day, when he made his speech welcoming the delegates to the meeting, he made reference to the fact that most of them were in Asia for the first time. When their ancestors had come to Asia, he said, it wasn't for cheap labor and raw materials, but to learn from what was four hundred years ago the most advanced industrial society in the world. Steelmaking went from Benares to Sheffield, and Indian textiles were copied all over Europe. Asia invented the best things in life, bridge, backgammon, chess, and polo. And the ethical principles the West thinks were the creation of its eighteenth- and nineteenth century philosophers can be found carved in stone in India from many hundreds of years before. Now, he added, you say we are trying to do twice as much as we could be trying to do with our limited resources. But you can go a block from here and see people for whom what we are trying to do is not half what they need, truly need—and if their leaders don't try for what they need, they will change their leaders. Sheperd and I thought it was a sound rebuke to us. It still is.

In the developed countries, we have to be prepared to face the bad news that some of the social programs promised by the politicians cannot be paid for. The postwar babies haven't been told that when they turn sixty-five in thirty years, it won't be possible to pay them Social Security benefits their parents are receiving.

There is still a danger of economic panic in this interrelated world, though we have in place excellent international mechanisms: the postwar creations, the World Bank, IMF, EEC, and the close cooperation of the leading central banks and governments. Without the international agencies, the LDC loan crisis of 1982 might have provoked a worldwide depression. (On the other hand, if the international organizations had been more strongly led in the 1970s, the OPEC bubble would not have done as much harm. We were very lucky that Jacques Delarosier of France was president of the International Monetary fund in 1982.) And we must spend money in our interdependent age to achieve technological redundancy everywhere—we cannot allow a situation to develop where a bomb in the telephone exchange will put everybody out of business. It *is* disturbing to see the disruption caused in 1986 by a single computer failure in a single not terribly important bank—Bank of New York, which was unable to pay for Treasury securities it was trading because some piece of machinery had gone blooey. No less than $26 billion in loans from the Federal Reserve System was required before Bank of New York could pay what it owed to other banks.

I do not subscribe to apocalypse theories or "long wave" analyses that tell us our postwar growth must be ended by a collapse, an economic breakdown, a debt deflation. You can do better than that by examining what John Naisbitt has called "megatrends," some of them negative but more of them positive. I do believe that there are cycles in economic activity, an inevitable aspect of a productive market economy. Yes, there are dangerous excesses; we cannot keep borrowing $100 billion a year from the rest of the world (which is what those arcane numbers about the "balance of payments" really mean); after a while prudent lenders will refuse us (which is what the experts mean when they talk about a "collapse of the dollar").

We have to face the fact that we have invited much of this trouble. I remember on my last tour of the Far East as chairman of Citibank arriving at Bangkok airport just as Jim Roche, then chairman of General Motors, was departing. In those countries the chairman of a big bank didn't ride the bus between airplane and terminal: a limousine picked him up at the foot of the stairs. As I was about to enter my Cadillac, I saw Jim arriving in a Chrysler. I twitted him about it, and he told me my people had rented the only Cadillac in Thailand. I said I had seen endless Toyotas in Bangkok but no GM cars at all, and he said they were going to start selling cars in Asia; their strategy was to manufacture for the Asian market in Europe. I said that if they let the Japanese take as much of the Thai and other Asian markets as they would naturally inherit if they were the only Asian manufacturers, General Motors would find that the Toyotas of the world would acquire enough capital and marketing muscle to push the American manufacturers around everywhere in the world, even at home. And that was what happened.

But there is also a closer link than my friends in the administration wish to believe between our budget deficit and this specter of our foreign borrowings. Much more must be done with the admirable recommendations made by Peter Grace's commission on government expenditures, and we also need, I think, new kinds of taxes, preferably a Value Added Tax on the European model. Some of the activity in the stock market in recent years has been uncomfortably close to the excesses we had in the 1920s, especially in the takeover and leveraged buy-out businesses, financed as they are by the issuance of dubious "junk bonds" that promise higher interests payments than the acquired assets can earn.

But the markets will make the adjustments. We are in the process of emerging, not without some pain, from the inflationary cycle that was abetted by OPEC. Shipping has already turned the corner: charter rates for Very Large Crude Carriers doubled between 1985 and 1987. The energy business is coming out of its crisis, and while one does not yet see the bottom of the farmers' sad adjustments, they are obviously in process. Metals and mining, because of vast overcapacity and the willingness of nations to subsidize uneconomic producers, are still in their down cycles. But the world needs economic growth, knows it now—you don't hear so much anymore from my friend Agnelli about "the limits of growth"—and will achieve what it needs. Not that I've given up on America. We're not dead by a long shot. We're still the leaders in most significant technologies. The venture capital funds with which I've worked find the overwhelming majority of the products they want to back in the United States. My friends at IBM tell me that while they make many of their transistors in Taiwan, for the most sophisticated chips they need they have to manufacture in the United States.

We've been hurt by the aftermath of the failure of our own Congress to consider the international trade commission that was proposed at Bretton Woods together with the IMF and the World Bank—the General Arrangement on Trade and Tariffs (GATT) is a pretty poor substitute. These problems, too, will correct themselves.

Should they live as long as I have, my children will know a world where more than half the earth's production is in the Pacific Basin, and the languages emphasized in school are Japanese and Chinese rather than French and Spanish. My advice is to watch the Chinese especially. Shigeru Yoshida of Japan, prime minister for most of the key period 1946–54, came calling on me in New York soon after my election as chairman of the bank. He was already a very old man, almost ninety. I asked him what he expected to happen in China, then still embroiled in its cultural revolution, and he said that everything in Japanese culture, economy, and politics had really originated on the mainland, and the Japanese had always improved on Chinese models rather than invented their own. The current disturbance in China was like several others that had occurred in the thousands of years of that great country's history. The Chinese would find their own new way to organize a more complex economy and society. "Then we will copy them," he said. "And so will you."

Many of the problems that now plague us, energy and pollution especially, will have found technological fixes. We will defeat hunger; the genetic engineering that will multiply food production is already a reality in the laboratories. We are immensely more resourceful today than we were in my youth. And the great accomplishment of my century, the dedication of developed societies to the economic, political, and moral betterment of mankind, will be sustained, with even better results than my generation achieved—and despite all the ignorant denunciations of our country and our time we have heard in recent years, I am proud of what my generation achieved.

I have seen three generations of fat cats disappear, and I know that individuals and even nations have no grounds for complacency. But growth is as certain as change. The world will offer new opportunities to entrepreneurs who are lucky and smart—but in any event brave. I know that the best is yet to come.

Sometimes I regret I won't be here to see it. Sometimes I think, what the hell, maybe I will stay around to see it. And participate, too.

Index